ADVENTURE *of* FAITH

Adventure
of
Faith

Shraddha Liertz

SCIENCE OF THE SOUL RESEARCH CENTRE

Published by:
G. P. S. Bhalla, Secretary
Science of the Soul Research Centre
c/o Radha Soami Satsang Beas
5 Guru Ravi Dass Marg, Pusa Road
New Delhi 110 005, India

For internet orders, please visit:
www.ScienceoftheSoul.org

For book orders within India, please write to:
Science of the Soul Research Centre
c/o Radha Soami Satsang Beas
BAV Distribution Centre, 5 Guru Ravi Dass Marg,
Pusa Road, New Delhi 110 005

First edition 2009

17 16 15 14 13 12 11 10   8 7 6 5 4 3 2

ISBN 978-93-80077-01-7

Printed in India by: Lakshmi Offset Printers

Contents

ADVENTURE OF FAITH TELLS THE LIFE STORY
of a person who was certain from her very youth that her
priority was God – and who consciously chose a life of celibacy
and devotion to support her priority. The book presents the
reader with a gripping account of the author's many steps in
her life's adventure as, driven by her faith and an unflinching
commitment to experience for herself its deepest meaning, she
watched her life unfold.

The reader travels with the author from her early childhood
days in pre-war Germany to her life as a Benedictine Catholic
nun living the secluded discipline of life in a convent. We
accompany her through her years spent as a Christian nun in
a Hindu ashram in central India, to her discovery of the inner
path of *Surat Shabd Yoga* and the need for a spiritual Master
to guide her in inner practice so she could learn from him to
experience God within herself. From India we return with the
author to her land of birth as she comes back to Germany at
her Master's request. She then leaves her religious order and
is called upon for the first time as an adult to live her life in
the maelstrom of normal worldly activity, while retaining her
priority of daily spiritual practice.

As the author reflects on the many challenges she faced on
the way, we witness her ever-widening perspectives and growing understanding of the relationship between the multiplicity
of outward-focused religion and the oneness of the inner world
of spirit. With our protagonist, we are confronted with the

contradictions presented by the many religions in the name of one God. Equally, we share with her the resolution of these contradictions as, through her association with her Master, her Christian faith comes full circle at a deeper level and she experiences the Universal Christ and the Word incarnate in a profound and inner way.

Spiritual reality cannot be described in words: this is the lesson of all teachers of spirit. What truth is at this most subtle of levels can only be hinted at, suggested, or at most, indicated. Even in normal life it is an experience shared by most of us that the same words are understood differently by different people, for our interpretation of meaning is necessarily conditioned by our individual experience. Even the grammar and structure of different languages – being intimately connected with the cultures they express – indicate through their variations the multiple perspectives of humankind.

Adventure of Faith is one person's perspective of her lifelong quest for God, expressed within the context of her particular background and Christian culture and her personal experience of the teachings of the Masters. As the author delves deeply into the issues of theology, philosophy, prayer and meditation with which she has had to grapple, she explores the universal behind the bewildering variety of religious doctrines, teachings and meditative practices, making the book most relevant to seekers of that truth which transcends differences and unites, rather than divides.

The book was translated from the original German by the author herself. Some of the quotations she included are from memory or from personal notes made during her life-long search for the divine, rendered, summarized or extracted from the source. Where sources were available, they have been noted at the back of the book, and are referenced by the page number where the quotes occur in this book. When English

translations of the material she used were found, these titles
have also been noted so English speakers can delve more
deeply into the wealth of spiritual litcrature that echoes the
author's adventure. A bibliography of references and their
English translations where available has been provided. In
addition, background notes on some of the main books and
authors cited have been provided.

This story is thrilling not only as the extraordinary travels
and personal reflections of a seeker of the divine, but as the
inner journey from the particular to the universal. For a sense
of the ultimate destination of the adventure presented by this
book, we may do no better than to refer to the inspiring words
quoted by the author: "I have learned so much from God that
I can no longer call myself a Christian, a Hindu, a Muslim, a
Buddhist, a Jew. The Truth has shared so much of itself with
me that I can no longer call myself a man, a woman, an angel,
or even pure soul. Love has befriended Hafiz so completely, it
has turned to ash and freed me of every concept and image my
mind has ever known."

J. C. Sethi
Secretary

Radha Soami Satsang Beas
February, 2009

God always remains an adventure
Whose outcome we do not know.

THIS EXPERIENCE, VOICED BY THE CONTEMPO-
rary Hungarian theologian and writer Ladislaus Boros,* runs
through my life like a brightly coloured thread. That is why I
have called this book *Adventure of Faith*, for the term describes
my own spiritual journey.

In my early youth I heard the call of God, and through
that inner experience God became my fate. That experience
completely changed the course of my life. Since that moment
my goal has been to encounter him – the One who called me
by name and demanded my undivided heart. In the following
years I realized more and more that it is truly an adventure to
get involved with God and surrender your life unconditionally
to him, because you do not know what He will make of it. It is
indeed an adventure to step onto the path of abandonment to
God, since the way ahead cannot be seen. Only in looking back
at the part of the path already travelled does one recognize it as
a path. If I had known in advance the countless twists and turns
and the steep ridges awaiting me, I would never have had the

---

*For sources of quotations given, please refer to the Source Notes at the
back of the book, where the sources are listed by the page number on
which the quote appears in this book.

courage to step on it. Yet the longer I followed this path, the clearer it became to me that there was no turning back.

Outwardly my way led at first into the 'garden inclosed"* of a Benedictine abbey, and sixteen years later into the 'promised land' of India. Metaphorically speaking, this way took me through deserts and over oceans and high mountain passes, until it ended at the feet of a living true Master. In an awe-inspiring moment I recognized him as the inner guide whom I had been following for so many years, but on reaching this point I realized that this was not the end of my journey. On the contrary, it proved to be the case that my life thus far had been only a phase of development and transformation, preparing me to meet my Master and to step over the threshold to a new dimension of my spiritual life.

This story, which I have written down at the request of my Master, Maharaj Charan Singh of Beas, is a personal one. But I see it as a metaphor for the endeavour of everyone who is sincerely seeking God, true happiness and inner peace. I also believe that my personal experience has much in common with the experience of anyone who is in search of answers to the fundamental human questions: What is the meaning of our life? Where do we come from? Where are we going? Why are there suffering and death in the world?

This book is addressed particularly to Christian readers. As a Christian I would like to share with them the overwhelming experience of discovering the mystic dimension of the Christian religion in the light of the teachings of the Masters: the mystery of the universal Christ and the mystic dimension of the teachings of the Master of Nazareth and of the great Christian feasts. For me, this has been an awesome and profoundly happy revelation.

---

*A garden inclosed is my sister, my spouse; a spring shut up, a fountain sealed. *Song of Solomon* 4:12

Beyond that, the path of the Masters provided me with the means not just to deepen my intellectual knowledge of these mysteries, but to make practical progress in coming closer to the fulfilment of the highest aspirations of the Christian faith.

Yet regardless of which religion one belongs to and regardless of one's philosophical or cultural background, this book may help one to realize why people start to search for the unnameable and unfathomable. It is because we are spiritual beings dressed in a human body. We have unlimited spiritual potential within ourselves. When we understand this, we consider it to be our highest task as human beings to tread the spiritual path, to free ourselves from existential ignorance about our true nature. Only then will our soul be able to proceed towards her origin, the primal source of all that exists.

The path of the Masters equips seekers of truth with the method needed to spiritualize their life, to attain true self-knowledge and finally to experience the ultimate reality. Realizing the potential of the path of the Masters was a fascinating experience for me, and sharing my experience with others was an important reason for writing this book.

This book is an account of how I, a devout Christian and a Catholic nun, found the path of the Masters. The book gives a short survey of the teachings of the Masters and touches also upon how I have tried to live these teachings in my day-to-day life. Although I learned the way from a contemporary Indian Master, that same way can be discovered in any religion. Most importantly, through my association with my Master, I discovered the mystic way within my own religion, Christianity.

My adventure of faith has not yet come to an end – it has only entered a new phase. The future is still unknown and the path is still steep, and as the years pass I find that it requires much perseverance, determination and an unflinching faith and confidence in the One whose call I heard so many years ago. I have no wish to hide these difficulties from the readers of this book. At the same time, I want to share with them my experience that perseverance on the path of the Masters confers a deep inner peace and an unfading joy that fills me with profound gratitude. The path requires daily meditation, constant vigilance and an untiring search for the Lord, and this cannot be done without a conscious 'Yes' to his will as it manifests itself in all the circumstances of our daily life.

Writing this book has been a wonderful experience for me, as I have watched my adventure of faith running once again like a movie before my eyes. I have become conscious anew of the divine guidance in my life. In looking back at the various phases of this way and in reflecting about so many events and experiences on it, I was able to see patterns that I had not seen before. Although the thought of making the experiences of my adventure of faith accessible to a larger circle had caused a feeling of uneasiness in me, in the course of time my main feeling was one of joy at making my way once again in the company of future readers. That is why I express my hope that this book may provide a captivating read, as well as inspire and encourage readers to pursue their own adventure in search of God.

Finally, I would like to convey my thanks to all who have followed the development of the book with interest and encouragement over the years and who have cooperated in a marvellous way. I especially want to thank the sangat of Munich, who have contributed much to the success of the book by their valuable advice and active support. Now I put this book at the feet of the present Master, our beloved Baba Gurinder Singh, whose guiding hand and encouraging words have enabled me to write and to complete it.

Shraddha Liertz

Munich, 7th February, 2009

PART ONE

Called by Name

CHAPTER ONE

When God Becomes Fate

IT WAS THE SPRING OF 1937. THE TRAIN CARRY-
ing the young girl home from school was just approaching the
station. She was already standing in the open doorway of the
carriage, ready to get off as soon as the train came to a halt.
She might have been thinking about that morning's lessons or
about her homework for the afternoon. Maybe she was also
thinking about the young boy from the grammar school who
came to school every day on the same train and to whom her
teenage heart had warmed. The one thing she certainly was not
thinking about at that moment was God.

Suddenly she felt as if an invisible light, coming from
above, was flowing over her. She was spellbound, completely
overwhelmed by what was happening. At the same time she
'heard' a clear and distinct voice inside, saying, "Preserve your
heart's capacity to love, for you know not whether God will one
day ask you for your undivided heart."

This experience was the beginning of my 'adventure of
faith', which is the story of this book. It lasted no more than a
few seconds. I did not have the slightest doubt that it was God
who had spoken to me. His voice had been insistent and at the
same time infinitely gentle and full of love. It seemed very clear

7

that I was entirely free to decide, but at the same time there was no doubt in my mind that I had to submit. The demand was inescapable, yet the decision was left to me. A deep feeling of happiness and inner peace filled me, and this made me sure that it was indeed the voice of God which I had heard.

I was just thirteen and a half years old. Nothing like this had happened to me before and I had no idea how it was going to affect my life, yet I obeyed unquestioningly, immediately renouncing my feelings for the boy, without giving any thought to how God would one day claim my undivided heart.

This experience of light and of the voice that came with it caused a complete about-turn in my life. Although I was unaware of it at the time, it redirected my life towards the transcendent, the absolute. It carried within itself a potential for spiritual growth that was to unfold progressively over the course of my later life. The divine sower had planted the seed of spirituality in my heart and he would make sure that it would sprout and grow.

God was no longer an anonymous being. He had spoken to me directly and unmistakably. He had 'called me by name', as the prophet Isaiah says: "I have called thee by thy name; thou art mine." He had laid his hand upon me and had thus become my personal God, to whom I surrendered my life unquestioningly and unconditionally, not knowing what the consequences would be. As Ignatius of Loyola said, speaking of his own experience, "Nobody knows what God will make of a man if he responds to his grace."

It was clear to me that I could not talk to anyone about this experience. Seeing light and hearing a voice! Nobody would believe me, or – even worse – people might call it the hysterical exaggerations of an adolescent.

Our parents were devout Catholics and had educated us in the ways of the religious life. At home we said our morning and evening prayers together and there was a thanksgiving prayer before and after each meal. Together with our parents we attended church on Sundays and religious holidays. However, that day's experience would hardly fit into their religious framework. I did not speak to them about it and there was no other confidant with whom I could have shared my story. In any case, I did not really feel the need to do so. The experience had changed my innermost being. I locked it away in my heart and kept it there as a precious treasure.

This first encounter with God was a key moment in my life, for now God had put me on a road where there was no turning back; it was my first 'point of no return'. This theme was to come up again and again in the course of my later life. Many times I was to be reminded that my unconditional surrender meant that there was to be no turning back. *He had become my fate* and from then on my life was inseparably connected with him.

From the very beginning I felt that my spiritual life was an adventure of faith. In his book, *To Experience God in Life*, Ladislaus Boros says, "God always remains an adventure whose outcome we do not know." In spite of all the faith in God that I have gained in the course of the years, it is still an adventure to live in accord with the conviction that it is God who is so often responsible for the turning points in my life. Time and again there have been twists and turns that were caused not by external circumstances but by inner impulses. During the course of my life it has become ever clearer that submission to God is an 'adventure' that means total insecurity but, paradoxically, provides absolute security at the same time.

With the twofold experience of light and voice, God had entered into my life in his own inscrutable manner. When he wishes to encounter a person – and the mystics assure us that his longing to unite an individual soul with himself is infinitely greater than our longing can ever be – he is free to choose any means by which to catch our attention. He may move our hearts by joyful events or painful experiences, by words of the holy scriptures or human words. He may give us a flash of insight into divine truth and reality in order to evoke in us a deep yearning for God, or he may send us the experience of his divine light or divine voice. God's call can come to a person in so many ways. What counts is not the way in which the call comes to us but the way we answer that call.

Growing up to be a Christian

At the time of my first encounter with God, my family's material living conditions were severely shaken by the political situation in Germany, where Adolf Hitler and his National Socialist Party had come to power. Since my parents were devout Catholics, and as such were strongly opposed to the Nazi regime, they had to endure extreme economic hardship. We often had hardly enough to live on – there were six of us children at the time – and had to depend on the help of friends and various other benefactors. But my parents could not be shaken in their religious convictions and even the reprisals of the local party leaders could not intimidate them.

There were two fundamental attitudes that shaped my parents' lives: an unshakeable faith in God and submission to his will, which they recognized even in the inescapable and fateful circumstances they were going through. Their faith and confidence in God was often severely tested, but the fact that they had to endure all these trials and troubles, chiefly on account of their religious convictions, only served to strengthen them in their faith. It gave them the courage to take as their main guide in life Christ's injunction in the Sermon on the Mount: "But seek ye first the kingdom of God, and his righteousness;

and all these things shall be added unto you." Never once did I hear a word of complaint from them about the trials that were sent to them. As the eldest child they let me share their worries, but by watching them I also learned how to live by faith.

In the small town where we lived the pressure of the Nazis was suffocating, but in 1938 my parents managed to escape. They moved to Munich, my mother's home town, hoping thus to be able to live in peace and to educate their children in the anonymity of a big city. Soon after our arrival I came into contact with a Catholic youth organization, the *Heliand* (old German for *Heiland* – saviour). Together with my girlfriends I spent many hours reflecting upon our life as young Christians. We worshipped together and passed many joyful days on excursions into the mountains. Belonging to this group was important for all of us, for in this way we learned to integrate religion into our daily life, and practising our religion was always a source of joy for us.

In those years I also started to seek pastoral advice about my quest to come closer to God. Although my discussions with various priests were very important to me, it was the books I read that influenced my religious development more than anything else, for I found books that contained invaluable guidance for my quest. Even so, I always knew deep in my heart that my soul's real guide was *inside*. I felt this anew every day. It was just as Teresa of Ávila says in her autobiography:

> Since I did not have a spiritual guide, I read the books mentioned, hoping slowly to understand some of their contents. But soon I was forced to realize that I could not learn much from books unless the Lord himself would teach me, for I hardly understood anything until the moment that his Majesty taught me by experience.

Many times I found that I had only to submit to tender but irresistible inner impulses in order to feel the nearness of God. I experienced these impulses not just during prayer but also at other times during the day. By submitting to them, I learned to trust my inner guide implicitly.

It was *he* who taught me how to pray. At first I prayed with familiar set phrases, then later with my own words, and eventually with just one word, which was enough to bring me into the presence of God, invisible and yet so near. By this last form of prayer I was able to remain in his presence and to 'behold' him. In hindsight, it seemed to me this youthful experience was like that of Johannes Marie Vianny, the holy pastor of Ars. He used to sit silent and motionless in his church. When asked what he was doing, he replied, "He beholds me and I behold him."

Jesus Christ in the centre

In the years that followed our move to Munich, my spiritual life took a new turn. My devotion became Christ-centric, that is, Jesus Christ more and more became the centre of my life. Increasingly my search and my prayers were directed towards Jesus rather than towards God, as before. Until now I had not made any connection between Christ and my experience of the inner light and the inner voice. The voice had explicitly spoken of God, for whom I should preserve my heart. 'God' meant 'our Father in heaven', to whom we addressed our prayers and in whom we placed our confidence. Of course, from my early childhood Jesus was familiar to me as 'our beloved Saviour', the one whom my parents received into their hearts at Holy Communion. My mother had explained this to me when I was a child of three.

As an adolescent, I found that receiving this sacred bread created a close and intimate bond between Jesus and my soul

– a bond that grew ever more intense. Inwardly, I focused more and more on him and I developed a very personal relationship with him. I had a fervent desire to go to Mass every day and to merge my heart with Jesus through Holy Communion. I loved to enter a church during the day in order to be with him, for my faith told me that he was present there in the form of the consecrated wafer. My love belonged to the incarnate Son of God, who became more and more familiar to me through readings from the Gospel during the celebration of Mass.

The next step on my spiritual path came when I read the autobiography of Thérèse of Lisieux, *The Story of a Soul*, given to me by a priest. I found it completely fascinating and I read it so often that in the end I practically knew it by heart. Maybe it was under the influence of this book that I first considered joining a convent so that I could dedicate my life completely to God and to Christ. When I talked to my parents about my wish, they were quite understanding, because both of them had had this desire in their youth. At that time, however, they considered me too young to put my wish into practice.

Not wanting to put off dedicating my life to God till I was able to enter a convent, I asked my spiritual adviser for permission to take a private vow of celibacy, as I knew that young people quite often did this at that time in order to preserve their heart's undivided love for God. Such a choice can be traced back to the early days of Christianity, when the Christian community of Corinth asked Saint Paul for his advice on this subject. He dealt with the question extensively, answering as follows:

> But I would have you without carefulness (free from anxiety). He that is unmarried careth for the things that belong to the Lord, how he may please the Lord. But he that is married careth for the things that are of the world, how

he may please his wife. There is difference also between a wife and a virgin. The unmarried woman careth for the things of the Lord, that she may be holy both in body and in spirit; but she that is married careth for the things of the world, how she may please her husband. And this I speak for your own profit...that ye may attend upon the Lord without distraction.

I was granted permission to take the vow of celibacy, and on taking this vow I felt even more intimately connected with Christ. By now I was eighteen, had finished my professional training and was working as a secretary in an office.

CHAPTER TWO

Living in the Face of Death

ONE YEAR AFTER OUR MOVE TO MUNICH, THE Second World War began and my father, being a reserve officer from the First World War, was called up at the age of fifty-two to serve in the army. After a few months of training he was sent to Russia, much of which was then occupied by the German army, and at the end of 1941, while in service, he contracted a severe disease and subsequently died after a few days in a field hospital.

The death of her husband and the father of her seven children, the youngest of whom was then only four and a half, was such a deep shock to my mother that for several months we feared for her life. On his last leave, my father had asked me to stand in for him during his absence. Now I had to actually replace him to a certain extent. I stood, as it were, as a partner at my mother's side, and together we overcame all our grief and sorrow and the events of the war, which became ever more threatening, with that unshakeable faith that had been our anchor in times of need for so many years.

Munich was being bombed by the British and American air forces, and the terror of the bombing taught us to *live in the face of death*. During one especially heavy air raid, we were all cowering in the basement while the house was shaken to its foundations. We had no hope of escaping alive from the inferno. In this extreme situation I felt that our only safety lay in anticipating death, as it were. Inwardly I hid myself in the bosom of God, convinced that I would have to appear before him at any moment. Faced with certain death, I remained silently in the safety of his protection. But we were all spared, and even our house in the city centre was hardly damaged at all, although all around many bombs had fallen, causing great devastation.

Many churches that I used to visit had been reduced to ruins. For me they had been a spiritual refuge, for there I had felt the nearness of God in a special way. They were places of recollection and prayer, and the services I had attended there were almost like participating in the mysteries of God that were celebrated in the liturgy. And so the destruction of these churches hit me harder than anything else, because it deprived me of the places where I could be with God. It was many months before I could pass by some of these ruins without shedding bitter tears at the thought that their smoke-stained walls were all that was left of them.

As a reminder of how to cope with the horrors of war, I had pinned to the wall of my room a poem by Reinhold Schneider:

> Only by praying can we divert
> The sword over our heads
> And wrest the world free
> From the forces of justice
> By living a life in holiness.

The war, with all its horrors, fears and sorrows, with all its death and destruction, had swept over us like an apocalyptic judgement. In his poem Reinhold Schneider speaks of the "forces of justice". But who were those who by their excess of sins had brought this immeasurable suffering upon us? We ourselves pleaded not guilty. We felt that we were innocent victims and we prayed to God that he might spare us.

But were we really so innocent? After the war there was much talk about the 'collective guilt' of the German people. We could find no answer to the question of how God's love and justice could be reconciled with all we had gone through. However, we found solace and peace of mind in submission to the inscrutable will of God. Taking refuge in God we tried to put Reinhold Schneider's words into practice and to lead a "life in holiness", following Christ's directive to seek first his kingdom and all else would follow naturally. The origin of suffering and death in the world and the fact that all too often the seemingly guiltless are punished is one of the most pressing questions facing humanity. It was only later in life when I found the teachings of the Masters that I was able to find some answers that satisfied both my head and my heart.

CHAPTER THREE

In Search of the Way

THE IDEA OF JOINING A CONVENT HAD RE-
mained alive in my mind throughout the war and I was
determined that one day I would make it a reality. In fact, I
thought of nothing else. The experiences of the war and my
father's death had left on my mind an indelible impression
of the transitory nature of all things. I now wanted to enter a
strict cloister, a place where I could lead a life detached from
the world, without being involved in teaching, nursing or other
such charitable works. My only desire was to dedicate myself
to a life of prayer and contemplation.

The Story of a Soul, mentioned before, had awakened my
enthusiasm for the Carmelite Order and I wanted to become a
Carmelite nun. But a visit to a Carmelite nunnery made it clear
that this was not the place for me. Although the meeting with
the prioress went quite well, I was frightened by the metal grille
in the parlour, 'decorated' with iron spikes, and the curtain that
concealed her from me. I was so afraid that after a few hours I
took flight and ran down the hill in order to get away as fast as
I could. In this way external considerations made me give up
in just a few moments an ideal that I had been carrying in my
mind for so long and with such great enthusiasm.

This experience had at least taught me something about what was *not* my way. Next I turned to the Benedictine Order, with which I had felt a special bond ever since my youth. In recent years I had spent a number of Easter holidays with a group of young people in the Neresheim Abbey in the Swabian Alps. Together with the monks we had celebrated the liturgy and participated in the communal prayer. The Benedictine way of living was entirely dedicated to what the founder, Saint Benedict, had called the *opus Dei*, the work of God. By this he meant singing psalms and celebrating the liturgy. All this now filled my heart, so I looked for a Benedictine convent where I could seek admission.

However, my first contact with a Benedictine abbey proved a disappointment. The nuns were unwilling to accept me as a choir sister because my schooling did not meet the standards applied to members of that community. I could have joined as a lay sister, but I could not agree to this, since lay sisters at that time were not allowed to participate actively in the liturgy and the communal prayer. A second attempt with another abbey was equally unsuccessful, for the same reasons.

This search for a place where I could take the veil was my first attempt to find out what God wanted me to do. Until now it had only been a question of how to fulfil his will, for I had not had any difficulty understanding what his will was when it had manifested itself in that call from within the light. Now, however, and in times to come, I had to try to discover his will, for it was not always shown to me in a clear and obvious way.

Meanwhile, the war had ended, and in order to escape office work I began a course of professional training to become a social worker. The financial situation of our family meant that I needed to earn money for several more years before I could think of joining a convent. As part of my practical training I had to spend some months in a placement in the town of Fulda. Before I went there, an old friend asked me to wait for him to finish his studies, because he wanted to marry me. I declined his proposal, saying that God had beaten him to it. He was quite disappointed and jealous, and he wanted to know what Christ meant to me. But how was I to explain this to someone whose aspirations were diametrically opposed to mine? By now Christ had become the very foundation of my life and my love for him filled my whole heart. There were other young men who saw in me their future companion, but I turned down all their proposals. I was determined to dedicate my life exclusively to Christ by living as a nun and belonging only to him.

Images of Christ

During my stay in Fulda I went every day to the church of the Benedictine abbey to participate in the convent service. The apse of the church was covered with a more than life-size mosaic depicting Christ as Pantocrator (Christ in Majesty). I was strongly attracted to this image and I became so much absorbed in it that it stood before me throughout the day. This was a novel experience for me. I was doing a kind of pictorial meditation, which had been known to Christianity for as long as there had been pictures of Christ. In the course of the Christian meditation movement that began in the 1970s, pictorial meditation became an important part of 'object meditation' – meditating on a particular object, such as a burning candle or a picture of Christ or of some saint. During my stay at Fulda I experienced for myself the value of this form of meditation. The faithful contemplation of Christ's image touches the heart and moves it to love him. Just as the love for a human being must be cherished to be kept alive, so also must the love of God be cultivated if it is not to wither. There is no doubt that this pictorial meditation keeps love alive if the contemplator turns to Christ within with an open heart.

After returning to Munich I could no longer renew this contemplation every day, and this particular image of Christ slowly faded away, only to be replaced by another one. It was a picture of Veronica's veil that I had in my room and loved to look at. This picture has a special meaning for many pious Christians. Legend has it that on his way to crucifixion, Jesus left an imprint of his face on a piece of cloth given him by Veronica (a name that means 'true picture' in Latin) to wipe his sweaty, bloodstained face. This inspired lovers of Christ to pray to him to impress his face into their hearts, as described in the words of one unknown writer:

> We, who are all Christians, carry Veronica's veil in our heart – the veil imprinted with the divine face. Whatever we do or don't do should stand before this imprint. And not only this – we should all carry something of this imprint in ourselves and radiate it around us.

This phase of contemplating on images of Christ continued for several years, and even after I became a nun I loved to mark the books for our communal prayer with such pictures.

CHAPTER FOUR

Leaving the World

IN THE SPRING OF 1949 MY BEST FRIEND JOINED the Benedictine Abbey of Saint Erentraud at Kellenried, near Ravensburg in Baden-Württemberg. She invited me to visit her there and look around. Was this the place to which God was calling me? I went there in order to find out. My friend spoke with great enthusiasm about the monastic life. Three other young women had entered with her, joining a number of novices already there. At that time the community numbered seventy members. I was able to meet the Mistress of Novices and to tell her why I wanted to become a nun. First and foremost was my wish to dedicate my life unconditionally to God. I was, as I have said before, particularly attracted to the Order of Saint Benedict, to their solemn chanting of the psalms and the liturgy.

The Abbey, with its lofty buildings and baroque church towers, seemed to me like a 'city on the mountain' where one is a little closer to heaven. After a few days I applied for admission to this cloister, which was granted. Convinced that God had led me to this place, I planned to enter Saint Erentraud in the autumn.

When in September 1949 it was time for me to say goodbye
to my former life, I did not find it easy to leave my home and
everything that had been my life up to then. I had wished with
all my heart to become a nun and there had been ample time
to weigh my decision and to prepare myself for this step – yet
my heart felt heavy now. Leaving my mother was especially difficult, and it was also hard for her to let me go. We had suffered
and survived together through the horrors of the war years,
through the pain of my father's death and all the difficulties
of the post-war period. This had created a very intimate bond
between us, but my mother would never have come in the way
of my vocation. I was her firstborn, and from the moment of
my birth she had prayed that her little daughter might become
a true child of God. When I dedicated my life to God, she saw
her prayer fulfilled.

And so, on the day that my long cherished wish to take
the veil was to be fulfilled, I was not in a joyous mood. Rather,
it was a feeling of dying that took hold of me and, of course,
a feeling of profound uncertainty about what this new phase
in my life would bring. There it was again – the 'adventure of
faith' that had begun when I first submitted to God's claim on
my undivided heart.

Giving up myself

Strangely enough, before entering the monastery I had never
reflected on the possibility that my life would thereby undergo
a fundamental change. For many years now I had wanted most
ardently to be free for God. In leaving the world and leading
a life of prayer and contemplation, I hoped that God would
more and more take possession of my thinking and feeling, of
my whole heart.

I had never imagined that being free for God would mean the giving up of myself, yet that was exactly what I had to do in order to submit to him. I felt that in order to be free for God I had to leave the world, as hundreds and thousands of Christian men and women, as well as followers of other religions, had done before me. What I had completely overlooked was the fact that simply stepping over the threshold of the monastery would not automatically make me free for God. Outwardly I would be leaving the world, but inwardly I would still be carrying it with me.

It is the human mind that carries the world within itself because like a computer it stores all the impressions supplied to it by the senses. In addition to that, it ceaselessly seeks new impressions and it hankers insatiably for the satisfaction of all the desires that the senses awaken in it. It is, in truth, the most formidable obstacle to surrendering our life to God. These tendencies of the mind suffocate what Saint Augustine (354–430) refers to in the first chapter of his *Confessions* as a human being's restlessness for God.

Therefore, if somebody really wishes to belong to God, he has to conquer the mind. Time and again lovers of God have striven to control their minds through renunciation, self-abnegation, asceticism and mortification. The monastic life, especially fulfilling the vows, has long been considered a suitable means of gaining control over the mind and making the seekers of God free for him. The vow of poverty (having no personal possessions) should make the heart empty for God, and by obedience they should renounce their own self-centred will and live according to the will of God, as manifested in the commands of the Abbot. Voluntary celibacy for the sake of love for God should preserve their hearts undivided for the Lord.

The crucial question, however, is whether or not asceticism and self-abnegation can bring about detachment from the world and bestow upon the practitioner complete mastery of the mind and the senses. Can it truly make him free for God? In practice, it can at best purify the mind. Human endeavour alone will always remain imperfect. Real detachment from the world will be accomplished only through the experience of its nothing-ness, and only an irresistible pull from the divine will create a real freedom for God. At the time of my leaving the world and entering the Abbey of Saint Erentraud, I was far away from entertaining such thoughts and having such insights.

CHAPTER FIVE

The 'Garden Inclosed'

WHEN I ENTERED THE BOUNDS OF THE ABBEY of Saint Erentraud in Kellenried, I was embraced by the Mother Abbess, and my friend gave me an impetuous hug. Then I was led into the church, where I knelt down and said to God, "Here I am."

As the big front door closed behind me, a new world opened before me – a world to which I had to now adapt and in which I had to grow. From now on this new world would shape my thinking and determine my actions. It would transform me in the spirit of Saint Benedict and the fourteen-century-old tradition of his order. New norms, new attitudes and new values would from now on define my life. New dimensions of spirituality would open up before me, but for the time being I felt somewhat dizzied and overwhelmed by all the new impressions.

The first thing I had to do was get acquainted with the monastic routine. Every day the aspirants and novices gathered round their mistress, the Magistra, who would be with us for the next five years, preparing us for the final vows and introducing us to the way of life in the convent. Every day we would read together one of the seventy-three chapters of the *Rule of*

Saint Benedict, the *Regula*, which he had compiled more than fourteen hundred years ago. It commences with the words, "Listen, my son, and bend the ear of thy heart." This would be one of our foremost duties in the coming years of preparation, which would be followed by the final vows, setting the seal on a life of dedication to God, a life of listening and putting into practice whatever we heard.

Daily life in the monastery is regulated in every detail from morning till evening. It is punctuated by communal prayer in the church, which is recited at fixed hours during the day, and by the celebration of the liturgy according to the *Rule*. At five o'clock in the morning the chanting of psalms started. In the forty-third rule, Saint Benedict says that nothing should take priority over this *opus Dei*. In those days in our monasteries, the psalms were still chanted in Latin and the liturgy was sung in Gregorian chant.

This service to God, lasting for at least five hours each day, is considered by the monastic family to be its main task. The monks and nuns of the Order of Saint Benedict believe that they offer this prayer to God in the name of the Church and on behalf of all Christians. It is their conviction that by their prayer they can have some influence on the fate of the world and that it will bring blessings on humankind. This belief is supported by the Church's teaching of the community of saints, the mystical body of Christ, according to which every member of the Church participates in the spiritual merits and the prayers of all the other members, because through their affiliation to Christ they are one body. As Saint Paul writes: "Now ye are the body of Christ, and members in particular."

I loved this chanting of the psalms and did my best to make it my personal prayer, or at least to merge with its atmosphere. Over the years the beautiful words of the psalms became very familiar to me. In so many ways they express what moves the heart of a seeker of God. Above all, there were the psalms that express the longing to encounter God, to behold his face, such as: "Make thy face to shine upon thy servant." Another verse I often repeated during the day was: "My soul thirsteth for God, for the living God: when shall I come and appear before God?" In this way the communal prayer became a source of nourishment for my own religious life and its deeply moving words were my daily inspiration.

Becoming a Benedictine nun

Adapting to the monastic way of life was not always easy for me. From my earliest youth I had been accustomed to taking responsibility and making my own decisions. Now I exercised obedience, adopting other people's thinking and being one among many with my fellow sisters. Renouncing part of my individuality and identity was a daily struggle and certainly not an easy one. This fact most probably had not escaped the attention of my superiors. In any case, I had to remain an aspirant for nearly a whole year before receiving the monastic habit and being allowed to start the novitiate. Waiting for such a long time was extremely difficult and I began to wonder whether doubts might have arisen in the minds of my superiors as to the earnestness of my resolve to dedicate my life to God. Life in the monastery thus became a part of a process of self-denial that was all the harder because it was a new experience for me. This struggle continued even after I took the final vows. It took me quite a while to realize what an essential part of spiritual life this struggle is.

At the end of the novitiate I was permitted to take the monastic vows for three years, as is customary in the Catholic orders. Saint Benedict demands unconditional obedience to the abbot, who takes the place of Christ in the monastery.

Furthermore, he demands that one should promise to remain in the same monastery; this was a preventive measure, since in his time there were wandering monks who went from one monastery to another. Finally, there was the vow to lead a monastic life, including poverty and celibacy.

By now I had a better understanding of what I was committing myself to by taking the final vows, and I promised with all my heart to live accordingly. This was to be my way of dedicating my life to God. It would be my way of surrendering myself to him.

In spite of the difficulties I have mentioned, I felt like a fish in water. I felt fulfilled and I had no doubt that I was where God wanted me to be. He had led me to this convent to make me his own. The convent was, for me, his 'garden inclosed'.

Bride of the divine Word

After nearly five years of preparation, on 22nd July 1954 I was allowed to take the final vows and receive the Consecration of Virgins. It was indeed a day of great joy, and I had been longing for it for many years. The ceremony of the Consecration of Virgins is like a wedding celebration in which the nun is the bride who marries her beloved Lord. The rite put momentous words into my mouth, which I sang with fervour: "He has imprinted his seal on my forehead, so that I would not admit another lover." After receiving the wedding ring, I sang: "With his ring my Lord Jesus Christ has wedded me and like a bride he has crowned me." These texts are taken from the legendary biography of Saint Agnes, who died a martyr's death at the beginning of the fourth century. In the ceremony, I was first asked by the bishop, "Do you want to be blessed and consecrated and wedded to our Lord Jesus Christ, the Son of the Almighty?" My answer was, "Yes, I do."

As beautiful and inspiring as the ceremony had been, I was quite conscious that it was merely symbolic in character. The wedding ring that the bishop had put on my finger and the veil that I carried were nothing more than outer signs of something that I still had to realize within myself – the union of my soul with God. Although this day had filled me with great happiness, the ceremony alone did not make me a true bride of Christ, for it was but the symbolic anticipation of something that cannot be created by words or ceremonies. The mystic union with God could be accomplished only in the depth of my soul and only there could I experience it.

The reality was that I still felt myself far removed from the experience of divine union. Moreover, though I was now a 'bride of Christ', I did not experience the romantic feelings sometimes associated with this status. I was far from the state of the 'bridal mystics' of the Middle Ages, such as Bernard of Clairvaux, Gertrude of Helfta and her fellow sisters Mechthild of Magdeburg and Mechthild of Hackeborn, Catherine of Siena and many others.

Those men and women took their inspiration mainly from the texts of the Song of Solomon, which probably dates from the second half of the fifth century BCE. They were filled with ardent love for Christ, and in their visions and ecstasies they experienced what the often daring words of this song hinted at:

> *The bride*:
> Thy love is better than wine.
> Because of the savour of thy good ointments
> Thy name is as ointment poured forth,
> Therefore do the virgins love thee.
> Draw me, we will run after thee:
> The king hath brought me into his chambers.

The bridegroom:
Rise up, my love, my fair one, and come away.
Let me see thy countenance, let me hear thy voice;
For sweet is thy voice,
And thy countenance is comely.

The bride:
By night on my bed I sought him
Whom my soul loveth:
I sought him, but I found him not.
I will rise now, and go about the city in the streets,
And in the broad ways I will seek him
Whom my soul loveth:
I sought him, but I found him not.
The watchmen that go about in the city found me:
To whom I said:
Saw ye him whom my soul loveth?
It was but a little that I passed from them,
But I found him whom my soul loveth:
I held him, and would not let him go,
Until I had brought him into my mother's house,
And into the chamber of her that conceived me.

The bridegroom:
Thou hast ravished my heart, my sister, my spouse!
Thou hast ravished my heart
With one of thine eyes,
With one chain of thy neck.

How fair is thy love, my sister, my spouse!
How much better is thy love than wine!
And the smell of thine ointments than spices!

> A garden inclosed is my sister, my spouse;
> A spring shut up, a fountain sealed.

> *The bride*:
> I am my beloved's,
> And my beloved is mine.

> Set me as a seal upon thine heart,
> As a seal upon thine arm:
> For love is strong as death;
> Jealousy is cruel as the grave:
> The coals thereof are coals of fire,
> Which hath a most vehement flame.
> Many waters cannot quench love,
> Neither can the floods drown it.

The mystics interpreted these verses exclusively in allegoric and symbolic terms, explaining their mystic meaning in various commentaries, of which one of the most famous was that of Bernard of Clairvaux.

The nuns of Helfta composed songs overflowing with love for their 'Bridegroom', which at that time moved the hearts of many people, including people outside the cloister. Here are two examples, composed by Mechthild of Magdeburg:

> I rejoice in loving him
> Who loves me,
> And I desire to die of love,
> To love ceaselessly and boundlessly.
> Rejoice, my soul,
> Because your life has died of love for you!

Do love him so much that you could die for him,
Thus you will burn forever unquenchably
As a living spark
In the great fire
Of the exalted Majesty.
Then you will be replenished with the fire of love
That nourishes and stills you already here.

The soul to the mind:
You can no longer teach me anything.
I cannot turn away from love anymore.
I must give myself as a captive to it,
Because otherwise I cannot live anymore.
Where love is, there must I be,
In life as well as in death.

I wish to die of love, if this I could do,
Because him that I love I have seen
With my enlightened eyes,
Standing in my soul.
The bride who has sheltered her beloved,
Need not to go to distant places.

Compared with these great mystics, my bridal state was
quite sober. But even though I did not experience any high-
flown feelings, being a bride of Christ was much more than
just an intellectual matter – it was a source of deeply felt joy
and happiness.

CHAPTER SIX

In the Sign of Fire

TAKING THE FINAL VOWS AND RECEIVING THE Consecration of Virgins was for me the culmination of many years of striving. I had always thought of this as my final goal, but in reality it turned out to be just a milestone on my spiritual path. But I did not realize this until after the 'wedding ceremony'. I would have liked so much to keep alive the exalted mood of that special day, but after a while those feelings faded away and the daily monastic routine took over, in which I had to prove my dedication to God hour by hour.

The path ahead of me seemed to be well marked out. It would be straight and clear, passing for the most part across level ground, perhaps ascending here and there onto a plateau, but probably without any remarkable ups and downs. In the peace and remoteness of the monastery I would try to come closer to God, till one day my life would merge into him at the hour of my death. I would serve my monastic family and con-tribute to the earning of our livelihood, as the founder of our order demands from his disciples. The *opus Dei*, participation in the liturgy, would constitute my main concern. Above all, however, there would be the ceaseless search for God. I wanted to grow into a deep spiritual life of prayer and contemplation.

Such were my life expectations. What God would make of my life, which was no longer my own, I did not know. How could I foresee that it would one day take a completely different turn? Actually, there would be no smooth path ahead of me, no straight and well-trodden way. On the contrary, the road ahead would prove to be steep, with many twists and turns – truly an adventure. And this unforeseen path would demand a measure of obedience to God that even the strictest rule of any religious order could not require.

For the time being, however, the course of my life was indeed even. I spent five to six hours of each day chanting psalms and celebrating the liturgy with my fellow sisters. Between the Lauds (morning prayer) and Mass there was a gap of about half an hour that was set aside for contemplation, for pious reflection on God, his attributes and his works, and on the mystery of Jesus Christ and his teachings. In the evenings we had twenty minutes of free time for our personal prayers, for our own 'search for his countenance'. One hour each day was allotted to the study of theological and religious books. Four hours were given to working for our livelihood in the gardens, on the land, in housekeeping or in the various handicraft and art studios. I worked in the orchards and learned everything about the cultivation of fruit trees and the harvesting and storing of fruit; in the winter I took care of the pruning of the fruit trees and the berry bushes like a real expert.

After it was discovered that I had an artistic vein, I was put to work in the embroidering studio for some years. I designed and made garments for use in the liturgy, as well as wall hangings and flags. Later, when somebody was needed to manage the flower garden, I was chosen for the job, as I was young, healthy and strong. Since I knew nothing about growing flowers, books on horticulture piled up on my table, taking the place of theological works. I became responsible for decorating the church and making the cloister look nice with flowers, besides looking after the flower gardens and the greenhouse.

I loved all those jobs and tried to learn all about them. In summer we all worked on the land, helping to bring in the harvest. Twice a day the community gathered for recreation. This was a time when we wandered through the fields, meadows and woods within the monastery walls, or sat together doing some manual work. Those were happy times and we all felt sure that the sun shone brighter within the walls of our monastery than it did in the world outside.

One year after taking my final vows, however, I started to become restless. I was afraid that my life in the monastery would peter out or become stuck in mediocrity. For the first time, the idea of a more austere way of life came to my mind. I envisaged a life much more strictly and one-pointedly devoted to the search for God. This had happened to other seekers before me, including the great Christian teachers Thomas Merton, Charles de Foucauld and John of the Cross, who I was to learn of later. At first I did not try to analyse this vague feeling of dissatisfaction. Maybe it was a reaction to the intensity of those earlier years when I was preparing for the final vows. Perhaps I was sometimes dissatisfied with the routine nature of my monastic life, for there was a lack of novelty, a lack of any striking new developments, but I could hardly have expected otherwise. The daily routine, designed to facilitate a life of prayer and devotion, possibly led in my case to a feeling of stagnation.

I certainly did my best to live a more intense religious life. I tried to concentrate on God even during my work, to be more attentive and aware during the community prayer and to come to a more intimate contact with God in my personal prayer. But I felt that all this did not advance me one bit in my desire to love God more. I felt a powerful urge to come closer to him, or rather to immerse myself more deeply in him, but I was at a loss as to how this could be done. It is exactly this wish to come closer to God, this longing to be with him, that is the foundation of our spiritual life. This yearning is planted into our hearts by God and we may rest assured that he himself will fulfil it in his own way and in his own time.

In my case, that time came during a week of recollection at the start of 1956. A single sentence brought about the turning point. During one of his sermons, the monk who led the spiritual exercises said, "We must have the courage to say to God: 'Do with me as you like.' You may be sure that God will respond." I gratefully took up this suggestion and prepared myself as well as I could to offer this prayer to God. It had to come from the depth of my heart. I wanted to put into it my whole desire to belong to God. After resolute preparation, I prayed to God using the words the monk had suggested, and opened my heart to his response.

God's response came after just a few days. It fell upon me like fire, in just the same way that it had in my youth. Again, it lasted only for a fraction of a second – like a flash of lightning – and God had taken possession of me. At least I was convinced that it was he who had attracted the eyes of my soul to him by this experience. It was no longer *me* longing to belong to him; now it was *he* who wanted to 'possess my undivided heart', as he had intimated all those years ago. I could not have brought about such an experience myself; this is something that only God can do, for only he has access to a person's innermost being.

On a fragment of parchment sewn into his clothing and found after his death, Blaise Pascal describes an experience I very much related to:

On 23rd November, in the year of grace 1654, on the day of Saint Clement, Pope and Martyr, which was also the day of other martyrs, on the eve of Saint Chrysogonus, Martyr, and others, between half past ten and half past twelve: *Fire.* God of Abraham, God of Isaac, God of Jacob, not the God of philosophers and scribes. *Certainty. Certainty.* Sentiment. Joy. Peace.... Forgotten the world except God.... The people do not know you at all. But I do know you. *Joy! Joy!* I had separated myself from him. Him, who is the fountain of living water, I had forsaken. My God, will you forsake me? May I not for ever be separated from you.

Once again my contact with the transcendent, which was the driving force behind my adventure of faith, had been only momentary, but it was impossible to run away from it, for I was already far too involved with the One who had called me by name. My only choice was unconditional submission. After this experience, days, weeks and months passed in silent submission to God. I found that it was impossible to divert my inner gaze from God. I was quite unable to turn away from the inner light that radiated imperceptibly from his hidden face. All I wanted was to respond to his gaze, without words or thoughts. This experience put an end to my pictorial meditation, for I found that I no longer needed Christ's image to contemplate upon. Not only had it become superfluous, but it even, paradoxically, covered up the face of God.

In a desert of ice

This blissful state, however, was not meant to last. After some time I found myself in a conflict of conscience between my duty of monastic obedience and my irresistible inner urge to remain in silence before God. It was obligatory in our community to use a book for morning meditation to help us in thinking about the divine. I felt it my duty to obey this command; at the same time, however, I felt unable to do so, since his 'gaze' arrested my inner attention. This conflict crushed me inwardly, since my superiors did not understand my wish for silent prayer and insisted that I use the book instead.

Under this pressure my heart slowly froze until in the end it felt dead, and I was caught up in a terrible desert of ice. God seemed to be very far away; only a gloomy longing for him filled my heart. Many years later I happened on an article that dealt with similar experiences. The author describes the attempt to resist the urge towards contemplative prayer as a suicide of the soul, and that is just what it felt like; I had been brought to the limits of my physical and mental strength. The radiant beginning ended in a catastrophe in which I all but drowned. The moments when my encounter with God flashed up again became increasingly rare. I wandered quite lost through the fearsome desert of ice, even though in my innermost heart I was sure that all the time God was embracing my life from all sides and that he was imperceptibly ever present.

This ice phase lasted a long time. It was a great help to me to read, among other books, *L'Abandon à la providence divine (Abandonment to Divine Providence)*. This book of letters of Père de Caussade of the Society of Jesus was one that I kept with me for many years. It helped me to learn a form of submission to God that I had not consciously practised before. This form of submission means letting oneself be *an instrument of God's will*. Until now it had always been *I* who had tried to fulfil his will; now *God* would act upon me to fulfil his will. During this new phase I learned that to practise 'Thy will be done' by no means implies an attitude of passivity; on the contrary, it is a very intense and active process, in which the will of a person embraces God's will with all his strength and makes it his own.

How I had yearned to abandon myself to God! And yet how little had I known what this truly meant! I was now learning this lesson in a way that could not have been more painful but was at the same time highly effective. The letters of Père de Caussade made a profound impression on me. Again and again I took up the book, soaking up the inspiring thoughts. A small paragraph reads like an entire program for spirituality to which nothing needs to be added:

> The comprehensive and solid foundation of a spiritual life lies in giving up yourself to God, so that he might dispose of you in every respect. It means forgetting oneself to such an extent as to consider oneself as sold and delivered and as something to which one has forfeited all rights.

As I began to implement this advice, my heart came back to life and I gradually regained inner peace of mind.

CHAPTER SEVEN

On a Pilgrimage to God

THE NEXT FOUR YEARS OF MY MONASTIC LIFE passed in this state of peace. Among the various books that were then my spiritual companions, Père de Caussade's *Abandonment to Divine Providence* had become the most important guide of my spiritual life. His words of counsel and instruction revealed to me the secret of encountering God in one's daily life: "The present moment is like an ambassador who transmits God's orders. The heart incessantly pronounces its fiat – let it be done." Then Père de Caussade explains how to be always close to God. He says, "Man's unconditional submission coaxes God into his innermost heart."

In those years I also received much spiritual nourishment from a theological work about the central mystery of Christianity, *The Mystery of Jesus Christ* by Matthias Scheeben. I felt the need to penetrate deeper into the mystery of Christ, the Word Incarnate, on account of which I had dedicated my life to God. It was many years now since Christ had become so close and intimate to me when I had contemplated the mosaic in the Church of Fulda Abbey. Scheeben's comprehensive work, which presents the doctrine of the Catholic Church concerning Jesus Christ, now helped me to create for myself an intellectual concept of the Son of God.

I made a very thorough study, trying to grasp the various aspects of Christology. This I did mainly with my heart, because I wanted to be still more intimately connected with Christ. This book was my constant companion, especially during the preparation for the liturgical celebration of the birth of Christ, and in reading it I received much benefit for my spiritual life.

Although the study of theological books can create a disposition in the human mind to turn to God, it can by no means transmit any *experience* of God. Although I found, as I said, that Scheeben's book helped me to create my own intellectual concept of Jesus Christ, it should always be clear that the image such studies create is a mental one, a picture of God with human features. In order to come to true knowledge and a living experience of God, mystics and teachers of spirituality unanimously insist that, at least during contemplative prayer and meditation, one must leave behind any picture of God fabricated by the mind – or any image created by the hand for that matter.

Such advice is found in scriptures written as long ago as the fourth century CE by the fathers of monasticism, the Fathers of the Desert. Evagrios the Solitary, who died in the year CE 399, demands of his disciples:

> You desire to see the face of the Father. Then under no circumstances search for a mental picture at the time of prayer.

Nine hundred years later, Meister Eckhart (1260–1328) expressed it in a similar way:

> Man therefore should not satisfy himself with a *thought* of God, for when the thought disappears, God disappears

as well. Rather one should have an *essential* God, who stands far above the thinking of humanity and above all creation.

But it is not only the contemplatives and mystics who have stressed the need to leave behind every concept or mental picture of God if one wishes to encounter him. Even such a brilliant thinker and theologian as Saint Thomas Aquinas, author of the *Summa Theologica*, realized at the end of his life that nothing can be known, thought or said about God, and he refused to complete the *Summa*. When asked for the reason, he replied, "I am no longer able to write, because everything that I have written appears like straw compared to what has been revealed to me now." His biographer reports that during the celebration of the Mass the saint was suddenly struck by something that moved him deeply and changed him completely.

Celebrating feasts for the Lord

The monastic life according to Saint Benedict is shaped first of all by the *Rule*, by the observance of which the seeker will "speed up the way of the precepts of God in an unspeakable bliss of love", as he promises in the preface of his *Regula*. Secondly, it is marked by the daily celebration of the liturgy, the *opus Dei* or work of God, especially the great religious feasts of the ecclesiastical year, which are the high points of monastic life.

Most of all I loved Advent, the weeks of waiting for the coming of Christ. It was the time of preparation for the liturgical celebration of the birth of Jesus at Christmas. I found my own feelings perfectly expressed in the communal prayer, the psalms and the readings, hymns and prayers for the coming of the Saviour, which we sang and recited every day. All those texts echoed my own yearnings.

There was, for instance, the Introit of the Mass where Jerusalem symbolizes the soul: "Jerusalem, rise up and stand on a high place and see the joy that comes to you from your God." The words exhort us most urgently: "Now is the time to wake up from sleep," and "The Lord comes! Hurry to meet him and make level his way." At the end of this time of preparation for the coming of Christ we heard the words, so full of promise: "Today you know that the Lord will come and tomorrow you will behold his glory."

Full of longing and expectancy, my fellow sisters and I awaited the advent of the Word of God, which, according to our faith, was to take place under the veil of the liturgical ceremony, and it was with great joy that we celebrated the memory of his birth on that holy night.

I have to say, though, that despite all their splendour, these celebrations always left me with a certain feeling of disappointment. We had all enjoyed the festive mood – but had anything more significant actually happened? Had the Lord come secretly, without anyone noticing it? Had the birth of the divine Word occurred in me without any indication at all, even though I had prepared myself with all my heart? Why wasn't I aware of his coming? I was at a loss to answer these questions, but I relied on my faith, which told me that the outer celebration could and must effect within each of us the grace of the birth of Christ; otherwise, everything would have been in vain. As Angelus Silesius says in his *Cherubic Wanderer*: "Were Christ to be born a thousand times in Bethlehem and not in you – you would be lost forever."

We prepared for the feast of Easter with the same intensity as we did for the birth of Christ. At Easter we celebrated Christ's victory over death, his resurrection and the redemption of humanity through him. The weeks leading up to Easter were filled with more recollection, more prayer, more study of the divine truths and even more turning towards God, to whom we had dedicated our lives.

Easter Eve, as it was celebrated in the monastery, was a beautiful feast extending over many hours, with scriptural readings, chanting of psalms and hymns, and rites full of profound meaning. We were filled with gratitude and joy at Jesus Christ's victory over the powers of darkness and death. We always anticipated with a special joy the singing of the Exultet ('Rejoice'), a hymn for the consecration of the Easter candle, sounding as it did almost ecstatic in its expression of boundless jubilation; it praised even the sins of humankind: *O felix culpa, quae talem ac tantum meruit habere redemptorem* (O happy sin that has deserved such an exalted Redeemer).

As at Christmas, so too at Easter the historical events in Christ's life were given prominence, because it was – according to the Christian faith – through the liturgical celebration of these events that the world would receive the divine grace of salvation, which Christ earned through his birth, death and resurrection. But just *how* this grace would be bestowed on us, just *how* we would participate in it and *how* it would affect us – all this remained a mystery of faith. At Easter, as at Christmas, a certain mental elation followed the liturgical ceremonies, but we had nothing 'tangible'. After the Easter celebration we were exactly the same human beings as before; nothing had changed, at least nothing that we were aware of. As before, I had to rely on my faith in the reality of salvation after death. But isn't the path of salvation something real, something we can experience? If the liberation from the slavery of the 'prince of this world'* and the return of the soul to the house of the Father cannot be experienced within us, can it be real?

With the third great feast of the ecclesiastical year, Pentecost, the feast of the Creator Spirit, who "fills the whole

---

*"Now is the judgment of this world: now shall the prince of this world be cast out." *John* 12:31

world, and...knows every word that is said", we celebrated the descent of the Holy Spirit upon the Apostles of Jesus Christ on the fiftieth day after his death and resurrection. Although the liturgical texts possess a compelling urgency, I had but little access to the mystery of this feast. Again, the liturgy aroused intense prayer in our hearts: "Come, Holy Spirit, gift of the Most High, fountain of life, burning fire, love, sevenfold gift of God." But *who* is this spirit of God and *how* could I experience his coming? This again remained a mystery of faith. It wasn't until many years later, through the teachings of the Masters, that I received an answer to my questions concerning the mystery of these Christian feasts.

During these years I familiarized myself more with the Benedictine Way of Contemplation, as presented by a fellow brother in the Order of Saint Benedict, Father Vincentius Stebler. This path proved to be a complex system of observations and actions, putting the vows into practice, exercising the *ora et labora* – pray and work – and reciting the *opus Dei*, which might lead one finally to the *oratio pura* – the pure prayer – as realized by Saint Benedict. This last stage is the contemplative, wordless prayer: God consciousness in the depth of the soul. During all those years of my monastic life it was this inner awareness of God that I aspired to with all my heart. God had awoken this in me early in my youth and rekindled it again and again. Every once in a while I was allowed to experience his presence for short moments, albeit in a very hidden way. Most of the time, however, my pilgrimage progressed in the darkness of faith.

My companion on the way was my inner guide who had been with me for so long. It was he who taught me to turn to God again and again and to find repose in him. It was he in whom I put my trust, in order to follow – according to the advice of Père de Caussade – the guidance of the Holy Spirit who is present in us all.

CHAPTER EIGHT

God Alone Suffices

WITH THE PASSING OF THE YEARS, LIFE IN THE monastery had slowly and imperceptibly become routine. I fulfilled my monastic duties as a matter of habit, so that once again the routine nature of my life led me into what I experienced as a state of mediocrity. My spiritual life had lost its depth and, without my being aware of it, I was lost in the fulfilment of my day-to-day duties. How long this lasted, I do not recall. In autumn 1961, however, without any visible cause, God made himself fall upon me like a judge, and in the light of God's incorruptible brightness, I saw myself as I really was. I was shown, more clearly than ever before, the countless defects of my character. Shocked and utterly dejected, I started to list all these defects – amounting to more than fifty.

The list no longer exists, but it can be easily reconstructed from the promises I made to God once I had recovered from the shock caused by this self-knowledge. There were no major shortcomings, just many little acts of spiritual negligence, creating a state of indifference that was lethal to true spirituality. There were so many little concessions in order to gratify the senses; so many moments spent with trivialities when I should have been turning my heart to God – moments meant for prayer. When such habits take root they can become an insurmountable hindrance on the spiritual path. Above all, there was the neglect of those soft and gentle impulses of God's grace that had invited me to stay with him and that I had perceived only too well.

This examination of my conscience was also inspired by a small booklet that Père Lallement had written about the life of monks and nuns. In one chapter he deals with the 'second conversion', describing life in monasteries. Recognizing myself in his exposition, I was deeply shaken. I did not want to suffer the fate of those who lost all perspective in their lives, who held back from dedicating themselves to God and rejoiced in the satisfaction of their selfish desires.

In her autobiography, Teresa of Ávila eloquently depicts this condition, which she herself had experienced. She describes her life in the cloister as drifting in an impetuous sea that lasted twenty years. She saw herself constantly falling, rising up and again falling. She admits that worldly things, sensual pleasures, conversations, and a thousand vanities had fettered her in spite of the practice of contemplative prayer. Often she asked the Lord to help her, but she had not put her full confidence in him. She had searched for a remedy and made efforts to improve, but she had not realized that all this would be of little use unless she gave up completely her trust in herself and put all her trust in God.

Teresa confesses that she lived in this condition as if in the shadow of death. She realized that God could not give her what she was longing for and that he could not help her, because every time he led her back to him she left him again. She describes her second conversion in her autobiography as follows:

One day, when I went to the oratory, it so happened that my look fell on a picture…. This picture showed Christ,

covered with many injuries, and this awakened such devotion in me that I was very much taken aback to see the
Saviour maltreated like this; because it vividly expressed
to me what he had suffered for us. When I considered the
ingratitude with which I had repaid him for these injuries,
my grief was so great that my heart seemed to break. I
threw myself down before him, shedding streams of tears,
and implored him to give me strength so that I would not
insult him any more.

In addition to this description Teresa writes:

I started now with a greater inclination to devote more
time to keeping company with God, and I began to keep
away from wayward opportunities (such as worldly friendships and chatting in the parlour); then, as they were out of
my sight, I returned immediately back to His Majesty!

Once again I had reached a milestone on my pilgrimage
to God. I wrote down my resolutions in the form of a prayer:
not to deny God a single wish, to dedicate my whole being
to God unconditionally and to be completely at his disposal.
Realizing well my weakness and inconstancy, I prayed to
God that I might at least live in the fear of once again losing
the grace of conversion. I wanted to shun neglect, infidelity,
forgetfulness and everything that might displease God, while
openly confessing all my faults. With a wakeful heart I would
live before his face and do nothing that might divert my gaze
from him. Over the prayer I had written, "for daily contemplation," adding that "God might help me to keep my promises
and again take possession of my life".

When I drew up this *magna carta* of my spiritual life, I was
well aware of my shortcomings and weaknesses, but I thought

that this, my second conversion and its practical implementation, would depend mainly on my own good will and determination, and on my own initiative and high-mindedness. Consequently, I fell into a kind of 'high-voltage' mental state, a phenomenon well known to the fathers of monasticism in the early days of Christianity, who observed that when the bow is overstretched it ends up breaking. Full of enthusiasm and eagerness, I began by modelling my life according to the resolutions I had made. In hindsight I would see that my inner guide allowed me time to experience where my ambition for high-performance spirituality would lead me. I still had to learn another lesson that, as yet, I knew in theory but not from personal experience – that *everything is his grace*.

Some months after my conversion I fell prey to a temptation that swept aside all my resolutions and everything that had begun so promisingly. Driven by ambition and blind eagerness to do something extraordinary, I threw myself into a task I would not normally have been able to cope with. It was the design and manufacture of a whole set of pontifical vestments – robes for the celebration of the ecclesiastical service in a Benedictine abbey. The execution of this project demanded an effort that absorbed all my time and energy for about a year and a half, and I was literally unable to think of anything else. I followed the communal prayers mechanically and I practically gave up my personal prayer, so that the inner contact with God loosened more and more. The divine horizon in my life had vanished and the world of faith hardly touched me anymore, although I was practically surrounded by it. I lost myself in a desert of God-forsakenness, even though I was living, so to speak, under the same roof with him. Well aware of my situation, I left things as they were because I felt powerless to change them.

In the summer of 1962, the project was completed and I found myself facing the ruins of my spiritual life. Filled with horror, I stared into the burnt-out place that once had been a God-loving heart. This was the end of my life with God – that much was clear to me. I was paralysed and knew that a new beginning was impossible. I had neglected him too much. Too often I had waved aside his invitations to stay with him. At that time I found myself incapable of a single thought that might bring me close to God again. I thought that from then on – I was thirty-nine at the time – my monastic life would be a mere façade. Behind it, death, emptiness and darkness would reign. This would indeed be hell.

For several weeks I remained in this deadly emptiness, filled with an immense mournful loneliness. My reckless ambition had destroyed everything that had developed in all those years since my first encounter with God. But I was not forsaken; the Lord saw my hopelessness and despair. Although I had strayed away from him, he was as close to me as ever. I had to go to the very brink of the abyss in order to realize my utter inability to come to God by my own strength. Only then would I experience his mercy and grace.

This desolate condition may have lasted two months. Wrapped in utter darkness, I sat in my meditation place, feeling as if I were dead. Suddenly the words *'Todo es nada – sólo Dios basta'* (All is nothing – God alone suffices) came into my heart, perhaps reflecting something I had read by Saint Teresa.* By these words I understood that other than God, all is nothing. At first it was just a remote echo resounding within me. Gratefully, I took hold of it, convinced that it was God who had made it come alive in me. How could I have had such a thought myself when I was so far away from understanding its meaning?

---

*The words are similar to a verse Teresa of Ávila wrote in her breviary: *"Todo se pasa...sólo Dios basta."*

God alone suffices – these words dropped into my burnt-out heart like a tiny spark of light. I clasped them to me and repeated them incessantly. In the course of the days and weeks that followed, this tiny spark grew bigger and bigger until it became a bright flame and finally a blazing fire that took possession not only of my heart but of my whole being. God had rescued me and restored me to a life with him.

God alone suffices. From now on, this would determine my life in the monastery. With great zeal I set out to really put God in first place in my life. Of course, for a nun this goes without saying. For me, however, it represented a huge decision. I used every minute for silent prayer and called upon my newly-awakened spiritual strength for the encounter with God, who had once again become the centre of my life. My life had been restored to me. Now I wanted to turn it into an incessant prayer and I asked the Lord to teach me. God heard my prayer in a way that I could never have imagined. Thus began a new phase in my adventure of faith.

CHAPTER NINE

Incessant Prayer

THIS REBIRTH TO A LIFE OF PRAYER TOOK PLACE in August 1962. Yet I still did not know how to turn my life into an incessant prayer. I made great efforts to think of God all day, but this quickly tired me. To direct all my thinking permanently towards God seemed impossible. As I wrote in my diary, "Sooner or later the mind gets weary of continuously thinking of God and capitulates."

But love yearns to dwell with God and one feels the desire to belong to him. Looking for a solution, I found some books in our library on inner contemplative prayer, *Abandonment to Divine Providence* and also the letters of Abbot J. H. Chapmann, mentioned earlier. They were of great help in understanding the mysteries of the relationship between God and the soul, which we call prayer. But I found nothing about incessant prayer. In a conversation with one of my fellow sisters who, like me, was in search of inner, ceaseless prayer, she drew my attention to the Jesus Prayer. She told me that it had opened up a new way of connecting with God and had taught her to pray incessantly.

The classic book on the Jesus Prayer is the *Philokalia*, meaning love for spiritual beauty. It is a collection of texts by more than thirty different authors of early Christianity from the fourth to the fifteenth century CE. First published in Greek in 1782 in Venice, it was later translated into several other European languages. The volume I found in our library was a selection in German.

The *Philokalia* immediately fascinated me. As I read it my heart absorbed the words of those saintly and venerable writers, soaking them up page by page, like a sponge. Then I began to practise the Jesus Prayer, first using the classic formula, "Jesus, Son of David, have mercy on me," the prayer of the blind man in the Gospel of Mark.

The first days with the Jesus Prayer were blissful and encouraging. I felt its effect almost immediately. I was filled with a profound inner peace and an inclination towards good, which made me realize its inherent power. Soon, however, I noted that incessant prayer demands complete self-denial on the part of the practitioner and that it would take immense efforts to concentrate my thinking on God by means of the Jesus Prayer. For the first time I became aware of the vast number of futile and superfluous thoughts that occupied my mind all day. Now it was up to me to conquer them with the Jesus Prayer, or rather not to allow them to surface. This needs wakefulness, or alertness of mind, to which the authors of the *Philokalia* attach great importance. Wakefulness is a term that is quite frequently found in their instructions. Hesychios of Sinai for instance writes:

> In my opinion the first step of wakefulness consists in the strict control of pictures of the imagination and the whisperings, for without exciting our imagination the devil cannot influence our thinking. The second step is to try to always maintain one's heart in silence and to prepare it in deep calm and without any haste for the prayer. The

humble and ceaseless Prayer of Jesus…I call the third step.
A further step is the constant remembrance of death. Like
good guardsmen, these exercises defend the soul against
the entrance of all bad thoughts.

From this point on, these fathers of monasticism became
my great teachers and I regularly turned to them for advice
and help. Their first and foremost instruction was: "Be patient.
Chase away the scattering thoughts from your mind." They
also advised: teach your mind not to run outside. I also found
inspiring words in the instructions of a contemporary teacher
of the Jesus Prayer who wrote, "This incessant prayer is like
a filter through which our thoughts must pass; only what is
compatible with the holy name of Jesus is allowed to pass."

Yet after a short time it became evident that I was unable to
identify with the classic formula of the Jesus Prayer. To express
my love and devotion to Jesus, I had to formulate my own text.
For some days I experimented in order to find the words I
wanted to say to God. Finally a short sentence emerged centred
around the name of Jesus, the inclusion of which is, according
to the instructions, essential.

Now that I had found my own 'prayer of the heart' I practised
it with great intensity within and sometimes spoke it out loud.
The term 'prayer of the heart' refers to the method by which the
ceaseless Jesus Prayer was practised by the monks of early Christianity. For instance, the instructions of Gregory of Sinai read
as follows: "Sit with lowered head on a low stool. In this position let your breath flow, as it were, into your heart and hold it
there…and practise the Prayer of Jesus without interruption."

Much importance was attached to the breathing technique
by the Hesychasts (from the Greek *hesychia* – to be in peace, in
calmness) for the practice of the Jesus Prayer. It served to bring
the mind (the attention) back inside the body and make the

mind collect within itself in order to practise the Jesus Prayer in complete recollection. The teachers of the Jesus Prayer point out that the outer technique is only a means. The essence of this practice lies in the undivided, pure and concentrated acclamation of the Lord in the heart, which in this connection means the depth of the soul.

I also tried to practise the breathing technique recommended by the teachers of the Jesus Prayer, but soon gave it up because it proved disturbing. The recommended concentration on the heart centre also soon proved to be unnecessary, because the invisible light focused on my forehead like a ray and held my concentration there.

At that time I was charged with insulating the pipes of the heating system in a new wing of the monastery, a work that did not require much concentration on my part. It meant that I was on my own for long periods of the day and therefore could give my full attention to the Jesus Prayer. About ten days after I began practising with my own prayer formula I was irresistibly drawn inside into a meditative depth that I had never experienced before. First the little spark of the name of Jesus flared up to a blazing fire, followed by a feeling of having touched a power current and receiving an electric shock. Simultaneously, I felt a fountain springing up within me, an entirely novel experience.

Awakening of the soul

Until now my spiritual activity had come mainly from the mind, the emotions and the senses. Now it felt to me that the consciousness of my innermost self was awakening. According to the testimony of the mystics, the entering of the transcendent into human consciousness brings about a profound change in the human being – like a person who has been sleeping and has now awoken. The term 'awakening to the self' or 'awakening to mystic consciousness' signifies the moment when a human being becomes aware of transcendent reality that often enters into his life as an experience of light. He may feel as if struck by lightning or filled to overflowing with light. After such an experience he is no longer the same being, as is testified by many mystic practitioners. In a fraction of a second he has gone through a transformation process that he could not have brought about by any amount of effort on his part. According to those who have had such experiences, the entry of the transcendent, divine reality into a person's life is absolutely irresistible and final; there is no room for hesitation or doubt. This experience often involves a radical turnaround in the life of such a person, as was the case for instance for Saint Paul, and had been my own experience as a young girl of thirteen years.

Several times in the course of my life God had 'touched' my soul and each time I had experienced the transforming effect of his touch.* These profound experiences had branded me, so to speak. I emerged from them as another being and felt as if nothing was quite the same as before; this would soon prove to be true once more.

From that moment I felt an overpowering urge to kneel down at this fountain of living water within me and to drink from it. But the monastic schedule allowed me few opportunities. The official worship that had meant so much to me before

---

*The experience of being 'touched' by the transcendental, for example, seeing transcendental light and hearing inward voices, is not an everyday experience, but neither is it an altogether extraordinary phenomenon that only saints and mystics speak about. Even people in the modern era, such as the French poet and playwright Paul Claudel and Parisian journalist André Frossard, both avowed atheists at the time of their experiences, tell of seeing supernatural light. André Frossard also heard an inner voice, which he describes in his stirring book, *Dieu existe: Je l'ai rencontré (God Exists: I Have Met Him)*.

felt now like a curtain between God and my soul, a curtain that I was all the time trying to pull aside. The many hours that we were spending each day on the liturgy, the *opus Dei*, seemed like time lost.

The rites and ceremonies of the ecclesiastic worship, the sacraments and the communal prayer had not been able to open this fountain to me and their spiritual nourishment now appeared like tasteless food. At the richly laid table of traditional piety and religiosity in the monastery I began to hunger and thirst for food for the soul. More and more I realized that this experience had uprooted me from the religious life I had been leading up to this point. But just as there had been no turning back when God had intervened in my life at an earlier time, so too there was no way back now. What had happened was irrevocable.

The experience of transcendence did not transport me into a state of trance, yet somehow I knew that it can suspend one's everyday consciousness and help one to rise to a higher state of consciousness, where contact with the divine transcends all previous encounters.

The encounter with profundities of my consciousness caught me quite unprepared. Unable to interpret what was taking place, I lived in a mist of light. It was indeed a kind of inner light experience and in moments of inner stillness I sometimes had a vision of a moon-like disc before me. In a way, the inner light had 'materialized' and become visible to the physical eye. At times it was a blazing light that blinded me and I had to try and protect my eyes with my hands.

By the experience of the deeper layer of spiritual life and the invisible presence of God within, my habit of contemplating on pictures of Jesus Christ that I had cultivated for many years was swept away. These pictures had become a veil between God and my soul and I could not bear them any more.

I therefore turned them round in my prayer books, where they served as markers.

In the ensuing period I continued studying the *Philokalia* very intensely. In order to have the book always at hand when I needed its advice for practising the Jesus Prayer, and because I had to return it to the library, I copied all of it by hand. I read the book so often that finally I almost knew it by heart and its content was always with me. The Jesus Prayer gradually took possession of me and changed me completely. While before my lively temperament had led me to seek satisfaction in outward activities, this energy was now drawn inside and all I wanted was to devote myself in silence to inner prayer.

CHAPTER TEN

The Call into the Desert

ONE YEAR EARLIER THE WORDS *'TODO ES NADA – sólo Dios basta'* (All is nothing – God alone suffices) had brought about a profound change in my spiritual life. Although I was then unable to grasp their whole significance, this new experience of a deeper dimension made me feel their reality. In spite of my own limitations, I now felt certain that God alone suffices. The deeper the truth of these words penetrated me, the more I also realized that all is nothing. All the time, I felt as if the "fashion of this world passeth away", as Saint Paul wrote to the Christian community at Corinth.

I experienced this 'nothing' as a desert – a desert in the metaphysical sense, meaning the absence of all that we can perceive with our senses and conceive with our intellect. In this state, one is confronted with the *nakedness of the Absolute*, as described by Meister Eckhart and experienced by all mystics. Meister Eckhart speaks in his sermons on several occasions about this desert. He says that a person who has transcended his physical body and the diversity of time will dwell in eternity, in unity and in the desert, meaning in the divine Being. He also speaks of the 'silent desert' into which the soul wants to merge – in the single ground of divinity.

Antoinette Bourignon also speaks of this desert, saying that she asked God in her prayer: "O Lord, what must I do to please you?" Thereupon she heard a voice saying: "Give up all earthly things. Renounce your love for the creatures."

"When shall I be completely your own?" she asked the Lord. She believed that she heard the answer: "When you shall no longer call anything your own and will be dead to yourself."

"And where should I do this, O Lord?" He answered: "In the desert."

I felt this desert very intensely, yet was unable to make sense of it until a year later, when I came across a phrase by Père René Voillaume, founder of the Little Brothers and Sisters of Jesus:

> Only in the nakedness and bareness of the desert do all the illusions dwindle away that keep us from really seeing what is buried in our hearts. To walk alone in the desert is simply unbearable for someone who is not simple and poor and who expects from life anything but God alone.

Although I had already read this statement several times, this time it penetrated my core like a flash of lightning; the mists dispelled and I instantly understood that it was God who had sent me this desert experience, that this desert was not a place but a state, and that it was he who had led me into this desert just as he had led others before me.

The desert will not suffer compromise: God and man stand face to face. One is simply overwhelmed by God's power and it is impossible to escape or hide. In this merciless desert we cannot possess anything except our own naked existence – and even this we will lose to God. But the desert conceals a secret, which is that the ultimate insecurity, the final experience of being handed over, actually confers the most profound security, the ultimate never-to-be-lost freedom, the genuine, the true life – God. I came to this insight after approximately one year of 'desert life' and noted it in my diary in order to keep a record for myself about the state I was in. In these notes, frequently taking the form of a dialogue with God, the expression 'God's total claim' appears repeatedly. It was no longer just the undivided heart of my youth that he demanded; it was the *total surrender of my entire being*, of my whole existence, to him.

The desert experience may come by way of a deep mental shock, by a heavy blow of fate, by some other deeply stirring event or simply by the 'touch of the absolute'. Regardless of how it comes, those to whom it comes fall under the law of the desert, where the choice is understood to be between eternal being or not-being, truth or illusion, reality or unreality, the Creator or his creatures. When that happens, evaluation of one's thoughts and actions no longer takes place by a process of intellectual reflection. There is no room for weighing right and wrong. The law functions automatically and incorruptibly, so that a person is instantly called to account for every act, and the consequences of each act are unavoidable. There still remains a certain measure of freedom to decide, but the consequences of each decision stand before one, as in a glaring light. The true significance of each choice is crystal clear. Does one choose true being or not-being? Does one choose truth or illusion? Reality or unreality? The Creator or his creatures?

From now on this was the law that governed my life. Not that I always had the strength to decide in favour of eternal being, of truth, of reality, of God; but every time I opted for not-being, for illusion, for unreality, for created beings – in other words, every time I opted for my own self, I was immediately aware of it, even in very trivial matters. And so the law of the desert became the measure of my life, as is so aptly stated in a poem I discovered at that time:

Who once has found the desert,
Shall not lose it again –
It is not a place: it is a condition.
The desert is the stillness,
That does not make one deaf,
But gives hearing.
The desert is a solitude
In which one does not lose oneself
But finds oneself.
The desert is not passive waiting,
But an active going towards God.
In that desert nothing is negative:
Silence is not the absence of speaking,
Fasting is not the absence of eating,
Solitude is not lack of company.
That desert is empty of all earthly things
And full of divine love.
In that desert those disillusioned with life
Have no place.

As it was unavoidable, I applied the same measure to our own monastic way of living. I compared our lives, our daily routine, the big buildings in which we lived, with the desert experience. 'God alone suffices' was now the criterion. A great many things in my environment, which before had seemed so indispensable, did not stand the test.

Gradually the ground of our monastic life, which had once seemed so solid, began to move beneath my feet. I couldn't understand why those with whom I lived attached any importance to those things that didn't seem to bring them any closer to God-realization. But that was not all; the whole visible world now stood between God and my soul. Many people, including great saints, see this world as a beautiful reflection of the Creator, but to me it seemed like a dense mist. I longed to push aside everything that stood in my way and to penetrate the mist in order to finally stand before the ultimate reality, before the uncreated light. I wanted to leave behind everything that was not God – not just in my mind, but in a very concrete, very real fashion. I wanted a life in true poverty, completely bereft of all earthly objects as far as was humanly possible here on earth, and my desire grew stronger and stronger.

During this phase of reorientation, the writings of the fathers of monasticism of the Christian East, collected in the *Philokalia* mentioned earlier, were of prime importance to me. Many of these monks had lived in the Syrian desert, in Asia Minor, in Egypt, near the Bosphorus, and later, on solitary Greek islands. In their writings I found an ideal of monastic life that imprinted itself on my heart. Seeing the exclusiveness and determination with which these men had made the search for God the sole purpose in their lives, and the one-pointedness with which they had followed their vocation, I began to view our way of life as an intolerable compromise.

The desire to lead such a life in the absoluteness of the early monastic tradition became more urgent every day. More and more I came into conflict with the life that hitherto I had considered the ideal of monastic existence. Serious doubts seized me and threw me into a state of deep uneasiness. Our way of life became more and more incomprehensible to me and I was no longer able to identify with it. I could neither ignore nor refuse the 'call of the desert'. Little did I know that withdrawing the senses from the world, entering into the great silence before God and detaching oneself from all transitory things must be accomplished in a totally different way.

CHAPTER ELEVEN

The Ridge Walk

EVER SINCE MY 'DESERT EXPERIENCE', I HAD been leading a double life in the midst of the monastic community. After a while it became clear that I could not go on like this for the rest of my life – I was now thirty-nine – because I would not be able to stand the mental pressure for much longer.

One day I was overwhelmed by an intense longing for inner peace and suddenly the solitude of the Carthusian monastery stood before me. Deeply alarmed, I wondered whence this thought had come. Was it God who had inspired it or had it sprung up in my imagination? I had already thought about joining a stricter order some years before, but at that time it had not been a serious matter. Now it seemed clear that my outer life would have to change as a consequence of the desert experience.

For months on end I pondered the issue, analysed my experiences and wrote down my reflections and conclusions in search of clarity. I needed to look objectively at my inner evolution and then examine whether I had drawn the right conclusions from my experience. Until I was sure about what prompted me to leave the monastery – the call of God or my own wishes – I felt unable to act. My conscience would not allow it. After having minutely analysed all the pros and cons, I was convinced that part of my recent experiences was a true 'call into the desert' – a call that I had to follow. But how was I to do this? The 'how' was shrouded in utter darkness.

Many months passed until finally, after the demise of our Mother Abbess, I was able to speak with her successor about my vocation. She was understandably shocked when I told her about my intention of leaving the monastery and changing to a stricter order, but she left me free to find my own way. My request for admission to the Carthusian nuns brought a kind and sympathetic answer containing, however, such a definite and final decline of my request that there was not the slightest hope for me of changing over to that order. Although I had been prepared for a negative answer, the refusal was such a stunning blow that for days on end I was unable to think calmly and reasonably. I felt deeply troubled, thinking that now I had to give up the desert ideal forever. For the first time in my life I felt as though I was hanging over an abyss.

Some ten days later I calmed down sufficiently to recall that experience of the desert which had been such a turning point in my life. With all my strength I fought against my inner despair and, in an act of faith and blind confidence, I threw myself into God's arms. I came to understand that I could thank him for suspending my life over an abyss and thus giving me the chance to leap into the void and deliver myself utterly to him. This was not to be the last time that God demanded this 'death-leap'; it seemed to be his method of education, preparing one for an unquestioning surrender to him. It became clear that this unconditional submission to God was from now on my only chance of survival, although for me it felt more like death than life. And such a moment does indeed evoke a feeling of *exinanitio*, of being extinguished or annihilated, an agonizing emptying of oneself. It is not the fear of physical death, but rather the fear of giving up everything that we consider vital for the maintenance of our self-consciousness: our feeling, thinking, knowing and wanting. The mystics of all religions make mention of this experience, put into words by Bernard of Clairvaux: "O Lord, it is a constant dying when one desires to gain you." And the same is meant in the Katha Upanishad when it says: "The path to God goes over the edge of a sharp razor." In order to encounter God, the seeker must – according to a frequently used expression from the Middle Ages – cross the 'bridge to the beyond'. In an analogy for physical death, which entails leaving behind all transitory things, including one's own body, the seeker here must abandon *himself* before being able to cross the threshold to a life with God.

The road to the Carthusian convent having been blocked, I made another attempt to gain an inch of desert for myself and contacted Père Voillaume, whose words about the call to the desert had had such a profound effect on me a few months earlier. His answer was very kind. He suggested the possibility of applying for admission to a strictly contemplative community in the south of France. Still, what he wrote remained quite vague and I realized that I still had a long way to go in order to reach a goal that was still shrouded in darkness. My second letter to Père Voillaume, written in October 1963, was not answered. I did not know that he had been in North Africa for several months and that his mail had not been forwarded to him.

In the meantime, by reading magazines found in our library I became aware of the many efforts being made within the monastic orders to reinvigorate monastic life by returning to the simplicity and strictness of earlier times and giving more emphasis to the *oratio pura*, the contemplative prayer that Saint Benedict speaks of in his *Rule*. It was no small consolation to me to find that I was not alone, and I felt encouraged to persevere in my search for a life nearer to this ideal. In those magazines I also found some articles about 'life in the desert' and I received permission to contact one of the authors, Soeur Marie from Paris.

India on the horizon

While I was still waiting for an answer from Père Voillaume, my mother sent me a circular letter from one of my former friends in the youth organization, who some years back had set up a leper colony in Northern India. *India?* The country's age-old spiritual tradition was known to me from the writings of Rabindranath Tagore. Although my knowledge was quite vague, I knew enough to take this letter as a hint from God.

I wrote to my old friend asking her about life in India, but without mentioning my real reason for writing. Having no idea of what had moved me and without answering my questions, she wrote about the visit of a Christian monk, Père Le Saux, who was leading the life of a *sannyasi*, a renunciant who seeks the Divine within, in India. He had taken the Indian name Swami Abhishiktananda, which signifies 'joy in the Anointed One' (Christ). To adopt an Indian name and to wear the clothing of an Indian sannyasi was for Christian monks the outer sign of integration into the culture of India. Together with his companion, Abbé Monchanin, he had founded the contemplative Christian ashram, Shantivanam (forest of peace) in the south of India. About this ashram and its concept they had written the book *Eremites du Saccidananda (The Hermits of Sachchidananda),** which had recently been published in German. My friend's letter literally brought me down on my knees. Did God want me in India? I must be out of my mind, I said to myself, for even considering that possibility. Nevertheless, this day turned out to be the day on which my vocation for India was born. A few days

---

* *Sachchidananda* is a Sanskrit term in Indian philosophy describing the essence of God. It is a compound term combining *sat* (being, truth), *chit* (consciousness) and *ananda* (bliss). This name is employed by Indian Christian theologians as a synonym for the Holy Trinity: the Father, the Son and the Holy Spirit.

later, when I held the book in my hands, I realized that these two monks were living exactly the kind of monastic life that I envisaged for myself.

Then, to my complete astonishment, in the middle of January 1964 I received a letter from Père Voillaume in Marseilles. He was proposing to intervene on my behalf with the responsible bishop in order to facilitate my joining the contemplative community in the south of France, which he had mentioned before. However, because my vocation was now pulling me towards India, I disregarded this proposal and turned instead to Swami Abhishiktananda. From reading his book, I felt as though I already knew him quite well, and I wrote to him about my desert experience, asking him whether he saw a way for me to follow the call into the desert in India. I had to wait for three months for his answer, which was sobering, "Wanting to come alone to India as a member of a strictly cloistered order is an adventurous idea," he wrote back. He was surely right, yet he ended with a decisive sentence, "But if God wants you to be here, it will be shown." I clung to those words as one would cling to a prophecy.

On 26th February 1964 I received a letter from Soeur Marie from Paris, to whom I had turned for contact with a hermetic monk. The answer given was, "If the Lord wants a change in your vocation, he will intervene at his hour and in his way." I was quite convinced of the truth of this, and I awaited God's intervention with unshakeable confidence.

At Easter 1964 there was another completely unexpected turn of events. An acquaintance who knew about my problems wrote to me about a small monastic community, the Sisters of the Virgin of the Poor, which was in Bouricos in France. There the ideal I aspired to was being put into practice. The sisters led a strictly contemplative life based on communal poverty and complete remoteness from the world.

What to make of this hint? Did God want me there, after first having put the idea of India into my mind? My path seemed to be full of sudden turns and they always made me afraid that the next step would take me into the void. Each time it proved to be just a sharp turn in the path, after which I still had firm ground under my feet – but only just enough ground for my next step and never more than that.

Before contacting Père Ermin le Clerk, the founder of the small community at Bouricos, I wanted to wait for Swami Abhishiktananda's answer, but it was a long time coming, so I finally decided to write to Père Ermin. He replied, "Unfortunately our sisters do not accept professed sisters from other orders or congregations." They had had too many unfortunate experiences with such conversions and they did not want to take the risk again. Not wanting to give up so quickly, I wrote them a second letter with more details about my motives.

While waiting for their answer I received a letter from India at last. My letter had been travelling around the Himalayas for ten weeks before it finally reached the wandering monk. In his reply, Swami Abhishiktananda painted a gloomy picture of the problems that would await me in India and I myself felt apprehensive about the problems I might face as a Catholic nun coming to India without any specific plan to found a cloister. Since I had in the meantime contacted the community of the Sisters of the Virgin of the Poor and was still hoping that they would grant me admission, I gave in to the fear that the Swami's letter had awakened in me. I wrote back to him, saying that under the circumstances I did not see how I could go to India; the obstacles seemed insurmountable.

However, the reply to my second letter to the community at Bouricos contained a loving but final refusal, and before I could answer it, there was another letter from Swami Abhishiktananda in which he tried to soften the effect of the previous one. He wrote to say that I should take everything into consideration and then, if I still felt like coming to India, I should make a decision. More than ever I now felt like a plaything in God's hands. Some years later I would read in the teachings of the Masters that we are all puppets in the hands of the divine puppet-master and that the whole creation is his *lila*, his play.

Since all other roads were barred, and only the way to India was left open, I was determined to take it. I had no other choice, for even the slightest thought of abandoning 'the desert' forever filled me with dismay and made me feel that desperation was pulling me into an abyss, for I knew that if I renounced the desert I could never find inner peace. As Père Voillaume had once written to a brother who was in a similar situation, "You will only find peace by answering the call of God."

For a long time I had felt as though I was walking along a narrow, steep ridge. My path to God had become a 'ridge walk' and the abysses on both sides were equally threatening. On one side there was a feeling of desperation; often the thought came up in my mind that the whole thing was only self-deception, that there was nobody who had called me and that there was no goal that I was striving for. On the other side, and no less frightening, there was the temptation of what in German is called *Selbstherrlichkeit*, which means making one's own decisions in an arrogant and self-centred way, instead of living in a state of submission. It felt like walking on a razor's edge, for in spite of my desert experience I was never absolutely sure whether I was on the right way. Had not thousands of men and women dedicated their lives to God in the Order of Saint Benedict and followed the 'way of perfection' according to his *Rule*? Why should I be any different?

Sometimes during this 'ridge walk' I was tempted to stop and to turn, at least for a moment, in order to look back at the years when I had been happy in my monastery. But then I felt as if somebody was standing behind me with a drawn sword in his hand – someone who wouldn't even let me turn my head. He would rather kill me than let me look back. Again and again I was tempted to say to myself, "Enough of this! Take your life into your own hands again." On one occasion I did give in to this temptation and I fell into the abyss.

Often I felt like an uprooted plant, lying on the ridge in the scorching sun. I prayed insistently to God, begging him not to leave me with my roots withering, but to plant me where I was destined to grow. I fervently longed to be rooted in soil that would nourish me, but another twelve months would pass before this happened.

It was like an experience of death, an experience through which I had to go. Every time I affirmed my willingness to persevere on the ridge, I had to lay down my life at God's feet. I went through this death a hundred times a day, in fact. Every time I thought about my situation, I felt as though I was face to face with death, but death turned into life as soon as I surrendered unconditionally to the will of God.

In spite of everything, the walk along the ridge was also glorious, for it made me experience God's invisible presence and it obliged me to look at him ceaselessly. It was *his gaze* that drew my gaze to him and that cured me of my vertigo in the face of the abysses on both sides of the path. This 'eye-to-eye contact' with my invisible companion on the ridge was a permanent source of strength that helped me to persevere through this phase and made the next step possible. Not that I ever actually saw any face or eyes looking at me, but there was a clearly felt yet invisible gaze that I was able to respond to and that made me certain of the presence of that unknown One to whom I had dedicated my life.

CHAPTER TWELVE

Who Are You, O Lord?

FOR TWENTY-SEVEN YEARS I HAD BEEN FOL-
lowing the unknown One whom I called God. First he had
demanded my undivided heart and then he had led me into
the 'garden inclosed' so that I should belong to no one but him.
After that he had enticed me into the desert. Finally he made
me walk the razor's edge in order to bring me to the place
where he wanted me to be.

By now I had encountered him in countless hidden ways
and had ventured to follow him so many times that he truly had
become my destiny. But *who* was he? In May 1964 I put before
him my question about his identity, in the form of a prayer:

> Who are you, Lord?
> You, to whom I abandon my life,
> Whom I follow on a steep and dark path –
> Step by step,
> You, who enticed me into the desert.
>
> Who are you, Lord, for whom I go
> Through fire and water,
> For whom I suffer
> To the limits of my strength?

Who are you,
That you have such power over me,
That you chain me to you,
That you do not leave me free,
That I cannot avert my gaze from you?

Who are you,
That you have become my fate?
Who are you,
Who became the centre and the object
Of my life and my thoughts?
Who are you,
That I cannot leave you,
Even if I were to lose my life?

I do not know you, Lord –
Yet you are close to me.
I have never seen you –
But your countenance shines over me.
I have never heard you –
But I know your voice.

Lord, it is you
Into whom I plunged.
It is you
Who fell upon me like fire.
You are that eagle
Who dropped on his prey.

You intervened into the depth of my life.
It is you
Whom I encountered in the desert.

It is you
For whom I wait,
Whom I set out to meet.
It is you in whom I put all my trust,
To whom all my love belongs –
You my Lord and God.

This prayer was an attempt to find an answer to my question to the unknown One. But there was no answer other than my remembrance of his work as I had experienced it. The question of who he was remained unanswered. I was sure of only one thing: he was not the God of the theologians and scribes, of the philosophers and the scholars of religion. He was the 'living God'. He had broken into my life forcefully and there was no escape.

The question in my prayer can only be answered fully at a higher level of consciousness, where the unknown One reveals himself to the soul. But this does not mean that such prayers are useless, for when we try we find that our efforts awaken within us a longing to know God, and this longing is at least a preliminary answer to our prayers.

This longing is of great importance in the spiritual quest. There is a story told by Sri Ramakrishna, a fervent seeker of God and a spiritual teacher in India:

An ardent disciple asked of his Guru, "When will I have the vision of God?" Instead of giving a direct answer, the Guru took the novice to the seashore and held his head under water for a while. Then he asked him how it felt. "I thought I would die for want of air to breathe," came the answer. "Such a longing for God would reveal him immediately," was the answer given by the Master.

To the Promised Land

Now all doors were barred – only the door to India remained open and I had no doubt that India was my 'promised land'. God would take me there – of that I was sure. The long ridge walk had made me fearless. Every obstacle that blocked my way now made me stronger and filled me with even more inner assurance. Intuitively I sensed that I was on the right path, although I could not have given a rational explanation for this. Not that there was ever a way in the sense of a perceptible path, for at best I was able to see only the next step. My inner guide did not let me see more than this. As Père de Caussade confirms:

> When God gives himself as a guide to a soul, he can rightly demand that she follow him unconditionally, without getting uneasy about the way on which he will lead her. The soul will be prompted without seeing the path ahead. The way ahead is neither where the soul sees it nor as she expects it to be. Seeing the way ahead is the way of the ego, which cannot do otherwise – it cannot take the risk. God's 'ways, however, are always new. He does not ride on beaten tracks, but always paves new ways. Under his guidance a

soul does not know where the journey goes. Neither books nor reasoning are of any help. The workings of the Divine constantly reveal the next move. Under his impulse alone she goes on her way.

All that I knew of the way were the steps that lay behind me.

By now I was in regular correspondence with Swami Abhishiktananda. In one of his letters, received on 16th September 1964, he took up the question of my vocation for India. His impression was that I had chosen India for the fulfilment of my personal 'vocation for the desert'. While such a vocation was a necessary prerequisite, it would not be enough. Whoever has a vocation for India, he wrote, comes in order to fulfil an *ecclesiastic mission*, helping to make real the presence of the Christian Church – either by living the monastic way of life or in some other way. Swami Abhishiktananda did not mention a definite missionary task; he had never envisaged that for himself, and I would never have accepted any missionary work in India. In his letter he demanded to know if I had received some clear indications from the Lord that would allow me to proceed on a course that seemed otherwise unwise and adventurous.

If he thought that I had chosen India for the fulfilment of my personal vocation, Swami Abhishiktananda no doubt was right. At the same time, I was also convinced that *God had chosen me for India*. His intentions were unknown to me; they would be unveiled step by step once I was actually living in India. Nevertheless I reflected on Swami Abhishiktananda's serious objections and thus discovered another dimension of my vocation for India: wherever I found myself in the end, it would be my task to bear witness that 'God alone suffices'. I was to live my vocation for the desert. When I had read *Eremiten von Saccidananda (Hermits of Sachchidananda)* I had realized that such a testimony was of fundamental importance for the Catholic Church in India.

In my reply to Swami Abhishiktananda I explained that I envisaged a life of prayer, contemplation and true poverty, in accordance with the ideal of the early monastic tradition as it is presented in the *Philokalia*. I also told him that I believed the 'desert experience' had predestined me for India. This exchange of letters seemed to be taking me into a new phase. New horizons opened before me and I sensed a wonderful inner freedom and ease, as I had now diverted my attention away from myself and was seeing my future in India in a wider context.

In the summer of 1964, while such reflections on my vocation still continued to occupy my mind, I had a visit from my uncle, Dr Klemens Tilmann, a Catholic priest. My mother had told him about my problems and he was very concerned. After a long talk, however, he said that he was also convinced that God stood behind it all and that he was willing to intervene on my behalf with the Church authorities in Rome. In a letter to me later on he summed up his conclusions from our discussions, "I came to you with a number of questions and doubts, but our talk has made it abundantly clear that the events you mention are not an illusion. When everything works out so perfectly in all aspects, it can only come from one source, from God. I felt a deep joy about your vocation and I am glad that I can contribute in a modest way towards its realization. With all my heart I shall accompany you on your path."

After receiving this letter I wrote to Swami Abhishiktananda again, for I was now able to show him that there really were clear indications that God had called me to India, as he had demanded. His reply to my letter came as a great relief. "In this way you have successfully countered all my objections," he wrote. The fact that my uncle was himself convinced about my vocation impressed him very much. Dr Tilmann was the co-author of the new German Catechism that had been published after the Second World War. Moreover, he was an *experitus* (expert) at the Second Vatican Council in Rome (1962–1965). Swami Abhishiktananda told me that he had heard enough about Dr Tilmann to realize that "he was not an ordinary man". After all the years of searching, waiting and worrying, this was the first positive reaction to any of the countless letters I had written. With immense relief I could now focus on my goal.

During the preceding weeks Swami Abhishiktananda had arranged a visit by Dr Bettina Bäumer, a young theologian from Vienna with a degree in Indology, who had been in India. She told me about her experiences and we quickly became friends. It was our hope that in a few years' time, we and other sisters from Europe might be able to lead together a life in the spirit of the Hermits of Sachchidananda. Our plans turned out to be impracticable because the differences in our respective backgrounds and in our concepts of community life were too great. Later, when we met in India, it soon became clear we would each have to go our own way.

A deep fall

In 1965 it was time to take up the matter of my going to India with the Congregation for Religious – the relevant Church authority in Rome. For help in formulating my request, I turned to a fellow brother of the Abbey of Beuron, Father Paulus. I knew this Benedictine monk from his articles in various religious magazines, and at the end of March he was able to come to Kellenried. Before that, our Mother Abbess had discussed my plans with the senior sisters of our community – without me present, alas. It was here that the idea was first voiced that I should apply for dispensation from my vows, in order to be free to do what I considered to be the will of God. To me it seemed unthinkable that a member of an order could ever even conceive of such an idea and I was shocked by the thought of having to take back my promise to God.

When we met, Father Paulus himself made the same suggestion within the first quarter of an hour. He had previously promised to help me, but under the influence of the Mother Abbess he must have retreated from that position. In the most insistent of terms he now pointed out all the dark sides of my 'adventure' and confronted me with a choice between remaining in the monastery or getting dispensation from my vows. For him there was no alternative.

Since he judged me unable to take such a decision at that moment, he suggested to me that I should spend some time in a Benedictine abbey in another country in order to gain some distance from the whole problem. This seemed to be a reasonable proposal, and since it was made in such a kind and concerned way, I immediately agreed to it. In reality, it was an arbitrary attempt, even if made with the best of intentions, to intervene and change my plans. I was so exhausted, physically and mentally, that the prospect of spending a year in a haven of peace appealed to me immensely – so much so that I accepted without hesitation. Quite unawares, I had for a moment lost 'eye-to-eye-contact' with the invisibly present One, and I had tumbled instantly into the abyss of *Selbstherrlichkeit*. I felt magically attracted by its depths before I realized what dangers were lurking there.

India was by now lost from sight, as I concentrated all my energy on the new project. I immediately began to study French, since in the week of Pentecost I was to go to Valogne in Normandy. Recently, this Abbey had founded a new monastery in Africa and I was told that perhaps one day I would be able to go there. This was all done to take my mind off India.

What took place in my mind in the weeks that followed is simply indescribable. Once separated from the goal God had fixed for me, I became a plaything of my own imagination. Countless ideas for the future arose in my head, all somehow ending in a mist of very vague ideas. I also realized that Valogne would be a real trap for me, where I would only retrieve my inner peace if I decided at the outset to forget about my experience of the desert. The ridge walk would have been no more than a vain escapade, something to be forgotten as quickly as possible. Some weeks passed in this way, during which I shed more tears than ever before.

One day, horror gripped me in the face of the dense mists in which my life was floundering and I realized that God was in no way truly present in all these considerations. I gathered all my strength, shed the projections of my fancy and placed myself inwardly before God. Over and over again I asked him for forgiveness for my presumptuous planning and prayed to him fervently to save me once more from going my own way. In this hour I retrieved my faith in his guidance and in my vocation for India. I gradually felt strong enough to follow this path, no matter how far away the goal or how much torment and frustration I would have to endure. Again I climbed up onto the ridge and directed my eyes towards God. Instantly the mists dissolved and from then on a wonderful certainty filled me; I was convinced that God would yet bring me to the 'promised land'.

The next day I confessed to our Mother Abbess that I was determined to continue on my way to India, whereupon she in turn told me what had induced her to consent to the plan to send me to Valogne. She had thought that such a postponement would be the end of my plans. However, as Père Voillaume had written to a brother in a similar situation, "Nothing weakens a person more and nothing is more barren, like an endless circle, than only to ponder with the intellect about truths and values, without ever putting them into practice in one's own life."

The last leap

After focusing on India once again, the first thing I had to do was apply to the Church authorities in Rome for permission to leave the monastery. What I needed was an *exclaustratio ad experimentum*, a kind of test period outside the monastery. In my case, it would have to be an exceptional permission, because it was normally necessary either to be a member of a founding group or to join an existing new monastery in India. Neither of these applied in my case. As was to be expected, my request was declined by the Congregation for Religious and they hinted at the possibility of my vows being suspended. While not actually feeling discouraged by the refusal, I was at a loss about my next step.

Two days later the Lord put me back on my feet. I shall never forget the moment. It was after the communal prayer in the afternoon. I had entered my room and remained for a moment in silence. My inner gaze was directed towards God and I asked, "What now, Lord?" Inwardly I was completely calm. I was sure that he would answer me in one way or another. Then I heard the voice that had spoken to me once before, long ago. In clear and distinct words it said, "Get back on your feet! Make a general attack! Fight! I am with you." Instantly I felt great courage and I knew immediately what to do. The Lord himself had taken up the banner and called on me to fight – no doubt about that. I later found in a book confirmation of my conviction that it was God who had spoken to me:

Whoever accepts the possibility that the Creator can contact man in the form of unarticulated suggestions or inspirations, by which the Divine Spirit influences the soul and mind of a human being, to him it will not appear impossible that this same Divine Spirit can even reveal himself with an articulated voice that is inwardly audible.

First I asked my uncle, Dr Tilmann, who six months ago had offered his help, for a letter of reference. Then I asked the former principal of the Catholic Organization of Social Work for Girls for a recommendation, as I had worked under her and she knew me well. I also asked Father Paulus from Beuron, who was a member of the mission-council of our order, but he felt unable to write a recommendation for me. (Years later, however, he did facilitate my participation at the Congress of the Monastic Orders in Asia, which took place in Bangkok.) On 21st June 1965, I again sent in my application for exclaustration to the Congregation in Rome, along with the recommendations I had obtained.

Next, I attacked the matter of a visa for India. I planned to go first to my friend Agnes Kunze in Dehra Dun in northern India, in order to help her with her work there. She had founded a leper colony there six years before and was doing admirable work. From there I was going to try to make contacts that would bring me closer to a life in the spirit of the Hermits of Sachchidananda. Unfortunately the help in getting a visa that had been promised by a supporter of the leper colony failed. However, Bettina Bäumer, when visiting me some time earlier in Kellenried, had happened to mention a possible way of getting a visa for India. In spring 1965 she had met a Greek nun, Sister Lila, who belonged to the International Secretariat for Study and Service Exchange in New Delhi. The aim of this organization was to promote the encounter between Hindus and Christians. Its founder, Major Ramachandra, was a disciple of Mahatma Gandhi. Now Bettina Bäumer's passing remark was to prove most providential. Soon we would experience for ourselves the meaning of the words of Jesus Christ: "Said I not unto thee, that, if thou wouldest believe, thou shouldest see the glory of God?"

Bettina Bäumer wrote immediately to Major Ramachandra and received in reply a kind and personal letter that was very encouraging. A few days later I also received a letter from him. He suggested that, together with Sister Lila, I should visit a number of ashrams in India and then decide on the one that suited me best. He himself had a specific ashram in mind and much later, after having taken quite a circuitous route, I did indeed end up there. The Indian Consulate gave me an entry visa that could be extended every year.

In the meantime, Rome had granted my *exclaustratio ad experimentum*, so that there was now only one last problem to solve: I needed money to make the journey and to meet the cost of living in India, at least for the first few months. Even in this matter I experienced God's help in such a tangible way that it was astounding. Within two weeks I had enough funds for my flight and plenty to spare.

Our Mother Abbess gave me a few weeks' holiday so that I could get some rest before my departure and prepare myself for the entirely new life that lay ahead of me. I already had the plane ticket in my pocket and my suitcase was packed when, five days before the actual departure, I received a letter from Swami Abhishiktananda that read, "There is war between India and Pakistan; don't come now!"

It isn't hard to imagine the shock this letter caused in me. I had burned all my bridges. What to do now? I adopted the approach that had worked for me so many times before and threw myself into God's arms, saying, "Lord, I had to arrange the date of my departure, but *you* will determine when it actually happens." Still, I was deeply disturbed, not least because our Mother Abbess was unwilling to let me come back to the monastery. She may have feared that I would cause a disturbance. But I insisted on returning and some days later I was on my way back to Kellenried.

Two days before the date of my departure, a second letter from Swami Abhishiktananda arrived, saying, "The war does not seem to escalate; if you have courage, come." Furthermore, he gave me directions for my arrival in Mumbai (Bombay), in case he could not meet me at the airport because of the war. Actually, however, India and Pakistan ended their hostilities on the day of my departure – another reassuring sign telling me to surrender completely to God's will. Never was I to feel that I had the situation in hand. *He* had destined me for India, and the reasons would be revealed to me one by one, once I began living there.

The evening before my departure I was deeply moved as I said farewell to my fellow sisters in the monastery. Most of them had had no clue about my plans. Some shed tears, some gave me their good wishes and promised to pray for me, and some were truly upset. I also felt the pain of parting because I loved my fellow sisters. Although friendships between us were strictly forbidden, I felt deeply attached to some of my companions. Now I left them after sixteen years of communal living in the monastery. It was especially painful to go away without giving them any reason, because I had not been allowed to explain anything to them. So we embraced each other in silent sadness. My monastic family would stay behind, walking their well-marked path, while for me there was a new beginning, travelling alone on an unmarked road.

During that last night in the monastery where I had spent the last sixteen years of my life, it became clear to me that the next morning was going to be for me a 'moment of truth'. Until now my spiritual journey had all taken place inside me. In a sense it had been unreal, like a figment of my imagination that might evaporate into thin air at any moment. Even the concrete steps I had taken, especially the voluminous correspondence and finally the packing of my bags, had all taken place within the four walls of the monastery. Tomorrow everything would be different, for I would leave the safety of my monastic home and step out into a completely unknown future. Except for an address and some vague plans, I had nothing to give me any feeling of security. The next morning I would know the truth about the One in whom I had believed and in whom I had put all my trust. Now I would find out whether I had been chasing a phantom or following my true vocation. Were it not for the fact that God was standing behind all this, I would surely have been filled with fear.

What would await me the next day I knew not; I only knew that I would have to face once more the full consequences of my adventure of faith. I had no idea whether it would be joy or fear, relief or anxiety. But when I finally let myself drift away into sleep, I was quite calm.

When I actually crossed the threshold of the monastery the next day, I felt as if someone received me with open arms – someone I did not see, yet whose presence I felt very intensely. It was out of the question that I might have created this feeling in myself; not only was I far from expecting or even desiring any such experience, but it was far beyond anything I could have imagined. The inner security it brought would never leave me for the rest of my life.

As I left my monastery on 25th September 1965, the ridge walk was at an end. Now, in India, the tightrope was awaiting me.

CHAPTER FOURTEEN

Recognizing the Will of God

IN ALL THE YEARS OF WHICH THESE PAGES GIVE account, I was often confronted with the question of what God wanted me to do. How could I know his will? What right had I to say that something was his will when I made decisions that did not fit into the traditional framework of recognizing and executing the will of God? Certain experiences and events led me to draw a number of very personal conclusions. These conclusions were no doubt subjective and others might question them, but for me there was no alternative.

Most of the time I acted intuitively, and sometimes I acted contrary to accepted notions about the will of God, but I always tried to be clear about my own motives, as I have explained in previous chapters. Apart from the two occasions when I received direct instructions from a distinct inner voice, I had to depend largely on my intuition.

But what is this intuition? At that time I called it my conscience and felt it to have a radar-like capacity to receive impulses that come not from the sphere of sense perceptions and reason but from a transcendent reality, to which the senses and the intellect do not have access. Intuition is inherent in every human being, but I felt that my experiences of transcendence enhanced this capacity, and I became more receptive to the impulses of the power that I called God. I often experienced this power as overwhelming and inescapable, and I did everything I could to remain connected to it. I tried to look with a constant gaze at this invisible but very much present power, for not only did I receive inner guidance, but it was and continues to be the source of life for me.

Intuition cannot be controlled or evaluated by the intellect. That is why I was often told that my decisions were unwise, irrational and adventurous. Yet deep in my heart I knew that I could not have decided otherwise. Every time I gave way to 'rational' arguments I would become profoundly uneasy and bewildered. On the other hand, when I allowed my intuition to guide me, I received confirmation in my heart that I had drawn the right conclusions from my experiences. Time and again surprising avenues opened before me that indicated the next step on a path where I was profoundly convinced God was leading me. If, however, for some reason or other the path was blocked, I knew that it was not the will of God that I should proceed. Such knowledge did not come from any rational process of thought, but from an attitude of acceptance of events I could not influence.

But I did not rely exclusively on my intuition; I would have considered that to be presumptuous, for on many occasions there was no generally accepted norm against which I could evaluate decisions. Instead, I looked for guidance and advice from experienced men and women who were themselves members of an order. Most of all, I searched the books that I had at my disposal, looking for ways in which I could find out the will of God. Père de Caussade had taught me submission to divine providence, which comes by way of unavoidable fate; that is Père de Caussade's definition of the recognizable will of God, to which one must submit or rather surrender. This acknowledgement of God's will may be called *passive*.

However, we are often forced to take *decisions*, and sometimes these decisions, which we want to be in accordance with the will of God, have far-reaching implications. Here Père de Caussade's letters failed to provide an answer to me. His letters appeared to give no advice about the *active* recognition of the will of God. They seemed to be addressed to readers who were mostly members of a religious order and no longer had to take any decisions themselves.

I did, however, find an article about 'guidance through the Holy Spirit' in a periodical published by the Jesuits. It presented the rules of Saint Ignatius of Loyola concerning the recognition of the will of God. In speaking about the two ways to recognize the divine will, he gives very concrete instructions.

The first way consists in pondering upon and reflecting on what benefits and advantages one might receive and what disadvantages and dangers could arise if the decision is made exclusively for the praise of God and the salvation of one's soul. One should also reflect on the advantages and benefits, and the disadvantages and dangers, which would arise if one chose another route. Next, one should observe to which side reason inclines more, and follow the intellect rather than the senses. Once the decision is taken, one should fervently pray to God to accept his choice and to let him know whether his decision was taken according to God's will or not.

The second way to recognize the will of God is meant for those who are already experienced in the spiritual life. The love that motivates and pushes a person to decide in favour of a certain action must come from above, prompted by the love for God. One must first perceive in oneself whether or not the particular preference for the chosen objective is aimed exclusively at God.

As a help in taking a decision, Ignatius of Loyola particularly emphasizes the experience of inner solace or forlornness. According to him, the decisive means of knowing is the experience of divine consolation, a kind of 'objectless solace' that does not pertain to earthly things. The soul is filled with an unearthly joy and deep inner peace, without knowing its origin, and she simply feels a powerful pull towards God and all things divine. Great strength emanates from this solace. Ignatius further adds, "The one lesson God himself teaches us (in order that we may know the will of God) consists of the consolation that expels all confusion from the soul and draws it exclusively to the love of God."

One thing, however, must be particularly emphasized: such consolation is obtained only through the inner connection in which one's 'gaze' invisibly meets the 'gaze' of God. When one is connected to God in this way one is entirely free of worries about the course of events, because now it is up to God to ensure that his will is fulfilled.

I hardly ever prayed that everything I considered to be God's will would be fulfilled; I believed and trusted that God himself would accomplish his work. Certainly one develops a feeling for what is the will of God, provided there is a sincere wish to know and to fulfil it, just as it is possible to sharpen the conscience to sense what is contrary to his will. It is this sensitization of the conscience that is of primary importance. It is a learning process through which the seeker of God has to go. When one's thinking and will are directed towards God, one learns to listen to those inner impulses that make one *more sincere* in one's intentions, *purer* in one's attitude, and *more selfless* in one's actions. This will bring one *closer to God* and one will find it ever easier to know the will of God. And when one keeps receiving the confirmation that one's decisions were true to God, one's inner certainty in the recognition of God's will grows accordingly.

Theologians and scribes of the world religions may think they can give us hard and fast rules concerning the will of God; their lists of dos and don'ts are all broadly similar. However, the question then arises as to whether those who don't care about the will of God are still living in his will; or is it possible that they avoid fulfilling his will by ignoring or simply overlooking it? In the case of such people, God's will is *simply executed*, just as it is in the case of any irrational creature, and just as it is throughout the entire creation. Anyone who tries to resist the will of God will have to learn by experience.

PART TWO

In the Promised Land

CHAPTER ONE

On Hold

ON 26TH SEPTEMBER 1965, I SET FOOT ON THE soil of India in the metropolis of Mumbai. Two days before, our Mother Abbess, in her motherly concern, had insisted on accompanying me to the train for Zurich, where I was to take the plane to India. Once more she had embraced me and then, with tears in her eyes, she had to leave me to my fate.

But after my experience of coming to the end of my ridge walk, my heart was filled with the profound peace and tranquillity of my new-found security. I had turned my eyes to the Lord, whose hidden face radiated a wonderful light. I did not cast a single glance at what I was leaving behind, for I felt it was God who had said to me, just as he had once said to Abraham: "Get thee out of thy country, and from thy kindred, and from thy father's house, unto a land that I will shew thee." These words had accompanied me over the passes of the Himalayas, which I had crossed – figuratively speaking – to reach my promised land of India.

This was terra incognita for me; I was entering an unknown land and facing an unknown fate. I had not chosen this fate – it had chosen me. Yet God's intention in leading me there was still a complete mystery to me. It would be another six years before I realized why he had chosen India for me.

Swami Abhishiktananda was awaiting me at Mumbai airport. The war between India and Pakistan, which had nearly thwarted my journey, had ended on the very day of my arrival. This had been my first flight ever and equally the first test of my knowledge of English, which as yet was quite inadequate. Some days before my arrival, a French Carmelite nun from Lisieux had also come to Mumbai. There were vague plans that at some stage we might both join some other nuns who were already living in India and live together in the spirit of the Hermits of Sachchidananda. As it turned out, however, the two of us were never to meet.

In Mumbai I was confronted for the first time by the thousand faces of India. India is a country that both fascinates and confuses the Western visitor. I saw a Parsee, a follower of the Zoroastrian faith, in his meditation room, where there were images of Buddha, Shiva, the Sacred Heart of Jesus and various icons – all together in one room and in one heart. From Mumbai we travelled for thirty-three hours in a third-class sleeper compartment to New Delhi. During the long journey I typed my first letters to my mother and to my monastic family. In Delhi I changed my European dress for an Indian sari, which from now on was to be my monastic garb.

The next morning I had a long interview with Major Ramachandra, the founder of the International Institute for Study and Service Exchange, who had signed his first letter as "Your dear Brother". It turned out that he had not yet found a place for me; the ashram that he had had in mind was not acceptable to Swami Abhishiktananda, because had I gone there it would have been impossible for me to attend daily Mass, which he considered unthinkable for a Catholic nun. And so it was that

I had 'solid ground' under my feet only for a few days and the 'tightrope walking' began almost at once. It was to last for quite some time, and this made me very aware of that adventure I had undertaken. Not for a moment was I to forget that only unconditional submission to the will of God would help me survive. In this respect, God was inexorable. I knew this from my previous experiences and fully expected that he would continue to demand submission, for only in this way would I be able to reach the goal he had set for me.

Finally it was decided that I should go to Dehra Dun for the time being to see my friend Agnes Kunze. From there I would go to Sat Tal (Seven Lakes) in the Himalayan foothills. Sister Lila, the Greek nun mentioned before, lived in Sat Tal, though she was in New Delhi at the time. So it was that after three days in Delhi I travelled alone to Dehra Dun by bus, a journey that took seven hours in a vehicle with no shock absorbers. We travelled through the heat of the plains of northern India toward the mountains. At one point the driver stopped on a bridge that spanned a deep ravine and pointed down. The wreck of another bus was lying there. It had fallen into the gorge a few days earlier – a truly macabre sight for us travellers and an unmistakable hint to give a generous tip after our safe arrival in Dehra Dun.

The leper colony Kripaon ki Mata (Mother of Mercy), situated on the outskirts of Dehra Dun, was founded by Agnes in 1959. I had expected to start my life in India there. There was a change of plan when Major Ramachandra offered to find a suitable place for me, but I would still have to go to Dehra Dun the following spring, for I had agreed to replace Agnes when she went to Germany for a holiday. This arrangement had been made with the Institute of Missionary Physicians in Würzburg, which had partly funded my fare to India.

Experiences at Rishikesh

While staying in Dehra Dun, Agnes and I went to visit Rishikesh in the Himalayan foothills, where the young Ganges flows into the plains. Rishikesh is a centre of Hindu ascetic life with many ashrams, great and small. It had been the express wish of Major Ramachandra that I should visit this place, which is so important to Hindus. We were guests of the Shivananda Ashram, the centre of the Divine Life Society, which had established a number of branches, mainly in the USA. Swami Chitananda, the president of the society, granted me an interview and told me that he had visited many monasteries and abbeys in Europe and that he had visited Germany as well.

I was accompanied to the interview by a young woman from Germany. She had been living in the Shivananda Ashram for the last five years as a nun and had become a strict devotee of Shiva, the Hindu deity responsible for the decay and the dissolution of the material creation. She had dedicated herself to seeking God and her young heart had an unshakeable faith in him. Her greatest desire was to live alone in a cave in the Himalayas; some years later, she was to fulfil this wish.

We had much in common in terms of our spiritual aspirations and there was an immediate mutual understanding between us. I had no ambitions to retire into a Himalayan cave, but we did feel a strong connection. It must have been based on our shared longing for the absolute, for complete abnegation of the world and for encountering the ultimate reality.

Swami Uma Shankar, as my young compatriot was known in India, took me to see the hermits who lived in caves on the other side of the river Ganges. It was a wonderful experience for me to sit in front of them and to listen to their words, which my companion translated from Hindi. They reminded me of the words of the Fathers of the Desert that I had read in the *Philokalia*.

One morning I went with Swami Uma Shankar to her music master, who conducted a kind of musical prayer with his students. Accompanied by the veena, an Indian stringed instrument, they sang texts from the Upanishads and various other songs in Sanskrit. We all sat cross-legged on the floor, according to Indian custom, and a wonderful atmosphere of recollection and prayer filled the room. We also visited Hindu temples and sites of pilgrimage in Rishikesh, which is one of the most famous places of worship in India.

And so, within the few days that I spent there, I saw some of the thousand faces of India pass by and tried to sort them out, although without much success, numbed as I was by the flood of impressions. After our return to Dehra Dun, Agnes and I made the long journey to Sat Tal, my temporary destination, where I was to stay for two months whilst Agnes returned to the leper colony.

Sat Tal Ashram

In Sat Tal the Methodist Church of America organizes a big gathering every year for its members in India. An Indian doctor and his wife were living there in order to attend to the medical needs of the farmers living in the surrounding mountains. There was also a Greek Orthodox monk, Father Lazarus, as well as Sister Lila, the Greek nun I already mentioned, and Sister Lalita from England. I very soon developed a warm friendship with all of them, and to our great joy we discovered that we all practised the Jesus Prayer. Father Lazarus had even published a book about it.

While we were in a state of anticipation for news from Major Ramachandra, Sister Lila proved to be a most sincere and true companion, who understood my situation better than anyone else. Again and again she encouraged me to have faith and confidence in God's ways. She had herself experienced his wonderful workings many times and was convinced that he had a task for me in India.

Every morning the residents of the Sat Tal Ashram met for an hour of Bible reading, in which the guests also took part. My English was still quite poor and, since I never knew which Bible verses I would have to read, I always prepared the whole chapter that was to be read that morning. This was an excellent training and in this way I progressed quite well in learning the language.

The weeks in the Sat Tal Ashram, surrounded by impressive mountain scenery, finally gave me a chance to find myself again after the precipitous events of the last few weeks. With the help of the Jesus Prayer, I was able to descend once again into the depths where the call to the desert had been born. I also regained that wonderful experience of inner clarity that I had felt on the morning of my departure from my monastery.

In the meantime, Major Ramachandra made every effort to find a place for me – but to no avail. We really had no time to lose, because the expiry date of my six-month visa for India was drawing closer by the week. Yet I was calm and sure that a path would open before me, as it had so often done in the past. I was convinced that God, who had arranged every detail of my voyage to India, was keeping a place for me in this country. He seemed not to expect anything else from me but an unquestioning faith and an unperturbed confidence in him. Even so, Sister Lila and I often prayed for me to be shown the right place. This place had been waiting all along – but at the time we did not know it. All we knew was that the road to Benares, where Major Ramachandra still wanted to send me, was more and more blocked. And actually, I felt quite disinclined to live there, because it would throw me into the world, into surroundings that would hardly be in keeping with my monastic vocation.

One day I had to take an important letter to the nearest post office and the long walk led me through some lonely mountain woods. Some ten minutes after I had left the ashram in the early morning, I realized that I had left the letter in my room. I went back to fetch it, not realizing that this little delay probably saved my life. My path crossed a small estate surrounded by a wooden fence. The house was uninhabited, but sometimes cattle were kept in the neighbouring stable. As I was approaching the fence on the far side of the estate, my heart suddenly skipped a beat when I saw a huge tiger coming up through the clearing ahead of me, which I would have been passing through just a few minutes later. If I had not been forced to go back to fetch the letter that I had forgotten, I would have walked directly into his jaws. The tiger continued slowly on his way, less than twenty yards from where I was standing, spellbound. The fence between us was a sham. Had the tiger been interested in me, he could have leapt it without even stretching. He must have taken a calf down in the village and no doubt was no longer hungry, for he must surely have detected my scent long before I saw him. After the tiger had disappeared up the path, I continued on my way by the same path the tiger had just used, assuming that no second tiger was on the way. Later I was told that this tiger was probably a man-eater. Soon after, the farmers of the surrounding mountains organized a night hunt for him, fearing not only for their cattle but also for their own lives.

Shortly after this there was some movement in my affairs. In the beginning of December Sister Lalita returned to England. She was longing for a regular religious life in a convent, with community prayer and the liturgy, and she had never quite been able to understand why I had left my monastery. The day after her departure, a letter addressed to her reached us. It came from Sushila Agarwal, her Indian friend, who lived in an ashram for ladies. The letter contained a request to Sister Lalita to write an article about Christ for the ashram's magazine. With it came an invitation to spend some time in the ashram and to join them in celebrating the birth of Christ. Sushila Agarwal, as Sister Lila told me, was the head of the ashram Brahma Vidya Mandir (house of the knowledge of God) at Paunar in central India, which had been founded by Vinoba Bhave, a most eminent disciple of Mahatma Gandhi.

It was only now that I learned that this was the very ashram that Sister Lila had had in mind for me when she first heard from Major Ramachandra that I was planning to come to India. It had long been a wish of the ashram community to have a Christian woman, preferably a nun, amongst them. The idea had been dropped because Swami Abhishiktananda, for the reasons already mentioned, had deemed that ashram not suitable for me. Sushila Agarwal had asked Sister Lalita repeatedly to join them, but she had not been willing to live in a Hindu ashram, because she needed a Christian community to live in.

After reading this letter, we knew this was the sign for us to take action and we were filled with great joy. Once again Christ's words were confirmed: "If thou wouldest believe, thou shouldest see the glory of God." These words where originally spoken in a different context, but we found, and rightly so, that they fitted my situation. We wrote at once to Sushila Agarwal, asking her whether I could come to the ashram instead of Sister Lalita. Then we waited with burning impatience for her reply. It came after twelve days with a cordial invitation to come to Paunar. A few days later I started the journey to Wardha, more than a thousand kilometres away in the state of

Maharashtra. On the way, I interrupted my journey to meet Swami Abhishiktananda and inform him about the latest developments. Now he had no option but to submit to this clear sign from the Lord.

In the course of the years to come, experience showed me more than once that one cannot intervene in the realization of the divine will, either in one's own life or in the lives of others. Swami Abhishiktananda must have had good reasons for his decision, but it was obvious that God had his own plans.

CHAPTER TWO

House of the
Knowledge of God

AFTER A TRAIN JOURNEY OF TWO DAYS, I AR-
rived on 18ᵗʰ December 1965 in Wardha, where the Mumbai-
Kolkata railway line crosses the line from Delhi to Chennai
(Madras). Sushila Agarwal was waiting for me at the station
and it was as if we had known each other for ages. We instantly
became friends. She told me that the community of Brahma
Vidya Mandir had for many years wished to have a Christian
companion amongst them and that they were convinced that
God finally had brought us together. We rode the seven kilometres to Paunar in a rickshaw and the members of the ashram
gave me a warm welcome. I immediately felt at home.

Three months had passed since my arrival in India, and
now I had reached my destination – albeit in a roundabout
way. Deeply moved, I entered the compound with its low
houses built around a square. At once I knew that in Brahma
Vidya Mandir I had found the place where I could put down
roots again and continue with my monastic life. I was firmly
determined to stay there, because it was obvious to me that
God had put me there. Indeed, as I came to realize later, when

I became better acquainted with India, there was no other place more ideally suited for me in the whole of the country.

At the time of my arrival, the ashram had only been in existence for six years and was to a certain extent still taking shape, for none of the twelve founding members had had any experience in this kind of community life. Most of the young women there had left behind a promising professional career and a comfortable life, and had travelled with Vinoba Bhave from village to village through large parts of India in order to serve his movement of voluntary land reform. It had been Vinoba's intention to persuade landlords to donate agricultural land to their farm labourers, who could then grow their own crops. These young women had mainly looked after the mothers and children in these villages, while the men took care of the distribution of the land and the acquisition of agricultural tools.

Vinoba Bhave himself had left his home and university in his youth in order to dedicate his life to *brahma vidya*, God-realization. For many years it had been his fervent wish to create a place for Indian women who shared his desire to lead a spiritual life dedicated to the search for God. It was his intention that Brahma Vidya Mandir should be a spiritual power-house that would send its energy throughout the country.

Some time after my arrival at Paunar, I asked the sisters for an Indian name. I did not want them to call me by my German name, which would always remain foreign to them. They deliberated together for some days and then decided that my name should be Shraddha. This Sanskrit word means 'faith and confidence in God', so that whenever they called me by this name it would remind them of their need for faith and confidence. In a wider sense, Shraddha also means devotion. Because I was a nun, I added the word *ananda* (bliss) to my new name, in accordance with Indian tradition. I saw my new name in the light of the words of Elizabeth, the mother of John the Baptist, who had said to Mary, the mother of Jesus: "And blessed is she that believed." This name set a seal on my adventure of faith and was an omen for my life in India. I carried it with great joy and I was always conscious of its deep meaning.

The ashram rules

Sushila Agarwal took it upon herself to introduce me to ashram life. She explained the daily routine, showed me the different chores in the house and garden and accompanied me to community prayer in the temple. In particular, she spoke about the eleven vows that Vinoba Bhave had set out as guiding principles for the life of the ashram community. Five of these vows came from *ashtanga yoga,*‎* where they figure as fundamental principles of spiritual life. The other six vows were taken from the ashram rules of Mahatma Gandhi. These eleven vows served as an orientation for the community, not as a formal pledge. The only condition for admission into the ashram community was the aspirant's firm intention to live according to these principles. Only *brahmacharya* – a celibate life – was obligatory for every member. The ashram rules and the activities in the ashram were meant to lay the foundation for the spiritual life of the community and support the striving of each member to attain *brahma vidya* – knowledge of God.

The five principles taken from *ashtanga yoga* are:

1. ***Ahimsa*** – non-violence, love and reverence for all God's creatures. This means renouncing not only physical but also mental violence – in other words, not imposing one's will or

---

* *ashtanga yoga*: the eightfold yoga path that goes back to the Yoga Sutra of Patanjali (circa 3rd–2nd century BCE), which later was called *raja yoga*.

opinion on anybody else. As a matter of course, *ahimsa* excludes the killing of any creature, human or animal. For this reason a strictly vegetarian diet was obligatory. I had already practised the vegetarian way of life in my monastery, ever since the day when I had felt a strong aversion to taking meat and my superiors had permitted me to take milk instead. Looking back, I see now how even then India had already been waiting on the horizon, though it was still so very far away. All those years ago I had hardly suspected how important vegetarianism would one day turn out to be for me. The principle of non-violence was held in high esteem in Brahma Vidya Mandir. One shrank from inflicting pain on any creature, even a poisonous snake. Indeed, we had a cobra living with us in peaceful coexistence and, some critical moments notwithstanding, nobody was harmed in all those years.*

2. ***Satya*** – truthfulness, honesty and sincerity in word and deed. *Satya* also includes not just having faith in one's own conscience but also showing respect for the consciences of others – meaning that one should never try to force anyone to change their mind.

3. ***Asteya*** – not stealing; not taking anything that belongs to others. Mahatma Gandhi said that taking things, even with the permission of the owner, was a form of theft if one does not

---

*One evening, as I sat in meditation on my bed, I was startled by a heavy thump. I fetched the torch that was always ready to hand and was terrified to see a big cobra winding its way across my bed, making for the door of the veranda. That evening, in spite of all warnings, I had forgotten to put up the mosquito net and the snake, on its usual path over the timber work of the roof, had fallen onto my bed. I had often heard the noise of something falling onto the mosquito net, thinking it was probably a rat. My dreams that night were more like a horror film, but my fellow sisters were not very impressed when I told them the next morning about my adventure. Serpents in India are considered a symbol of Vishnu, and to meet them is valued as being in effect a meeting with that deity.

need them. To increase or expand one's wants is also considered an offence against the principle of *asteya*.

4. **Brahmacharya**[*] – physical and mental sexual abstinence in order to dedicate one's life to the search for God. I had already made this promise in my youth and had taken a solemn oath at the time of the Consecration of Virgins years later.

5. *Aparigraha* – not to accumulate things, not to keep things that are superfluous, either as an individual or as a community. *Aparigraha* is a very concrete and practical vow of poverty. I was always deeply impressed by the consistency with which this principle was practised in the ashram and sometimes felt ashamed of not being able to realize it in the same way as my fellow sisters. Meister Eckhart speaks to his novices about this same spirit of detachment in his *Talks of Instruction*. He says:

> Whosoever can do without all things and does not need them is much more fortunate than the one who feels the need for them and wants to possess them. That man is the best who can dispense with what he does not need.

The remaining six principles were part of Mahatma Gandhi's ashram rules, which he created for practical, ethical and partly political reasons. They are: physical work, control of the palate, fearlessness, equality of religions, loyalty to one's country and abolition of the untouchability of the casteless Hindus. In order to keep these eleven vows constantly in mind, the ashram community recited them twice every day after prayers in the temple. Sushila's explanation of these principles moved me deeply, for not only did she speak with great conviction, but she herself was a living example of their implementation.

---

[*] *Brahmacharya* was originally a phase of life of a Vedic student and lasted twelve years.

As Sushila was explaining the ashram rules, I realized that the five *ashtanga yoga* vows did bear Christian traits, although they were formulated centuries before the Sermon on the Mount. In his teachings Jesus Christ again and again stressed the principle of non-violence and confirmed it by his own example. Because he was "meek and lowly in heart", he could ask his disciples to follow his example.

In the same way, the teacher of Nazareth demanded purity and sincerity in thought and deed from his disciples; their speech should be an uncompromising "Yea, yea; Nay, nay". Jesus Christ, who by his own testimony did not possess even a place to lay down his head,* also attached great importance to having modest needs and a carefree faith in the fulfilment of life's necessities, because our Father in heaven gives to each one according to his needs.†

The implementation of these eleven vows, especially that of genuine poverty and great simplicity of living, would from now on form part of my life at Brahma Vidya Mandir. This was what I had so much desired in my monastery after the 'experience of the desert'. It was in truth how I now wanted to live, though I found that life in Brahma Vidya Mandir had a degree of ascetic sparseness beyond anything that I could ever have imagined.

The ashram rules followed by the community differed from the *Rule of Saint Benedict*, which had hitherto shaped my monastic life. Whilst Saint Benedict minutely regulates community life, Vinoba Bhave left it to the founding members to mould for themselves their life together. The authority lay with the community itself and decisions were only valid when taken unanimously. The supreme rule at Brahma Vidya Mandir

---

*"The Son of man hath not where to lay his head." *Luke* 9:58
†"Your heavenly Father knoweth that ye have need of all these things." *Matthew* 6:32

was love, and in order to show the measure of love that should prevail amongst the sisters and brothers, Vinoba Bhave had chosen Christ's words: "This is my commandment: That ye love one another, as I have loved you." Sushila Agarwal emphasized that this love should show in our practical living: we should live for one another and selflessly serve the community. She herself epitomized this ideal to the point of total self-denial. She was also very interested in the way of life of my erstwhile monastic community, and quite often I told her about our life at Saint Erentraud. In this way, our mutual experiences in community life complemented each other.

Saint Benedict demanded that his monks earn their living by the work of their hands. It was the same at Brahma Vidya Mandir. For four hours a day we worked for a nearby publisher, where Vinoba's books were published in various Indian languages. We folded the sheets and prepared them for binding. For this work, the community received the customary modest wages. Apart from this, we grew our own vegetables, and no food was brought in other than oil, cereals and milk. Every month the ashram edited a small magazine for Indian women that had subscribers across the whole country. It dealt with the cultivation of a religious life and the development of a sense of social responsibility.

Brahma vidya

Our day started early in the ashram. At 4:30 we gathered in the temple for the first community prayer, followed by a one-hour lesson in Indian philosophy. Unfortunately, I could not go to this as it was held in Hindi, which I did not understand sufficiently. After a modest breakfast, each of us then worked in the house and garden for two hours. Every day we had approximately four hours to ourselves, which we used for study, meditation and spinning cotton yarn for our clothing. One group of sisters gathered each evening to sing with great fervour the beautiful songs of Mira Bai, the famous Indian princess and mystic (1498–c.1563). Her songs express her burning love for Krishna, the eighth incarnation of Vishnu, the preserver god in the Hindu trinity of Brahma, Vishnu and Shiva and one of the most celebrated heroes of Indian mythology. In the Bhagavad Gita Krishna is often depicted as a shepherd playing the flute and is the great teacher of the seeker of God, Arjuna.

Three times a day the ashram community assembled for prayer in the temple for twenty to thirty minutes. I participated in this prayer from the first day, but since I didn't know the language I could not recite the text with the sisters. In any case I also had some doubts about praying to a God who – so I thought at that time – was not the God of the Christians. I practised the Jesus Prayer instead.

In the early morning the community recited the Ishavasya Upanishad in Sanskrit. Upanishad means 'secret teachings', the knowledge of the ultimate Being, the creation and the soul that is to be conveyed only to initiates. Upanishad also means 'to sit nearby in devotion' at the feet of the Guru in order to be introduced into the secret knowledge of Brahman, the supreme Being, that is passed on from person to person only.

In the middle of the day we recited the *Vishnu Sahasranama (Thousand Names of Vishnu)*, the names listed for Vishnu, the preserver god of Hinduism, in the ancient Indian epic, the Mahabharata. In Hinduism it is believed that chanting these names with sincere devotion bestows peace of mind and noble virtues.

In the evening, part of the second chapter of the Bhagavad Gita was recited. The Bhagavad Gita, probably composed during the third century BCE, is as highly regarded in India as the Bible is in the Christian world. Like the Bible, it has been translated into nearly all the languages of the world. Even today, it shapes the lives of millions of Indians, who know the sacred texts by heart and recite them during their work in the house, in the fields or on the streets.

The Ishavasya Upanishad is comprised of only eighteen verses. In the beginning, the Upanishad describes the nature of the all-pervading One, the absolute Lord:

> All this, whatever moves in the changing universe,
> Is enveloped by God....
> The non-dual *atman* (Self) is one
> Swifter than thought.
> The senses do not reach It,
> As It is ever ahead of them.
> Though Itself standing still,
> It outstrips those who run.
> In It the all-pervading air
> Supports the activity of beings.
> It moves and It moves not;
> It is far and It is near;
> It is within all this and It transcends all.

Then the unknown author of this Upanishad points to two practices that are diametrically opposed to the attainment of the true knowledge of the supreme Being: "Those who are devoted to *a-vidya* (ignorance or rituals) enter into blinding darkness and those who delight in *vidya* (theoretical knowledge of the deities) enter into still greater darkness."*

---

*In Vedic times it was believed, as Radhakrishnan explains in his introduction to the Bhagavad Gita, that by means of sacrifices, cosmic forces were 'set in motion'. When rites were performed with knowledge, the expected benefit would result. The primary motive in offering sacrifices, Radhakrishnan adds, was the desire for earthly and heavenly gain.

The Upanishad reaches its culmination with the seeker of God imploring the sustainer of life to show him his face:

The face of Truth is covered
With a brilliant golden disc;
Do thou remove it, O Sustainer,
So that I, the seeker of Truth, may behold it.

The golden disc refers to the disc of the sun, which here symbolizes the material world that fascinates us and hides God's face from us. But it is not just the material world that comes between us and God; our mental pictures also cover his face. The intellect and the experiences of the senses, as well as everything we see, veil the eternal truth that we can only behold with closed eyes and a mind made completely motionless.

It is the eternal truth itself that conquers the created light with the uncreated light. Therefore the seeker of God prays directly to the sustainer, the seeing one, the ruler of the world, that he may withdraw the rays that veil his face: "Through thy grace, may I behold the most blessed form of thine."

At first, the true meaning of the Ishavasya Upanishad was a mystery to me, because it was a whole year before I could study the text in more detail. But to really understand such a text is only possible if one has experienced what it talks about.

The communal prayer that plays such a central role in the daily routine of the Benedictine monasteries had its importance in Brahma Vidya Mandir as well, though it was not given the same prominence that Saint Benedict gives it. The members of the community were free to choose whether or not to participate, but Vinoba Bhave had pointed out that to neglect this part of our daily program would have definite consequences for our spiritual life. Whoever neglects prayer and meditation, or whoever gives it insufficient time, will not develop spiritually.

One can gain the experience of the infinite only if one remains in active contact with God. The spiritual basis of Brahma Vidya Mandir was the *advaita* philosophy. *A-dvaita* means 'non-duality' and signifies that the supreme Being, God, is the only principle of existence. He is the One without a second. According to *advaita* the entire creation is but an emanation of the highest, absolute Being. This paramount tenet is expressed in the prologue of the Ishavasya Upanishad, which was sung by the ashram community every morning:

> This is fullness – that is fullness.
> Fullness emanates from fullness.
> Although fullness emanates from fullness –
> Fullness remains undiminished.

This mystic verse is a description of the creation in a nutshell. With a few abstract terms, the Upanishad speaks of the inexhaustible divine Being (the fullness) from which the creation, also called fullness, flows forth in an uninterrupted emanation. Since the creation does not have an independent existence, and since by its coming and going it forms an endless cycle, the emanated fullness does not diminish the emanating fullness, which is the ultimate Being. God's creative power emanates from him and merges back to its origin. To realize the truth of these words is an overwhelming experience.

There was a moment when I had an inkling of this experience, and in August 1967 I noted in my diary, "My life is very simple. God draws me more and more into the mystery of his threefold life and I have nothing more to do than let myself be 'begotten' by him and give back my life to him through his Son in the profound silencing of words and thoughts." And I added, "Every·day my experience is the same: I do not feel my existence. Things are passing me by and I do not really notice them. Even when I am studying or thinking any thoughts, I am not the doer."

This is a Christian interpretation of an *advaita* experience, which is the experience of the soul's identity with God. Whether this is the oneness of the soul with God, *atman* with Brahman, as *advaita* postulates, or whether it is *union*, the soul's merging with him, as Christian theology says – is merely a matter of theory. Whoever has had the experience has no need for analysis, for once we attain *brahma vidya*, once we have actually experienced that only Brahman, the supreme Being, God, has true existence, we realize at the same time our oneness with him and then we *know*: *aham Brahman asmi* – I am that One.

This is in perfect agreement with the words that Jesus spoke to his disciples on the eve of his crucifixion: "I and my Father are one." In his farewell speech he returns once more to this mystery of his oneness with the Father – this time in a prayer directly addressed to the Father: "That they all may be one; as thou, Father, art in me, and I in thee". Meister Eckhart also speaks of the oneness of the perfect soul, in terms similar to those of the Upanishad: "Therefore, when I am transformed in God and he has made me one with himself, then – as truly as God lives – there is no difference between us.... God and I are one." Whoever has attained direct experience of the oneness of God and the soul has become a *gyani*, a knower, one who possesses the highest realization; such a one has attained the purpose of human life and has reached the end of his or her course as a created being.

The sisters at Brahma Vidya Mandir, however, were not following the path of knowledge *(gyana yoga)*. Although they received lessons in *advaita*, they were following the path of *bhakti* (devotion). They were devotees of a God who had taken the human form as an avatar (incarnation) and who thus had become a personal God.* Just as Christians are devoted to Christ, so most of them were devotees of Krishna. There are many parallels between the life of Jesus and that of Krishna, whether viewed historically or mythologically. The spiritual goal of the community was to attain God-realization through *bhakti*, the way of devotion to God, and through *karma yoga*, as taught in the Bhagavad Gita. *Karma yoga* means selfless, desire-less and disinterested action, which includes prayer, meditation, devotion to a deity and the study of spiritual scriptures.

Becoming an Indian

Such were the conditions in which my new life began. It was not long before I was participating in the complete daily routine of the ashram: working in the vegetable garden (very familiar to me); sitting in front of the low, open fireplace in the kitchen; cleaning the houses and fetching water from the well. In addition, I was eagerly studying Hindi, the basics of which I had already acquired in the monastery, but the main language for me was English, which was understood by most of the ashram sisters.

---

*The holy scriptures of India mention two aspects of God. The first of these is the formless, attributeless, absolute Being (Brahman), who can be known only by experience; that is, by the merging of the individual *atman* (soul) into Brahman. The second aspect of God pertains to the divine Being in relation to the creation and is referred to as Ishvar (Lord of creation). Ishvar, in turn, has three aspects: the creator, sustainer and destroyer, personified in the three deities known as Brahma, Vishnu and Shiva. According to Indian tradition, Vishnu incarnates from time to time in human and other forms, and as Krishna, who is considered to be his eighth incarnation.

It was not always easy to adapt to life in Brahma Vidya Mandir, for the contrast with my previous way of life was just too great. I found it especially hard to adapt to the diet, and I ate only when hunger compelled me. The total absence of tables and chairs in the ashram was also very hard for me; practically the whole daily routine took place on the floor, whether it was working in the printing press, eating, studying or praying in the temple. For many people in India this is nothing unusual, and it was by no means intended to be an ascetic exercise, but for me it took a lot of getting used to.

The sisters, however, felt that I adapted to the ashram very quickly, and to them this was a confirmation that I had lived in India in a previous life. This was a view that I could not accept at that time. The concept of reincarnation was just too strange and it would take years before my intellect was able to open itself to something that had been taken for granted in early Christianity. It was only after the Second Council of Constantinople in CE 553 that reincarnation was no longer generally accepted by Christians. But the sisters never made any attempt to convert me to their way of thinking.

A few days after Christmas 1965 I fell sick with paratyphoid fever. In order to cure the illness, fasting was advised – only water was permitted. This was a difficult test for me and my mind revolted. Of course a doctor was called, who gave me homeopathic medicine, and I was lovingly nursed by the sisters. Indeed, the weeks of illness brought us closer to each other than would otherwise have been the case.

After three weeks the fever left me, but I was weakened. Nevertheless, I decided to forego any tonics and rejected all thoughts of my habitual German food. I still found the plain ashram food difficult to take, but I slowly recuperated and after a reasonable period of convalescence I was able to participate again in all the activities of the ashram.

Living in the desert

Four months passed, reeling off like a film in which I was both actor and spectator at the same time. In just a few weeks, everything that had been my life for so many years fell away. As soon as I entered my promised land, the framework of my former monastic life ceased to exist. The conditions in which I now continued my search for God were fundamentally different. In particular, there was no longer any outward support for my Christian spiritual life that I could hold on to.

Now God really led me into the desert which I had so fervently longed for while I was in the 'paradise' of our Benedictine religious life. Since my experience of the desert, I had left behind everything that had become a hindrance on my spiritual path, a veil between my soul and God, whose touch I had felt for a moment. Now I found myself in the nakedness of the desert of which Père de Voillaume had spoken. But in this desert I knew there was the fountain that had welled up inside me when my consciousness had been drawn into that deep spiritual awareness. I had carried this fountain with me during the exodus from my former life and now I was being given the opportunity to drink freely from it.

Above all, I was accompanied into the desert by the invisible inner light I had known, and by *his grace*, which was the source of life for my soul. *He* had remained with me, the *One* by whose command I had left the land of my fathers – my monastery. The world might be turning around me and countless impressions might be pressing in upon me, but as long as *he* was near, I was not moved by any passing events. The incessant Jesus Prayer accompanied me as well, and a wonderful strength emanated from it as it continuously repeated itself within me. In this way, I was excellently equipped for life in the desert.

During my ridge walk, an unconditional submission to the will of God had been my only chance of survival; now, for some time, an absolute confidence in God became the foundation of my life in the desert. Without it, all sense of meaning in my life would have vanished like water running into desert sands. This confidence in God did not even leave space for hope, for hope is based on ego, one's sense of self; every hope is nothing but a wish that God may grant fulfilment of one's own desires and imaginations. If one can put one's confidence wholly in God, then the person no longer has any wishes of his own, so the question of hope that they may be fulfilled does not arise. Such confidence is the gift of a longing to unite one's will with the will of God, to lose oneself in God.

Even so, I did sometimes wonder what the future might have in store for me. What were God's plans for my life? Why had he brought me to this country? I did not know, nor did I care to know. Had he not taken over the direction of my life long ago and had he not, ever since I entered this promised land, arranged everything so well? All I had to do was to lose myself once again in this adventure of faith.

What I did not know then, what I could not even faintly imagine, was that in the years that lay before me, I would have to go through many phases of inner development in order to reach the threshold of the real promised land that awaited me in God's plan. Many new spiritual horizons had yet to appear before I arrived at that point. It was, however, of little importance that I was not aware of the direction in which my inner guide would take me – what counted was that I should abandon myself to his guidance, which I was experiencing in so many ways. Only after the completion of this process of transformation would God lift the veil and let me look at the goal that I was unknowingly striving for, and I would have to spend more than six years in India before this happened. But every day in

India new perspectives opened before me, and every day my horizon expanded beyond anything I had previously imagined, so that my trust in God's guidance grew and grew, confirming my faith more and more. Only a few weeks after my arrival at the Paunar ashram, I was to receive an overwhelming proof of the way in which God was clearing my path.

CHAPTER THREE

With the Blessings
of the Church

As I had left my monastery for India with the permission of the highest ecclesiastical body, I had to place myself under the jurisdiction of the bishop of the area in which I lived. This obligation, Swami Abhishiktananda had warned me, might possibly turn out to be a source of problems for me. He had written to say that a bishop would be more than a little hesitant about taking responsibility for an exclaustrated nun who wanted to come to India on her own, without a Church mandate and without concrete plans for founding a religious community. As a precaution, they might demand that I have a companion with me, or the bishop might employ me for missionary work, meaning that I would be unable to live according to my vocation.

However, once I was certain that India was indeed my promised land, all such concerns disappeared, for I was convinced that he who had called me to India would surely take care of those problems as well in order to realize his plan. I had already received the first evidence of how divine providence was governing my life in that country and I had seen how wonderfully my path had been levelled before me.

At Brahma Vidya Mandir, I already felt like a member of the ashram community, but now it was time for me to contact the bishop in whose diocese the Paunar ashram was situated. I had to place myself under his jurisdiction, and in particular I needed his permission to live in a Hindu ashram. When I had first arrived, after leaving the railway station at Wardha to go to Paunar, I had noticed a small church in the town. I attended Mass there on the following Sunday, walking the eight kilometres from Paunar to Wardha on foot and introducing myself to Father Matthew, an Indian priest who administered there. He was, like the bishop, a member of a branch of the Carmelite Order of Kerala. The residence of the bishop was about five hours away by train.

Father Matthew promised to report my visit to the bishop, but then the contact was interrupted since I fell ill and could no longer attend Sunday Mass. A few weeks later, however, Father Matthew visited me at Paunar and told me about his meeting with the bishop. To my great astonishment I learnt that Monsignor Januarius, the Bishop of Chanda, not only approved of my stay in Brahma Vidya Mandir, but had always had a strong desire to have a contemplative community in his diocese. He was very interested in meeting me, said Father Matthew, and would surely visit me at Paunar some time.

My first meeting with the bishop took place a few weeks later at Wardha. I was deeply impressed by his personality and instantly trusted him. Monsignor Januarius told me that he had taken a degree in Indology in order to extend his knowledge of Hinduism. At that time this was quite an unusual thing for a Catholic Indian theologian to do. Since he had himself acquired firsthand knowledge of the Indian holy scriptures, he advised me to start by studying these scriptures in order to obtain an authentic insight into Indian philosophy. He advised against reading books about Hinduism written by other, mostly

Western, authors. So I not only received the blessings of the Church for my life in a Hindu ashram, but I also was instructed by the bishop to study the holy scriptures of India. This was far more than I could ever have imagined.

When I told Monsignor Januarius how, when I was still in Germany, Swami Abhishiktananda's letters had made me tremble about my future bishop in India, he laughed heartily. In my clumsy English I then told the bishop the story of how I had come to India. Once more he astonished me by confessing that he had been praying for years for someone like me to come to his diocese – a member of a contemplative order wanting to integrate into the spiritual tradition of his people. I was literally the fulfilment of his prayers. The bishop also suggested that I could perform a very important service for the Church as a mediator. We then spoke about the future and agreed that we would wait for a sign, for we were both wholly convinced that God would manifest his will at the right time. I was much relieved by the bishop's attitude. I felt quite reassured that he would not one day arbitrarily assign to me another task in his diocese, as Swami Abhishiktananda had feared.

In the course of our conversation the bishop also inquired about the form of prayer I practised. To help me answer, he first spoke about his own inner striving and deeply impressed me by his words. I then tried to speak about my own spiritual experience – what God's life-giving gaze meant to me, how I wanted to respond to this gaze with my whole being in the silencing of my thoughts and how his invisible light would shine inside me.

This experience of the inner light was to become my spiritual life from Easter 1967 onwards. My diary notes of those years regularly refer to this phenomenon. In 1968, for instance, I wrote, "It is the divine light, the all-permeating, *seeing* light. I feel how this light not only flows over my body, but how it 'dissolves' it, so to speak. All that remains is the light – the body dissolves into light. Not that I am not permanently conscious of my body – but I feel that the light eliminates it. All I have to do is let my whole being be permeated by this light. No mental activity is needed – the light is there and sometimes it engulfs me with great force."

I also mentioned to the bishop my practice of the incessant Jesus Prayer, but it was unknown to him. Finally, I assured him that I would not only continue to recite the breviary, but would also keep up my daily Bible reading. The bishop seemed satisfied with my replies. At the end of our talk, Monsignor gave me a very important piece of advice: I should always keep my aim clearly in view so that I would not be distracted and driven by all the events of the day, but at the same time I should not have a concrete plan – this was his directive. He said that above all I should try to implement that for which I had applied for the exclaustration, "because the value of your experiment will be measured only by the spiritual depth into which it will lead you".

What was this aim that I should keep clearly before me? It was *he himself*, the still unknown One, the One who had become my fate and had taken possession of me. Now I must live with him not in the 'garden inclosed' of the monastery but in the desert, until *he alone* would be there, and this *me*, that still continued to exist, would merge into him. To live with *him* in the desert had been my only purpose for coming to India and my sole legitimate reason for living here, though it was not mentioned in my application for the exclaustration. And God's intentions were still unknown to me. My whole striving was aimed at this goal and I wanted to reach it through a life of intense prayer and meditation. The incessant Jesus Prayer had long been a proven means of directing my heart to him throughout the whole day; it was my way of answering *his gaze* and exposing myself to the rays of the invisible light. That is what my spiritual life consisted of.

Not to develop any concrete plan meant that I had to read his will from his eyes, as I had done in the past. My sole concern should therefore be to remain in 'eye-to-eye contact' with my inner guide, in order to find out what his intentions were in any given situation. I would have to continue to feel my way forward on the path that lay before me but was hidden from my sight. Anyway, it was much too early to make any plans for the future; later I was to find that my life in India developed its own dynamic and presented me with tasks that were not of my choosing but that I could not evade.

Four weeks after this first meeting, the bishop asked me whether I was receiving sufficient nourishment for my spiritual life in Brahma Vidya Mandir. He had noticed a very deep spiritual craving in my heart and he was not sure, he said, whether this could be fulfilled in the ashram. I confessed, in all frankness, that because I was still adapting to my new life I was as yet unable to realize all that I was striving for – an intense spiritual life with many hours of silent prayer and contemplation. The language barrier and all the different things I still had to learn were preventing me from making best use of all that the ashram had to offer.

Even so, from the beginning I had a wonderful feeling of freedom in my new living environment in Brahma Vidya Mandir. There was no longer any curtain between God and my soul such as I had experienced in the monastery, especially during the long hours of obligatory prayer in the church. The daily routine in the ashram left me a lot of time for contemplative prayer and meditation. In addition, it was a great relief to be rid of the feeling (which had so much depressed me in the monastery) of having to keep up a tradition.

The bishop's question had related to the absence of any Christian religious framework, generally considered indispensable for the maintenance of a spiritual life. But it was exactly this framework that had felt so alien to me for so many years, since experiencing deeper levels of consciousness. I did not miss the exterior forms of the Christian worship at all since I had already found them to be a hindrance to drinking from the fountain of living water. Nor did I miss the sacraments, because my form of communion was the divine light. I did not say this openly to Monsignor Januarius, fearing that, as a bishop and member of an order, he might not be able to understand it. Yet from the beginning I had made it clear to the ashram community that I would attend Mass every Sunday in the parish church. This obligation of a Catholic Christian was well known to the sisters and they never put up any obstacle to my fulfilling it.

Bishop Januarius continued to follow my progress with great interest. From time to time he used to come to the ashram. He was a welcome guest there and soon came to be a friend of the community. I did not consider it merely a matter of luck that it was exactly this bishop in whose diocese Paunar was situated. To me it was yet another fulfilment of Christ's promise: "If thou wouldest believe, thou shouldest see the glory of God."

Occasionally I spent a few days at the bishop's residence to attend to his correspondence with houses of various religious orders in Germany who envisaged founding communities in his diocese. On one of these occasions I was introduced to Mr H. Singh from Nagpur, who was a guest in the neighbourhood. We talked about Brahma Vidya Mandir and I mentioned that I was a nun. This made him ask me what I had gained for my spiritual life by leaving the world and joining a convent. Somewhat surprised, I answered that I considered this my vocation, since I had felt the wish to devote my life to God from my early youth. Mr Singh then wanted to know whether I had ever experienced the audible life stream, the sound of the Word of God. Never having heard of anything like this, I had no answer. But it was clear to me that it must be an extraordinary experience. I was then unaware of the fact that this phenomenon, albeit described in different words, was also known to Christian mystics.

Although I had not suggested it, or even hinted at it, Mr Singh offered to visit me in the ashram, about seventy kilometres from Nagpur, in order to bring some literature on the subject. Some time later, he came and left a book on the teachings of the Masters, in which I would find information about the sound current, as he called the audible life stream. After this, the contact with Mr Singh continued, although I was not really interested in the teachings of the Masters. Mr Singh had offered me the hospitality of his family in Nagpur and sometimes, when I had business there, I would visit them. He never missed the opportunity to furnish me with more literature on the teachings of the Masters and, not wishing to be impolite, I would sometimes glance at it.

This seemingly accidental and trivial meeting with Mr Singh proved later to be crucially significant. Although I did not realize it at that time, our short meeting at the bishop's residence was my first step towards a whole new phase in my spiritual life – the path of the Masters – for which my inner guide had brought me to India.

In Brahma Vidya Mandir I now had solid ground under my feet and within a few months I felt I had received over-whelming proof that my life in India was part and parcel of a clearly designed divine plan. It seemed clear that he had everything under control, so to speak. Nevertheless, I sometimes still had the feeling of walking on a tightrope, and the drop below caused me even more giddiness than when I was on the ridge. On the ridge, I had had my accustomed environment, which provided at least a certain visual support, whereas on the tightrope only *his gaze* gave me any feeling of security. I knew he would not let me fall into the depth – *provided I trusted him*. This realization would fill me with a joy that made me forget the depths lurking below.

Kripaon ki Mata

At the end of March 1966 I had to begin my service at the leper colony at Dehra Dun in northern India. I had taken this upon myself in order to replace my friend Agnes Kunze during her home leave in Germany. In this colony there lived about a hundred lepers, some of whom were families with children. They kept their own houses and whoever was able to work could do so by spinning and weaving wool and cotton in the colony's workshops.

Apart from administrative work and housekeeping, my assistant, who was also German, and I had to be present during the doctor's visits to dispense the medicine and to supervise the dressing of wounds caused by leprosy. The rest of the nursing was done by residents who had received some training. There was no real risk of my being infected, since those who lived in the colony had already passed the contagious phase.

The atmosphere in the colony was not at all depressing. In fact, people were joyous and grateful to receive not only a roof over their heads and their livelihood, but also respect for their human dignity. Marriages were held, children were born, feasts were celebrated and provisions for their possible return to normal life were made. I took part in everything and did my best to look after the many worries and needs of these people.

My stay at the colony lasted six months in all. During this period, I had to do work that was diametrically opposed to a contemplative life, and in truth I felt overtaxed. But in spite of the excessive burden and the turbulence, I felt a deep inner peace. I hardly noticed the world spinning round me. Things passed me by and sank away again. My daily work was done wholly in the presence of God and in the practice of the Jesus Prayer. When, after five months, Agnes returned from her holidays, I started my journey to Kolkata to meet Mother Teresa, as Major Ramachandra had enjoined me to do. Little did I imagine at that moment what turbulence the meeting with Mother Teresa would trigger.

CHAPTER FOUR

Meeting Mother Teresa

IN KOLKATA I WAS ABLE TO SPEND TWO EXTRA-
ordinary days with Mother Teresa. She took me to Kali Ghat,
formerly the pilgrim hall of a temple dedicated to the goddess Kali. This was where they brought people who were found
dying in the streets of Kolkata. They were the poorest of the
poor, for whom there was not even a place in the three thousand official slums of Kolkata. They were taken off the streets
so they could at least pass away in peace. Many of these piti-
able people lay completely apathetic on their beds, cowed like
animals, unable to speak or eat. A German woman doctor who
had joined Mother Teresa's Order of the Missionaries of Charity went from bed to bed asking them about their condition
and treating them with the same respect and courtesy as if they
were privileged patients or even beloved parents and friends.

Afterwards, we visited one of the homes for young orphans.
They had been abandoned by their mothers, who were too poor
to feed them. These half-starved little ones were nursed by the
sisters with great care. For those who survived, sponsor parents
were sought to look after their education, visit them, invite
them to their houses and take care of their needs.

The next day I was allowed to accompany Mother Teresa to the Kolkata docks, where her presence was needed in order to receive a cargo of rice that had been donated by Misereor (a charitable organization of the Catholic Church in Germany). Mother Teresa wanted to have it loaded into the waiting lorries and take it with her. However, she met with endless difficulties because she did not have all the necessary paperwork. The problems were solved only after she had gained entry to the office of the head of the dock administration and they learnt who she was. It took four hours to settle the affair, so there was no time left to visit the buildings housing the lepers who were cared for by Mother Teresa's community.

I looked up to Mother Teresa with admiration. She was a charismatic personality who possessed the power to inspire others and stimulate them to exceptional service. The motivating power behind her dedication, the secret of her success, was a profound love for Christ that filled her whole being. In 1983, when she was lying sick in a hospital bed, she wrote a meditation on Christ's question to his disciples: "But whom say ye that I am?" In her meditation she wrote, "Jesus is my only love. Jesus is my one and all." It was to Jesus that she had dedicated her life of service to the abandoned, to those whom no one else cared for. With absolute consistency she put into practice the words of Jesus: "Verily I say unto you, inasmuch as ye have done it unto one of the least of these my brethren, ye have done it unto me."

During my two days in Kolkata we hardly spoke about personal matters, but I still felt a certain intimacy between us. We had gone similar ways – because God had intervened in our lives, both of us leaving our convents, knowing we had to obey. This experience connected us. Apparently, Mother Teresa felt the same, because when we first met, she said, "You are not a novelty to me." Her way had led her into the slums of Kolkata, while mine had led into the desert.

Two days after this memorable stay in Kolkata, I wanted to travel to the south of India, to visit some Benedictine monasteries. Mother Teresa also had to go south, so she invited me to travel with her and two of her sister companions. However, circumstances obliged Mother Teresa to postpone her journey for some days, so I waited for her and this brought about a sequence of events that would have been hard to imagine.

Halfway to Chennai – we had been travelling for about ten hours – the train was stopped by striking students who wanted to enforce the setting up of a steel plant in this area. When it became clear that the train would be held up for a long time, Mother Teresa became active. She took the ringleaders to task and insisted they organize a van for her and her companions and drive us to the next town, one hour away. Since it was Mother Teresa who demanded this, the young men hastened to comply with her request. They organized a jeep and took us to a big convent school, where we were received with great hospitality. For the sisters there it was a great honour to render a service to Mother Teresa. It was ten days before we were able to continue our journey.

A Christian ashram

In those days of forced rest, Mother Teresa repeatedly brought up the subject of the founding of a contemplative community. She told me she had reflected quite often about my present situation. In her opinion I had now gained sufficient experience in Brahma Vidya Mandir and it was time to start something on my own. Actually, I had spent only three months in the ashram and had only begun to familiarize myself with their way of life and their spirituality. Mother Teresa confessed that it had long been her wish to have a contemplative branch of her order in addition to the Missionaries of Charity, who served the poorest of the poor. This contemplative branch would support the work of the 'external branch' of the sisters by prayer. This vision is generally accepted in the Catholic Church and is also shared by the Benedictines and members of all other contemplative orders.* Mother Teresa considered me to be the right person to establish such a community with her help. She said she already had a suitable house at Kolkata and she would support me in every way. I should come to her and not return to Paunar.

Mother Teresa must surely have been concerned about the salvation of my soul, which in her view was in danger in this non-Christian ashram. In keeping with her character, she now wanted to take action. She remembered a nun from Mangalore in the State of Karnataka who wished to enter a contemplative order; she could be my companion from the beginning. I should write to this sister in Mother Teresa's name and then visit her.

The founding of a prayer branch of her order was already as good as settled for Mother Teresa, and she became more and more enthusiastic about it. However, this was an enthusiasm that I found difficult to share. I voiced my doubts and reservations about her idea very clearly, but she was not ready to listen to my objections. "Do the first step in faith; think of nothing else," she advised me. This is what she had practised herself when founding her own community. The difference was that she had had an inner calling on which to base her faith,

---

*To support this conviction, an event from the Book of Exodus is noted: Whilst the Israelites were fighting against the Amalekites, who resisted their passage through their country, Moses climbed to the top of a hill with Aaron and Hur, and lifted up his arms in prayer. As long as he remained in this position, the Israelites were victorious; but as soon as he put down his arms, the enemies triumphed. *Exodus* 17:10–13

whereas I did not feel any calling to set up a contemplative branch of the Missionaries of Charity.

Certainly, Mother Teresa's plan to entrust me with the founding of a contemplative community was no small proof of her confidence in me, but it frightened me. Of course there had once been a vague intention to start a community according to the ideal of the Hermits of Sachchidananda and I might well have joined that group, but I had never intended to found a community on my own. Moreover, I was convinced that God had led me to Brahma Vidya Mandir for a reason and that my place was there.

Yet Mother Teresa insisted on her plans. I agreed to write to the nun in Mangalore and to visit her. On my way south, I was to discuss the issue with Father Francis, the founder of Kurisumala Ashram in the Nilgiri Hills in southern India. Some years ago he had started a monastic community according to the *Rule of Saint Benedict*, so he should be able to offer valuable advice. Mother Teresa expected a lot from his counselling and said, "Do what Father Francis tells you to do." She herself had always submitted obediently to her superiors, to her spiritual guides and to the bishop; she was convinced that in this way the will of God was made manifest to her. I for my part was not so sure of this, because in my life God's plans had been revealed differently.

The subsequent conversations I had with Father Francis made it abundantly clear that founding a contemplative community on the basis of Indian monastic and spiritual tradition should be preceded by a thorough and profound preparation. Father Francis was convinced that I would need to gain more experience if I wished to start such a project from a solid base.

Mother Teresa would probably have considered such preparation superfluous. We had never discussed what kind of religious life the prospective community was to live by, but to her it was surely self-evident that the prayer branch would lead the conventional religious life of a Catholic convent. She definitely would have rejected any adaptation to the Indian spiritual tradition. To her it would have been unwise to experiment in this way with young women from traditional Catholic families in India.

Another conversation, this time with the General Prior of the Apostolic Carmelites at Kerala, to whom my bishop belonged, led to similar conclusions. Furthermore, the General Prior, who had once visited Brahma Vidya Mandir with Monsignor Januarius, was of the opinion that my stay there could well be a lifelong task for me.

After all these discussions it was clear that my proposed trip to Mangalore would no longer serve any real purpose, but I wanted to comply with Mother Teresa's wishes and visit the nun she had mentioned. Very soon, however, it became evident that the situation was not at all as Mother Teresa had thought. Sister Immaculata would not have been a suitable companion for me to start a contemplative community with. We did agree on many points about a contemplative life, but at the same time we were both so much shaped by our different backgrounds and experiences in religious life that it would have been hard to find a common basis for a community life. I was very much relieved that the subject of founding a prayer branch of the Missionaries of Charity was clearly out of the question and I informed Mother Teresa about the outcome of these various conversations. But whenever I met her in later years, she always took great interest in my life in India. It was only in 1978, after another ten years, that she realized her plan to start a contemplative branch of her order.

After this episode I left Mangalore for Bangalore. There I visited, as planned, my fellow brethren in the Benedictine Order in their monastery Asirvanam (Forest of Benediction) and discussed the events of the last few days with the prior. He confirmed my own conviction that I should live at Brahma Vidya Mandir. Since God had led me there in such a wonderful way, it seemed clear that this was where I should be. This was the second time within a year that I had found that man-made plans for my life did not always conform to the will of God. In such cases the plans were doomed to fail, even if made with the best intentions and religious zeal. For me it was further evidence that I should fix my gaze firmly on my inner guide and follow the inner call, for only in this way would I be able to find my path. When I informed Monsignor Januarius about Mother Teresa's ideas, he was also of the opinion that my place was in Brahma Vidya Mandir, and he gave me a comprehensive study program, which he had already mentioned at our first meeting at the beginning of the year. Full of joy, I returned to the ashram on 18ᵗʰ December and was cordially welcomed by the sisters. It was exactly one year since I had first arrived there. I had been away from Brahma Vidya Mandir for more than six months and it had been quite a turbulent time. I was much relieved to be able to merge once more with the peace and quiet of the ashram and to devote my life exclusively to spirituality.

Requests to start a Christian contemplative ashram reached me several times in the following years. These were serious proposals; some of them even came from Indian bishops. While I was well aware of the importance of such communities in the Indian Catholic Church, I felt very clearly that it was not God's intention for me to undertake such a task. With the experience of the desert, *he* had uprooted me from the traditional form of religious community life and it would have been impossible for me to fit again into such a framework. Such could not be the will of God, I felt quite clearly. More importantly, how was I to lead young people to a form of life with which I was unable to identify? I knew that my way was a different one. Even if I did not see it before me, I had to keep myself prepared to walk it when the time was ripe. It was wrong, I felt, to anticipate God's decisions about my life by starting a community on my own and thus creating a *fait accompli*.

CHAPTER FIVE

In the World of Vedanta

IN THE BEGINNING OF JANUARY 1967 I BEGAN following the instructions of my bishop to study Indian philosophy. His intention was that with my studies I should build up a sound basis for dialogue between Christianity and Hinduism. There was, however, a far more significant reason for this study, which probably neither the bishop nor myself were aware of at that time. This was the development of my own spiritual life, which was entering an important new phase. My teacher was Swami Sevanand (bliss through service), one of three monks who were also living in the ashram community in accordance with Vinoba Bhave's wishes. He proposed that we begin with Shankaracharya's commentary on the Brahma Sutra, a collection of aphorisms based on the philosophy of the Upanishads about the nature of Brahman, the supreme Being; about *atman*, the individual Self; about creation; and about the means to attain God-realization and final liberation. This commentary is one of the main works of this great Indian philosopher and it was the object of the daily philosophy lessons in the ashram, which I had been unable to attend because of my insufficient knowledge of the language.

To begin with, Swami Sevanand explained the purpose of Vedanta and, by implication, the object of our study, the Brahma Sutra. Vedanta, a school of philosophy based on the teachings of the Upanishads, is concerned with the course of self-realization by which one understands the ultimate reality, Brahman. It considers that its task is to destroy humanity's innate illusion that everything we perceive with our senses constitutes reality. In countless variations and examples, the Upanishads seek to prove that all empirical knowledge is *a-vidya* (not-knowing), ignorance. Similarly, all purely intellectual knowledge about the One, all that we can acquire by the study of the holy scriptures, is ignorance as well. What Vedanta wishes to convey to the seeker for truth is *vidya* – true knowledge. It wants to open the seeker's eyes to reality – to the experience of Brahman, the supreme Being. So the Brahma Sutra begins with the phrase: "Now, therefore, the desire to know Brahman...".

The aphorisms of the Brahma Sutra cannot be understood without a commentary – they are texts of archaic conciseness, which are almost impossible to decode. Yet Shankaracharya's commentary, too, is anything but easily accessible and would be a closed book for most Western readers. With his explanations, my teacher allowed me access to these texts. From the first lesson this was a wonderful experience. We spoke about the Sutras' assertion of the sole and absolute existence of God, in comparison to which the material creation is non-existent. This thesis that the material creation does not possess real existence is the foundation of the *advaita* philosophy.

I was so fascinated by what I had heard that after the lesson I spent the whole evening in contemplation of God's existence, especially his immanence in the creation, of which I had never before been so conscious. In the course of the following weeks I received abundant insights. My perspectives widened to embrace new horizons that I had never seen during my study of Christian theology. To my amazement, I realized that the teachings of even the greatest of our Christian theologians represent no more than a limited view of the divine truth. The barriers of the Christian, occidental way of thinking about divine truth began to crumble as I entered into the teachings of the Advaita Vedanta.

I had never imagined that the mysteries of God could be approached otherwise than through Christian theology. In the beginning many questions arose, since I was unable to classify what I heard within the categories of Christian theology. When my questions were not sufficiently clarified during the lessons, we decided that I should begin by just listening and taking in, giving time for what I learned to sink in. This proved to be good advice, because in the course of time many questions were solved by themselves.

From the very beginning, the *advaita* philosophy fascinated me immensely because it expressed precisely what had been indelibly impressed on my consciousness by the experience of the desert: *All is nothing – only God exists*. I was strongly attracted by the emphasis on personal experience of God rather than mere intellectual knowledge – a point that is constantly stressed in the Brahma Sutra. For me, my personal encounter with the transcendent had swept away in a flash all discursive thinking about God and had given me a different sense of the absolute. From that moment onward, I wanted nothing else but to submit wholly to the effect of this experience, which had transformed my entire being.

Time and again, my teacher pointed out that the Vedas and the Upanishads are based on experience and that there can be no real understanding of them if one lacks personal experience. He referred to Shankaracharya, who expresses this quite clearly in saying:

Brahman cannot be known by the perception of the senses, because he should not be considered an object amongst other objects. Nor can he be known by logical reasoning, because no logical reasoning leads to him. Brahman can only be known through *anubhava* (experience).

I cannot say how many of the five hundred and fifty-five sutras I studied with Swami Sevanand. He did not proceed systematically, but selected subjects of special importance. I shall, however, never forget the last sutra, which reads, "There is no return for the released souls, according to the scriptures." As a commentary on this sentence, Shankaracharya quotes a number of texts from various Upanishads, according to which anyone who has reached the ultimate goal by attaining true knowledge of God need no longer come back into creation after death, because they have transcended the cycle of transmigration.

But it was not this promise of final liberation that moved me; rather, it was a mental association triggered by the word 'return'. Several times in the course of my life, my own experience had shown me that there is no return – no going back – on the way to God. Having once set foot on this path, under the irresistible attraction of the absolute, one can never turn back.

Qualification for brahma vidya

Shankaracharya demands from the student of *brahma vidya* the fulfilment of a number of conditions. These conditions are a *sine qua non* for anyone who wishes to attain God-realization. My teacher also spoke to me about these prerequisites and I was deeply impressed by the high standards that Shankaracharya sets for all seekers of truth. At the beginning of my studies, however, I was unable to appreciate fully the significance of his words.

It was only the study of Vedanta that opened my eyes and enabled me to realize the attitude needed in order to approach the science of God-realization.

Shankaracharya's first prerequisite is that students must have a sense of the difference between the absolute divine reality *(sat)* and unreality *(asat)*, or at least must strive with all their might to gain this experience, especially by concentration *(dharana)* and meditation *(dhyan)*. They should already have experienced transcendence in some way, already have been touched by the absolute. The words *'Todo es nada – sólo Dios basta'* that had such an impact on my spiritual life refer to this experience. This is the experience of the desert that any student of *brahma vidya* (God-realization) should have had before he can begin to acquire direct knowledge of God.

Shankaracharya does not mention the reasons for these conditions, but they are easily understood if one looks at the texts that speak about *brahma vidya*. These texts reflect experiences that can only be had on a spiritual level; such experiences are inaccessible to the intellect because its capacity is limited to empirical perception and cognitive processing of what it perceives. These texts go beyond the limits of the mind's powers of comprehension. The intellect is always at risk of falling prey to the fatal illusion that it has acquired genuine knowledge of God, when it has in fact merely acquired theological learning.

Shankaracharya's second condition for the study of *brahma vidya* is the renunciation of the desire for any rewards for our actions. This applies both to earthly rewards in this life and to rewards in any future life. This requirement is based on the teachings of Vedanta, which points out that if we are reborn in order to be rewarded for our good deeds, then we are still caught in the cycle of birth and death, and so cannot attain true God-realization. The student therefore must not have the expectation of any reward – acting exclusively for the sake of God-realization.

The third precondition is the practice of the six virtues, which are the ethical prerequisites for the study of *brahma vidya*. The student must possess inner balance and content-ment, self-discipline and control of the senses; there must be patience in the face of hardship and difficulties, as well as a capacity for inner recollection and faith in God.

The fourth precondition is a longing for salvation. Salva-tion means liberation from the cycle of birth and death, which requires that we overcome our existential ignorance, *a–vidya*, of the fact that our innermost being, our true Self, is *atman*, the soul. I cannot say whether there was ever a time when these preconditions were strictly applied in the selection of applicants. For a long time the sacred texts were transmitted orally and it was up to each teacher to accept or refuse a student. Nowadays, anyone can go to a library and study the books, but it would be wrong to call the results of such study *gyana* (knowledge). The real knowledge of God referred to in the Upanishads and the Brahma Sutra is something quite different.

The Bhagavad Gita

Some time later, when I had already acquired some knowledge of Sanskrit, I began to study the Bhagavad Gita – the 'Song of the Exalted One'. I had a German as well as various English translations at my disposal, but they often differed considerably from the original text, so I decided to make my own translation and a commentary on the eighteen chapters.

My study of the Bhagavad Gita familiarized me with the teachings of Hindu philosophy on *karma*, creation's law of cause and effect, and *samsara*, the phenomenon of transmigration.

However, it would take me several more years, and many conversations with Swami Sevanand and Sushila Agarwal, to integrate these fundamental concepts into my thinking. The Western world mostly dismisses them as fanciful, even though the idea of reincarnation was once accepted in Christianity.

The verses of the Bhagavad Gita that were recited every evening in the ashram temple describe the characteristics of one who has attained steadfast wisdom and whose consciousness is merged in the transcendent. Here Arjuna asks his teacher: "How does a man behave who has attained imperishable wisdom?" In answer, Krishna describes the behaviour of a man who has reached the goal of his spiritual path and attained *brahma vidya*. It had been Vinoba Bhave's intention that seekers of God in Brahma Vidya Mandir should use the model that Krishna outlines in these verses, keeping it constantly before their eyes like a mirror. Krishna says that the person who has attained this wisdom has abandoned all the desires of his heart and found his satisfaction exclusively in God. Here it resounds again, this '*Todo es nada – sólo Dios basta*', so similar to the words of Saint Teresa.

Then Krishna continues: "A man of steadfast wisdom will not be perturbed by the adversities that life brings about; he does not look for earthly happiness, nor does he have any attachment to the world." This means that anyone who is united with God no longer grasps onto the objects of the senses and also no longer has any desire for them, because he has beheld the ultimate reality.

Later in life I was to hear this same idea expressed as follows: if you try to take away from a beggar the copper coins that he has collected, he holds on to them with all his might, but if you offer him a piece of gold instead, he will open his fist and drop the coins without hesitation. Once anyone has been touched by the absolute, all the beauty of the world, its wealth, honour and power, are worthless compared with the precious spiritual wealth they have found.

In his parables of the kingdom of heaven Jesus makes the same point when he says: "Again, the kingdom of heaven is like unto treasure hid in a field; the which when a man hath found, he hideth, and for joy thereof goeth and selleth all that he hath, and buyeth that field. Again, the kingdom of heaven is like unto a merchant man, seeking goodly pearls; who, when he had found one pearl of great price, went and sold all that he had, and bought it."

Krishna describes the behaviour of a person who is still entirely attached to the world. His mind will be carried away by the senses and he will hold on to whatever gives him sensual pleasure. It is from such attachments that vice originates, confusing the mind and finally dragging one down into ruin; all peace of mind is lost and all power of discrimination is swept away on the breaking waves of sensual pleasures. For those who have attained wisdom, the very opposite is true:

> That which is night to all beings,
> In that the disciplined man wakes;
> That in which all beings are awake,
> Is night to the sage who sees.

These are mystical words, containing a truth that Vedanta expresses in many ways. He who is ignorant considers the world of the senses to be real, whilst the one whose inner eye has been opened to the transcendent recognizes that the creation is unreal. The verse points to the experience of the 'desert dweller', whose consciousness, touched by the absolute, has crossed the threshold to the world beyond. One who has experienced that divine light knows that the light we see with our physical eyes is darkness. Krishna's words gave me a glimpse of the dimension I was to explore. Never before had I found such a compact but clear description of this experience.

The Upanishads

My third study program was the Upanishads. A fellow sister, who had been a teacher of Sanskrit, introduced me to the world of these ancient mystical texts, which soon drew me under their spell. In the Upanishads, the great Indian *rishis*, or seers, set out their own experience of the transcendent, of the ultimate reality. They gave voice to their experiences beyond the boundaries of philosophical and theological learning.

Again, an unknown territory opened up before me when we started reading these wonderful texts together. At first they seemed strange and hardly accessible, but then I began to feel a familiar attraction because, as with the Bhagavad Gita, I had some limited personal experience that I could relate to the text.

We had selected the Katha Upanishad because I wished to explore a central theme of Vedanta, the teachings about the *atman*. This concept has a double meaning in the Upanishads: first, *atman* is that spirit of God which permeates the whole creation and from which the creation has sprung. In this context, the concepts of Brahman and *atman*, as used in the Upanishads, are synonymous. *Atman* is, however, also the essence of every human being; it is our innermost, eternal, imperishable Self, the soul of our soul; it is that which is truly divine within each of us. The Katha Upanishad describes the nature of *atman* in this twofold aspect as the originless Being that is both the origin of creation and the innermost Self of all beings.

We made our own translation of the texts from Sanskrit. Realizing that it is all but impossible to render their pithy words in another language, we decided to make a loose translation that resembled the archaic character of the original text, even if it was not strictly literal. The verses below are taken from this free translation.

> The knowing Self,
> Unborn, deathless,
> Originless, without a second,
> Eternal One, who ever is.

> Infinitely small,
> Exceedingly great,
> Living in the heart of every creature.
> Immobile – he moves far,
> Motionless – he goes everywhere.

> Without body himself,
> In bodies he dwells.
> Not given to decay,
> Even if the body disintegrates.

> The Lord, the One,
> Innermost Self *(atman)* of all that exists.
> The One, who became visible in multiple forms.

> The eternal One
> In changeable things,
> In the change of time.
> The knower of the knowing ones,
> The One amid the many.

> One who recognizes this *atman* in himself,
> This enlightened one, and only he,
> Receives eternal bliss
> And everlasting peace – no one else.

This *atman* cannot be attained by study
Of the scriptures,
Nor by intellectual power,
Nor even by hearing learned discourses;
By him it is attained,
Whom it chooses.
To such a one the *atman*
Reveals its own nature.

This chapter has given only a glimpse into the world of Vedanta, to which the study of the Brahma Sutra, the Upanishads and the Bhagavad Gita introduced me. One of the most important insights that I gained by the study of the holy scriptures of India was something I had not envisaged. I became aware of the universality of the spiritual, mystical experiences of humanity. I realized that the Christian mystics and the unknown authors of the Upanishads were speaking about similar experiences. This realization was an important step on my spiritual path in India, because it extended my horizon beyond the limits of the Christian understanding of divine experience. Not that this universality of mystic experience was in any way a new idea; great theologians, philosophers and scholars had reached the same conclusion long ago, but at that time I did not know their writings. I discovered them only later through my research for this book.*

At first, my realization was limited to Christianity and Hinduism. Some years later, through the literature of the teachings of the Masters, I came into contact with the scriptures

---

*The German philosopher Arthur Schopenhauer, and Paul Deussen, who translated the Brahma Sutra into German, have pointed out these parallels. They have also been mentioned by Rudolf Otto in his book *Mysticism East and West* and by the former President of India, Sarvepalli Radhakrishnan, in his books on the Brahma Sutra and the Bhagavad Gita.

of other great Indian saints and Muslim mystics, above all Jalaluddin Rumi (1207–1273), known in India as Maulana Rum, and Hafiz (1326–1390). I gradually came to understand that God-realization is universal in nature and beyond the distinctions and limits drawn by religions. It became clear to me that spiritual and mystic experiences at a higher level of consciousness do not differ, because there is only one divine truth and one reality.

As I became more familiar with the texts of the Upanishads, I realized that while theological statements about the nature of God in the various religions may differ and may even be contradictory, the actual experience of God will be the same for all, be they Christian, Hindu, Buddhist, Muslim or Jewish. During the first stages of the spiritual path, seekers of God carry the imprint of their own religion; they may continue to follow this religion after the breakthrough of their consciousness into transcendence (or rather the entering of the absolute into their life), but their experience of the metaphysical and the divine is independent of their particular religion. This is very impressively expressed by Daniel Ladinsky in one of his poems inspired by Hafiz:

> I have learned so much from God that I can no longer call myself a Christian, a Hindu, a Muslim, a Buddhist, a Jew. The Truth has shared so much of itself with me that I can no longer call myself a man, a woman, an angel, or even pure soul. Love has befriended Hafiz so completely, it has turned to ash and freed me of every concept and image my mind has ever known.

CHAPTER SIX

Sachchidananda Community

On several occasions i had turned down suggestions that I should found a Christian contemplative community for sisters in India, but over the years something like an invisible community developed around me, which I began to call the Sachchidananda Community – a reference to the Hermits of Sachchidananda. This was a circle of friends that constituted a second family for me – second to the ashram community of Brahma Vidya Mandir. This circle became an important factor in my development in India.

It was, of course, hardly a community in the full sense, since most of its members hardly knew each other and they rarely met. With some of them I only exchanged correspondence, while others came occasionally for days or even weeks to Paunar. Common to all its members was an interest in the dialogue between religions, in the integration of the age-old Indian philosophy into Christian theology, and in the adaptation of forms of worship of the culture of India to the Catholic church service.

The origins of the Sachchidananda Community go back to the beginning of my stay in India. Only a few months after my arrival, the first contacts and friendships were made.

This happened in May 1966 at a seminar of Indian music in Mussoorie, a small hill station close to Dehra Dun. My friend Agnes Kunze had booked a place for me at the seminar.

The participants came from many parts of the country. They were mostly Indian seminarians, Catholic theology students, young priests, mainly members of Catholic orders, and Indian Catholic sisters. When they heard that I was living as a Catholic nun in a Hindu ashram community, there was no end to their questions, but in general my reception in the group was quite friendly and some of them showed great interest in my 'experiment', as they called it. I answered all their queries and in the two weeks we spent together we had some very good conversations. At the end of the course, many of the participants asked for my address and proposed to visit Brahma Vidya Mandir or invited me to their own convents and monasteries for discourses and discussions.

Since I only returned to the ashram at the end of 1966, the first group of my newly acquired friends did not come to Paunar until June of the following year. Our guests were students of theology, members of the Jesuit Order at Pune. As my friends, they were cordially received by the ashram community. Moreover, this visit offered an opportunity to implement one of the most important principles of Vinoba Bhave: harmony between the different religions. The three students shared our life from morning till evening. As they had many questions to ask, we met one evening under the star-clad sky for a discussion. There was a wonderful atmosphere of peace and stillness, and we all sensed the presence of the Lord, who was the invisible centre of our small group. They wanted to know what had led me to India and I started to relate my story. At the end it was clear to all of us that living with God can be a breathtaking adventure, an adventure of faith and love, if one gives way to him.

This was a subject that moved my friends very much. They had dedicated their lives to God, but at the same time they felt the complete insecurity of their existence. So many things had been stirred up in the preceding years in the Catholic Church that they found themselves facing an incalculable fate, an imponderable future. They felt insecure in their vocation and in their chosen way of life. When they heard how I had been living in search of an uncompromising response to the call of God, they felt encouraged to try a new approach themselves. We spoke about how the only way to rise above fear is through faith in God, full trust in him and surrender to him. This means giving oneself wholeheartedly to God; there is no other way to become master of our own lives.

I was deeply touched to sense through their questions the existential fear of these young people. They had not yet learned from experience that unconditional trust in God and unquestioning surrender to him are the most stable foundations for life. Nor did they know that surrender brings us face to face with God – albeit in a hidden way.

My young friends also wanted to know what I considered to be the meaning and the purpose of my life in India. At that time, it had already become clear to me that I would not found a community of my own, but would remain in Brahma Vidya Mandir. It was here that I wanted to continue my life in search of God, convinced that he had placed me there. I told my friends that I was ready to serve the Church of India through my life here, and that only God knew what his plans for me were.

In this discussion it was important to me to make it perfectly clear that I had neither an ecclesiastical mission nor any concrete plans for the future. I had not chosen India, nor did I wish to choose any task for myself or to work out any plans just in order to prove to myself or to others that my presence in this country had some meaning. Ever since I experienced God's total claim to my life, there was nothing left for me to do apart from a wholehearted acceptance of his will.

Another student asked what I was living on. He was asking me how my Christian religious life was nourished, since in Brahma Vidya Mandir everything that makes up the life of a Catholic nun was absent: the daily Mass, community prayer, the Christian environment. I admitted that it was not the sacramental encounter with Christ that nourished my soul, for then I would have been living on starvation rations. My 'bread of life' now was rather the experience of the divine light inside; my spiritual life consisted in letting my whole being be permeated by this light. I also mentioned the incessant Jesus Prayer, the daily Bible reading and attending the Sunday Mass at Wardha.

Finally, one of the young prospective shepherds of souls asked what message I had for them. Soon they would be sent out to preach God's word; like many ministers of the Church, they were questioning their own understanding of their vocation. I definitely did not have any messages to give them, but I had an answer that had been formulated before on many occasions: "In the present times, which are so action oriented, we must emphasize the need for a spiritual life, a life of inwardness and a living relationship with God. What we need today are men and women who speak about God on the basis of their own experience. Only words that originate from such an experience bear the power of conviction. A messenger of God should reflect his encounter with God."

To illustrate this point I told my friends the impressive story of Upakosala in the Chandogaya Upanishad. There we are told that this young seeker of God had, together with his fellow students, served his Guru Satyakama for twelve years, during which they all received instructions from him about the sacred wisdom. After twelve years the other students were allowed to go home; only Upakosala had to stay back, since he had not yet attained ultimate knowledge of Brahman. The young man was deeply grieved, became sick and refused to take food. Finally, during the absence of his Guru, the knowledge of Brahman was conferred upon him by Agni, the god of fire. When the Guru eventually returned, he saw the transformation that had taken place in his student and he told him: "Your face, my dear, is shining like that of a man who has attained the knowledge of Brahman."

After the visit of that first group in June 1967, the Sach-chidananda Community grew continuously. At the end of October 1967, three more theology students from Pune came to see us. They had obtained permission – by no means a matter of course – to come to Brahma Vidya Mandir for their prepara-tory retreat, prior to consecration into the priesthood. For ten days they shared our life, and from the first moment they were like members of the ashram community – they worked with us in the garden and in the houses, took part in the philosophy lessons and joined in the community prayers in the temple.

Swami Sevanand, my philosophy teacher, was their mentor and he devoted himself to this task with dedication. The stay of these three friends was an enrichment for the whole com-munity; it tangibly intensified the atmosphere of joy, love and peace amongst us and the sisters were deeply impressed to see that so many young men were dedicating their lives to God. When they left, we all felt a very big gap.

Another group consisting of equal numbers of theology students and young priests once participated in our Christmas celebration, which the ashram community observed every year since I came to live with them. The sisters had learned Christian Christmas songs, which they sang with devotion at the midnight celebration of Christ's birth. They had decorated a statue of Christ, which had been carved by a grateful guest; it depicted Jesus as a shepherd, who – like Krishna – was playing on a flute. At his feet lay a lamb and one of the sisters said to me, "This is me." Whether Christians or Hindus, the celebration of Christ's birth made us one big family and we felt like children of the one divine Father, whom we worshipped by different names and in different ways.

These visits carried on over the years. Quite often, Indian Catholic nuns would come too. Most of them were superiors and mistresses of novices who came to find inspiration to guide them in adapting the way of life in their convents to the Indian cultural context. Very soon a cordial friendship connected us and I was always generously received in their houses in Pune and Bangalore whenever I happened to visit those places. On such occasions I was always asked to speak about our life in Brahma Vidya Mandir or to give a discourse on prayer and meditation. Thus our relationship grew over the years, helped by the fact that we occasionally met at the various conferences and seminars that I attended at the express wish of my bishop.

Every once in a while, we at Brahma Vidya Mandir were even visited by religious sisters from Europe. They had come to India with the intention of founding a religious community, but some of them secretly entertained the hope of being able to live in our ashram. But I had to point out that this would not be possible without a 'vocation to the desert'; otherwise, they would soon miss the Christian surroundings they were used to and their religious life would most probably suffer damage.

The community life of the Sachchidananda Community was, of course, limited to just a few days here and there, whenever we happened to be together. Only once did it last longer, when a young Carmelite priest spent a whole month in the ashram, together with his Sanskrit teacher. The priest belonged to the diocese of my bishop and the sisters christened him Prasannabhai (pleasing brother). Whenever he came to the ashram, we decided to lead a veritable Christian religious life together – celebrating the Eucharist every morning, reading the Bible and working on a *Sachchidananda Liturgy*. We spoke about many things concerning the renewal of the Church in India, which was of great concern to him. We also spoke about our way to God and about our duty to bear witness to Christ among the Hindus, which for him, being a priest, was quite important.

It was not just theology students and young seminarians who came to Brahma Vidya Mandir, but also their professors and those who served as tutors to the novices. They had heard such enthusiastic accounts from their students that they wanted to see the ashram for themselves. In a way, they also belonged to the Sachchidananda Community, although in a different fashion. These experienced priests and monks very soon became true friends. I could talk to them about my problems with the doctrine of the Catholic Church and with the practical application of the sacraments. Like my bishop, they proved to be very understanding and supportive, especially when I had to spend some months at Bangalore, in southern India, on account of a health problem. Over the years, a very fruitful cooperation developed between me and these distinguished friends. Whenever my travels brought me to their cities, they always welcomed me into their monasteries and colleges as one of the family.

During these visits we often discussed the 'Indianizing' of the Catholic Church in India. For various historical reasons it is marked by decidedly European features, and this is one of the reasons why Hindus consider it to be a foreign element in their country. In particular, we spoke about how the liturgy might be adapted to more Indian forms of worship. Still more important was, of course, the reshaping of the actual texts of the liturgy, which are exclusively Catholic and occidental in nature. We felt that the Catholic Church of India should outgrow its Mediterranean cradle and integrate into the cultural and spiritual life of India, a country that possesses such profound knowledge of God and has brought forth so many saints and mystics. Therefore, the idea of creating an authentic Indo-Christian theology on the basis of the *advaita* philosophy occupied our minds very much.

Meeting all these people and enjoying their friendship was of great importance to me. First, there was the human aspect of these encounters – these people accepted me and my unusual position, and they helped me find my own identity in India. Indeed, the importance of their help in this respect cannot be overestimated. The desert experience had extracted my roots from the traditional religious life, and by leaving my monastery I had physically uprooted myself from the ground that had nourished me for so many years. These experiences caused a profound change in me but, since my friends had not known me before, their reactions to my person, my thinking, my words and deeds, were related to Shraddha and not to Sister Praxedis (as I had been known in my monastery). My friends confronted me, so to speak, with the here and now of my life in India. This helped me to attain a new understanding of myself, to establish a new identity and to regain solid ground under my feet.

Beyond that, the members of the Sachchidananda Community performed an important role in assisting me in the process of inner development during those years. They were brothers, sisters, discussion partners, fellow-travellers, advisers and also from time to time helpers in times of need. Through my conversations with them and through the exchange of letters, many things became much clearer to me. By sharing with them my experiences and insights and by speaking to them about my own way of searching for God, I gained a deeper understanding of all the steps I had already taken. Sometimes I became conscious of important matters only through the process of confiding in others, one example of this being the development of my thinking about the priority that one should give to one's own conscience. Also, by conveying to my friends the insights obtained by the study of Vedanta, Brahma Sutra and the Bhagavad Gita, my horizons widened and new perspectives opened before me.

With some of the members of the Sachchidananda Community, I was united in deep friendship. This was an experience that was new to me since the forming of friendships had not been permitted in our monastic community. The power of these relationships lay in the fact that we belonged not to each other but to the Lord. This gave to these relationships a peculiar momentum – through our friendships our love of God deepened and our happiness in belonging to him was enhanced. This made us even more eager to search for him and helped us to experience his presence in our midst. Sometimes we spoke about these things and were full of joy and gratitude that we had experienced such spiritual love.

Monsignor Januarius's personality was such that I regarded him as very much a part of the Sachchidananda Community. He was an understanding, far-sighted, wise and solicitous fellow-traveller and a true friend, even though, on account of his position as a bishop, he stood outside the circle of friends.

Outside the Sachchidananda Community there were a number of prominent personalities in the Indian Church who occasionally visited Brahma Vidya Mandir in order to learn about our life. Vinoba Bhave and the whole ashram community appreciated this very much and explicitly approved of it. Even Cardinal Gracias of Mumbai once came to Paunar and was received as befitted his rank. He was much impressed by the cheerful and happy faces he saw.

Most of my friends were members of the Catholic Church of India, but I also had some very good friends amongst the Hindus. Some were well-known Indian personalities who considered my life as a Catholic nun in a Hindu ashram to be a matter of some importance. Vinoba Bhave himself always followed my life in his ashram with great interest and noticed with satisfaction how I became part of the community. He also followed with close attention my publications in various magazines, and when I was asked to give a lecture about Brahma Vidya Mandir at the Monastic Congress in Bangkok in 1968, he asked me for a copy of the text.

Through the mediation of Major Ramachandra, with whom I had remained in contact, I made the acquaintance of one of the great spiritual leaders of modern India – Sri Kakasaheb Kalelkar. He had been a disciple and friend of Mahatma Gandhi, and had devoted his life to the promotion of understanding and harmony between the different religions in India. Sometimes we met at conferences and seminars organized to promote the dialogue between religions, and he was pleased to see that I was helping this important work with zeal and a sense of duty. Before my trip to Europe in the spring of 1971, he even took the trouble to make the long trip from Mumbai to Paunar in order to speak with me about the 'familyhood of religions' and to suggest that I might deal with the subject in my lectures in Europe.

CHAPTER SEVEN

Life between
Christ and Krishna

LIVING AS A CATHOLIC NUN IN A HINDU ASH-
ram meant that I was bound to be involved in the dialogue
between religions. In Brahma Vidya Mandir, I found myself in
a position that entailed much more than just the occasional talk
with a member of another religion or an occasional attempt to
muster some mutual understanding. As was said earlier, Vinoba
Bhave, the disciple and great exponent of Mahatma Gandhi,
had set out with the clear intention of making his ashram a
meeting place of religions, where harmony between Hindus,
Muslims and Christians should be put into practice. Though
historically India was known as a land of tolerance and of
many beliefs, the reality was that more often than not relations
among the various religions were anything but peaceful.

In the eighth century Muslims invaded India as conquerors,
and even today Hindus and Muslims regularly confront each
other in bitter clashes. In the case of the Catholic Church, from
the beginning of the sixteenth century, when the Portuguese
came to India, its relationship with Hindus has always laboured

under the burden of its fateful historical identification with colonialism.* In addition, India was and still is considered by Christianity as a target for missionary activity, even though for nineteen hundred years there have been Christian communities in southern India who call themselves Thomas Christians. The foundation of their communities goes back to the apostle Thomas, who is believed to have reached the Malabar coast in the year CE 52, at a time when there was frequent commercial traffic between Egypt and India. In the middle of the fourth century, Christian refugees from Syria or Mesopotamia came to the western coast of India, where flourishing Christian communities developed over the centuries.

When I came to India in the autumn of 1965, the Catholic Church was showing signs of being ready for a dialogue. The Second Vatican Council had just come to an end, and during this Council, the Catholic Church had, amongst other things, reflected about and redefined her relationship with other world religions. In a declaration about her relationship with the non-Christian religions, the Church turned away from her traditional attitude towards these religions and expressly mentioned the recognition of the experience of God in these religions and encouraged dialogue and cooperation with their followers. In addition, the Church declared that the cultural values of such religions should be recognized, preserved and promoted. In the previous year, during the preparation for the Eucharistic

---

*Neophytes were given Portuguese names and European clothes. In keeping with Portuguese colonial custom, their status as employees brought with it certain privileges. The British colonial power, on the other hand, tried to prevent any religious propaganda that might hurt the feelings of the Hindus. The British held back from any direct patronage of the Christian religion, and this principle of religious non-interference and neutrality was observed right up to Indian independence on 15th August 1947.

Congress at Mumbai, Pope Paul VI addressed Hindu deputies. Anticipating the final resolution of the Council, he said:

> Yours is a country with an ancient culture, the cradle of great religions, the homeland of a nation that searches for God in ceaseless longing, deep contemplation, silence and fervent hymns of prayer. Seldom has the yearning for God been expressed in words so full of expectation as it was in your holy scriptures many centuries before Christ: 'From the unreal lead me to the real, from darkness lead me to light, from death lead me to immortality.'

Such were the circumstances in which my 'life between Christ and Krishna' in Brahma Vidya Mandir began. Apart from the fact that India was then – and still is – exposed to the missionary activities of the Christian churches, I knew nothing about the situation in India when I first arrived there. Monsignor Januarius, of course, was well aware of this situation. By his study of Vedantic philosophy, he had himself anticipated the declaration of the Council by some years and was fully attuned to the dialogue between religions.

Naturally, the ashram community knew about these matters, at least in general terms, but we never mentioned them. We preferred to look for common ground and to emphasize the links connecting our religions. We felt united in the search for God. I sensed how God was leading these young people and I encountered him in their hearts. "I am in such a hurry to come to God," one of my fellow sisters once confessed. We wanted to walk together on this path of searching for God. Vinoba Bhave put special emphasis on the principle of *samyukt sadhana* – leading a spiritual life in community with others.

In particular, we knew that we were one in our faith, that we were all children of one God, even if we called him by different names. This common consciousness, to be one in God in the essence of our being, was the basis of our living together. Wherever we differed in the practice of our religion, we exercised mutual respect and regard. Thus, for instance, it had been understood from the beginning that I attended Sunday Mass in Wardha and that I spent Easter with a Christian community. I was sometimes asked by the sisters why this was so important to me and why I could not celebrate Easter with the ashram community – but without anyone ever suggesting that I should revise my decision. Occasionally the sisters did express their hope that one day I would realize that I no longer needed to take part in outer worship. But although my spiritual life was no longer nourished from this source, the contact with my fellow believers was still important to me, and my bishop would definitely never have permitted me to stay away from Sunday Mass as a general principle.

The ashram community did not conduct *puja*, a ceremonial offering, or worship any deity, as is customary both in temples and in private homes in India. Vinoba Bhave considered that these things were obsolete. Often he repeated his conviction that the time of religions had passed and only spirituality would endure: "The religion of the future is spirituality," as he used to say.

Even though at the time I felt this statement to be quite extreme and could not agree to it, it made me think. From my own experience years ago in my monastery in Germany, I knew of a deeper level of consciousness. I knew also that rites and ceremonies may have their limitations in leading one towards the experience of God, but it is surely the case that not all people are called upon to walk the path of spirituality and mysticism, and for them the exterior forms of worship can be a help in lifting up their hearts to God. On the other hand, Jesus does point out that "the true worshippers shall worship the Father in spirit and in truth," and Saint Paul reminds the

Christian community of Corinth that they are the temple of God and that the Divine resides in them.*

Over the years, my study of the *advaita* philosophy and Vedanta familiarized me with the spiritual world inhabited by my fellow sisters in Brahma Vidya Mandir. I became convinced that the eternal wisdom had built itself a house in India and that, by means of its holy scriptures, it had put a precious diamond into the soil of this country. I came to realize that the Vedantic scriptures do not represent 'purely natural knowledge of God' in the somewhat patronizing way that Christian theologians concede when considering the non-Christian children of our heavenly Father. Rather they are the authentic experiences of great mystics and saints, to whom God revealed himself as the one, eternal and only Being, from whom every creature has received its existence. Meeting God in another religion was for me a truly great discovery.

Vinoba Bhave had, after years of study of the Old and New Testaments, published a selection of the Gospels and the Epistles of the Apostles, a compilation betraying great love and deep sensitivity. The titles of the different chapters are in Sanskrit and thus point to the inner relationship between the Gospels and the holy scriptures of India. This Hindu disciple of Jesus was always deeply moved when Jesus's name or texts from the Gospels were quoted.

The sisters in the ashram suggested reading these selections from the Bible together. We met every day and exchanged views about what we had read. Occasionally we happened on passages that my Hindu sisters found quite inaccessible; the doctrine of the resurrection of the dead on the day of judgement was particularly incomprehensible to them. Their reaction

---

*"Know ye not that ye are the temple of God, and that the spirit of God dwelleth in you?" *1 Corinthians* 3:16

to my explanation made me realize that on this point Christian teachings stand in complete opposition to the Hindu faith. Bodily resurrection from the dead, as taught by the Church, has no attraction for Hindus; to them, death means liberation from the physical body, so that having to return into a physical body after death is a form of imprisonment. When I reflected about these matters, I wondered whether the teachings of the Church about death and resurrection from the dead were perhaps too simplified and needed to be reinterpreted.

Testimony to Christ

Whether the members of the ashram community gained anything towards their spiritual growth by having a Christian nun in their midst, I cannot say. They respected what they saw as my undivided and steadfast search for God. I shared their life, which was dedicated to *brahma vidya*. To what extent I thereby gave testimony of my faith in Christ was a question that was sometimes asked by Christians, especially by priests and members of religious orders in India. Mahatma Gandhi encouraged Christians in his country to give this testimony, saying, "Let your life speak to us."

Most of all, it was no doubt my faith in Christ and my love for him that gave this testimony. At least that was what one of the sisters in the ashram must have felt, because she told me, "I believe in Christ because you believe in him and because I see what he means to you and how you have dedicated your whole life to him." In practice, to bear witness to Christ must surely mean putting into practice in our daily life his exhortation to his disciples: "Love one another as I have loved you." These were the words that Vinoba Bhave gave as a guiding principle to the founding members of the ashram. It was a commandment that united us in the spirit of Christ.

But alas, I often realized that by my sometimes arrogant attitude and impatience with my fellow sisters, I offended against this command. This alarmed me very much and once I wrote many pages in my diary about love in everyday life. They were all beautiful texts from the Gospels and the Epistles of the Apostles. Jesus makes it quite clear how he wants his command to be understood: "And if any man will sue thee at the law, and take away thy coat, let him have thy cloke also. And whosoever shall compel thee to go a mile, go with him twain." This was precisely what I was not always willing to do – and I persuaded myself that there were good reasons for my unwillingness; there was my constantly growing correspondence, the articles I had to write, the speeches I had to prepare and the time I spent studying Vedanta and Sanskrit. Because of all these activities, I often failed to find time to render any additional service to the community. In this way I not only lost precious opportunities to give testimony of the love of Christ but, more importantly, I failed to set the good example that one could expect from a Christian.

Moreover, the harmony between religions that we wanted to realize in the ashram did not always work without tensions; sometimes situations arose that cast a shadow over us. Early in 1969, when a group of young theologians with their mentor visited the ashram, a number of sisters said that they would like to participate in our worship. Some of them were not unfamiliar with the liturgy of the Catholic Church since they had been educated in Christian schools. But the majority of the sisters did not know anything about our service. I tried to dissuade our guests from letting the sisters participate in the Mass without any preparation and suggested instead a para-liturgy with readings from the Bible and prayers. But my friends were full of enthusiasm and eagerness and invited everybody who wanted to join our worship.

The sisters sat with us around the celebrant, who spoke the texts of the liturgy in English. When he came to the consecration of the bread and wine, the sisters took offence at the words: "Take, eat; this is my body. ... Drink ye all of it; for this is my blood." To Christians these words are quite familiar and they believe in the symbolism involved, but to the sisters it was a shock to hear the words 'flesh and blood of Christ'. Some of them could not calm down for a long time, although I tried to explain the symbolic character of the liturgical act. Although they quite understood the idea of distributing and consuming blessed food during worship because this is common practice in Hindu temples, the words used were very offensive to them. This experience shook my feeling of oneness with my Hindu fellow sisters. To my deep regret I was compelled to realize that even if we were united in our search for God, we were separated by religion, by the outer forms of worship. This realization perturbed me. Should the differences between our religions be a hindrance to our being one in God? We wanted to live in harmony, but now religious differences were coming between us.

This event made me realize that the plurality of religions in the world has, for more than a thousand years, given rise to hatred and enmity between human beings and led to cruel wars amongst them. In most cases political interests were involved, and the representatives of the various religions were struggling for power. They were killing each other in the name of God. But what has God to do with it? What was the meaning of the plurality of religions from the Lord's point of view? I wondered what message there was for us in all this, but I was unable to find an answer.

After the episode mentioned above, I always celebrated Mass with my Christian visitors behind closed doors. The ashram sisters no longer asked me to celebrate Easter with them and during the years that followed, I always spent the holy week with some Christian brothers or sisters who had invited me to celebrate with them the mystery of Christ's death and resurrection.

All this created in me a feeling of isolation from the ashram community, which put a great strain on me. After some time, I asked Vinoba Bhave for a talk, but it was not very satisfactory, and his reply to a letter of mine, which had been read by some of the other sisters, did little to clarify the matter. Maybe the problem was just too intricate and complicated to be solved. Most probably a solution could only be found on a higher level – on the level of spirituality.

The religion of the future

There was yet another matter that was coming to occupy my thoughts more and more during those years. As mentioned before, no *puja* with rites and ceremonies was celebrated in the ashram, but every now and then I had the opportunity to attend a Hindu ceremony in a temple or private home. Oil lamps were lit, rites of purification and ceremonies were practised, little bells were rung or gongs struck, hymns were sung, prayers spoken and food was offered to the deity and distributed to the participants as *prashad*, blessed food.

All this was familiar to me from my own Christian practice. When I found in Hinduism the same basic forms of outer worship as are found in Christianity, I realized that there is a general inclination, shared by all humanity, to worship God with outer signs. In Christianity, as in other religions before it, it is evident that these rites and ceremonies had evolved over time and were therefore of human origin.

Yet for us Catholics, these rites and ceremonies are sacred performances that have to be accurately observed by the priest who conducts them, because they are part of the established ritual and considered to be the channel through which, according to the teachings of the Church, the grace of God and the salvation of the soul flows to the believer. When I found similar rites with similar claims in other religions, this raised a number of questions that I never had to face before. I had to ask myself whether other aspects of the Christian religion, with the exception of Christ's message, might also have been fashioned by the hands of human beings. I had to look at the whole theological structure, the dogmas of the Church, the hierarchy and Church legislation, and ask myself whether or not all this was of divine origin and truly a means of salvation. Apart from customary theological argumentation, I had no answer to these questions.

I grew up with the claim that Christianity is superior to the other world religions, which, with the exception of Islam, are much older than Christianity. I was also familiar with the missionary zeal of Christianity. This claim had now lost much of its absoluteness for me, but I found that in Hinduism there is also a certain sense of superiority over other religions. I began to wonder – in spite of the prejudices I had been brought up with – whether the various religions might not all have an equal right to claim to lead people to God and to offer a path to salvation. Or perhaps none of them could really do this?

All religions refer to the revelation of the mysteries of God by their great prophets and teachers. Do they all possess the truth, or have the other world religions received only 'a ray of light', as many people in the Christian Church believed? Or have the followers of all religions, including the Christian one, perhaps largely lost sight of a dimension from which the great teachers came? This dimension is the mystic experience of God, the realization of God by direct perception of the divine mysteries and the divine Being. According to the testimony of

Christ, eternal life consists of this God-realization: "And this is life eternal, that they might know thee the only true God, and Jesus Christ, whom thou hast sent."

The great mystics of all the world religions have penetrated into that dimension, and the descriptions of their experiences are so much alike that they can to a large extent be interchanged. For example, Guru Ram Das (1534–1581), one of the great mystic teachers of India, says:

> My mind is restless because I do not behold God,
> Like a man dying of thirst is restless without water.
> My mind was pierced by the arrow of thy Name,
> And no one dwells in my heart but the Lord.

These exact words could easily have been spoken by one of the renowned Christian mystics. At any rate, the well-known German Jesuit Karl Rahner (1904–1984) considers that Christianity's only chance of survival is to advance into the spiritual, mystical dimension of religion. His often-quoted statement, "The pious one of the future will be a mystic, one who has experienced something, or nothing at all," points in the same direction as does Vinoba Bhave, who sees no future for religion without spirituality.

All these questions were by no means just academic. To acknowledge them and to voice them in speeches and publications was not without risk, but I was no longer able to push them aside; instead, I subjected them to a critical analysis. However, although these questions were relevant to my faith in the Church, they did not affect my spiritual life as such, which was nourished from another source that God had opened inside me. They were of secondary importance because they did not affect my experience of God's existence, which was indelibly imprinted upon my mind and soul.

That I was not alone with my doubts was something I realized repeatedly during conversations with fellow Christians. Many a missionary, many a priest or theology student were troubled by similar questions. For them, they were questions of existential significance, and they were bound to face them because they concerned their self-image as servants of the Church. All tried to find a way through these difficulties, taking into consideration not only their faith, but also their conscience.

CHAPTER EIGHT

Christ in Indian Garb

WHEN I CAME TO INDIA IN THE AUTUMN OF 1965, a unique atmosphere of awakening reigned in the country's Catholic Church. Nearly twenty years earlier, India had attained her independence after five hundred years of foreign rule under the Mughal emperors and the British Empire. For the first time in its history, it was a united country with a government of its own choice and it had become the world's largest democracy. The Indian nation – at least the educated classes – had awakened to a completely new self-assurance that expressed itself in many different forms.

The Catholic Church in India was now much concerned with finding a new identity. Christianity had already taken root in southern India in the middle of the first Christian century, where it had developed organically and had adapted itself completely to the local culture, so that it was now indigenous to that part of India. In central and northern India, however, the Christian religion was still mostly something foreign, for it had developed under colonial rule, enjoying at first the protection and then later the tolerance of the respective European powers. For hundreds of years the care of souls in these Christian communities had been almost exclusively in the hands of foreign missionaries, who equated Christianity with Western culture and a Western way of thinking. Those who converted to the Christian faith became foreigners in their own land – a situation that had hardly changed over many generations. To finally free itself from this odious situation, the Catholic Church in India was now beginning to recall the cultural values and the spiritual tradition of the country. There was an increasingly urgent emphasis on the need to adapt the ecclesiastical and religious life of the Catholic Church to Indian culture, and on the need for an Indo-Christian theology based on Vedantic philosophy.

The demand for a cultural adaptation also had a missionary aspect, which Vinoba Bhave had expressed as follows: "It is not that Christ would be unacceptable to Hindus – but the Church has failed to present him in an Indian garb." Such an adaptation could not, of course, undo the fatal mistakes of the past. Even so, it was hoped that it would provide a fresh impetus, not only to the Christian churches in India but also to the understanding of Christianity on the part of the Hindu population.

This was the state of affairs when I entered my promised land and, without any preliminary stages or special preparations, I began putting into practice what for the Catholic Church of India was still just a vision of the future. I lived side by side with my Hindu sisters. I dressed like them, bore an Indian name, studied their holy scriptures and so I became one of them, as they repeatedly assured me.

Consequently, my Church soon considered me a 'pioneer in matters of cultural adaptation' and my life in Brahma Vidya Mandir was seen from this perspective. Yet I did not live in the ashram community with that purpose in mind; in particular, I was only too aware of the complexity of such a process. Without exception my visitors came from big cities, where a Western way of life had already become the norm. They might perhaps consider life in the ashram quite romantic – but that was simply not the case. Our way of life was similar to that of the simple folk in the Indian villages. Our only luxury in the ashram was electricity, but we had no fans to cool us in the very hot weather and the windows of our low buildings did not even have glass; the rooms had no ceilings, just wooden beams under the roof, on which all kinds of creatures crawled about and from which termites fell down on us. Some of my Indian visitors – nuns in leading positions in their respective orders – confessed that they felt guilty because, unlike me, they had never lived in such conditions. They returned to their houses full of new ideas, and my fellow sisters in Brahma Vidya Mandir were glad to see the impression that our way of life made on these people.

Sachchidananda Liturgy

One way in which the Catholic Church in India tried to give Christ an 'Indian garb' was in the matter of the liturgy. With the sanction of the ecclesiastical authorities, some seminaries and religious communities had begun to compose new texts for the celebration of the Eucharist. These texts adopted concepts and words from Vedanta. My friends belonged to this group, and during their visits to Brahma Vidya Mandir I worked with them.

After some time, I felt the urge to compose texts of my own that would reflect both the Christian experience of God and that of the Indian rishis, or seers, laid down in the Upanishads. I called these texts the *Sachchidananda Liturgy*. *Sat-chit-ananda* (meaning truth, consciousness and bliss) offers a kind of conceptual approach to naming the unknowable absolute that is the highest Being. These were concentrated texts, expressing core ideas only, which most people probably could not adopt for their liturgy. They had been composed not for everyday use but for small groups who wished to meditate upon the mysteries of God in this particular way.

In the course of time I created texts for the whole Mass, which we used on certain occasions. A small selection of them may give the reader an idea of how I tried to synthesise the Christian and Vedantic experiences of God. In the introductory text I gave expression especially of my experience of the desert, which had moulded my spiritual life in such a decisive way. The spirit of the Katha Upanishad resounds in these lines:

> Eternal truth – ultimate reality –
> Pure spirit – formless – invisible One –
> Nameless – unthinkable –
> Unborn and immortal One –
> Without beginning and without end –
> For whom our hearts crave.

> Immeasurable void* – boundless desert –
> Unfathomable abyss – inexhaustible mystery –
> Unsearchable silence – timeless eternity –
> May I lose myself in You.

> Eternal wisdom – all-knowing One –
> All-pervading – encompassing all –
> Innermost soul of every being –
> Source of life – cause of all that was created –
> May I abide in You.

---

*The term 'void' refers to God. During a journey through India I once came to Bodhgaya, the holy place where Gautama Buddha received enlightenment. There I met a Buddhist monk and in the course of our conversation he asked me whether I had ever had the experience of the 'void beyond the void'. I was not familiar with this Buddhist expression, but I believe that I understood the question. Perhaps this void beyond the void is identical with the desert which I had experienced.

Another aspect of these texts was the 'cosmic liturgy' that encompasses not only human earthly existence but the entire creation, and that reveals the central position of the divine Word that became human in Jesus Christ. It was important to me to point out this dimension as well, and equally to show the *immanence of God in creation*, which had impressed me so deeply at the beginning of my studies of the Brahma Sutra:

> Supreme God, beyond all comprehension,
> Your uncreated Word resounds in a thousand
> Words in time and space.
> This universe reflects in countless forms
> The unfathomable richness of your Being.
> You have expressed yourself in matter and in form,
> In the elements and in the laws of nature;
> They all obey you and sing your praise.
> The forces and the mysteries of life,
> The powers of the elements released,
> The tiny atom and the immeasurable worlds,
> The beauty and the splendour of the universe –
> They all reveal your glory in this fleeting time.
> We offer You this cosmic praise
> In our changing, transitory world.

I had spent many months creating these texts, integrating them with my own experiences and insights so that I was able to identify with them. They constitute a theology in the form of a prayer that addresses not just the intellect, but above all the heart. I used these texts to get closer to the mysteries of God – if not by experience, then at least by the yearning of my heart. It was very important to me to keep my faith alive in this way. My bishop took great interest in the *Sachchidananda Liturgy* and he showed it to the Liturgical Commission of the

Indian Conference of Bishops. On account of this I was asked to formulate a commentary for a meeting of this commission and to present my ideas to it in some detail. My publications came to the attention of the preparatory commission of the All-India Seminar and I was invited to work with them.

Renewal of the liturgy

This cooperation resulted in an invitation to participate on a large scale in the seminar of the Catholic Church in India that took place in autumn of 1969 in Bangalore. The task of this seminar, with its six hundred and thirty delegates and observers from India and abroad, was to study in sixteen different workshops the renewal of the Catholic Church in India. I was assigned to the workshop dealing with the renewal of the liturgy. The team concentrated mainly on the 'Indianization' of the rites of the Mass, meaning the adaptation of the outer forms of devotion in order to give them a more indigenous character. This was not unimportant, but it was nevertheless superficial compared to some other matters under discussion.

To me the inner renewal of the liturgy seemed much more important and I tried time and again to point this out. But the team was so much occupied with other issues that it constantly lost sight of this theme. There was little hope, therefore, that we would be able to agree upon the content of a submission on this issue that could be included in the documentation of the seminar. Therefore the board of the seminar suggested that I should submit to the plenary a private resolution that read:

> The great concern of every reform of the liturgy is a pastoral one: the sacred celebration should be renewed in its rites, ceremonies and texts in such a way that their meaning can be understood by the faithful. The liturgical action should

be performed in such a manner that the participants can identify with it. Great importance should be given to ensuring that the community gathered round the altar will, by participating in the holy event, come to know the mystery of salvation, whose remembrance is celebrated, so that they may attain through it the grace of redemption.

In my opinion, meaningful and inspiring texts were needed to achieve this – texts that would invoke in the participants an atmosphere of prayer and strengthen their faith in God and their love for him. What lies beyond that – to be seized by the mysteries of God in the depth of the heart and to be thrown into the experience of God – is entirely in his hands. But the liturgical celebration could at least prepare the ground, and the longing to meet God might thus be awakened. My circle of friends and others certainly had this experience time and again when using the texts of the *Sachchidananda Liturgy*; we felt nearer to Christ and the divine mysteries when, with deep recollection and a loving heart, we allowed the texts to sink in.

In those days, Catholic and Protestant churches in India had to a certain extent adopted Mahatma Gandhi's suggestion to show Christ to his people in an Indian garb. I had played my own part in this by living as a Catholic nun in a Hindu ashram. Mahatma Gandhi's words had a symbolic significance. At that time I could hardly have imagined that later, on the path of the Masters, they would become literally true for me.

CHAPTER NINE

Monastic Perspectives

ANOTHER ASPECT OF THE ASSIMILATION OF Indian culture by the Catholic Church was the reorientation of monastic life and spirituality. This also concerned the Church in some other Asian countries with ancient monastic traditions where Western Christian monasticism was trying to gain a foothold. Once again it was my life as a Benedictine nun in a Hindu spiritual community that led to my being invited to the Congress of the Superiors of Monastic Orders in Asia that took place in Bangkok in December 1968. The organizers asked me to give a lecture about my experiences in Brahma Vidya Mandir and to point out the relevance they might have for Christian monasticism in the countries of the Far East.

The ashram community had not reacted very favourably to this invitation, and some of the sisters had even tried to convince me that it was not necessary for us to participate in meetings and conferences. Following the example of Vinoba Bhave, so they said, the practice in Brahma Vidya Mandir was one of *sukshma karma* – spiritual action – and their conviction was that through our spiritual life subtle waves of energy radiated into the world. This was something I could only agree with since in our contemplative monasteries we follow the same principle.* But they left it to me to decide whether or not to participate, and I felt that I should accept the invitation. Father Francis Acharya from the Kurisumala Ashram, whom I had visited in December 1966 and who had also visited Paunar in the meantime, had urged me to take part in this meeting.

Before my departure I had shown Vinoba Bhave the text of my lecture, "Brahma Vidya Mandir: Monastic Experiment, Symbol of Harmony between the Religions, Challenge to Christian Monasticism". He approved of it even though I had presented some points from a Christian perspective, for instance that the non-Christian religions will find their fulfilment in Christ. Nevertheless he let it pass as my personal point of view. Moreover, he knew that I was far from trying to influence in any way my Hindu fellow-travellers to God in Brahma Vidya Mandir.

The preparation for the journey to Bangkok was one big obstacle race, which ended at Kolkata Airport when I was denied permission to leave the country because I could not present the voucher for having paid my income tax. When this problem was solved the next day, I learnt at the passport control that I would have to obtain a new entry visa in Bangkok if I intended to return to India. At that moment I was on the point of giving up the whole thing – I could not bear to think about what would happen if I could not obtain a visa. This worry, however, proved unfounded, because the Indian Embassy in Bangkok granted me an entry permit to India without any problems.

As I arrived at the congress centre late at night, there was some surprise the next morning about the newcomer in an

---

*Père Etienne de Saint Marie, a French Carmelite, writes for instance in his book *Conversation avec Dieu*: "A soul that belongs to God without any reservation radiates him, as it were, by herself. The radiation of our soul reaches far beyond our sphere of consciousness. Wherever a God-loving person lives, a hearth of divine warmth is created. One holy thought, even if it remains hidden, radiates like a bright shining light into unknown distances."

ochre-coloured sari.*There were questions without end – some of them well meaning and interested, others critically investigating. On the whole, the illustrious assembly received me cordially and respectfully. I had come to Bangkok with mixed feelings, because there I would meet monks and nuns whose ideals of monastic life I no longer shared. Up to now I had been considered a deviant who had chosen a rather adventurous way to realize her self-designed ideals. The invitation to the monastic congress had, in a way, rehabilitated me, especially in the eyes of my fellow sisters at Kellenried. Now I was suddenly considered a pioneer and asked to present new perspectives for monastic life in Asia. But I did not feel like a pioneer – this was the interpretation of others. Nor did I feel any satisfaction about the unexpected change in attitudes towards me. God had led me on this way and his reasons were still as unknown to me as ever. I had always refused to offer any justification for being in India because it would have hindered me in the realization of God's inscrutable plans for my life. I was ready to fulfil certain tasks assigned to me, but all this – in my view – did not legitimise my presence in India. Living in India was part of my adventure of faith. No rational explanation could be given for it and I never tried to offer one.

During the congress I was able to speak to many of the participants, but not to my fellow brethren from India who a number of years ago had founded Asirvanam near Banga-lore. Nor was I contacted by the Mother Abbess from Ryde,

---

*According to the Indian tradition, an ochre-coloured garment is an outward sign of *sannyasi*, renouncing the world, which is the last stage in the life of a Brahmin. The other stages are *brahmacharya* (celibate), *grihasta* (householder) and *vanaprastha* (inhabitant of forests). *Sannyasis* very often live as wandering monks and beg for their daily food. *Sannyasinis* (women who have renounced the world) mostly live in ashrams. In Brahma Vidya Mandir the sisters wore white garments. Whenever I needed to identify myself outside the ashram as a nun, I dressed in an ochre-coloured sari.

England, who was preparing to found a community in India. Years later I visited the new convent, but I could not imagine living there, nor would my fellow sisters from Brahma Vidya Mandir have felt at home there.

One member of the organizing committee was Father Paulus, who had once successfully diverted my attention away from India. Now it was his task to organize my participation in the congress. I only thought, *tempora mutantur* – times are changing – and greeted him with great happiness.

On the list of experts, I had discovered amongst others the name of the Trappist monk Thomas Merton, author of the book *The Seven Storey Mountain*, whom I was very much looking forward to meeting. Alas, it was not to be. A few hours after his moving discourse, "Marxism and Monastic Perspectives", he was struck down by an electric shock in his room. We were all deeply shocked by his death, but realized that this fervent seeker of God had now found what he had long been seeking. His pilgrimage on earth was over. Only a few days before his sudden demise he had written about his experiences in the Far East, where he had spent some time just before the congress. His words almost sounded like an anticipation of what was soon to come – "I believe that I know and I have seen what I was unconsciously looking for. I do not know what is yet to come, but I have pierced through the surface and looked behind the shadows of disguise." He had touched the absolute, or rather the absolute had touched him, and he emerged from this experience another being. Thomas Merton was described in an obituary as a "monk between yesterday and tomorrow", and I felt deeply connected to him. His books point towards new horizons of Christian life and to many they are an appeal for a new beginning.

My discourse had been scheduled for the last day. It was the first time that I had to speak about Brahma Vidya Mandir to such a large and eminent audience. While delivering the lecture I became aware of how much I already identified with the ashram community. I spoke about the life and the principles that we followed, not as a detached observer, but as a member of a community of seekers of God. First, I gave an account of the history of our ashram and pointed out that in founding Brahma Vidya Mandir, Vinoba Bhave had initiated a new form of spiritual community life for women in India.

Design of a new way of monastic life

It may have surprised my audience to hear that we had neither a mother superior nor a regular statute for the order, whereas in Benedictine monasteries the abbot and *Rule* are the pillars. I explained that in our ashram authority rests with the community; the pillars are the sense of responsibility of each individual member of the community and the unanimity of all decisions about community life. It was Vinoba Bhave's intention that this would help the sisters to grow together into oneness and become one heart and one soul. Without this spirit of oneness, a community life in the ashram would have been impossible. The unifying power should be love. I was able to testify wholeheartedly that there was indeed a spirit of love and mutual acceptance at the heart of our community.

Then I presented to the Assembly of Monastic Superiors the ashram rules, described the daily program, explained our community prayer and spoke about *advaita* philosophy and the Bhagavad Gita, which are the basis of the spiritual life of the community. In particular, I spoke about the preconditions for the attainment of *brahma vidya*. The goal of *brahma vidya* is to meet God, which Shankaracharya emphasizes in his commentary on the Brahma Sutra. This is also the goal of monastic life.

In the second part of my lecture I began by describing Brahma Vidya Mandir as a symbol of harmony between religions that had become a place where Christians and Hindus could meet. I pointed to one of the most important conditions for a dialogue between religions – to meet God in the heart of the other person. I confessed that every time I found God's countenance in another religion it was an overwhelming experience. I also explained how much I had gained through my encounter with another religion and how profound an impression Indian philosophy and spirituality had made on me.

At the end of the second part, I touched upon the subject of the fulfilment of the non-Christian religions in Christ. This was no doubt of great interest for the participants at the congress because it concerned their own role as founders of monastic communities in Asia. I expressed my conviction that the 'Universal Christ' is present in all the religions of the world in a concealed form and that the divine Word or Logos* is also manifest in the holy scriptures of these religions. I considered it our task as Christians and monks to live the religions of Asia in a Christian way in order to fulfil them in Christ. We would

---

*The term *logos* was a key concept in the philosophical school of the Stoa in Athens, founded by Zeno of Kition in about 300 BCE. According to the Stoa, Logos is the cosmic order, willed and installed by God. Through the writings of Philo of Alexandria, a famous religious philosopher and contemporary of Jesus, the authors of the Gospels may have been familiar with the concept of Logos. In the prologue of the Gospel of Saint John, this term is used in a far more comprehensive sense as the Word of God that always was with God and that at a certain moment in history became man in Jesus Christ in order to preach the message from the Father in heaven. The doctrine of Logos can also be traced back to the Jewish idea of Wisdom *(hokhmah)* in the time after their Babylonian exile in 538 BCE. It is also called *sophia*. For all eternity this Wisdom has been with God as his 'co-creator': "I was beside the Master Craftsman, delighting him day after day, ever at play in his presence." (*Proverbs*, 8:30) This Wisdom is present in a hidden form in the entire creation and thus rules the universe. At the same time, it is also a manifestation of God, a "breath of the power of God, and a pure emanation of the glory of the Almighty". (Jerusalem Bible, *Wisdom* 7:25)

then experience his presence there. I added that it was even more important to love Christ with all our heart and with all our strength and to give testimony to him through our lives. In my opinion, I said, this is the only legitimate way to preach Christ among those who did not share our faith. For me, this was no mere academic subject that I was talking about; I was trying to live in Brahma Vidya Mandir according to these insights, and that is why I was able to speak with conviction.

In the third part of the lecture, I spoke about the consequences for Christian monasticism in Asia that would result from the points mentioned above. After having lived now for three years among Hindu seekers, I had come to believe that the spirituality of Vedanta and the Bhagavad Gita is a challenge for Christian monasticism in India and in Asia as a whole. The Church in these countries had presented almost exclusively her active side as a provider of education and charitable work, but she had sadly neglected her other essential aspect – a profound spirituality and the mystic experience of God. Hindus and Buddhists would ask not what we *know* about God, but rather whether we have *experienced* him. This was the great challenge for those of us who have made the search for God our life's task.

At the end of my discourse I also spoke about the adaptation of the form of life in our Christian monasteries to Asian traditions. I pointed out that not only our way of living but also the spiritual aspects of our monasticism bore the stamp of Western civilization. The *Rule of Saint Benedict* reflected a purely Roman spirit. I expressed my fear that, without major changes, Christian monasticism would remain alien in Asia. I considered it indispensable that Christian monks and nuns should not only adapt to the way of life in the Asian countries but should also be introduced to the basics of the ascetic-mystic teachings of the Asian religions. New ways had to be found, which would be nothing less than a new creation in the spirit of Christ of the ideals of the early monasticism and the great spiritual heritage of the religions of Asia.

Although I had spoken quite frankly, my words were very well received. Many of the participants offered their congratulations and the Bishop of Bangalore, in whose diocese one Benedictine monastery already existed and a convent was under construction, told me after the lecture, "This is exactly what the Church in India needs today." Father Paulus of Beuron asked me for a translation of my lecture for the monastic magazine in Germany, and Father Enomiya-Lassalle, a well-known German Jesuit and Zen master who had also lectured at the conference, expressed his agreement with what I had said with the words, "I congratulate you, you have spoken the truth." Actually, I had merely shared with my fellow brothers and sisters in the Order of Saint Benedict what had become part of my life in India, where the adventure of faith had led me. For this reason I did not feel like an adviser, but more like a witness of our life in Brahma Vidya Mandir.

Some people might have expected that I would now want to gather a group of women around me in order to realize the ideals that I had presented to the audience, but I did not feel the wish to do that. I had been asked to offer perspectives for Christian monastic life in Asia, but I had no desire to take it any further. In any case, only three years had passed since my arrival in India and I was still a beginner.

Before returning to Paunar, I was able to visit Mother Teresa again and tell her about all that had happened since our first meeting. She seemed very pleased and satisfied with the course that my life had taken. The subject of a prayer branch of her community was not mentioned again. One week before Christmas I was back in the ashram. A few days later, our friends from Pune arrived, with whom we celebrated the birth of Jesus Christ.

CHAPTER TEN

On the Threshold
of a New Horizon

FOR FULLY FIVE YEARS I HAD NOW BEEN SHAR-
ing the life of a Hindu ashram community. With the study
of the Brahma Sutra, I had entered the world of Vedanta and
assimilated the mystic texts of the Upanishads and the Bhagavad Gita. Again and again I had contemplated the ideal of a
desert dweller – one who has attained the ultimate wisdom of
which the Brahma Sutra speaks. This whole process not only
changed my thinking but also transformed me; I emerged from
it with a new identity.

At the same time, meeting so many people, developing the
Sachchidananda Community, carrying out the different tasks
given me by the Church of India, writing a large number of
articles for Indian and German magazines and attending to a
voluminous correspondence had all opened up new horizons
to me. I never saw these activities as the real reason why God
had led me to India, but even so they had become an important
element of my life in this country.

All my experiences in the course of the years, all the insights
I had gained, had now created a wide-open space within me,

spreading out before my inner eye like a magnificent panorama. While presenting new perspectives for the Church in India and for monasticism in Asia, I myself gained more of a distance from the traditional picture of Christianity. While pointing out the necessity of a change of thinking in the Church, I myself experienced an inner transformation. And by questioning the old thought patterns and opening up new perspectives, I created a space within myself that would allow me in due time to advance toward new horizons.

It was wonderful to see how my spiritual life was able to unfold unhindered by the rigid framework of a traditional religious life, which I had outgrown through my inner experience of the desert. Brahma Vidya Mandir gave me the freedom to expand my understanding of God and I was nourished by this experience. Because of this, and in particular because of a mysterious and indescribable experience of union with the invisible inner light, I found myself transformed and created anew. On 22nd July 1970, the anniversary of my solemn vows and the Consecration of Virgins, I wrote in my diary, "In this light I live and this light keeps me alive." For a long time I remained in this blessed state of deep inner peace and sometimes I even thought I had reached the goal of my spiritual life.

One day I suddenly realized that this could not be the end of my way to God and that I was far from having reached the summit of union with God. Notwithstanding that the invisible inner light had created a wonderful feeling of living in the presence of God, I had the impression that my spiritual journey had come to a standstill. I felt like I was standing on a ridge, unable to move any further because it gave way under my feet. Of course, this experience was not new to me, but now the situation was completely different. Before, my 'ridge walk' had pertained not to my spiritual path but to finding out where God wanted me to go. The ridge on which I was now standing was part of my spiritual path, my way to God. In the *Philokalia*, which had been my guide for so many years, I found nothing to help me. The incessant Jesus Prayer had led me to the light; as late as 1971 I had written, "My life is submerged in light." But shortly afterwards I realized for the first time, as I noted in my diary, that this light now came to me as a dark light. Although I continued to feel its presence, it was no longer a bright light and it was beyond my power to make it shine again. So I fixed my eyes on the dark light and practised a 'dark contemplation', as described by Saint John of the Cross in his work *The Dark Night of the Soul.*

In this situation and for the first time, I felt the need to find a spiritual guide. It seemed to me that my path had been blocked and all my endeavours to overcome this were of no avail. But whom should I approach? The obvious thing to do might have been to submit my query to Swami Abhishiktananda, who had gone a similar way and who certainly possessed much spiritual experience. But he was the one who had frustrated Mr Ramachandra's plan to send me to Paunar, and so I had lost confidence in him, even though he was such a great and renowned personality in India. We no longer had any contact and I rarely met him. Whenever we did, we hardly spoke about spiritual matters, or about the tasks that had been given me.

In the course of the years I had certainly met several deeply religious priests, above all my bishop. However, I doubted that they would be able to assist me with my spiritual problems. I had often spoken with them about meditation and spent time with them in seminars on prayer, and so I was able to assess their position, but I could not make up my mind to approach a Christian spiritual guide. My main fear was that they might try to persuade me to return to the method of discursive meditation, and I knew from my experience of the desert that this would be a step backwards. To seek guidance from a spiritual guide in Germany by correspondence was out of the question because I did not know anyone. Nor could I hope to find a solution in books, because the problem I was confronted with demanded the personal guidance of an experienced person.

In former years, when I had not yet been looking for a spiritual guide, I had come across several Hindu gurus. I had met the leader of the Shivananda Ashram in Rishikesh and Sri Rajneesh Chandra Mohan, later known as Bhagavan Sri Rajneesh or Osho, as well as Mata Ji, who lived in Mumbai and who was worshipped as a goddess by her followers. But I had never felt that any of these teachers was to be my spiritual guide. Also my relationship with Vinoba Bhave was such that I could not speak to him personally about my spiritual path. Opportunities to meet him had been rare since he often was away from the ashram; nor had I read his books, which were only available in Indian languages.

On the other hand, there was Mr H. Singh from Nagpur, whose acquaintance I had made under the strange circumstances described earlier. I knew that he was a convinced follower of a so-called 'living Master', and I took this as a hint from God to contact this Master. Ever since I had first met Mr Singh in the spring of 1967, he had always furnished me with literature on Sant Mat, the teachings or path *(mat)* of mystic saints *(sant)*. During my occasional visits to his family home in Nagpur I had also seen a picture of his Master, of whom they all spoke with great love and respect.

The main reason for my decision to meet his Master, however, was my inner impulse. I had always followed it, even if I did not have any rational reasons for doing so, and it was this trust in my inner guide that finally made me decide to approach the Master. For reasons known only to this inner guide, he had led me to the extreme edge of the ridge, and I felt it was not for me to ask questions. One day I would receive an explanation, and when it came it would be overwhelming, even answering some questions I had never asked.

From Mr Singh I learnt that his Master, Maharaj Charan Singh, would be coming to Nagpur, a town about 113 kilometres from Paunar, in January 1970. I wanted to take this opportunity to speak to the Master about my meditation problems and to ask him a number of questions that had arisen while I was reading the books on the teachings of the Masters. These questions concerned the descent of the soul from her place of origin and her return thither by means of the divine Word, which could be heard inside in the form of a sound current. I also wanted to ask the Master about the origin of my inner experiences of light, which I had lived with for so many years.

Until then I had not yet spoken to Monsignor Januarius, my bishop, about my intention to contact a spiritual Master. It did not seem necessary, since what I wanted was merely an informative talk with the Master, and the bishop had given me wide-ranging freedom to make my own decisions. Moreover, my meetings with the bishop were few and far between.

However, I was not to meet the Master in 1970. I was too late asking for an interview with him and the available time had already been booked. But at least I saw the Master during his discourses and I was deeply impressed by his personality. I had never before experienced such radiance in any spiritual teacher known to me.

I had to wait another year to get a chance to speak to the Master. In fact, I needed this waiting period because it was during those twelve months that the necessity of a spiritual guide became ever clearer. During this time, a kind of dark block had formed within me, which I was unable to overcome or penetrate even with the greatest of efforts, and during meditation my own thoughts kept echoing back to me.

What had happened? Had I become negligent in my search for God? Had my activities become too diverse and too extensive? Had my spiritual life suffered from them? No doubt my life had at times been extremely busy; I had been entrusted with a number of tasks and had done my best to comply with them. But fascinating as these tasks had often been, I had resisted the temptation to accomplish them at the cost of my spiritual life. Admittedly, there had been moments when the work nearly crushed me, but with rare exceptions I always made time available for meditation, prayer and reading spiritual literature. The tasks given to me never became the main purpose of my life – in fact, had I made them my main concern and allowed them to take me away from the centre of my spiritual life, I would not have been able to accomplish these tasks. More than ever, it had been the experience of the invisible divine presence and the inner light that had saved me from getting submerged in external activities. But now, every-thing changed. The inner path seemed to have come to an end without me reaching my goal; or, more accurately, it seemed to be blocked by a barrier that grew more insurmountable day by day. The light came back to me as darkness and I did not know whether I still loved God. This question distressed me most of all.

What had happened, and whether I was in any way respon-sible, were questions to which I had no answer. In any case, it was not in my power to remove the obstacle within me and to make the light shine again. The inward light had been a gift of his grace that I had received, but had been unable to keep. In the deepest ground of my soul I was entirely calm. Had I not found so often before that God blocked one way in order to open up another? Perhaps my journey through the desert had come to a point where a new form of 'living with God' was to be introduced? Had I reached the threshold of a new dimension in my spiritual life? I did not know it, but my inner guide knew the way ahead of me, and all I had to do was to submit once again to the adventure of faith.

Meeting the Master

Such were the thoughts that occupied my mind when, in January 1971, I was finally able to meet Maharaj Charan Singh in Nagpur, where he used to come once a year, since he had a large following there. During the interview, the Master was exceedingly kind and therefore I did not find it difficult to ask my questions. First, I said that the book *Science of the Soul*, the last one Mr Singh had given me, seemed to me like a sealed book. The Master answered that this book had not been written for me, and he gave instructions that the abridged edition of *The Path of the Masters* by Dr Julian Johnson should be sent to me.

Concerning my experience of light, the Master said that such experiences are remembrances from a previous life that are imprinted on the mental body, or mind, and are now manifesting consciously. I was too surprised about this answer to ask the Master for further explanation, and I did not even reflect on it later, nor did I return to this matter in later conversations with the Master. If I had asked the Master then and there for some further explanation, it would have given me a much better understanding of my spiritual path. It is only now, while writing this book, that all of a sudden the meaning of the Master's answer stands clearly before my eyes. The Master was referring to a period of nearly thirty-five years, from my first experience with the transcendental light in my youth all the way to the year 1971, when this experience had come to an end. So this whole period had been a 'phase of remembrance' of light experiences that I had had during a previous life in a different physical body, which were 'stored' in my mental body. According to the teachings of the Masters, this mental body survives the death of the physical body. It reincarnates in another physical body, accompanied by the soul, in accordance with its destiny.

The Master's answer did not appear to be based on theory, speculation or reasoning. Rather, I felt that he could *see* with his inner eye the condition of my mind and soul, and so his answer was based on direct perception. He was speaking factually, just as we speak factually whenever we say, for instance, that the sun is shining. Mr H. Singh had sometimes hinted that the Master could see deeper into the heart of a human being, but I had not paid particular attention to his remark, nor had I taken it into account while speaking to the Master.

Now this phase of remembrance had come to an end. Seen in this light, it is not surprising that I felt as though I were standing at the edge of a ridge, unable to take even a single step forward. I had reached the point where I finished going over the old ground from an earlier life; now my spiritual path was about to take me into the unknown. I felt that I was at the threshold of a new dimension of spiritual life, the path leading within.

The loss of my remembrances from a previous life was meant to evoke in me a burning desire for the union of my soul with God. The phase of remembrance was now behind me, but for many years it had been the reality of my spiritual path in this life; it had marked and shaped and transformed me. Although at the time I was ignorant of all this, I am firmly convinced that the Master saw not only my previous lives but also the road ahead of me. Concerning my meditation, the Master advised me to concentrate on the point at the forehead, which had been familiar to me ever since I started using the Jesus Prayer. It was unusual for the Master to give such advice; normally he discourages meditation before initiation, lest one should get accustomed to a wrong method, but I was unaware of that at the time.

As for the inner blockage and the echoing of my thoughts in meditation, the Master again gave a surprising answer. He said, "You are confronted with your own mind." I took note of this answer without really understanding it. I had a very vague inkling of what had happened, but I only grasped the full significance of the Master's words after a thorough study of the teachings of the Masters. Later I came to see that during my study of the Advaita Vedanta my own mind had caused me to succumb to the *intellectual fascination of this philosophy.*

Previously, the *experience* of God had always come first in my spiritual life, at least since the beginning of my desert experience; now I had fallen victim to the most subtle seduction of the human mind – to mistake intellectual comprehension for the realization of what was comprehended.

With the experience of transcendence and invisible light within, I had received a glimpse of the reality I was searching for – but it was just a glimpse. I had also been deceived into giving too much significance to the *intellectual anticipation* of a state that I was searching for but had not yet experienced. Because of this confusion, *my own mind stood in the way of experiencing the transcendent reality.* Although my studies of the Brahma Sutra had warned me, I had become a knower but not one who truly knows.

Even if I was unable to understand the deeper meaning of some of the Master's answers, the manner in which he had replied to my questions made me realize that he had experience on the spiritual path and knew more than I did. This was enough to fill me with confidence in the Master and to nurture my resolve to learn more about the teachings of the Masters.

I was about to travel to Europe for a few months, but at the end of our conversation the Master invited me to visit the Radha Soami Satsang* when I returned to India. This meditation centre is near Beas in the Punjab, in northern India. There I would be able to study the teachings of the Masters thoroughly and get clarification of all my questions and doubts before making a decision concerning a spiritual guide.

The book by Dr Johnson, which I received a few days later, offers a summary of these teachings in a systematic way, adapted to the mentality of Western readers. He gives an image of God and the world that I had not found before, either in Christian theology or in Vedanta. Some of his expositions were familiar to me, especially the teachings about karma and reincarnation, but there were other aspects that I was unable to integrate into my mental world. Through reading this book I realized that the teachings of the Masters were much more than a method of meditation, which was what I had originally been looking for. According to these teachings the path of the Masters is a way of life; above all, it is a way of redeeming the soul from enslavement to the 'prince of this world' of whom Jesus Christ spoke, and a way leading her back to the house of her Father. The living Master, as Dr Johnson says in his book, is not only a spiritual teacher but an adept of spirituality who has access to God's mysteries and is capable of revealing them to others. A Master, therefore, is a bearer of the spirit. He is a vessel of the divine spirit, invested with the power to transmit to us the Holy Spirit and God's abundant grace. The teachings of the Masters touched essential aspects of my faith and therefore I wrote to the Master, saying that my life was inseparably connected with Christ as I had experienced him, even if to me he represented not so much the historical Jesus of Nazareth as the divine light and the source of living water.

---

*Radha Soami Satsang: *radha* (soul), *soami* (Lord), *satsang* (true association). Radha Soami – Lord of the soul – is a name which Soami Ji of Agra gave to signify the supreme Lord.

In my letter I also explained that I had not renewed my search out of curiosity, nor even to save my soul, but for the sake of truth alone. This truth is identical with God.

After having studied Dr Johnson's book thoroughly, I decided to accept the Master's invitation and go to Beas after returning from Germany. During my stay in Europe I would have ample opportunity to discuss with others the relevant questions, and in Beas itself I would be completely free to decide according to my conscience.

Two months after meeting Maharaj Charan Singh, I had a chance to speak with my bishop about my decision to go to Beas. Monsignor Januarius showed interest and said, "You go and inquire and then come and tell me." I mentioned that the Master imparted the method of meditation by initiation, leaving open whether or not I would apply for it. So I went to Beas with the knowledge and the consent of my bishop. I also explained to him where I stood spiritually and I asked him whether he could guide me. Monsignor answered that he had never had any experiences like mine and therefore was not in a position to show me the way.

Before travelling to Europe, I was able to meet Father N., a well-known German Jesuit in Pune. I talked to him about the possibility of initiation into the path of the Masters and put to him some questions of a more theological nature, which had come up partly in relation to Dr Johnson's book. We also spoke about the sacramental structure of our ecclesiastical and religious life and I openly voiced my doubts about the teachings of the Catholic Church on the sacraments. For me they seemed to be only empty structures, lacking the life-giving spirit of God. In particular, I had major doubts about baptism. I could not accept that it was an actual initiation into the mysteries of Christ, the rebirth in the Holy Spirit about which Jesus spoke when he said to Nicodemus: "Verily, verily, I say unto thee, except a man be born of water and of the Spirit, he cannot enter into the kingdom of God." I did not doubt that in the early days of Christianity baptism had been just such a 'baptism in the Spirit' – this is shown by many examples in the Acts of the Apostles.

Father N. agreed with this, but he insisted on the need to maintain the hierarchical and sacramental structure of the Church so that the spirit of God could be brought back into it. Father N. most probably wanted to say that he saw the Church organization as a structure or vessel, a receptacle into which new life could be poured. I told him that for me the big question was – how is that to happen? I was no longer convinced that the 'office bearers' in the Church were also 'bearers of the spirit', able to impart the spirit of God to the people. Another question that had long occupied me concerned the position of Christ as a redeemer of humanity and how this salvation was to take place; but this I wanted to clear up with theologians in Germany.

So many things had been set into motion in the last few months. I felt that I was standing on the threshold of a new horizon, at the beginning of a path that would lead me into unfamiliar territory, which perhaps would turn out to be the real promised land.

CHAPTER ELEVEN

Dialogue between Religions

IN THE SPRING OF 1971 I BEGAN MY VISIT TO Germany, which was to last for six months. The reasons for this journey had recently crystallized more and more, so that I now realized it was important and even necessary.

In the first place, I had to clear up my status as an exclaustrated nun with the Church authorities in Rome. In order to maintain this status, I needed an 'exclaustration at the disposition of the Holy See'. The permission is valid for a lifetime, but it is granted only in exceptional cases. This matter I wanted to settle personally in Rome. To remain a nun was very important to me, because I still considered my monastic vows to be an expression of the dedication of my life to God. Moreover, belonging to a religious order in accordance with canon law seemed quite important for my future tasks in India.

Secondly, since I intended to apply for Indian citizenship, I wanted to see my monastic community and my family in order to take leave of them for good. I had no intention of visiting Germany again after having become an Indian citizen. Inwardly I was already an Indian. Thirdly, I wished to establish personal contacts with some German publishing houses that had shown interest in translations of the Upanishads and other holy scriptures of India. As mentioned earlier, I had, together with a fellow sister of the ashram who had been a Sanskrit teacher, made some promising translations of those texts, which I could present to the publishers. My fourth aim was to have discussions with various theologians in Germany in order to clarify various questions about the Christian faith. As the previous chapter has shown, this was very important as a way of helping me to understand my religion.

Finally I wanted to consult a number of competent people about the possibility of initiation into the path of the Masters. This was a decision I did not want to take alone because of its far-reaching consequences, and I wanted to give my Church a fair chance to participate in my decision and to present possible alternatives. So I had many reasons for going to Germany, but in the end I followed an intuitive inner impulse that again could not be explained rationally. It was a question of fate, as would become apparent one year later.

My first destination was Rome. Father Engelbert, a fellow brother of the Benedictine Order and at the same time my contact person with the Congregation for Religious, had assured me that there would be no problem in obtaining final permission to live as a nun outside of the convent. It was all the more hopeful because at an audience in Saint Peter's, Pope Paul VI himself had shown great interest in my 'experiment' when I told him about my life in Brahma Vidya Mandir, and he told me to give his greetings to the ashram community.

Two years earlier, my bishop had had an opportunity to inform the Holy Father about my life at Paunar. His reply was, "I have always wanted somebody to do something like this; the Church will benefit greatly from this." Then he added, "Protect her."

Besides settling my personal affairs in Germany I expected that my visit there would contribute to the dialogue between

Christianity and Hinduism. Even before setting off, I had been asked to give a number of lectures on that subject, since I had already published several articles in German Catholic magazines. During the six months of my stay in Germany I gave nearly fifty lectures and sermons.

When I arrived in April 1971, I was soon confronted with the fact that the West (Europe and America) had become a field of missionary activity for the Eastern religions. The Christian Churches were no longer confronted with Hinduism and Buddhism only in Asia, where they did missionary work, but also in their own backyard, so to speak, in the Western hemisphere. It was no longer sufficient merely to acknowledge that Eastern religions had become an *object of fascination for Christians.* The competent Church authorities had already realized that there was also a *challenge* that had to be faced. Some leading theologians in Germany had already stated that the encounter with the religions of Asia could be of epoch-making significance for Christianity as a whole, comparable to the encounter with the culture of ancient Greece during the first centuries of Christianity.

Fascination and challenge

The Catholic and the Protestant Academies of Bavaria had made "The Fascination and Challenge of Eastern Religions for Christians" the subject of their joint conference, which took place in Tutzing, Bavaria. I had been asked to open the discussion with a lecture on the dialogue with Hinduism. Since the speaker who preceded me had treated the subject of the fascination of Advaita Vedanta, I concentrated mainly on the *challenge* they presented. In my opinion, the meeting between Christianity and the religions of the East gave the Christian Churches a unique opportunity.

This was a subject that the Catholic Church in India and the Sachchidananda Community had been dealing with for several years. In Brahma Vidya Mandir I had partly put into practice what I was now presenting to the audience. My practical experience lent to my words a power of conviction that a purely theoretical presentation could not have conveyed.

My own horizons had been broadened by encountering Hinduism in general and the world of Vedanta in particular. It was my view that Christianity as a whole now needed to broaden its understanding of the diversity of religions, and by so doing see itself in a new light. This could not be just a question of shifting the emphasis in the relationships between the Christian Churches and the other world religions, which the Church authorities had already begun to do; it was also a question of establishing a dialogue on an existential level. To merely aim at a peaceful and friendly coexistence of religions is not enough. The real challenge lies in trying to discover the common roots so that ultimately we may rise to the level of universal religion as mentioned by Vinoba Bhave – the 'religion of spirituality', in which the experience of God replaces theological assessments about God. It is precisely a desire to experience the divine that has motivated many Christians to turn to what the Eastern religions have to offer.

In my lecture I pointed out that for Christianity the first step in the direction of a universal religion would be to become aware of its own spiritual and mystic tradition and make efforts to return to it. The writings of mystics within the Christian churches point in the direction of universality, for they are similar to the accounts that have come from the great mystics of the other world religions. This similarity is all the more remarkable because they did not know anything about one another. Today, when we compare their descriptions of their experiences, it is surprising how similar, or even identical, they are, even when separated by many centuries. I was able to speak from my own experience about how fascinating and spiritually inspiring this discovery could be.

A breakthrough towards the religion of the future will, however, not be accomplished on the outer level of rites, ceremonies and theological structures. It will be accomplished on the inner level of consciousness – of a spiritualized, interiorized religion based on the experience of God. The outer forms of different religions will surely continue to exist side by side for a long time, but a growing number of Christians will try to cross the threshold to the religion of spirituality.

I was able to express these thoughts only because I had already travelled some distance on my way towards this religion of spirituality, in which the experience of God takes the place of intellectual knowledge of God and exterior worship. For me, turning to the path leading within had not been the result of a process of reasoning; it grew out of my own experience of the transcendent. While studying Dr Johnson's book, I realized that the teachings of the Masters lead in the same direction.

On the eve of an Indo-Christian theology

I spoke to Catholic and Protestant students of theology, who came from various universities and from a number of religious communities, about the necessity of a Christian theology rooted in the spiritual heritage of India. This view had been put forward very strongly by some well-known theologians, including Dr Raimundo Panikkar and Stanley Samartha. Because I am not a theologian, I could not take part directly in the creation of a Vedantic-Christian theology; this had to be done by Christian theologians and Indian pandits (teachers). But it was a subject I was particularly interested in, because to a certain degree I had already integrated Vedanta and *advaita* philosophy into my way of thinking as a Christian.

I was therefore able to give personal testimony that there is great promise in the attempt to create a theology that combines *advaitic*, Vedantic and Christian elements. Now that the Christian Churches were ready to leave the traditional avenues of their theology, new approaches to the experience of God and new ways of understanding the holy scriptures would be opening up to them that hitherto were outside the range of interpretation of Western Christian traditions. The Christian churches would thus discover new features in God's countenance that until now had been hidden from them, and God's mysteries would shine in a new light.

I had come to this conviction through the study of the Brahma Sutra, the Upanishads and the Bhagavad Gita. The Western churches will come to realize that they do not know all there is to know about the unfathomable depth of God, that there is more than can be explored with the intellect, and that God has also revealed himself to human beings outside of Christianity. I had long since realized that non-Christians do not at all 'sit in utter darkness and in the shadow of death' and that they have by no means merely grasped a 'ray of the divine light', as many Christians still believed.

Through my studies, I also arrived at the conviction that creating an authentic Indo-Christian theology based on Vedanta and the *advaita* philosophy was relevant not just for the Christian Church in India; it would also be of major importance to the universal Church. It is a mistake to believe that creating this new system of theology is of concern only to the Church in India. It is to be expected that such a theology will influence the thinking of the universal Church, as was the case in the thirteenth century, when Thomas Aquinas adopted the philosophical system of Aristotle as a basis for his *Summa Theologica*, his main theological work. The effect was to spread Aristotle's thinking widely throughout the Christian Church. From this point of view we are surely justified in asking whether Christian theology today can afford to limit itself exclusively to the scriptures of the Old and New Testaments as a basis for its exploration of the divine mysteries and the nature of God, and whether it can afford to employ only classic occidental thinking patterns to find the truth.

During the years of dialogue with another religion I also came to the conclusion that it was a fatal error for Christianity to keep believing itself to be the exclusive retainer of the truth and the only legitimate holder of God's message to humankind. With this attitude Christianity has, I believe, cut itself off from those other fountains of God's revelation that flow so abundantly outside the Christian framework.

In an earlier conversation with my bishop about this subject, he had pointed out that we cannot construct a theology; that can only be done by a genius who is at the same time both a saint and mystic. Such an endeavour would require both intelligence and intuition of an exceptional kind. Above all, as was pointed out by Thomas Aquinas, it would require personal experience of God *(cognitio Dei experimentalis)* – known in India as *gyana*, true knowledge. Every attempt, therefore, to create such a theology could only have a preparatory character until such a person appeared.

In my lectures I repeatedly emphasized that the real source of knowledge of God is the experience of God. As testified by Meister Eckhart:

> Man should not be content with merely thinking of God, because when the thought disappears, God also vanishes. He should rather have an essential God, who is far above the thinking of man and all creatures.

This corresponds with Shankaracharya's words, quoted earlier:

> Brahman cannot be known by sense perceptions, because he should not be understood as an object amongst other objects. Nor can he be known through logical conclusions, because none of them leads to him. Brahman can be known only through *anubhava* (experience).

In search of an answer

On arrival in Munich, I was happily reunited with my mother, brothers and sisters, who had already arranged for me to give some talks about India. Apart from many friends and interested relations, I also met my uncle, Dr Klemens Tilmann, who in the past had been very helpful in obtaining permission for my exclaustration. When we discussed my ideas about the teachings of the Catholic Church and about theological and dogmatic questions in general, he remarked that my "contours had become blurred". This was a reproach I was to hear more than once from other theologians in the months to come. But it was not my contours that had become blurred – it was my horizons that had been widened. I found that it was impossible to explain to Church officials in a single conversation the details of my inner spiritual journey of recent years. To do this would have required much more time to talk and an interest in a different way of thinking.

On 16th May I was finally able to see my fellow sisters at Kellenried again. The closer I came to my monastery, the more mixed my feelings became, but the joy of meeting again was so great on their side, and their reception was so cordial that I immediately lost all feelings of restraint. Two years earlier, my bishop had visited the abbey while he was in Europe. He had given a talk and slide show about Brahma Vidya Mandir that had won the hearts of all the sisters. This had reconciled them to the fact that I was now an outsider. I had also kept contact with my monastic family by correspondence and they had read the various articles I had published in German papers, especially my Bangkok lecture.

Topic number one in our discussions was meditation – a little-used term during my time at the monastery. It was the older sisters in particular who asked about it. Many things had changed since I had left Kellenried in the autumn of 1965. A special meditation room had been provided, courses on Zen meditation had been organized for the sisters, and the abbey itself offered meditation courses to people from outside. In the light of these developments, some sisters thought that it would not have been necessary for me to leave if only I had exercised a little more patience. But this did not touch the core of the matter, and during my visit I never spoke to them about the true reasons for my going to India.

It was a matter of great regret to me that in spite of all our discussions about meditation I was unable to really share with my fellow sisters the whole richness of all the insights and experience I had gained in Brahma Vidya Mandir. It was just not possible. Somehow, an invisible wall stood between us that kept me from saying more about these matters. The sisters must have sensed the new direction my inner life had taken, and they may have felt unsettled when they saw that it was possible to live an authentic spiritual life outside of the monastery.

Walking around the familiar halls of the monastery and seeing the same faces again, I realized how much I had changed. I felt that I no longer belonged there, where I had been at home for so many years. I felt a strange sense of unreality, and whenever I closed my eyes I was back in the ashram. The sisters took this to be a good sign. I could not imagine returning to a life in the monastery – but this question did not arise, since all of us knew that my place was in Brahma Vidya Mandir.

The following months were filled with speaking engagements in many places and contacts with publishing houses who had asked me for translations of the Upanishads into German. I also participated in some meditation courses in order to be up-to-date about what had happened in this field. The Christian meditation movement in Germany – meant as a response to what was being offered by the Gurus and Zen Masters from the East – was in its beginnings, taking its first hesitant steps on a way leading within, developing a synthesis of Eastern and Western methods of meditation. In *The Cloud of Unknowing*, a book of unknown authorship, a Christian way within had been discovered, and some Catholic teachers of meditation were trying to combine it with the methods of Zen meditation. Dr Tilmann also had published a meditation guide that did not use any Eastern meditation techniques. He considered any approach that did not relate to the Christian faith as unsuitable for Christians.

As planned, I visited a number of priests and theologians during my journey. I wanted to clear up my doubts about certain points of the teachings of the Catholic Church and discuss with them the possibility of being initiated into the path of the Masters. My doubts mainly concerned the question of the salvation of humankind, which – according to the teachings of Christianity – was accomplished by Jesus Christ through his crucifixion and resurrection from the dead. My question was: who had demanded Jesus's death as atonement for the sins of humanity and to whom had Jesus paid the ransom? I was, of course, familiar with the answer given by Christian doctrine. This doctrine is founded on the teachings of Saint Paul, which are themselves based on the sacrificial theory and practice of the Old Testament. This no longer convinced me. I wanted to know how exactly the salvation of the soul occurs and how we go by baptism from death to life. As Saint Paul writes in his Epistle to the Romans:

> Know ye not, that so many of us as were baptized into Jesus Christ were baptized into his death? Therefore we are buried with him by baptism into death; that like as Christ was raised up from the dead by the glory of the Father, even so we also should walk in newness of life.

However, I was given only the old familiar answers that I already knew from theological books and that I had thought about for many years, so finally I had to accept that my questions were still unanswered. I found, too, that I was no longer able to accept on faith the truth of assertions that seemingly cannot be explained. My questions had become too urgent for that.

About the second subject, my initiation into a path of meditation by a non-Christian Master, I spoke to priests who themselves meditated, who gave courses on meditation and were in some cases authors of books on the subject. Almost unanimously they encouraged me to apply for initiation into the path of the Masters. They believed Christians had to explore such ways. This was the view of Dr Tilmann even though, as already mentioned, he did have reservations about Christians adopting Eastern methods of meditation.

I spoke with one of the priests in whose meditation course I participated about how my relation to Christ might be harmed if I were to be initiated by a non-Christian Master. I confessed that Christ was the foundation of my life and that he had become the all-pervading reality to me, although it was not at all clear to me how much my Christ was identical with the Christ of the theologians. But he reassured me, saying, "We need not worry about Christ." What he meant was that

Christ in his universality always is and always will be, and that a living Master is an instrument in God's hands. This answer dispelled my doubts and strengthened my resolve, so that I felt able to apply for initiation into the path of the Masters with a clear conscience. Two of the priests I consulted were, however, vehemently against initiation by a non-Christian Master; one of them even called it occultism. I rejected this categorically, because I felt sure that the path of the Masters was nothing of the sort.

After a lecture on Indo-Christian theology that I gave to a group of young Benedictine monks who were preparing for ordination, one of the participants asked me what I believed to be the task of monks in our age. I answered, at first jokingly, "Europe has already been civilized (this had been to a great extent the work of monks); the art of printing and also gunpowder have been invented (both by monks), so what remains to be done?" Then I added, "In the present times people are yearning for *witnesses of God*, for men and women who have met God. This is the real and original task of monks: to be windows between this world and the transcendent realms, through which the divine light may shine forth. Their most important task and duty is to enter the divine realm and to become permeated by its light. That is the standard by which the life and deeds of a monk will be measured."

My travels also took me to the south of France, to Switzerland and finally to Austria, where my stay in Europe ended with a series of lectures on the subject "The Cosmogony of Hinduism". A parish priest asked me to speak on a Sunday dedicated to religious vocation about the subject "Is living in a religious order still up to date?" He had declared himself not competent on this question, but believed that, as a nun, I surely would be able to give a number of reasons for dedicating one's life to God in a cloister. I gladly complied with his request and described to the congregation, gathered in the church for Mass, the road that had led me to the monastery. I also spoke about the bliss of belonging only to God, but I did not hide the fact that it is also a path of self-denial and renunciation, and that one has to have a vocation.

When, in the beginning of October 1971, all matters had been settled and all lectures had been held, I was glad that these turbulent and eventful months had come to an end. In order to remain unaffected in the midst of this turmoil, I had often used the trick of imagining myself in the ashram, sitting in meditation in my spartan room. In this way I succeeded in neutralizing the whole maze of thoughts, experiences and impressions. It often happened that I found myself mentally in Brahma Vidya Mandir as soon as I closed my eyes or had a moment of stillness. It was high time to return to a life of quietude and recollection, of prayer and meditation, for I sensed that during these six months my spiritual life had lost some of its substance. Nevertheless, it had been a fruitful time. I had met so many people, found so much interest in India and the subjects of my lectures, and had so many interesting conversations.

The whole experience had been far more than just an enjoyable time. It had improved considerably my own understanding of the matters I had been talking about and discussing. For me, these matters were not academic at all – they were of immediate practical relevance to my life, and especially to my spiritual path. For instance, it was only when I spoke about the promising possibilities that lay in the dialogue between Christian theology and *advaita* philosophy that I fully realized how much my spiritual life had benefited from the study of the Brahma Sutra and Vedanta, and how many new horizons of God-realization it had opened before me.

Positive as these results of my lecturing activities had been to me, their future importance would turn out to be far greater. I would now travel to Beas, and there I would study the teachings of the Masters with the same openness and readiness that I had demanded of the Christian theologians when I put to them the philosophical traditions of India. While reading Dr Johnson's book, I had already realized that the teachings of the Masters would take me beyond the insights of Advaita Vedanta, and that they might offer more by way of practical help in my efforts to realize and experience God. Seen within this context, the lectures I had given had been a preparation for the next step that I had to take – leaving behind old concepts and opening myself to new insights. I had not received convincing answers to some of my questions about the Christian faith, but this neither depressed nor disturbed me, because these questions did not concern the transcendent reality that I had experienced in my spiritual life. I was confident that I would find the answer some day.

During my stay in Germany, it had become abundantly clear to me that I had taken root in India and that I identified to a great extent with the country and its people. I left Germany firmly resolved to become a citizen of India, feeling no need ever to put my feet on European soil again. On 7th October 1971 I flew back to India. All my thoughts were concentrated on Beas and my next meeting with Maharaj Charan Singh. When the aeroplane lifted off, Europe had already been forgotten.

PART THREE

The Path of the Masters

CHAPTER ONE

On the Threshold

ON 10TH OCTOBER 1971 I ARRIVED AT DELHI
Airport, where I was met by Mr H. Singh of Nagpur, my
acquaintance of many years, who had first brought me in contact with the teachings of the Masters. In his company I made
the eight-hour train journey to Beas, a little town in Punjab.
Our destination was the Dera (an Indian word that means
'abode'), the spiritual centre of the Radha Soami Satsang. The
Dera is situated about six kilometres from Beas and forty-six
kilometres from Amritsar, the town with the famous Golden
Temple close to the border with Pakistan.

Maharaj Charan Singh lived at the Dera with his family
and several hundred *satsangis*, initiated disciples, almost all
of them Indians. The Dera had developed from the smallest
beginnings in 1891 into the sizeable colony that it now was. I
received a very warm welcome and was given a room in the
international guesthouse that was downright luxurious by comparison with the accommodation in Brahma Vidya Mandir.

The very next morning I was called for an interview with
the Master, who received me very kindly. I told him about the
reaction of some Catholic theologians to the possibility that
I might apply for initiation into the path of the Masters. The

Master did not show the slightest surprise or annoyance that I had asked these people for their views. Maharaj Ji,* as the Master was respectfully and lovingly addressed by his disciples, encouraged me to make up my own mind after spending some time studying the Sant Mat literature. By this he referred to the teachings of the saints – the mystics. The term *Sant* (saint) *Mat* (teachings) designates the teachings of mystics who practise and teach Surat Shabd Yoga, the yoga of the sound current, the audible Word. These mystics include Guru Nanak, Kabir, Jalaluddin Rumi, Hafiz and others, as well as the present line of Masters of the Radha Soami Satsang Beas, the first of whom was Soami Ji. The Master invited me to be a guest of the Dera for as long as I wished.

After the turbulent months in Europe I was in urgent need of finding inner peace and I therefore used the first few days to take stock of my present situation. I was conscious of standing at the threshold of a new phase in my spiritual life and, before crossing it, I wanted to be quite sure about my motives so that I could justify this step to my own conscience.

By this time, I had already made a provisional decision by accepting the Master's invitation to come to Beas, but as yet I had not made a commitment to actually step onto the path of the Masters. The Master had explicitly assured me that I had complete freedom of choice, and I did indeed feel completely free to take whatever decision I might recognize as God's will for my life.

On the other hand, I had not come to Beas by accident; rather, I was convinced that my inner guide had shown me the way. By trusting him I had arrived here, and each further step would be taken with my eyes fixed on him. It had been my

---

*Maharaj Ji: *maha* (highest), *raj* (king), *ji* (a word expressing respect and reverence). In India this title is commonly used to address a person of high spiritual rank.

guiding principle for many years to obey this inner impulse when taking the sometimes momentous decisions in my life.

In order to take stock of my situation, I wrote down everything that had been moving and affecting me for a long time. First and foremost there was the fact that my spiritual life had stagnated and I lacked the strength to do anything about it. It seemed clear to me that I needed the help of an experienced spiritual guide, and so I had approached Maharaj Charan Singh in the hope that he would grant me his help. This was the main reason that had led me to Beas.

Secondly, a number of questions about my Christian faith had arisen in recent years. In particular, the Christian dogma about the salvation of humankind by the blood of the crucified Jesus Christ had become a central question of faith for me. When I considered the state of the world, even after Christ's death on the cross, I was overcome with doubts about the truth of these teachings. Was salvation only to become effective in the hereafter, and was this earth to remain forever a valley of tears and a den of vice? I could no longer believe that the whole of humankind was already redeemed, and so it seemed justifiable to ask whether there is only *one* saviour, as Christianity maintains, or whether saviours are sent by God time and again in order to redeem the souls allotted to them. I had never been satisfied by the answers I received to this question from the Catholic theologians I consulted, but when I read the *The Path of the Masters* by Dr Johnson, I realized that the teachings of Sant Mat do indeed offer a fresh perspective on this question.

The Word of God

The third reason for my turning to a Master was the question that I had first asked many years back: "*Who* are you, O Lord?" *Whom* had I been following into the desert? *Whose gaze* had saved me from falling into the precipice when I found myself on the ridge and on the tightrope? *Who* had led me to the threshold where I was now standing? Who was this unknown inner guide in whom I had placed so much trust?

Certainly, I believed that it was Jesus Christ. I had dedicated my life to him and given him all my love; he was the foundation of my life. But was Jesus of Nazareth identical with the Lord to whom my life had belonged since my youth? Was Jesus really the power that had intervened in my life on so many occasions? Was he the one I had known for so many years in the form of light and whose voice I had heard within? I could not answer these questions with any certainty. Who could answer these questions? I vaguely hoped that I might find the answers in the teachings of the Masters.

Just a few days after writing down my questions I received the answer during my meditation practice. It was not an intellectual realization, but an intuitive understanding of the interconnectedness of a number of factors, which up to now I had not been able to see clearly. In a flash of insight I saw that the redeeming power that can rescue the soul from the powers of darkness and lead her into the kingdom of light is the divine Word, by which all things were made. This divine Word, the power of God, takes on human form in order to proclaim to the world the message of the Father and of the kingdom of God and to redeem souls. This Word of God that has become man is the mercy of God incarnate, which had manifested itself as Jesus of Nazareth, the Christ. At the same time, it stood like a revelation before my eyes that this Word had not been manifested only in Jesus of Nazareth, as Christianity believes. It can manifest itself in anyone if it so chooses, making that person into a Christ. The Word can take on human form again and again without detracting in the least from the greatness and uniqueness of former incarnations.

The Sant Mat teachings – as Dr Johnson's book had indicated – speak with a wonderful clarity about how this Word of God takes a human form. They do so without getting lost in theological and dogmatic speculations about the nature of this divine Word and without turning it into a myth. According to these teachings, the Word did not come to earth in human form just once as Jesus Christ; again and again "the Word was made flesh, and dwelt among us." Sant Mat teaches that these are the true living Masters, the Satgurus,* chosen by the Word to become saviours of souls. Such a Master is a Christ of his own time. As Jesus said to his disciples: "As long as I am in the world, I am the light of the world." This is true of all true living Masters; they are the light of the world for those disciples who are living at the same time.

Admittedly, it may be difficult for a Christian to accept the teaching of Sant Mat about the repeated incarnation of the Word because the tradition of the uniqueness of Jesus Christ as the saviour of the world is a fundamental part of the Christian faith. On the other hand, the teachings of the Masters offered to my searching mind an explanation for the fact that humankind is still so clearly in need of salvation, even after Jesus Christ. And did not Christ himself say, "I am not sent but unto the lost sheep of the house of Israel"?

My intuitive realization about the nature of Christ as the Word made flesh also gave me the answer to another of my questions: *"Who are You, O Lord?"* I saw the Lord as that same Word of God, that same Word that I had experienced within as light and an inner voice. In the hour of my conversion, it

---

*Satguru: true teacher, true Master, living Master. In the teachings of Sant Mat, this expression denotes a spiritual teacher who teaches Surat Shabd Yoga (yoga of the sound current), who has himself ascended to the highest realm (Sach Khand or Sat Desh), and who has been appointed by the supreme Lord to lead his allotted souls back to him.

was this Word that had touched the depths of my soul, kindled the spark of divine fire in my heart and made the fountain of living water spring within me. This was the inner call that I had followed when I left the 'house of my fathers' in search of my promised land.

This sudden insight strengthened my conviction that the teachings of the Masters were not in conflict with my faith in Jesus Christ. I could cross the threshold on which I was standing and turn to the path of the Masters, to Surat Shabd Yoga, the foundation of which is the teaching on the divine Word, the same divine Word of Christianity. *Surat* is a term for soul and *Shabd* refers to the divine Word as audible sound; *yoga* means 'to yoke or to join'. Surat Shabd Yoga is the spiritual method of uniting the soul with the divine Word. I was filled with great joy and a deep peace within and I experienced again the same inner security that had been given to me when I had first embarked on my adventure of faith. The Lord had answered my questions in a way that I could never have expected; I was sure that it was his answer.

I now believed that I was ready for initiation and could ask the Master to accept me as his disciple. But in fact I had as yet scarcely begun to explore this new dimension that was now starting to open up before my eyes. It soon became apparent that I had many lessons still to learn and many hurdles still to overcome, of whose existence I had as yet not the slightest inkling. Only nine days had passed since I had arrived at the Dera and I had hardly even begun to understand what it means to tread the path of the Masters.

A few days later, when I asked the Master for initiation, he told me to study a little more. When he gave me this advice, I felt sure that he was not telling me to concentrate on further intellectual study. The Masters of our time do insist that one should first satisfy the intellect before applying for initiation, and Maharaj Charan Singh knew that I still needed to deepen my understanding of Sant Mat – especially about the role of the Master in Surat Shabd Yoga. Above all, I still had to fulfil one of the most important preconditions for this path – to have faith and trust in the Master. The Master's answer to my request for initiation was at first a disappointment. As it turned out, I would have to repeat my request several times, and some months would pass before the Master would grant it.

Today it is clear to me that it was my new relationship with the Master that had helped me on that morning by giving me this intuitive realization about the Word – the realization that the Master and the Word of God are one. By doing this he helped me to develop my understanding by giving me a glimpse of the truth – not through intellectual comprehension but through a vision of reality adapted to my capacity at the time. He knew my questions even before I asked them, and he answered them in his own way. No words were needed.

CHAPTER TWO

Taking Hurdles

FOLLOWING THE MASTER'S ADVICE, I CONTIN-
ued with my studies of the Sant Mat literature. I started with
the original, unabridged edition of Dr Johnson's book, *The
Path of the Masters*. This helped me to gain a much clearer
understanding of the teachings of the Masters. It was a voyage
of discovery that brought me many new insights. My horizons
widened day by day and the teachings took shape more clearly
in my mind. Slowly, the various aspects of the teachings of
Sant Mat came together, like the pieces of a mosaic coming
together to form one beautiful picture that fascinated me more
and more.

After studying Dr Johnson's book for some weeks, I turned
to the original literature of the Masters of the Radha Soami
Satsang of Beas. These works included, among others, five
volumes of *Philosophy of the Masters* by Maharaj Sawan Singh,
as well as discourses and letters of the various Masters to their
disciples all over the world and selected extracts from question
and answer sessions at meetings of international guests with
Maharaj Charan Singh.

As I read these books I began to comprehend that the
unfathomable depths of the teachings of Sant Mat can only

be grasped by a student who actually walks the path leading within under the guidance of a living Master. The words of the Masters were charged with spiritual energy and they radiated a wisdom that only a true knower can have, one who possesses the *cognitio Dei experimentalis*, knowledge of God by experience, as Thomas Aquinas puts it.

In the writings of the Masters I repeatedly found parallels with *advaita* philosophy and quotations from the Upanishads and the Bhagavad Gita. Maharaj Charan Singh often pointed out that all great spiritual teachers preach the same truth. However, the religions that emerge from these teachings evolve under the influence of their particular historic environments and, in doing so, they depart more and more from their original source. This process cannot be undone, but on the level of spirituality it is possible to discover their common origin, which consists in the experience of the divine truth and reality by those great teachers.

One important point of agreement between Vedanta and Sant Mat is the primacy of the experience of God over intellectual knowledge of God. Both of these schools of spirituality also teach that the soul is a drop of the inexhaustible ocean of absolute Being. The spiritual path of a human being and his liberation consist in again becoming conscious of the divine origin of his soul and merging into this ocean of divine Existence.

A few days after my arrival at the Dera, I was able to start meditating in the way that the Master had shown me in Nagpur. It was not the proper Surat Shabd Yoga exercise – just a preliminary concentration exercise since I did not yet know the precise words for the meditation. These words are imparted only at the time of initiation. As is customary in the Dera, I got up at three o'clock each morning when the siren sounded for meditation. I tried to meditate by concentrating at the point in the forehead that the Master had shown me. This point was already familiar to me through the practice of the Jesus Prayer and I was able to put my attention in the place where the divine light had touched me for many years.

Meditating, however – and this was the first hurdle – turned out to be difficult. My time in Europe had been tiring, and I had developed a severe headache like the one I had experienced in the monastery during my 'ridge walk'. This meant that I had to perform the concentration exercises with utmost care and that I was often unable to meditate for more than half an hour. The headache appeared especially when I tried to force my concentration.

Although I believed, after just one week in the Dera, that I had a clear idea about the path ahead, there was a second hurdle that was far more difficult to overcome than the headache. I had come to Beas with the idea of asking the Master for initiation, so that I could then just go away and meditate. I thought that once I was initiated I would leave the Dera and forget about the Master who, to my way of thinking, would have fulfilled his task by initiating me. In order to obtain the required knowledge about the path of the Masters as fast as possible, I spent all day reading and stuffing my brain with intellectual knowledge about Sant Mat.

For this reason, I saw no need to attend the morning satsangs, where the Master gave discourses in Punjabi, the local language. At the evening meetings with the Master in the international guesthouse, which were conducted in English, I sat in the back row, while the other guests competed for places near the Master. I was quite astonished to see how one-pointedly they would fix their gaze on him. Somehow I felt like a stranger among these people. I was unable to identify with them because I thought of myself as Indian and tended to avoid these 'foreigners'. In doing so, I isolated myself and deprived myself of the opportunity to talk with people who were already practitioners on the path.

There was another hurdle of my own making. I had decided to cultivate an attitude of reserve – an attitude of wait-and-see. When I had first arrived at the Dera, I noticed how bright the faces of the people I saw around me were as I made my way to the guesthouse. The inhabitants of the guesthouse also made a very happy impression on me; they seemed to be full of joy in being at the Dera. Observing all this, I resolved not to allow myself to make decisions based on emotions, but rather to begin by thoroughly studying the teachings of the Masters in a detached way. It was precisely because I found the Master so very likeable that I was on my guard. Consequently, I did not allow myself to be influenced in any way by the enthusiasm of the disciples I met. On one occasion, I was sitting at a table with two German-speaking guests who had been initiated one year back. They were visiting the Dera for the first time and they spoke with great enthusiasm about the path and the Masters. As I did not want to get caught up in their elation, I kept them at arm's length, and repeatedly contradicted them so that they became more and more taciturn.

Some weeks went by in this manner, until an Indian couple who were living in the guesthouse noticed how much of an outsider I was. Since I wore Indian dress, they approached me and, after a long talk about my life at Brahma Vidya Mandir and the reasons that had led me to the Dera, they took me under their wing. They accompanied me to satsang and explained to me many things about Sant Mat that I had not yet understood. Meeting Mr and Mrs D. turned out to be a crucial turning point for me, which helped me to overcome a hurdle that had become a serious hindrance on my path. Without my being aware of it, the Master had availed himself of these two satsangis in order to pull me out of my self-imposed isolation.

Lessons to learn

Soon after I started to study the Sant Mat literature, it became clear to me that it would not be practicable to receive initiation into Surat Shabd Yoga and then just forget about the Master. I realized that the Master has a central position on the spiritual path. He does not just impart the method of meditation to his disciple; he also accompanies him all the way, right up to the highest goal – the union of his soul with God. Without a relationship with the Master, a disciple cannot take even one step on this path.

Every day it became more evident to me that I might as well pack my bags and leave the Dera if I could not accept this fact. I had intuitively understood the key position of the Master and was intellectually convinced that the teachings of the Masters were not contrary to my faith in Jesus Christ. As mentioned earlier, I had already asked for initiation nine days after my arrival at the Dera, and that had been no momentary whim. But still I had thought that after initiation I would be able to leave behind the one who taught me the method of meditation. I had believed that it would be enough to understand Sant Mat and to desire union with the divine Word.

Now I had to choose. Either I could forego initiation or I could turn wholeheartedly to the Master. Since I was sure that I wanted to walk this path, I would now have to learn the most important lesson of all – to make the Master central to my thinking, my devotion and my contemplation. This, however, turned out to be extremely difficult because I had never followed a living spiritual teacher. I had always followed my inner guide, with whom I felt inseparably connected. Jesus Christ had become the foundation of my life – a foundation that I would never abandon. He was a reality in my life that I could not put aside, for that would mean that during all those years

I had been chasing a phantom, and it had all been nothing but a grand self-deception. But in the days to come the Master led me step by step towards realizing that I did not have to give up Jesus Christ in order to follow the Master.

To begin with, he made it very easy for me to concentrate on him. He was an exceptional personality who impressed me very deeply by his great kindness and humility. His face radiated light and his eyes had a supernatural lustre. Trusting in divine guidance, I tried to give myself entirely over to the Master's *darshan** and to visualize his form also during meditation.

This confidence was rewarded much sooner than I could ever have hoped. Only a few days after I began to look at the Master with a gaze full of confidence and love, a marvellous change took place within me. The inner blockage that had brought my spiritual progress to a standstill began to dissolve and the longing of my soul expanded immeasurably. From this experience I realized how dangerous my situation had been and that I never would have been able to remove that inner blockage by my own effort. Had I not met the Master, it would have remained there for the rest of my life, or perhaps I may even have given up the spiritual life entirely, despite my having gone so far, having overcome so many difficulties and having experienced divine guidance so often.

The second lesson I had to learn in those days was to extend once again my whole being towards the divine Word, the fountain of my life, which I had met in my youth in the form of inner light and an inner voice. The kind of meditation I had adopted under the influence of *advaita* philosophy had buried my intimate relationship with God. My heart was, as it were, paralysed and incapable of longing for union with God. This had

---

* *darshan*: sight or vision, seeing; looking with reverence and love at a noble and distinguished personality, especially a spiritual Master.

created a feeling of no longer loving him. Now I tried to open my heart by calling to the divine Word with the prayer from the first Epistle to the Corinthians: *Marana tha* – Come, O Lord. Together with my turning to the Master, this exercise bore the fruits that I have described in the preceding paragraphs.

All by his grace

A few days after this inner transformation – it was on 26th October 1971 – I was able to speak to the Master about my experience. The Master was indescribably kind and said that he was aware of my efforts and my progress; he encouraged me to continue my study of Sant Mat literature. When I again asked for initiation, he said, "I will do it when the time has come."

Given the Master's response, I felt that I should generate a strong desire for it within myself in order to show the Master how great my longing was. By doing this, I hoped that I would not have to wait so long. My main motive in wanting initiation was, however, very egocentric: I wanted to receive meditation instructions so that I could continue on my spiritual path. Other reasons – liberation from reincarnation, the salvation of my soul, the experience of the sound current – were still purely intellectual, quite colourless and without life. Nevertheless, I tried to create a kind of artificial desire, a desire that had not grown organically within me – there had been far too little time for that to happen. One day my efforts to create longing within myself were so exaggerated that the headaches came back and I was overcome by a great fatigue. This was certainly not the right way to prepare myself for initiation, but I had to go through this phase in order to learn the third lesson of the path of the Masters – that it is all his grace.

By the evening of that day I had finally made up my mind to wait calmly and leave it to the Lord to fix the time for initiation. When I considered how long God had been leading me towards initiation without my having any awareness of it, I could see how childish it would be to suddenly become impatient and try to hasten the process. When, with God's help, I regained my faith and trust, he made me realize that it is he himself who wants the return of that soul, that tiny drop out of the limitless ocean of divine Being. Who is anyone to desire union with God? It is God who infuses the longing into the human heart – it is the working of his grace. When I realized this, my inner balance was restored and I got back the inner security that had filled me when I had followed the voice of my inner guide and embarked on my adventure with God.

CHAPTER THREE

The Master in the Light of the Gospel

UNDER THE EYES OF THE MASTER, I HAD GONE through an intense and complex learning process in just a few weeks. The study of the Sant Mat literature had revealed to me a completely new image of God and the world. While studying the books, I had already overcome some hurdles on my way to the path of the Masters, and I had learned some fundamental lessons that were to prove indispensable for embarking on this path.

The first important lesson had been the realization of the nature of the divine Word and its incarnation as a Christ, which came to me during my first few days at the Dera. This opened my eyes to the mystery of the Son of God, who in the course of human history came and still comes again and again in human form as a teacher and a saviour in order to grant access to the kingdom of God to those souls allotted to him by the Father; of this I was now convinced. Jesus Christ clearly spoke of this on the eve of his crucifixion when he said in his prayer to the Father: "I have manifested thy name unto the men which thou gavest me out of the world: thine they were, and thou gavest them me."

After I gained this insight, three weeks passed by and then the idea came to me: that I might learn about the nature of a true Master, called in Sant Mat tradition a Satguru, with the help of the Gospels – especially by examining the words of the Master of Nazareth when giving testimony about himself. I would search the teachings of Jesus Christ, the Word of God made flesh, so that he himself could introduce me into the mystery of a true living Master.

To a Christian, it may seem very daring to apply the writings of the Gospel about Christ to a non-Christian Master. But as I was inspired to explore this idea from within myself, I felt sure the idea came to me as an inspiration from my inner guide, and so it was with great eagerness that I started to explore the mystery of a true living Master in the Gospel.

God and man

The prologue to *The Gospel According to Saint John* outlines in a few sentences and in archaic language the truly amazing mystery of the Christ, the Son of God, who became man. The Gospel reads: "In the beginning was the Word, and the Word was with God, and the Word was God.... And the Word was made flesh, and dwelt among us." According to the testimony of Saint John's Gospel, the "only begotten Son" *(unigenitus)*, the Christ, whom the Father had sent into the world for the salvation of souls, is both God and man. He is the Creator of the world. As a man he is a creature with an earthly body, a human mind and a soul; he is also one with the Word. These fundamental teachings of Christianity about the Word of God, the Logos, and its incarnation in human form are also the central ideas of the teachings of Sant Mat.

With bold words that scandalized those who heard him, Jesus himself pointed to the mystery of his person when he said to the Pharisees, "Your father Abraham rejoiced to see my day: and he saw it, and was glad." When the Jews objected that he was a young man and yet pretended to have seen Abraham, Jesus answered, "Verily, verily, I say unto you, Before Abraham was, I am."

In his prayer directed to his Father on the eve of his arrest, Jesus testified that he had been in the glory of the Father before the world was made.* In this prayer Jesus also says that the Father "lovedst me before the foundation of the world".

Time and again, Jesus emphasizes that he and the Father are one: "Believe me that I am in the Father, and the Father in me." For this reason, the Son knows the Father and the Father knows him. The Christ knows the mysteries of God because he is one with him. While going through the Gospel of Saint John, I found many such passages. They now carried a meaning for me that I could never have imagined without meeting a true living Master. Even today, I am filled with awe when I read Jesus's statements about himself and ponder the mystery of a Satguru, whose soul is one with the Word of God. There is no difference between his soul and the Word of God. A Christ is the Word in human form.

In the evening satsangs, the Master was quite often asked questions of a personal nature – who he was and how he saw himself. He rarely gave a direct answer to such questions, but preferred to quote one of the self-testimonies of Jesus. This was always like a revelation to us. It was these statements made by the teacher of Nazareth about himself that threw such a bright light on the person of the Master; we were always fascinated by the thought that they applied equally to the Satguru seated in person before us. When I first began to approach the

---

*"And now, O Father, glorify thou me with thine own self with the glory which I had with thee before the world was." *John* 17:5

Gospels from this angle I was not yet fully convinced, but the more I read them the clearer the concept of the Master became in my mind.

The fountain of life

In reading Saint John's Gospel, I came across many passages of great importance to understanding the true nature of a Christ. They were the passages in which Jesus manifests himself as the bearer and transmitter of divine life. Only one who carries life within himself can transmit life. The Master of Nazareth thus testifies: "For as the Father hath life in himself, so hath he given to the Son to have life in himself."

With manifold symbols, Jesus Christ refers time and again to the fact that he is the fountain of life for all who believe in him. Deeply moved, I read the description of his meeting the Samaritan woman at the well of Jacob. There Jesus speaks of the 'water of life' that bestows immortality: "But whosoever drinketh of the water that I shall give him shall never thirst; but the water that I shall give him shall be in him a well of water springing up into everlasting life." Through the experience of the deeper dimension of consciousness that was granted to me, I felt a fountain had welled up inside me from which I too could drink living water that would quench the thirst of my soul. This personal experience had given me at least a faint idea of what Jesus Christ had spoken about.

When I read this passage in the Gospel of Saint John, I already knew from my study of the Sant Mat books that the water to which Jesus refers is the divine life current, or the Word, the Shabd, which manifests itself as light and sound. It can be perceived by the eyes and the ears of the soul after she has been connected with the Shabd through initiation by a true living Master.

According to the teachings of the Masters, only a Christ, a Buddha, a Murshid – a Master of the highest order who has become one with the divine life current – is able to reconnect the soul of his disciple with the Shabd and so put her on the road leading to salvation. This is the greatness of the Masters and their unique position in God's plan for the liberation of souls.

On another occasion, Jesus calls himself the 'bread of life': "Verily, verily, I say unto you, Moses gave you not that bread from heaven; but my Father giveth you the true bread from heaven. For the bread of God is he which cometh down from heaven, and giveth life unto the world.... I am the bread of life: he that cometh to me shall never hunger; and he that believeth on me shall never thirst."

Sant Mat teaches that we can experience the life-giving divine power of the Word or Logos within ourselves as light and sound. The 'bread of life' means the supernatural light that nourishes the soul until she has grown up to "the stature of the fullness of Christ", as Saint Paul wrote to the Ephesians. I had experienced for myself the touch of this supernatural light as a gift of the bread of life long before I had ever heard about the concept of a living Master or Sant Mat. On the basis of my own experience, I had at least a faint idea of how Christ had transmitted the divine life of which he speaks.

The prologue to Saint John's Gospel speaks of the Word of God as "the light of men". Jesus himself testifies repeatedly that he is this light. Thus he says: "I am the light of the world: he that followeth me shall not walk in darkness, but shall have the light of life." This light cannot be perceived by the physical eyes; for this the eye of the soul is needed.

Jesus once revealed himself in his radiant or inner form to some of his disciples when he took them to Mount Tabor. It must have been an overwhelming experience to them, to see their Master in his astral form. This experience also awaits the disciple of a true living Master when, by means of the meditation exercises, he crosses the threshold to a higher level of consciousness. He will then see his Master in a resplendent light form, and from then on this inner form will be always by his side. This divine light will reveal itself to the soul during her ascent to the kingdom of God, ever brighter and more powerful, until she merges forever into the uncreated light of God.

The teacher of truth sent by God

Of all the insights I gained about the nature of a true Master, a Christ, through Jesus Christ's testimony about himself, I would like to share with my readers one more aspect that deserves special attention: this is the idea of the Master as the teacher of truth sent by God.

While reading through the Gospel of Saint John, I realized more and more that the Master of Nazareth had a very distinct sense of his *mission*. "Him that sent me" is an expression frequently used by Jesus. Time and again he emphasizes that he has not come on his own initiative, but that the Father has sent him in order to announce the message of the kingdom of God and that the Father "hath borne witness of me". Jesus Christ professed that he descended from heaven to fulfil the will of the one who had sent him, and he promised that "he that receiveth me receiveth him that sent me."

In his profound nocturnal conversation with Nicodemus, a Pharisee and councillor of the Jews, Jesus points out that God has loved the world so much that "he gave his only begotten Son, that whosoever believeth in him should not perish, but have everlasting life. For God sent not his Son into the world to condemn the world; but that the world through him might be saved."

Even in the hour of farewell from his disciples on the eve of his arrest, in his prayer to the Father he time and again comes back to the idea that he has been sent by God, as when he says: "But now I go my way to him that sent me."

Totally filled with this sense of mission, Jesus considered it his foremost task to give testimony to the truth, to the kingdom of God. This he confessed to the Roman governor Pontius Pilate, who later on would deliver him to the Sanhedrin, the Jewish judicial body, for crucifixion. He said: "For this I have come to the world, to bear witness to the truth." The Master of Nazareth not only proclaimed the truth, but according to his own words *he is himself the truth*: "I am the way and the truth and the life."

The personality of the Master of Nazareth and his recorded words left a deep impression on many of those who heard him. As the Gospel of Saint Matthew testifies, many of them were deeply moved because Jesus "taught them as one having authority". The people of his home town also saw this quality in him, for they asked themselves, "Whence hath this man this wisdom, and these mighty works? Is not this the carpenter's son? Is not his mother called Mary?... Whence then hath this man all these things?"

The mystery of the strong personal magnetism and the authority of Jesus is due to the fact that he lived as a human being on earth and at the same time was "face to face" with God.* At any given moment he was able to lift up his eyes to heaven and to raise his consciousness to the level of the Father, to the throne of God. Jesus, the Christ, had himself realized the truth that he preached. He confirms this in the meeting with Nicodemus mentioned earlier, where he says, "Verily, verily, I

---

*This expression Saint Paul uses in his letter to the Corinthians: "For now we see through a glass, darkly; but then face to face." *1 Corinthians* 13:12

say unto thee, We speak that we do know, and testify that we have seen."

In his human form, however, Jesus Christ could reach only his contemporaries, but not the generations coming before and after him. What about those who had lived outside the short period when Jesus was on earth? As it was said earlier, Sant Mat teaches that God has to send his Son again and again into the world, so that as a Christ he can show the way back to the Father to those souls that are allotted to him. The Word must take human form, because only in this form can he proclaim the message of the kingdom of God and redeem the souls. If it was necessary *once* that the Son of God, his Word, should come to earth, then it would *always* be necessary.

During the evening satsangs in the Dera, Maharaj Charan Singh emphasized repeatedly that the Masters themselves do not demand of their disciples that they believe blindly in the true nature of a Master. This will be revealed gradually to the student on his or her spiritual journey. In the beginning, the Master explained, it is sufficient just to accept him as companion, brother, father or friend, and to follow his instructions for meditation. In the course of his progress in meditation, the disciple will come to recognize the true nature of his Master. The Master's assurance that this is a gradual process was very important to me, for I was not yet able to accept in its entirety the Sant Mat teaching regarding the nature of a true living Master.

I spent some weeks studying the Gospels, listening to the testimony of Jesus about the true nature and mission of the Word of God made flesh. It became more and more clear to me that a Christ, a true Master, as presented in the Gospels through the person of Jesus and in the context of Sant Mat teachings, is a *mysterium tremendum* – an awe-inspiring mystery. In the light of the Gospels I began to understand the Sant Mat teachings much better. Through the self-testimony of Jesus Christ, the image of the Master began to take on a beautiful lustre. I was overwhelmed by the idea of what was taking place before our eyes: the eternal Word had taken human form and dwelt among us as a living being with whom we kept company. This filled me with deep reverence for the Master, but also with love and devotion to him. With my background in the Christian scriptures, I had come a little closer to him and he had become much more familiar to me.

CHAPTER FOUR

It Had Been His Gaze

BY THE TIME I FINISHED MY STUDY OF THE
Gospels it was the end of October 1971. It felt to me that in just
a few weeks I had gained so many insights. New worlds had
opened before my eyes, and on the 26th of that same month the
Master accepted me for initiation. Now the path lay before me
and the Master's place in my life became clear.

But the last and biggest hurdle remained; I still felt one
strong inner blockage that had not been removed by my study
of the Gospels. Intellectually, I had accepted the Sant Mat
view of who the Master was, but I had not accepted it in the
depths of my heart, where I felt inseparably connected with
Jesus Christ. During meditation it proved to be impossible to
look, as it were, with one eye at Christ and with the other one
at the Master. When I realized that I had to choose between
these two directions, agony gripped me. How could I ever avert
my gaze from Jesus Christ, whose eyes were constantly looking
at me? This inner conflict worried me deeply. I asked myself
whom I could speak to about it. Of course, there was the Master, but I shied away from asking him. He had always shown so
much understanding of my questions and he had always been
so full of kindness, yet I still did not have enough confidence to

ask a question that so directly pertained to his person. But the Master had heard my question without my asking him, and he answered it in a way that only a Master could.

One evening the satsang was given by Professor Bhatnagar, former secretary of the Master. The Master was present during the satsang while the Professor emphasized strongly that we should keep our gaze fixed steadily on the Master – not only during meditation, but for twenty-four hours a day. I was much affected by those words because just the day before I had considered giving up contemplation of the form of the Master during meditation in order to concentrate again on the darkness. During the satsang the Master was sitting silently before us, but he had surely showered untold grace on his audience – not the least on me. At any rate, while listening to the Professor's words I felt an inner urge to show, at least as a sign of good will, that I was prepared, albeit as yet unable, to make the last decisive step. I decided to sit in satsang the next morning in the first row and to fix my gaze on the Master as the other satsangis did. It was a cry for help to that power to which I had dedicated my life. Only two days passed before I experienced for myself what it means to make one step towards the Lord. When we do this, he will take a hundred steps towards us – as I had read in the writings of Christian mystics.

On that day, when the evening satsang was over, I felt a strong impulse to go immediately to my room and to meditate, even though I was very tired and had a headache. I felt that something was going to happen. As soon as I entered my room, I was thrown to the floor as if by an invisible force. This had never happened before. Lying on the ground, face down, I started to weep helplessly. With these tears, all my agony left me. At the same time, I felt the eyes of the Master fixed on me, holding my gaze.

It was at this moment that I recognized the Master's eyes as the same eyes that I had looked into while passing over the ridge, and I knew for certain that I was repeating an experience that I had been through many times in the course of the past years. I now realized, without the slightest doubt, that the Lord and the Master are one.

Finally, I had found *'my Christ'*. *He* was the one who had spoken to me in my youth, who had demanded my undivided heart and who had laid his hand upon me. *He* was the inner guide who had taught me the contemplative prayer. *He* was the one who had encouraged me to fight when I had been at a loss because of the refusal from Rome to grant me exclaustration so that I could go to India. *He* was the one who had stood behind me on the ridge with his sword raised high in his hand. *He* was the one who had received me outside the door of my monastery when I took my first step into an unknown future. And now, finally, *he* had led me to his feet, in the form of a living teacher, in order to teach me the path leading within, which I could not have walked without having first met him in his physical form.

Now he had disclosed his identity to me; now I knew who it was that I had been following since my youth. It had been the Word of God that takes human form. Maharaj Charan Singh assured us many times that the Word, the Master in his Shabd form, invisibly stands at the side of his future disciple from his birth or, rather, he is *inside* him. When it is his great good fortune, one day, in its own inscrutable way, this Word manifests to him as the shepherd of souls and takes him, openly, into his fold.

In a wonderful and unpredictable way, the question of whose face I should look at during meditation was finally answered. I needed to look neither to the right nor to the left, but to the centre. There I found the gaze that had been directed at me over so many years. The gaze of the Lord and the gaze of the Master had become one. Now I had experienced for myself that the universal Christ, the divine Word and the Master are all one. It was an indescribable experience that turned me into a disciple of the Master in a matter of moments, without my having to turn away from Christ.

The next morning – it was 7th November 1971 – I had the opportunity to speak to the Master. It was not necessary to tell him of the experience of the previous evening because he had brought it about. I only said to the Master, "When the Master uses his supernatural powers, the disciple cannot but surrender." The Master looked at me and then he said only two words: "I know." Later I would see for myself many times how the Master sees what is going on in the innermost recesses of a person. He sees into the depth of people's souls, even if he does not speak about it.

With this experience the prayer which I had directed to the Lord so often during our daily chanting of the Psalms, "Thy face, Lord, will I seek.... Make thy face to shine upon thy serv-ant," was fulfilled in a twofold way. The Lord had shown me a 'glimpse of his face' and I gained the inner security that in my Master I would behold the human form of the Word.

Beholding his face

What wouldn't I, and hundreds of thousands of human beings who have lived during the two thousand years since Christ's death, have given to meet him, to behold his face? I had always felt myself at a disadvantage compared to those who had been able to behold Jesus face to face.

Is not our longing to see God in human form legitimate? We are accustomed to perceive things with our senses. To this natural need God responded by manifesting himself in the form of the Word made flesh in Jesus Christ, as the Gospels tell us. But did God reveal himself in human form only once in the course of human history? Did he show himself to a small privileged group on just one occasion and never again?

I had had to be content with images of Jesus Christ that had been made by artists who had never seen him in his human form. Many of these images were certainly beautiful and able to evoke feelings of devotion and love, as I had experienced for myself while contemplating on the mosaic in the church at Fulda Abbey. Even after the desire to contemplate on the image of Christ had been extinguished by my experience of transcendence, the prayer "Let me behold your face" had not lost its actuality; now, however, I prayed not for a vision of Christ but for the realization of his presence in a form that had nothing to do with imagination.

To a certain extent, this prayer was fulfilled later, while I was going over the 'ridge' and while I was on the 'tightrope'. At those times I had met the gaze of that unknown One, whom I called 'my Lord', and I had felt that I was seeing God – although in a hidden way. In a similar way, the experience of light had been a vision of his face.

My own experience had now convinced me that God, in his loving mercy, sends his Son into the world in human form again and again. I was filled with indescribable joy when I realized that even today we can behold his face in a true living Master, a Christ. I could never have dreamt that the words "Let me behold your face" would be fulfilled in this way. Every day now I could experience for myself that for the disciple of a true living Master there is nothing more blissful than devoting himself to the *darshan* of his Master, to beholding his physical form and especially his face.

Maharaj Charan Singh, however, frequently pointed out that, by means of meditation, outer *darshan* of the Master should lead us to inner *darshan*, to the contemplation of the inner radiant form of the Master. Quite often he emphasized that the Master in his physical form is not the real Master, nor is the disciple in his human form the real disciple. Rather, the true Master is the Shabd and the true disciple is the soul. The body of the Master is a mere instrument and the body of the disciple is only a means to establish the connection between the two. In his real form, the Shabd or Word of God, the Master will liberate the soul of his disciple and lead it to its final goal in order to make it one with him. Then the soul has reached the state described as 'the fullness of Christ';* it has become the 'son of God'.

---

*"And he gave some, apostles; and some, prophets; and some, evangelists; and some, pastors and teachers...Till we all come in the unity of the faith, and of the knowledge of the Son of God, unto a perfect man, unto the measure of the stature of the fulness of Christ." *Ephesians* 4:11,13

CHAPTER FIVE

Towards Initiation

IN THE DAYS BEFORE THE OVERWHELMING experience described in the previous chapter, I had often tried to evoke love and devotion for the Satguru, the true Master, in my heart. Once, during the evening satsang, an Indian satsangi, a Dera resident, had spoken movingly about this subject. The Master himself often said that without love for the Lord we cannot make progress on the spiritual path. In saying this, the Master was certainly not demanding that we love him; he was speaking about his own experience of loving his own Master, for he himself had been, and still was, a disciple of his beloved Master, Maharaj Sawan Singh, known affectionately as Great Master. Though he was now a Satguru himself, Maharaj Charan Singh always referred to his own Master with such love and devotion that we were deeply touched. But I was unable to awaken such feelings in myself. It was only when my experience of the oneness of the Master of Nazareth and the living Master had transformed me into a disciple of the Master that my heart opened.

The realization that during all those years on the ridge I had been looking into the eyes of the Master enabled me to cross over the threshold at which I had been standing for many weeks. A boundless land of spirituality extended before me and I felt a strong urge to enter it and to pass through it quickly. I wanted to do the real meditation, because the meditation I was already doing with the Master's permission was only a preliminary exercise.

However, some months would still have to pass before the Master would initiate me. Although I regularly repeated my request for initiation, he did not fix a date. Moreover, he was sometimes away from the Dera in order to deliver satsang in remote places for those who were unable to come to Beas. For example, he was away from the Dera at the end of November 1971 for three weeks and, during his absence, the war between India and Pakistan flared up again. We could hear the artillery fire, because the front line was not far away. Then the alarming news reached us that the Master had suffered a severe heart attack and was in a hospital in Delhi.

When the Master finally returned to the Dera, I again asked him for initiation, but he just answered, "Don't worry, it will come." This was on the morning of 24th December. At the beginning of January, the time came for the guests to leave the Dera, making room for the next group. For this reason, the manager of the guesthouse had booked a flight for me to Nagpur. I was stunned at the idea that I should leave the Dera without being initiated, but then I was told that the Master had ordered the booking to be cancelled and provided another room for me in the Dera.

On 7th January 1972 the Master sent for me and asked whether I had any obligations in the ashram that would require my early return. Fortunately this was not the case. The Master then said that, because of his heart attack, his physicians would not yet allow him to speak for long, and since initiation would take at least one hour, he asked me to wait till the beginning of February.

But in reality, I was still not ready for initiation. Although I had learnt many lessons since I came to the Dera and I had put my longing for initiation into the hands of the Lord, I needed still more time to come to a deeper understanding of the grace of initiation. During the weeks to come, the Master was preparing me in many ways, even without speaking to me directly. This waiting period was a long night, but a night full of splendour; it was like Advent, the time of waiting for the coming of the Lord. The Master had become the centre of my life and all my thoughts concentrated on him.

At the beginning of February 1972, I was suddenly gripped by deep fear. It happened while I was busy smashing up old and badly baked bricks with other inhabitants of the guesthouse. While doing this *seva* (voluntary service for the Master and his sangat, his community), I was seized by a kind of despair. I felt that I would die if the Master did not initiate me. Although he had promised it several times, he kept postponing the date. After my initiation I told the Master about this experience and he said, "I wanted you to come to this point." So that had been the real reason for all the delays: I had to realize that without initiation my life would have been like a living death. It was very important to realize this before initiation. The Masters point out time and again that one should ask for initiation only when the longing for it has become irresistible. Such an experience is necessary to keep an initiate going on the long and arduous path of spirituality.

Then came 6th February 1972. We were only twelve guests, for a group of South African satsangis had not obtained their visas for India, and so the evening satsang was held in the reception room in Master's house. To be so close to the Master in a small room was a beautiful experience for all of us. We were allowed to ask questions, and I wanted to know how the Master finds his disciples, who are spread out over all the continents.

The Master gave an answer that I don't recall now, but that apparently did not satisfy me. I therefore asked another question and the Master gave me another answer. In this way, a kind of dialogue developed, during which I tried to concentrate on the Master's words and to keep my gaze fixed on him. In the end, however, I could no longer listen to the Master's answers. The surroundings seemed to fade away and I felt as if my soul was standing before the Master, whom I hardly perceived any more in his physical form.

The Master wanted to grant me this experience on the eve of my initiation. He wanted to show me how the Master finds his disciple: even if he is physically far away, he is present to the Master. Distance does not exist on the level of consciousness of a true Master. He knows his own. As Jesus says in the parable of the good shepherd: "I am the good shepherd, and know my sheep, and am known of mine."

I was quite dazed by this event. In a single moment I had again received an inkling of the greatness of a true Master that even decades of study could not have conveyed. Such experiences imprinted themselves indelibly in my heart and there formed the foundation of my faith in the Master and my trust in him, which I hope will never be shaken.

At that moment I did not know that the Master would initiate me the next day. This I only found out when, at the end of the evening satsang, I heard him telling the manager of the guesthouse to bring me to his office after breakfast on the following morning; then I realized what it meant – the Master would initiate me tomorrow.

The day of the new birth

The next morning in his office – it was 7ᵗʰ February 1972 – the Master handed me the initiation text in English and told me to read it carefully. After the morning satsang, which I was not to attend, I should come to him and he would initiate me. Full of joy I retired to my room and read the text with great attention.

Now the much-longed-for day of initiation had come. I tried to prepare inwardly for this significant hour, which would indeed mark a turning point in my existence as a being created by God. It would be the hour of rebirth in the Holy Spirit, to which the Master of Nazareth referred when he said to Nicodemus: "Verily, verily, I say unto thee, except a man be born again, he cannot see the kingdom of God."

According to Sant Mat, the new birth that Jesus Christ speaks of is brought about by the power of the Word, the Shabd, which has taken human form in a true Master. I was convinced that it was in this form that he would free my soul from the 'power of darkness'* and reconnect her with himself. At initiation the Master would take my soul out of the hands of the prince of this world and take upon himself the responsibility for her liberation and for her entrance into the kingdom of God.

In the last few weeks, I had read so much about initiation and its effects, and I had heard it discussed in the evening satsangs with the Master. It was still theory to me, but I had already experienced the greatness and power of a true living Master on several occasions, so that I looked forward with confidence to the gradual unveiling of the reality of the spiritual path. More important than all reflection about the possible effects of initiation on my life was that at that hour I should entrust to him my fate – my whole life.

When the time came, I went to the Master's house. Since the Master still had to attend to many other things, I had to wait for nearly an hour. When he finally approached me,

---

*"Giving thanks unto the Father…who hath delivered us from the power of darkness, and hath translated us into the kingdom of his dear Son." *Colossians* 1:12–13

he apologized for making me wait for such a long time. I was quite embarrassed and answered, "It is a grace to wait for the Lord."

The Master took me into his visitors' room, sat Indian fashion on the carpet and made me sit likewise on the ground in front of him. For a whole hour I sat in front of the Master with my gaze fixed on him while he explained the method of meditation, gave me the meditation words and made me repeat them until I knew them by heart. These are Sanskrit words, five names of God, which the disciple has to repeat inwardly during meditation with utmost concentration and without interruption, until he reaches such perfect concentration that his consciousness turns inside and is lifted up to a higher plane.

Then the Master explained to me the soul's path in her ascent through the various spiritual realms. He described different kinds of light and sound that the pilgrim will experience during his return to the eternal home. These manifestations of the sound current, the heavenly music, are to be seen and heard in meditation as the soul ascends to higher levels of consciousness. After explaining all this, the Master taught me how to listen to the Shabd. I tried to memorize all the Master's words and to open my heart to the grace of initiation. At the end of initiation, his last words were, "This is a path of love and love only."

Initiation into Surat Shabd Yoga is not a ceremony, but a process of instruction; it can be conducted by any person authorized by the Master. It is, however, far more than just an imparting of the technique of meditation and a description of the lights and sounds of the inner realms.

The fundamental significance of initiation is that the Master reconnects the soul of his disciple with the Word, the Holy Spirit, and awakens her to a new life. According to the teachings of Sant Mat, only a true living Master can do this. By initiating a disciple, the Master takes upon himself the responsibility for the disciple's soul and takes charge of his 'book of life', in which reward and punishment for his actions are recorded.

The methods of meditation may change over the centuries, and a true Master is free to choose the method by which the consciousness of his disciple is to turn inside. Should he wish to, the Master could do it with a single gracious gaze. Similarly, the Master is not bound to give particular words for the repetition or *mantra*, he can give a disciple any words he chooses for meditation. What matters is not the words themselves but the power that the Master puts into them. This power unfolds when the concentration of the practitioner has become stronger, so that finally the words repeat themselves automatically even outside meditation.

What happens inside the disciple during the initiation is hidden from most people until such time as they are able to raise their consciousness during meditation to a higher level, where they will meet the Master in his astral form, his subtle or radiant form. Only then will they realize what the Master has done and is still doing for them. Doubtless this will be a wonderful experience for the disciple. There are disciples who ascend to this level of consciousness right away at the time of initiation, but most have to work hard to reach this stage. Whether or not the disciple has inner experiences at the time of initiation and how quickly he progresses on the path depends on his own inner state.

For most disciples it is a long and arduous journey, as the Masters always emphasize. But nobody should lose heart when progress is slow, for the inner path is a retracing, in reverse, of the soul's long descent from her original home, which took place over an unimaginable span of time. When their disciples feel disheartened, the Masters console them by pointing out that the ascent by means of Surat Shabd Yoga is comparatively short.

During the evening satsangs the Master was frequently asked what happens to a disciple who does not succeed in covering the whole distance in this lifetime. The Master's answer was invariably that a disciple has to return to the world only if he still has very strong attachments to people and objects of the world or if he must still receive rewards or punishments for his actions that necessitate a life on earth. Otherwise, he will be able to continue his path of liberation on a higher plane.

As mentioned before, similar forms of meditation are found in other religions. In Christianity, for example, we find the Jesus Prayer and the practice of concentration described in *The Cloud of Unknowing*. It is, however, of decisive importance that a true living Master imparts the meditation technique. If someone sets out on this inner path without a proper guide, there is a great danger of floundering; even if he succeeds in reaching the astral region, nobody will be there to receive him and he is likely to succumb to the temptations, the so-called *siddhis** that lie in wait for him on that plane. Therefore, spiritual teachers strongly caution against trying to walk the inner path alone.

The disciple initiated by a true living Master will meet his Master in his radiant form at the threshold of the astral region, and under his guidance he will be able to continue on his way. Above all, he will now hear the Word, the sound current, which will irresistibly draw his soul upwards into the spiritual worlds.

---

* *Siddhis* are supernatural powers described by Patanjali in his Yoga Sutra, such as knowing the past and the future; understanding the language of all beings; knowing the thoughts of others; eliminating the feeling of hunger and thirst; making oneself invisible, as light as a feather, as small as an ant or as big as an elephant; materializing things out of thin air.

Preconditions for initiation

As a conclusion to this chapter the preconditions for initiation should be mentioned. Like the teachers of the wisdom of Vedanta, who demand from the candidates for *brahma vidya* the fulfilment of certain preconditions, the Masters of Surat Shabd Yoga insist on the observance of definite principles before initiation. These must be adhered to without compromise, both before and after initiation. Firstly, it is essential to adopt a *purely vegetarian diet* (no meat, eggs, fish or fowl), in order not to increase the already heavy burden of sins resting upon the soul by killing animals and eating their flesh. Secondly, the Masters demand *complete abstinence from alcohol and drugs*, because alcohol not only befuddles the senses but also weakens the mental powers, which need to be strong and alert for a spiritual life. Taking drugs leads to hallucinations, which are by no means true spiritual experiences. Thirdly, the Masters insist on a *flawless moral life*, since striving for the highest spiritual goal is incompatible with a life that is not in accordance with moral and ethical principles.

From the time of initiation onwards, there is the further obligation to devote at least two and a half hours every day to meditation. Meditation should come first in the life of a satsangi. This means that he has to adjust his daily routine in order to have sufficient time for meditation. This no doubt means cutting down on other activities and giving up a number of things that might have been important to him. The observance of these four 'vows' is indispensable but, like in the teachings of Jesus Christ, the most important quality on the path of the Masters is love and devotion to the Lord. This was emphasized by the Master at every opportunity. As was pointed out earlier, the last sentence the Master said to me at my initiation was: "This is a path of love, and love only."

"How is it possible to attain this love?" I once asked the Master during evening satsang. He pointed upwards and said, "He has to give it." We often asked the Master about the nature of that love for the Lord. He explained again and again that true love only comes when one meets the Satguru in his astral or radiant form inside. At our present level of consciousness, love is always either intellectual or emotional; neither kind is stable. At one time the intellect may be fascinated by the Sant Mat teachings, and at another time it feels indifferent. At one time we feel love for the Lord, then at another time we don't feel anything. Yet we should always try to nourish the flames of love by all means at our disposal: daily meditation, attending satsang, reading Sant Mat books, *seva* or service to the Master, turning to him mentally whenever our mind is free, praying to him and surrendering to the will of God – in other words, living according to the principles of Sant Mat.

CHAPTER SIX

Looking Back

WITH MY INITIATION INTO SURAT SHABD YOGA, a very turbulent phase of my spiritual path came to an end. It had lasted for nearly ten years. When I made the first steps on this path, I did not see it for what it truly was; it did not show itself to me. I only knew that there was no turning back, but the goal itself was not known to me. Now it stood clearly before my eyes and I could look back over the distance that I had covered so far. How much effort had been needed to take all these steps! Sometimes I was close to giving up my adventure of faith, but he had not allowed that to happen because the very salvation of my soul was at stake, even though I was not aware of it. This must surely be the experience of every traveller on the spiritual way.

The whole long journey had been necessary; every turn taken, every mountain face climbed, every phase of inner dryness endured, had been necessary in order to reach a goal known only to my inner guide. Looking back at all the affliction and hardship I had endured on the journey that now lay behind me, I could sense the amount of grace I had received to enable me to reach the feet of the Master. Each phase of the journey had had its own significance, starting with the first hesitant steps

I took as a youth after my first experience of the inner light and the inner voice. From that moment, my life belonged to God.

In the next phase of my journey, the sixteen years of monastic life in the Abbey of Saint Erentraud, I had learned what it means to search for God and to recognize his will. The unknown One, who had become my fate, was my Lord, and I belonged to him. The third phase of the journey, my life at Brahma Vidya Mandir, had opened before me new dimensions of the knowledge of God and had expanded my vision beyond the boundaries of my own religion. I had grown deeper into the religion of spirituality, towards which I had been led by contemplative prayer and by my experience of the transcendent during my life in the monastery.

The last phase was discovering the teachings of the Masters, which finally brought me to the threshold of the mystic path on which I would find everything that I had been longing and hoping for: the practice of merging my consciousness with the transcendent reality and the union of my soul with the infinite divine Being.

My journey had taken forty-three years. It had been – if I had correctly understood the Master – a 'phase of remembrance'. The experience of light and a deeper dimension of consciousness that I had during that time had given me valuable 'stock capital' that I could take with me into the new phase of my spiritual life. I knew from experience that there is a path leading within and that God, who is light, can be experienced in the form of light. These experiences were a great help to me in understanding the path of the Masters.

I had made my inner journey as a Christian, never questioning whether and how Jesus Christ had taught his disciples the mystic path, the path leading within. These questions only arose when I considered applying for initiation into the path of the Masters.

From the point of view of Sant Mat, there cannot be the slightest doubt that Jesus Christ, the incarnate Word, showed his allotted souls the path leading to the kingdom of God. These are his own words: "I am the way, the truth, and the life." Many of Jesus's mysterious words, especially those quoted in the Gospel of Saint John, indicate that he taught the path of the Word or Shabd. But only a true spiritual teacher well versed in the path of the audible Word will interpret these words in this way. They relate, amongst others, to the listening to the Word of God, as for instance: "The words that I speak unto you, they are spirit, and they are life." The words of Christ cannot be interpreted as relating exclusively to hearing with the physical ears, nor can they be understood solely in terms of their ethical and moral sense. Obedience to a moral code may cleanse the heart, but it cannot fill it with divine life. This divine life is the Word that can be heard inside, which Jesus variously refers to as 'light', 'fountain of living water' and 'bread of life'.

The way back to God

The spiritual path on which I was led in my early youth by the experience of a supernatural light had been a way of searching for God and, simultaneously, of finding him. It had been a time of longing for God during which I had, at my own level, time and again experienced moments or phases of union with him. It had not been my own decision to follow this path; in my youth, before that experience, I did not feel any desire to dedicate my life to God. It was *he* who had put his hand upon me when I was still too young to think of such things.

As the years went by after this event, I realized more and more that God had become my fate and that my life had become an adventure with him – an adventure from which there was no turning back. In reality, this adventure was my way back to him, to the house of the Father, which my soul had once left with its descent into creation. Now he had called her back. He had kindled the longing for union with him in my heart because he wanted to unite my soul again with himself.

It was only through the study of the teachings of the Masters that I came to understand that the spiritual path is the soul's way back to God, from whom she was separated an immeasurable time before. With amazement I read the descriptions of the soul's descent into the creation by Soami Ji Maharaj of Agra* – how she became a captive of the prince of this world and how she became weighed down by a great burden of sins that prevents her return to her true home. His description (which I paraphrase) shows how high and far is her original home:

> The first and foremost region is that of Radha Soami, which is the beginning and the end of everything and circumscribes all. Below the Radha Soami region is Sat Nam (true Name) or Sat Lok (true region), which is highly effulgent and pure and is the region of pure spirit and consciousness. Two stages below Sat Lok is the region of Sunn (void) or Daswan Dwar (tenth door) and below this lies Trikuti, the causal world and the region of Brahm. From here emanates *Ishwari-Maya* or *shakti* (power), the subtle material of the whole creation below. Below Trikuti lies Sahansdal Kamal (thousand-petalled lotus), whose power supports the regions below it – Anda (the astral region) and Pinda (the visible, material world).

---

*Born Seth Shiv Dayal Singh, Soami Ji (1818–1878), as he was called by his disciples, taught the way of the Word, the Shabd, as recorded in his two books, *Sar Bachan (Poetry)* and *Sar Bachan (Prose)*.

If the soul wants to return to God, she must retrace the long journey to her true home that she made in her descent from there into the material world. In returning to God – and here the faith of Christianity corresponds completely to the teachings of the Masters – the soul cannot rely on her own strength. She can only do it by holding the hand of the incarnate Word. According to the Sant Mat teachings, the saviour, the Christ, leads the soul back in his Shabd form after having connected her in his human form with the sound current, the audible Word.

The Christian Church does not emphasize this inner way of salvation. Christians believe they are saved by the death of Jesus on the cross. Long before I came into contact with Sant Mat, I had lost faith in this theory, which was developed by Saint Paul. It raises a great number of unanswered questions. To me, the teachings of the Masters offer a convincing answer. According to these teachings, the path of salvation is a practical mystic path that must be walked under the guidance of a saviour sent by God, a true living Master. Seen in this light, the spiritual path is much more than a beneficial technique, which is how the Christian meditation movement sees it. It is, rather, something that is essential for the salvation of the soul, for her liberation from the power of darkness. In Sant Mat, the spiritual path is a path of salvation and a path of action laid down by God himself – a point that Maharaj Charan Singh emphasized time and again in the evening satsangs at the Dera.

The position of religion

In this review of my spiritual path, one important question remains: what was the position of my religion on this path? With deep gratitude I confess that my religion gave me faith in God and in Jesus Christ, moulded my life from early childhood and gave it a solid foundation. It taught me to love God and to trust in him, giving me support even in times of misery and affliction.

I grew up in the bosom of the Catholic Church, living, as it were, close to its heart. I received from it much help and inspiration for my religious life. In my youth, the truly great and holy ones whom the Church has brought forth were shining examples of love of God, which I strove to follow.

Admittedly, it was an ideal image of the Church that I saw and revered. I saw no shadows on its face and I knew nothing of the dark side of its history: the Inquisition, the power struggles, the depraved lives led by a number of popes, cardinals and bishops. I had only a very vague knowledge of the terrible facts of the Crusades and the sometimes questionable or violent methods used in converting 'heathens' to Christianity. Today it is clear to me that throughout history parts of the Church establishment have been misused by the powers of darkness.

According to my Christian faith, I saw the Church as primarily a mediator between God and human beings, an administrator of the divine mysteries. I believed that God's grace flowed through the hands of the Church by way of its sacraments, rites and ceremonies. This is the Church's own view of her unique role. I adopted this view as my own, receiving the sacraments and participating in formal worship in order to meet God.

However, my own experience of the mystic dimension of spiritual life did not come to me through these religious forms. On the contrary, my experience showed me that they were no longer of use to me. In a single moment, all that I had hitherto considered an expression of my devotion to God and a means of gaining union with him was rendered obsolete. Once God had pulled me into the depths of my own soul, it was impossible to be content with the traditional forms of a Christian religious life; they rather seemed like a curtain between God and my soul.

I could not explain why I had met God outside the framework of the Church's worship and the sacraments. Why had the experience of transcendence not come through these channels? I eventually found the answer in the teachings of the Masters, which explain that religious rites and ceremonies are perceived by the senses, so that the attention is held outside and fixed there. But God is pure spirit and cannot be recognized and experienced on that level of consciousness where the human intellect and the senses function. In order to meet him, human beings must turn their attention inside, so that the consciousness expands to inner regions, in what Jesus Christ calls 'my Father's house'. By practising the Jesus Prayer I had started this inner journey, but without the support of the broader understanding that was to come to me through Sant Mat.

Through the experience of a deeper layer of consciousness, a phase of my religious life had come to an end: I had outgrown the exterior forms of devotion to God and of contact with him. This does not mean that in leaving behind the exterior forms and signs and turning to the path leading within, I had abandoned my religion. I had just moved on from the level of symbols to a deeper level of realization, and had thereby moved towards the religion of pure spirituality.

The Masters emphasize that it is not necessary to give up one's religion in order to walk the path of the Masters. They say very clearly that Sant Mat is not a religion, but a science of the soul by which it is possible to overcome one's ignorance about one's true nature and about God. The teachings of the Masters show the sincere seeker of God a dimension of spiritual life that the religions of the world have lost sight of. On the path of the Masters each will find the fulfilment of the highest aspirations of his own religion, whether it be Christianity or some other religion. Sant Mat teaches that the key point is the need for a true living Master, someone in whom the Word of God has taken human form. Jesus Christ himself emphasizes this point very clearly in referring to his mission as a saviour of souls during his lifetime when he says to his disciples: "No man cometh unto the Father, but by me."

So in turning to the path of the Masters I did not desert my religion, nor did I leave Jesus Christ. My love for him today is in no way diminished, because he and the Master are one. This is not just a statement of belief – it is something I have known ever since that evening when my inner guide revealed himself to me as the Christ in the form of the living Master. There are the words of the Master of Nazareth, as laid down in the Gospel, which evoke within me a deep feeling of connection with him. His words are still a light on the way to me, especially since those words of self-testimony helped me realize the nature of a true Master. Moreover, it was only in the light of the teachings of Sant Mat that I was able to understand the mystic meaning of Jesus's words, which only a true Master can recognize.

On that memorable evening when I realized that the inner guide was the Master, who had been standing at my side since my youth and had accompanied me over the ridge, I began to understand that nothing had been in vain on the way that now lay behind me. All the love and devotion that I had offered to the Lord in the course of my life I could now take with me on the path of the Masters; not a single word of prayer, not one gaze on him was lost. My love had been directed from the beginning to the same power. Now this power had revealed itself in the form of a living Master. More and more I came to see how the sixteen years in the monastery had been a unique preparation for the path of the Masters. It was a preparation that quite a few satsangis considered a blessing, as they had had to make their way through the thickets of a worldly life.

With my initiation I crossed the threshold into a new dimension of spiritual life. Holding the hand of the Master, I would now walk the path of Surat Shabd Yoga, onto which he himself had guided me from inside. He would continue to be my inner guide, but from now on in a way only possible for a true living Master. The unique relationship between disciple and Master has already been discussed.

From the moment of initiation onwards the Master is with his disciple in his inner form, whether the disciple sees him within or not. Maharaj Charan Singh often assured us of this. This shows clearly how wrong I had been in my initial intention of forgetting all about the Master after initiation. I had not known at that time that the Master takes his abode in the disciple in his radiant form at the hour of initiation. Even if a disciple later turns his back on the path of the Masters, the Master will never leave him. This is a point often stressed by Maharaj Charan Singh. The same point is explained by the Master of Nazareth in the parable of the lost sheep.*

With initiation, I had come full circle. I had at last met in human form the one who had called me by name in my youth and who had been my unseen guide on the way. He had led me through a process of learning and transformation in order to prepare me for meeting him in his human form, because it was only in that form that he could teach me to listen to his Word.

---

*"How think ye? if a man have an hundred sheep, and one of them be gone astray, doth he not leave the ninety and nine, and goeth into the mountains, and seeketh that which is gone astray?" *Matthew* 18:12

CHAPTER SEVEN

Sidelights on Dera

AFTER HAVING SPENT SOME MONTHS AT THE
Dera, I felt more and more at home. I had grown accustomed
to the daily routine, made friends with some of the foreign
guests and some of the Dera residents, and become increasingly familiar with the teachings of Sant Mat. Above all, my
confidence in the Master had grown and, with his help, I had
surmounted quite a few obstacles. Day by day I had absorbed
the Dera's prevailing atmosphere of peace and tranquillity, of
meditation, love and devotion. I had gone through a process of
transformation, although I was slow to realize it. Satsangis call
the Dera a paradise on earth. This is not quite true, of course,
because the Dera is inhabited by human beings and not by
angels, but the presence of the Master permeates, illuminates
and transforms life in the Dera, imbuing it with a sense of ease
and serenity that does create a paradise-like atmosphere.

Every day in the Dera began at three o'clock in the morning with meditation, which everyone practised alone. Collective meditation is not recommended in Surat Shabd Yoga.
After breakfast and some kitchen work, we gathered every
morning for the Master's satsang, during which he himself or
a designated speaker explained the Sant Mat teachings.

We foreign guests were unable to understand the discourses, since they were given in Punjabi, but any time spent in the presence of the Master, having his *darshan*, was very precious to us, and we fixed our gaze on the Master. Some advanced disciples may even have seen light emanating from his physical form.

Some weeks after my arrival, I had begun exploring the Dera in order to familiarize myself with it. The Dera had taken shape by the banks of the river Beas in the course of nearly eighty years, in a place that had previously been a barren wasteland, cut through by deep ravines. The inhabitants of the neighbouring villages shunned this region, believing it to be haunted.

When I arrived in October 1971, I found there a sizeable colony surrounded by a big wall. The centre of the Dera was dominated by the *satsang ghar* (satsang house). It is a seven-towered building in Mughal style, built by Maharaj Sawan Singh between 1934 and 1937 for the purpose of holding satsang. It was designed to hold two thousand people, but by the time it was completed, it was already too small for its purpose and satsang had to be held in the open. Fifty years later, a number of huge, steel-framed sheds were built for holding satsang, which also served as accommodation for the hundreds of thousands of Indian practitioners who gathered at the Dera several times in the year for the big satsang gatherings.

Today the Dera is more than a hundred years old and is almost urban in character. Modern houses, administration buildings and some large three-storey guesthouses have been constructed. In the village of Beas, Maharaj Charan Singh erected a charitable hospital with three hundred beds that opened its doors in 1986. The hospital serves patients from the surrounding villages, regardless of their religion, many of whom might otherwise have no access to medical care.

The centre of the Dera had formed around the house of Maharaj Sawan Singh, who was the Satguru of the Radha Soami Satsang Beas from 1903 to 1948. I loved the 'old Dera' very much. One can still see there the small satsang hall, the well that Maharaj Sawan Singh had dug for his beloved Master, Baba Jaimal Singh, and the buildings that served as the Sawan Singh Library, the old Publications Department and early residential buildings. The atmosphere radiated by these old buildings was indeed incomparable. In this older part of the Dera, there were also a naturopathy clinic and a dispensary where those who came to attend satsang, mainly Indians, could consult a physician.

Board and lodging is free of charge for all the guests of the Dera. We were only expected to help by cleaning vegetables, washing dishes or working in the garden. In the afternoon, all of us, Indians and foreign guests alike, did an hour of work, called *seva*. When I came to the Dera in 1971, the big ravines the river Beas had created along its bank were being filled up. Enormous masses of earth were being moved – hills were being pulled down, the soil used to fill the ravines and the ground levelled. The initial depth of the ravines was five to eight metres. An easy chair for the Master had been placed nearby, so that he could watch us as we passed by, each carrying a basket of earth on our head. In spite of all the dust that enveloped us, the Indian disciples sang at the top of their voices. The women had put on their best saris and the children carried small buckets with sand, just to please the Master. Of course, they could have used heavy machinery to do the work much faster, but this would have deprived us of the joy and the merit of *seva*.

This kind of *seva* for the Satguru has a long tradition. It goes back to the time of the Gurus in the line of Guru Nanak in the Punjab. *Seva* of any kind for the Master is considered an important component on the path of the Masters. The most important *seva* that a satsangi can accomplish, however, is meditation – as the Master repeatedly emphasizes.

Sometimes we did *seva* at the edge of the river Beas, cutting the head-high sedge grass, bundling it up and carrying it to a place where it was stored. This grass was needed to fuel the open fires in the big kitchens, where unimaginable quantities of *chapatis*, rice and vegetables were prepared every day. During the large satsang gatherings, the work went on round the clock, and always accompanied by the singing of devotional songs from the Sant Mat tradition. A *seva* we particularly loved was breaking up old bricks into small pieces to serve as a foundation for new roads.

Over time, as greater and greater multitudes poured into the Dera for satsang, the rough land by the river was transformed into fertile farmland. Entire village communities came for the weekends on lorries and worked in the fields. The river provided sufficient water and a large irrigation system was developed. In 1987 the river Beas overflowed its banks, destroying the fields; the water even entered some low-lying buildings and provision stores. In the following years, a high dam several kilometres in length was built to hold back the water in the event of another flood.

For those staying in the international guesthouse, the evening meeting with the Master was always the highlight of the day. At that time, the small hall on the first floor of the guesthouse was still large enough – now the meetings are held in a newly constructed hall built over an expanded dining area. The meetings provided an opportunity to ask the Master questions about the Sant Mat teachings. The Master answered these questions very patiently, even though they were quite often repetitive, and every day we were fascinated anew by his answers. We always had the impression that the Master heard much more in the questions than just the questioner's words. The questioner stood before him and without doubt the Master was able to read his thoughts, so that these dialogues had a very personal quality, despite the presence of so many other people.

Sometimes at the end of their stay at the Dera the guests wanted to thank the Master for his hospitality and for everything they had received. The Master always pointed out that there was no reason to thank him, because the Dera belongs to all of us. It had been built by the loving *seva* of all, and all could make use of the opportunity to spend some time there in order to recharge their spiritual batteries. The Masters make sure that the Dera remains a spiritual centre, the sole purpose of which is to communicate the Sant Mat teachings and encourage the practice of Surat Shabd Yoga. All activities of the Dera serve this goal, and the time that a guest spends there is directed towards bringing his life more fully into line with the objective of the liberation of his soul and the attainment of God-realization.

CHAPTER EIGHT

Surat Shabd Yoga

W$_{ITH}$ T$_{HIS}$ C$_{HAPTER}$ T$_{HERE}$ B$_{EGINS}$ A $_{SYSTEM}$-atic outline of Surat Shabd Yoga, the teachings of the Masters. The central themes have already been mentioned in the course of my narrative; they are the Word, the living Master and meditation. They have been presented hitherto in a somewhat fragmentary fashion; what follows is an attempt to present these teachings of the Masters as a coherent whole.

The path leading within

In the years before my initiation into Surat Shabd Yoga, I had longed with great intensity to merge again into the depths into which the experience of the desert had drawn me. But once my phase of remembrance had come to an end, I failed. Although I still vividly remembered this experience, I was not able to revive its effect; it did not carry me along any more. The time had come to travel the spiritual path on my own two feet. The way that lay before me was the path leading within, the actual spiritual or mystic path that initiation had opened up for me. In Surat Shabd Yoga, this path consists of three phases or practices.

First, by repeating the words given to him by his Master, the disciple must completely withdraw his consciousness from his body and concentrate it at the third eye, which is also called the tenth door. This is the place that Jesus called the 'single eye'.* It is the seat of mind and soul in the human body, and is situated in the subtle body between the eyebrows. In Surat Shabd Yoga it is the point of departure for the spiritual ascent of the soul.

The Master's instructions are to close all the lower doors of the body with this exercise of repetition – in other words, to withdraw the consciousness from them so that the disciple's mind cannot wander into the world, nor can the world of the senses enter into his consciousness. These lower 'doors' are the sense organs and the organs related to elimination and procreation.

The restless mind, which is like a turbulent sea, is to be calmed down by the uninterrupted, concentrated repetition of the words of meditation given to the disciple at the time of initiation. All the images that ceaselessly arise in the mind, all the wishes and desires brought in through the senses, the whirl of thoughts, are to be put to rest by means of the meditation. Finally the mind becomes motionless, like the glassy surface of a pond. By this repetition the mind is deprived of all food; just as an oven goes cold when its fire is deprived of fuel, so does the mind become still when the *vritti* (waves) are calmed and the *chitta* (thinking capacity) is no longer assailed by them.

By controlling the mind in this way, one also learns to keep the body motionless so that eventually the practitioner becomes quite unaware of it. When the disciple brings all his attention one-pointedly to the eye centre, he will meet his

---

*"If therefore thine eye be single, thy whole body shall be full of light."
Matthew 6:22

Master in his radiant form. This is a moment of supreme bliss
and happiness that every disciple yearns for with all his heart,
but that has its price, as Kabir, a great Indian mystic (1398–1518),
hints at in one of his poems:

> Narrow indeed is the path of true love
> For it can hold but one, not two.
> When I was – ah! the Master was not,
> But now the Master is, and I am not.

When the concentration in the third eye has become perfect, the consciousness of the disciple crosses the threshold to
another level. It expands to the transcendental reality, which we
are normally quite unaware of. The crossing of this threshold is
a *process of dying*, an anticipation of the experience of physical
death. In deep meditation, the consciousness withdraws from
the body, as it does during physical death, the only difference
being that after meditation the soul returns again to the body.
The Masters point out that this experience frees the disciple
from all fear of death and that he will even look forward with
joy to his own death. In this way, the sting of death will be
taken away from the disciple of a true Master, for his own
experience will show him that death is actually an awakening
to another, higher level of consciousness; it is, as the Master
assures us, like awakening from a dream. Jesus Christ also
speaks of this process of dying as a necessary process that has
to precede the attainment of life: "Verily, verily, I say unto you,
Except a corn of wheat fall into the ground and die, it abideth
alone: but if it die, it bringeth forth much fruit."

It requires little imagination to realize that the first stage of
the path leading within is difficult to tread and may take a long
time – to go through this stage may be the work of a lifetime.
Faith in the teachings of the Masters is needed as a working

hypothesis, so to say, and great effort and an unflinching determination are demanded. One has to adjust one's life for the whole twenty-four hours and one has to set aside time for meditation every day. But as Maharaj Charan Singh explained many times, the disciple's journey is easier and meditation will bear fruit when practised with love and devotion for the Master. More than anything else it is love for the Master that moves us forward on our journey.

The radiant form of the Master

When a disciple has perfected this first practice of his journey, often after years or decades, he will meet his Master, as mentioned before, in his astral or radiant form at the third eye. From here the second stage of his journey begins. This is the *contemplation of the inner form of the Master*, in which the disciple is to immerse himself in that form and finally become one with it, as described by Kabir in the poem quoted above. The purpose of contemplating the radiant form of the Master is to fix the attention of the disciple there during meditation. The radiant inner form of the Master captivates the disciple's attention so that during meditation it does not slip down into the world of the senses. Maharaj Charan Singh mentioned still another purpose of contemplating on it: "The radiant form catches our attention so much that we are not allowed to go astray. Otherwise you will be lost in those mansions – there are so many attractions, so many attractions."

As long as he cannot see the inner form of his Master inside, a disciple may wish to use a photograph of the Master to aid contemplation. This is a question frequently asked during the evening satsang. The Master strongly discourages this practice because a photograph is lifeless, and imprinting it on the mind cannot bring about any spiritual effect. The photograph of a

Master may serve to keep his memory alive. It may also evoke the desire to see the Master in his radiant form and encourage the disciple in his efforts to meet his Master inside.

One evening, the Master also referred to the possibility that a disciple sometimes may get a glimpse of the Master's face within long before seeing his inner form. This blissful experience will be a great encouragement to a disciple.

In beholding the inner form of the Master, my prayer "Make thy face to shine upon thy servant", which I had so often addressed to God, will find its fulfilment beyond anything that I ever could have imagined. On my spiritual path, the Lord has already answered this prayer of mine in manifold ways: first, there was the experience of his hidden presence; then there was his gaze, which was like beholding his face; finally, this prayer was answered in an even more wonderful way by letting me see the Master, my Christ, in his human form. The ultimate fulfilment of this prayer will take place when my soul reaches her real home and beholds the Lord face to face.

During the early stages of his journey, if the love of the disciple for his Master is still unstable and affected by doubts, then by turning the attention towards the Master's inner form, that love will unfold beautifully and fill his entire being. It is here, and not before, that true love begins, as Maharaj Charan Singh emphasized every time we inquired about the nature of true love.

The sound current

The sound current, or resounding Shabd, emanates from the Shabd form of the Master because the true form of the Master is the Shabd. Listening to the Shabd is the third aspect of the spiritual path that Surat Shabd Yoga teaches. When the consciousness of the disciple crosses the threshold into the worlds beyond, the inner organs of perception are opened. The eyes of the soul, hitherto blind, can now see the supernatural light; the ears of the soul, that so far had been deaf to God's voice, now experience the vibrations of the creative power, the Shabd, in the form of an enchanting music.

The capacity to see this light and to hear the sound of the Word is present in every human being. But these faculties can be used only when we cultivate them by appropriate means. We have to extend, as it were, our inner antenna and tune in our 'receiver' (the inner senses of perception) to the transcendent frequency of light and sound.

When I first read about the sound current or audible life stream in the book *Science of the Soul* by the Beas Master, Sardar Bahadur Jagat Singh, lent to me by Mr H. Singh of Nagpur, I closed the book. The statement that one can hear the Word inside oneself sounded too strange to me, and I did not want to have anything to do with such things. But that book was not written for me, as Maharaj Charan Singh explained to me when I first met him. It is meant for initiated disciples who already have a basic knowledge of the path of the Masters. It required intense study of the Sant Mat literature on my part before I could reach at least an intellectual appreciation of the central mystery of Surat Shabd Yoga.

The Shabd, the divine Word, the creative power of God that called creation into being, manifests itself as the audible life current, which has different sounds in the astral, causal and spiritual regions. Soami Ji of Agra, the great Master and mystic, exponent of Surat Shabd Yoga in the modern age, describes those sounds, comparing them with the sounds produced by musical instruments.

> The reverberating melodies
> of bell and conch resound
> with the enchanting music of *veena* and flute.

The *kingri* is played to the beat of the *mridang*,
the *dholak* and the *pakhawaj* play on and on.*

The music of the Shabd that can be heard inside, however, is
unstruck music; this means that it is not produced by any instrument or any physical means. Nor is it just some lifeless cosmic
vibration. As Maharaj Sawan Singh stresses in *Philosophy of the
Masters*, "He is omnipresent and…pure consciousness." In the
same book the Master also points out that the "heavenly music"
is so enchanting, so charming and so attractive that the consciousness of the one hearing it will instantly connect with and
merge into it. The harmonies of the audible life stream captivate
mind and soul to such an extent that they desire nothing but to
listen to this divine music. The fascination of the material, astral
and causal worlds fades away through hearing this sound.

Hearing the Word with the inner ear is a universal human
experience; people of all times and religions have heard it. The
Upanishads speak of it; the Greek philosophers mention it; the
Persian prophet Zoroaster and the Muslim Sufis knew about it;
we also find it in the scriptures of the Jews, in the Old Testament, which testifies that the Word of God has manifested
itself in various ways. The Theosophists also know about the
audible Word, and Christian mystics and saints have perceived
it as a beautiful melody.

There is no doubt that disciples of a true living Master may
have to go a long way before hearing the Shabd within. But just
as they may have a glimpse of their Master's face long before
reaching the third eye, so also they may be able to hear an echo
of the sound current or audible Word during meditation, when
their concentration has become stronger.

---

*The *veena* and *kingri* are stringed instruments; the *mridang*, *dholak* and
pakhawaj are different kinds of drums.

Upon making contact with the Shabd, the soul, which is tied down by the force of gravity of creation, will now be pulled upward by the irresistible power of attraction of Shabd. She will be able to ascend through the transcendental worlds, finally reaching the source from whence the Shabd originates – the throne of God, the supreme Lord himself. Such is the liberation of the soul from the power of darkness.

The Masters often point out that the sound current is the food of immortality, of which Jesus speaks very beautifully in the Gospel of Saint John: "For the bread of God is he which cometh down from heaven, and giveth life unto the world…he that eateth of this bread shall live for ever." The Masters tell us that when the soul partakes of this food it receives eternal life. This means that after the death of the physical body in which she lived on this earth, she no longer has to return to the circle of birth and death.

For me, the connection of my soul with the sound current also had a personal significance. The Consecration of Virgins, which I had received many years ago, had been a symbolic anticipation of the wedding of my soul with the divine Word. According to the testimony of the Masters of Surat Shabd Yoga, the soul is the bride of the eternal Word – a thought that is also very familiar to the Christian mystics.

The soul and the Word, so the Masters explain, dwell in the same chamber, the human body, which the apostle Paul describes as a "temple of the living God". Yet the soul and the Word do not see one another and they cannot come together, because an insurmountable hindrance separates the soul from her Beloved. This is the dense veil of the human mind, which covers the soul and prevents her union with the bridegroom. By initiation, the Master had connected my soul again with the sound current; to experience the mystical wedding will be the supreme fulfilment of my life.

The path leading within, the connection of the soul with the audible Word, her liberation from the prison of this world and her return to the house of her Father is the foundation of the Sant Mat teachings. In the following two chapters I would like to familiarize the reader with some broader aspects of the teachings of the Masters dealing with the state of the soul in this creation, and in particular with karma and reincarnation. These ideas can be difficult for people brought up in Western societies.

CHAPTER NINE

God and Creation

THIS PRESENTATION OF THE COSMOGONY OF
the Masters starts with the two questions to which many seek
an answer: Why did God create the world? Why are we here
on earth?

How often we had asked the Master these questions in the
evening question and answer sessions! In his answers, he always
referred to the inscrutable will of the Lord, who called this
creation into being. The reasons for this creation, the Master
added, are beyond our comprehension; we cannot understand
these things at our level of consciousness because they go far
beyond our limited range of experience. Only the innermost
self, the soul, is capable of knowing the Lord's purpose for
the creation.

Of course, the Master knew the answer well – of this we
were convinced, because the Masters are one with God and are
not separated from him even while they are in the creation. But
this knowledge cannot be expressed in words. For this reason
Maharaj Sawan Singh answered, when asked the same question: "The best answer that I can give is to repeat the words
of an ancient sage: 'Ask him who made it. I was not with him

when he created it.'" When the consciousness of the disciple rises to a higher level, the answer will reveal itself gradually to him as he progresses.

The second question – why God has sent the souls into creation – is answered in a metaphorical way by Soami Ji. In *Sar Bachan (Poetry)* he says that the Lord gave the souls to Kal, the personification of the negative power, to animate his material creation. Since the negative power can create only matter but not souls, he was given living beings (souls) to populate the lifeless worlds. The birthplace of these souls is Sach Khand (the true land), the realm of the true Lord of souls.

In *Sar Bachan (Prose)*, which contains records of Soami Ji's satsangs and dialogues, he mentions still another aspect of the souls being sent into creation: "The human soul, *jiva*, was sent into this world to see the show of life." It was the will of the supreme Lord that the souls should witness this show of the origin and development of creation.

The souls, however, were not sent into the world just to be spectators; they were also to be players in the theatre of the world. On leaving Sach Khand, each soul received from the Lord – as Sant Mat teaches – her *adi karma*, her first karma, which contained in seed form her role in the theatre of the world assigned to her by the Creator.

The cosmogony of the Masters

It was a fascinating experience for me to read about the beginning and development of creation as outlined by the Masters in Dr Johnson's book *The Path of the Masters* and in Soami Ji's *Sar Bachan (Poetry)*.

Unlike the detailed account of creation in the Book of Genesis, in which the origin and the development of the world is vividly described, Soami Ji draws the picture of the origin of creation and its unfolding with a few lines: First the supreme Lord created Sach Khand, where he reigns as Sat Purush, the True Lord. In this region the Shabd manifested as the Lord's all-encompassing and all-pervading power of creation, which called creation into being. Then the Lord created two other spiritual worlds below Sach Khand. In these regions were charted out the causal, astral and the physical worlds, referred to as the 'three worlds'. The verse continues with the supreme Lord saying:

> These three worlds were created
>> from but one drop of me,
>> while I remain the unbounded,
>> unfathomable Ocean....
> I do not live in the three worlds –
>> only the drop stays there.
> That very drop operates the entire system;
>> it is this drop the Vedas call
>> 'the limitless Brahm'.*

And then the Lord adds: "None can fully grasp the secret of this creative drop."

In the highest of the three worlds, which the Masters call Trikuti (three mountains), the creative power of the absolute Lord produced the two essential elements of these worlds: universal mind and matter. Universal mind consists of very subtle matter that has no life of its own, but draws all its energy

---

*The word 'drop' hints at the immense power of the ocean of divine Being – one drop of the creative power of God could bring into existence all three worlds. In reality, the drop is the ocean and the ocean is the drop, as the prologue of the *Ishavasya Upanishad* states: "When fullness is taken from fullness, fullness still remains."

from the divine life current, the Shabd. It is a super-cosmic, creative intelligence, the structuring and organizing force in the three worlds, encompassing, integrating and controlling everything. The universal mind carries in itself the seed of everything that has taken shape or will ever take shape in time and space in the three worlds. This power is, as it were, "the architect of the multiplicity and diversity that characterizes the causal, astral and physical realms", as it is defined in *A Treasury of Mystic Terms.*

The second essential element in the three worlds is matter. In Trikuti it exists in its most subtle form, whereas in the worlds below, the astral and the physical universes, it takes on coarser forms. Trikuti contains the two lower realms in seed form. For this reason it is called 'causal' – something that causes an effect. Soami Ji also refers in his story of creation to the *tattwas* or elements and the three *gunas* (qualities of nature) that already exist in Trikuti in subtle form.

The Masters declare that the light-flooded beauty of Trikuti cannot be described – it is visible only to the inner eye. Soami Ji depicts this experience in *Sar Bachan (Poetry)*:

> Many suns and moons are seen,
> And many galaxies of stars are beheld....
> There appear before the eye, forests, mountains
> and gardens;
> And in every garden do flowers bloom.
> Streams and rivers with clean current, and seas
> doth the soul by bridges cross.

The sound of the Shabd in the causal world is Om, which was known also to the seers of ancient India and which is mentioned in the Vedas as the creative Word of Brahman. In his description of the causal world, Soami Ji also speaks of the reverberating sound of the beating of a big drum and the thunder of clouds.

From the causal region, the creative power of the absolute One flows down towards the negative pole of creation from its origin in Sach Khand – the positive pole of creation – and produces Anda, the astral world. 'Anda' is a Sanskrit word that means 'egg'. This expression pertains to the oval shape of that region, referred to for instance by Hildegard of Bingen in her book *Scivias (Know the Ways)*. The astral world is made of subtle matter and all forms of the physical universes exist there in a subtle form and are visible to the inner eye. This astral world is the big 'power station' that sustains the physical worlds.

Then comes Pinda, the physical worlds, the lowest, negative pole of creation. Pinda emanates from Anda. In these worlds, coarse matter and the physical forces of nature predominate, while the powers of mind and even more of the soul are greatly reduced. For this reason, the physical creation functions in a state of relative negativity – in comparison with Anda and Trikuti, utmost darkness reigns in Pinda. This condition is – as we will see – the reason for the development of evil in the world.

All the worlds that have been briefly outlined here are reflections of the highest, absolute reality. They are *levels of consciousness* described with reference to our human experiences in time and space, because only in this way are they accessible to our intellect. The Masters emphasize that Anda and Trikuti can only be perceived by the eyes of the mind and the powers of the soul when we go within.

This short summary of the cosmogony of the Masters should not conceal the fact that the origin and development of creation is an extremely complex subject that scientists will never be able to unveil completely, and that these worlds extend immeasurably far beyond the reach of our imagination or intellect.

Mind and soul

As the soul was carried by the downward flowing current of the Shabd, she was equipped with the necessary tools to be able to enjoy the show of the three worlds as she entered each of them: on the causal level, the causal body; on the astral level, the astral body; and on the material level, the physical body. In addition, each soul was furnished with her own individual mind, covering the soul as causal, astral and physical mind (corresponding to the three bodies). The individual mind is, so to say, a drop of the universal mind.

In the Sant Mat teachings the term 'mind' (Sanskrit: *man*, Latin: *mens*) is a collective term for the three mind-coverings of the soul: in Trikuti the *karan man* (causal mind), in Anda the *andi man* (astral mind) and on the physical plane the *pinda man*,* which rules the physical body and senses. *Pinda man* is known as the human mind. These three minds are actually aspects of one mind, functioning at different levels.

In order to understand the teachings of Sant Mat, it is essential to understand the nature of the mind, whose origin is in the causal world, Trikuti. As mentioned before, the universal mind consists of extremely subtle matter that possesses no life of its own; it draws its energy exclusively from the divine life stream, the Shabd. The individual mind receives its life

---

*The *pinda man* has four faculties: 1) *manas*: faculty of cognition and perception, of receiving and storing of sensory impressions, especially of feelings, taste and hearing; 2) *chitta*: the faculty of recollection and of discerning of impressions that are conveyed mainly through the eyes, like form, beauty, colour, movement, harmony and perspective; 3) *buddhi*: the actual intellect, the power of discrimination that makes decisions from the impressions received by *manas* and *chitta*; 4) *ahankar*: the organ of execution of the mind that carries out the decisions of the intellect. *Ahankar* is man's will, the seat of the ego, of his individuality, through which he distinguishes himself from other persons and from the outer world.

force from the soul, to which it was given as an instrument. Sant Mat also emphasizes that mind and soul are inseparably connected as long as the soul is imprisoned in one of the above-mentioned bodies. As long as the soul is enveloped by these mind coverings, she identifies with them. Only when she casts them off on her way back to her origin, Sach Khand, the highest region, can she recognize herself as a being independent from the mind.

The soul is pure spirit (Latin: *spiritus*). She is a spark of the divine light, a drop of the ocean of divine Being, and therefore immortal. The created material mind, on the contrary, is only a necessary tool for the soul to enable her to function in the three worlds. As soon as the soul separates from it, the mind will stay back in Trikuti, its place of origin.

Without the coverings of body and mind, the souls, as pure spiritual beings, would not be able to operate in the three worlds. The mind, however, is a fundamental impediment to the self-realization of the soul; it dims her light and clouds her view of God. This fact accounts for her present condition in the world.

After her descent from the highest realm, and being equipped with her several bodies and her individual mind, the soul could at first enjoy the beauty of the regions that she traversed, experiencing the material world with the aid of the sense organs. It was a paradise-like state in which she lived. In the Indian tradition it is called the Golden Age, in which the *dharma*, the divine order, was still perfectly fulfilled. Humanity was adjusted completely to the order of creation and therefore lived in harmony with it.

The prophet Isaiah describes the state of creation at that time and pictures the final condition of the world that will come to pass when the descendants of Isaiah, on which the "Spirit of the Lord shall rest", will take up their reign:

The wolf also shall dwell with the lamb, and the leopard shall lie down with the kid; and the calf and the young lion and the fatling together; and a little child shall lead them. And the cow and bear shall feed; their young ones shall lie down together: and the lion shall eat straw like the ox. And the sucking child shall play on the hole of the asp, and the weaned child shall put his hand on the cockatrice' den.

As long as the Lord wills it – and no creature can question it – the creation must continue, and the souls will be tied by the negative power to the three worlds. It is in the order of creation that the souls should be bound by this power. A soul that once has descended into one of these worlds cannot leave it on her own strength.

The ruler of the three worlds

In his *Philosophy of the Masters*, Maharaj Sawan Singh speaks of the 'divine law', the *hukam*, which is the divine creative will that emanates like a wave from the ultimate One. By this wave the two poles of creation are born: the positive power; and the negative power, which manifests the three worlds – causal, astral and physical – and rules over them.

Indian mystics of the nineteenth and twentieth centuries call this negative power Kal (time or death), a name that can be traced back to the Vedas. In adapting to the comfort level and understanding of their audience, these mystics have chosen to personify the negative power; they speak of Kal as a being that fulfils the task allotted to him under the supremacy of the highest Lord. The personification of the various aspects of God as creator, preserver, ruler, judge or destroyer and so on is very common in the Indian philosophical and religious tradition, since the presentation of metaphysical and divine realities is only possible in terms of our human sphere of experience. In accordance with the usage of the Masters, in this book I have kept up this tradition of personification of the negative power.

Kal therefore represents the power and ruler of the three lower worlds. He exercises his rulership over these worlds in two ways: first, on entry to his realm every soul is 'covered' with an individual mind that is a drop of the universal mind. According to the inscrutable will of God, this individual mind is the most effective means of binding the souls to the creation.

Secondly, Kal's rule over the three worlds is based on the law of cause and effect, the law of karma, which regulates in every detail all that happens in the three worlds – the evolution of creation in its various phases, the orbits of the stars and planets, the development of life on earth and the individual fate of every single creature. It is not limited to the physical creation, but controls the astral and causal worlds as well.

While truth, bliss, love and mercy reign in the kingdom of the true Lord, justice rules in the realm of Kal. Justice is maintained by the law of karma, and the souls who live within the sphere of time and duality, the sphere of the negative power, are subject to it. The term 'negative' indicates that this power operates at the lower pole of creation, while the true Lord, the positive power, reigns at the upper pole.

CHAPTER TEN

The Souls in the Creation

AFTER THIS SURVEY OF THE COSMOGONY OF
the Masters, now comes the crucial question of how it has
come about that souls which originated in the Creator and
were meant to be happy enjoying the show of the creation
are now in a condition that is diametrically opposed to their
creator's nature. Why are these souls suffering?

Again it is Soami Ji who very impressively answers this
question. Following the sentence quoted earlier: "The human
soul was sent to this world to see the show of life," he goes
on to say: "but when she came here she became completely
absorbed in the show and lost all recollection of the Lord, like
a child who goes out to see the fair, holding on to his father's
hand, but lets go of the father's hand and is soon lost in the
crowd. Now he is no longer able to enjoy the fair, nor can he
find his father and wanders from place to place."

Whoever reads this explanation will immediately ask why
the soul let go of the hand of the Father and got lost in the show
of life. The starting point of this development lies – as Soami Ji
explains – in the fact that she is separated from God.

The soul is, as mentioned above, a drop of the ocean of
divine essence. As long as this drop was in the ocean, it was

one with the ocean. When the soul, in accordance with the will of the Lord, descended to the regions below her land of birth, the feeling of individuality covered her like a veil. For this reason she became susceptible to the attractions of the material creation, let go of the hand of the Father and lost herself in the tumult of the fair.

The following paragraphs try to explain why the soul became lost in the fair of creation, getting caught up in the net of *maya** and falling under the sway of the individual mind.

In the net of maya

Over an immeasurable span of time, the soul descended deeper and deeper into the creation. Under the influence of her individual mind, which had been given her to explore the world, she gradually succumbed to the fascination of the creation. For this reason, she fell more and more under the influence of the mind. As the coverings over her body and mind became denser, her light became obscured. Eventually she was surrounded – figuratively speaking – by utter darkness and sank into a deep slumber. She forgot where she came from, who her Father was and who she was herself.

Thus the creation became like a net for the soul, in which she became more and more entangled. This net is very finely spun, using threads that the soul was unable to recognize because, in entering the worlds of the negative power, her light

---

maya: ignorance; unreality; world of non-existence; the power of deception which makes us take the creation to be real even though it is perishable (*asat* – that which does not exist, the unreal). *Maya* has human beings believe that they have a free will and are free to do or not do what they like, whereas a *gyani* (a wise person) has realized that he is only an instrument in the hand of the supreme One, who carries out his plans for creation. In Indian mythology, *maya* is often personified.

was already darkened. Since it is the will of the supreme Lord that the souls should live in creation, this net is inescapable.

The strongest thread of the net is – as Sant Mat teaches – the fatal fact that, on the level of earthly consciousness, a person is unable to experience the existence of the soul and therefore believes that his individual ego is his true self. That is why he identifies with his mind, emotions and thinking, with his body, spouse and children, and with his property. His whole thinking and acting is directed towards finding satisfaction and happiness in these things.

To search for happiness is part of human nature; we carry within ourselves an insatiable longing for happiness. In his *Confessions* Saint Augustine says that the reason for this longing is to be found in the soul's subconscious remembrance of the bliss that it once experienced. The Masters add that human beings, instead of striving to return to this place of bliss, try to find the fulfilment of their longing by chasing earthly happiness.

The second thread in the net of *maya* is that people consider the material world to be real because they are unable to experience the worlds beyond; thus they live, without being aware of it, in a complete illusion, taking the shadow as truth, the appearance as reality. They live and act according to this existential illusion and get more and more enmeshed in the net in which they were caught so long ago.

The third thread is the fact that people do not remember their previous lives because their consciousness has no access to the 'computer', their mind-body in which are stored the karmas of the untold earthly lives through which they have already passed. If they were able to read this book of life, they would carefully avoid adding new sins to those committed in earlier lives, the consequences of which they have to bear.

The Sant Mat teachings point to yet another thread in the net of *maya*, which is that we are subject to the three qualities or attributes of nature, known in Indian philosophy as the three *gunas*. These three *gunas* are the first subtle building materials of creation and are the basis of all other substances, including the five *tattwas*, the subtle or esoteric elements: earth, water, fire, air and ether; and the twenty-five *prakritis* – the manifestations of the elements in our bodies and their effects on the human mind. In the physical creation the *gunas* are manifested as light, fire and darkness. The fundamental properties of the *gunas* are described in the Bhagavad Gita, quoted below. Unfortunately they are unknown in the West. The teachings of the Masters agree perfectly with the statements in this ancient book of Indian wisdom:

> *Satogun* is stainless and luminous. It binds by creating attachment to happiness and attachment to knowledge. *Satogun* sets the trap of happiness and knowledge and binds the soul by attachment to beauty; it puts golden snares on the soul.
>
> *Rajogun* is of the nature of passion, the source of thirst and attachment; it binds the embodied one fast by the attachment to action. *Rajogun* evokes the desire for everything that a person has not yet attained and binds him by attachment to the things that he has brought into his possession.
>
> *Tamogun* is born of ignorance and deludes all embodied beings, binding them fast through heedlessness, indolence and sleep. *Tamogun* effects lethargy, sluggishness and foolishness in a person; his actions are not directed by reason but by instinct. The senses of such a person are dull; he is not inclined to work and gives himself over to a great need for sleep.

According to the individual mentality of each human being, these qualities of nature have their different effects – in one the tendencies of *satogun* are predominant, in another those of *rajogun*, and everyone will sometimes go through phases in which *tamogun* prevails.

Still another thread of the net of *maya* is the imperfections of creation, an essential mark of its nature. Although endowed with so much power, Kal was incapable of manifesting perfect worlds. Rather, they are tainted with existential imperfections. They consist of many mutually contradictory components. At the end of his story of creation Soami Ji mentions the cause of that imperfection. He says: "Know that it is a compounded creation." This means that the three worlds are composed of opposing qualities. These opposing qualities (Sant Mat speaks of the pairs of opposites) are the play of *maya* and have their effect on the entire creation, for instance as light and darkness, heat and cold, movement and rest and so forth. We experience the pairs of opposites as joy and suffering, love and hatred, praise and reproach, honour and shame, satisfaction and disappointment, etc.

It is indeed this polarity, the duality with its opposites, which is characteristic of the three worlds below the highest plane; it exists only in them. Beyond the sphere of the negative power, in the realm of the highest Lord, there are no opposites, not even good and bad – these are projections of the mind. The Lord is, as the great German philosopher Nicholas of Cusa (1401–1464) puts it, the *coincidentia oppositorum* – the coinciding of opposites.

Human beings also bear this duality in themselves because they possess two natures: the divine one, their souls, and the material one, their individual minds and their bodies. On the one hand they experience the centrifugal force of the mind, the strong, outward tendencies that prevent them from coming into contact with the divine and make them slaves of the objects of the senses. On the other hand, there is the centripetal tendency, the inward pull, the longing of the soul for transcendence, for God. This longing, however, remains underdeveloped as long as they do not lead a spiritual life.

Another imperfection of the realm of the negative power is its transitory nature. It is in a condition of perpetual change – coming into being and passing away. The creatures of Kal's realm are subject to birth and death because it is beyond his power to give them life. Since the immortal soul lives together with the mind in a perishable body, she is condemned to reincarnate after the death of one body into a new one, because the death of a creature does not release the soul from its fetters of karma. Indian philosophy explains the creation in terms of eight million four hundred thousand forms of life. The soul is thus held captive in the creation as it reincarnates again and again in different forms. The Masters point out that in this endless cycle of birth and death, it is extremely rare to obtain a human form. They point out how precious the human birth is because it is in the human form alone that the soul can find release from the lower worlds and return to its divine source.

I have attempted to show in a concise manner the extent of the entanglement of the soul in the net of *maya*; for more details, the reader is referred to the Sant Mat literature. The Masters tirelessly point to these facts in their satsangs and letters. Their teachings about Kal and *maya* have opened my eyes and made me realize how inescapably my soul and the souls of all people are ensnared in the creation.

Under the sway of the mind

The second reason why the soul, after descending into the creation, let go of the hand of the Father is, according to the teachings of the Masters, *her individual mind*. Furnished with its several faculties, the mind enables the soul to operate in a physical body. By the faculties of *manas* and *chitta* it receives and stores the impressions that the senses of the human body transmit to it. Through mind and senses we are able to enjoy the glory and beauty of the world and to explore the mysteries of creation.

The Masters point out that the human mind has become completely dependent on the senses of the body. In this way it has become their slave, just as the soul has become the slave of the mind. Under the influence of the sense perceptions the mind has developed five negative qualities that are opposite to the positive qualities supplied to it by nature. The Masters call the negative qualities the five perversions of the human mind, the five vices, or the five robbers; Christian moral theology calls them the five cardinal sins. They burden human beings like a severe illness. These five perversions are:

Lust: Sexuality, which was given to human beings for the reproduction of the species, turned into voluptuousness, pulling them down to the level of animals driven by their instincts. In a wider sense, lust includes every form of hedonism, licentiousness and lack of restraint in satisfying the senses and the desires of the body, including the abuse of alcohol and drugs.

Anger, rage: People are social beings, and therefore it is a part of human nature to establish social relationships with others. These relationships are strongly disturbed by the second perversion of the human mind, anger and hatred. This vice destroys the harmony between people, creating quarrels and discord amongst them, and it is the cause of wars between nations. Anger is a raging fire that destroys everything noble in human beings.

Avarice, greed, covetousness: People have a natural desire to seek security in life by acquiring material goods; under the influence of the senses this desire degenerates into avarice and greed. By these negative qualities we are pulled down to the level of the things that we crave and are enslaved by them. Avarice makes people unscrupulous, ruthless and heartless in dealings with their fellow beings.

Attachment: The positive capacity of the human mind to persevere, and our sense of responsibility and duty, degenerate into attachment to other people and things. People are embroiled in the world because they are blinded by *maya*, the ephemeral world of phenomena. Attachment makes human beings slaves and prevents them from turning to higher, spiritual matters.

Egocentricity, egotism, pride, vanity: The fifth most severe disease of the human mind is the perversion of ego, or I-ness. The ego in human beings is part of their nature; it is the basis of their individuality and at the same time it is the individual mind's faculty of execution, its will. By the cancer-like growth of their ego, people become conceited and proud, self-righteous and self-opinionated. They close their heart to the love of God and their fellow beings.

Once the human mind comes under the dictates of the senses, it insatiably chases after sense pleasures, but these offer only short-lived enjoyment. As the Masters point out, the soul has to bear the consequences of this fatal error. The mind, which should be the soul's servant, becomes a despot. It is then the soul's worst enemy; under its influence the soul let go of the hand of her Father and now the mind does all it can to prevent her from taking hold of it again.

The law of cause and effect

When we look at our own lives and those of others, we get the impression that to a large extent we are governed by blind fate and that the course of life is often determined by coincidences and circumstances that are out of our control. Due to our experiences in life, we may come to the conclusion that fate is not only blind but also unjust at times.

This is indeed one of humanity's great unanswered questions, and is treated at length in, for instance, the Book of Job. Who is responsible for the fact that a seemingly blind and unjust fate reigns on earth and that often enough good people must suffer, whereas sinners remain unpunished? To a devout Christian, this paradox is insoluble. I, too, could not explain why God, whom my religion calls a loving and merciful Father, permits so much apparent injustice on earth. It is a question that puzzles all people, and I only found the answer in the teachings of the Masters in the law of cause and effect, the law of karma.

As long as the soul was master of her individual mind, she lived in harmony with the law of cause and effect. In the Golden Age she therefore could enjoy the creation and at the same time partake of the unending divine bliss. But with the passing of the *yugas,** she forgot the supreme Lord and the origin of her being; unconscious of her own existence, she got

---

*The Indian tradition, referred to by the Masters when speaking of the immensity of time, describes a cycle of four *yugas* (ages, epochs) revolving perpetually in eternity: *Satyuga* is the Golden Age, in which the divine law is still perfectly fulfilled. Human beings naturally adapt to this law. *Tretayuga* is the Silver Age, in which human beings start to act purposefully, meaning that they begin to act with certain goals in mind, as for instance in offering a sacrifice to gain the favour of a deity. *Dvaparyuga* is the Copper Age, in which lawlessness and disobedience against the divine law are prevalent. Illness and mishaps occur, desires creep in, and sacrifices are offered to the deities to prevent misfortune. *Kaliyuga* is the Iron Age, in which the divine law is hardly fulfilled and the world is drifting towards doomsday. The four *yugas* are said to cover a period of 4,320,000 years. One cycle of the four ages is a *maha yuga*, a great age. One thousand *maha yugas* are one *kalpa*, which is called 'a day of Brahm'. Then follows *pralaya*, in which the three worlds – material, astral and causal – are dissolved. Then the whole cycle recommences.

caught up in the net of *maya* and became a slave of the mind. Consequently, she was caught up in the mechanism of karma and oppressed by it.

According to the teachings of the Masters, every action a person takes, every word he utters, every thought he thinks, every experience he has, every motive by which he is led, his every desire – are all stored in his mental body like seeds. Nothing is lost, nothing is forgotten. Every seed must bear its fruit, as Saint Paul writes in his letter to the Galatians: "For whatsoever a man soweth, that shall he also reap." The fruits he must reap are the rewards for his good deeds, and the punishments are the consequences of his bad ones. Both will be determined by the law of karma, which is perfectly neutral and objective and works automatically, with unfailing certainty, absolute accuracy and incorruptible justice. The reward of one's deeds must be received and all debts must be paid. And the Master of Nazareth himself does not leave any doubt about this law.*

In particular, the Masters point out that whatever a person inflicts on his fellow creatures comes back to him like a boomerang. Each person must account for all the suffering he has caused others. This concerns not only his fellow human beings, but also his fellow creatures, the animals. Seen in this light, any cruelty to animals, any exploitation, vivisection or experimentation, as well as all killing (or having them killed) in order to eat their flesh, takes on an altogether new significance. For this reason, eating meat is avoided by disciples of a true Master, because killing a living creature causes serious consequences. The suffering and the agony of tortured creatures comes back in the form of wars, natural catastrophes and the like. There is a

---

*"For verily I say unto you, Till heaven and earth pass, one jot or one tittle shall in no wise pass from the law, till all be fulfilled." *Matthew* 5:18

direct correlation between the wars that flare up time and again in the world and the killing of people and animals.

Seen from this perspective, nobody suffers innocently in this world. My own family, for example, considered itself free of guilt when the events of the war swept over us, but we were not innocent. We may not have done anything in this life that justified such suffering, but what did we know about the liabilities we had taken upon ourselves in previous lives, which resulted in our suffering in this life?

It is not just our negative deeds that have their consequences. Good deeds that are not done out of selfless motives also create karma that must be received in the form of some kind of reward. Good actions tie the soul with golden chains, and bad actions tie it with iron ones – but both are effective in keeping the soul imprisoned in the creation.

The wheel of reincarnation

Sant Mat teaches that a person can neither pay off all his karmic debts nor can he receive all his due rewards in one lifetime. Some of it will be settled, but much new karma will accumulate on his account, and the soul that is burdened with this load will have to return to earth yet again in order to collect both rewards and punishments.

According to the kind of karma one has, it is not even certain that one will be born again as a human being; one may have to take an animal form or even a plant body in order to pay off debts or receive a chance to gratify sensual desires that remained unfulfilled in a previous life.

When I read about these matters in the Sant Mat books and heard about them in the Master's evening satsangs, I was deeply shocked when I realized the extent to which the knowledge of the law of karma and its consequences had been obscured in Christianity. Christians do believe that good deeds are rewarded by God and bad deeds bring suffering, and they believe that one must atone for grave sins by dwelling in hell forever. But Christians are ignorant of how the law of cause and effect really works. The key factor lies in the decision by the Second Council of Constantinople in CE 553 to ban the belief in reincarnation as heretical. After that, it completely vanished from the dogma of the Church and the consciousness of the faithful, but it had been very much a living belief in the first Christian centuries.

Jews may have believed in reincarnation, as is evidenced by numerous passages in the Bible. Jesus Christ was considered by some contemporary Jews to be a reincarnation of the prophet Elijah, by others of Jeremiah or of some other prophet. He himself called John the Baptist a reincarnation of Elijah. In the religions of the East (for example, Hinduism, Buddhism, Lamaism) the belief in reincarnation is an integral part of their tradition. While reincarnation is hard for many Westerners to accept, ignoring it does not make it go away.

It is one of the threads of the net of *maya* that humans cannot remember their previous lives. If they could look back on their past lives and see the consequences of the bad deeds they have committed, they would try to avoid them in the future and would do their utmost to escape from the domain of Kal. Still, in our age it is admitted by many physicians and psychologists that sometimes children do remember their previous lives or that people by means of re-birthing therapy can look back on former lives; there is a voluminous literature on the subject.

The Masters also point out time and again that reincarnation can explain many things in a person's life: somebody comes into the world gifted with very special talents, another with handicaps; everyone has their special inclinations and tendencies that cannot be explained exclusively by heredity. These are the *sanskaras*, impressions on the mind that have been caused by actions and thoughts in previous lives.

The sequence of many lives that a person has to go through is a process of learning and purification. By experience they learn their lessons, even if most of the time they are unaware of the lesson they have learnt or are learning at any given moment. These experiences are imprinted upon their mental body and make them shun what in the past has led to painful experiences, just as a child learns to avoid fire when he or she touches it and feels pain. The wheel of reincarnation is turning incessantly. The soul that got into this round of coming and going under the law of karma cannot free herself. Only contact with the Shabd, so the Masters say, can bring about liberation from the circle of birth and death.

Before my first contact with the teachings of the Masters, my study of the Bhagavad Gita and the patient explanations of my fellow sisters at Brahma Vidya Mandir had already convinced me to a certain extent that karma and reincarnation are facts that determine our lives; but only the Sant Mat teachings gave me a comprehensive and coherent insight into their workings.

The origin of evil in the world

One of the most worrying questions facing humanity concerns the origin of evil and the cause of suffering and death in the world. It always seemed to me that none of the great religions of the world nor any of the philosophers of the Mediterranean world were able to answer this question convincingly.

The Jewish tradition and the Christian teachings hold the view that evil originates from Adam and Eve's transgression of the divine order when they ate from the "tree of the knowledge of good and evil". After having ignored this commandment, Adam blames the woman that God has given him and Eve in turn blames the serpent. Referring to this story, Saint Paul in his letter to the Romans, however, calls Adam the originator of sin: "Wherefore, as by one man sin entered into the world, and death by sin; and so death passed upon all men, for that all have sinned."

On the grounds of this statement of Saint Paul, Christian theology developed the concept of original sin – the sinfulness that Adam, as the progenitor of humankind, is alleged to have passed on to all people. Insofar as a person comes into the world burdened with sin, the teaching of Sant Mat corresponds to that of Christianity. The essential difference, however, is that in Sant Mat the origin of sin, of evil in the world, is to be found neither in a devil nor in the primal father of humankind but in each individual being. According to the teachings of the Masters, every being carries the load of his own karma with him from one life to the next.

As can be seen from the description of the net of *maya*, the origin of what we call sin and evil in the world lies in the nature of creation, in its polarity, in the duality arising from this polarity, and in the degeneration of the human mind. Sant Mat teaches that sin came into the world when the child let go of the hand of the Father, when the soul lost control over the mind and the mind succumbed to the interplay of all the factors mentioned above.

In this chapter we have explained why the child – figuratively speaking – let go of the hand of the Father and wandered aimlessly through the bustle of the fair, why the soul got ensnared in the net of *maya* and why she became a slave of the mind. It was shown how everything the human mind experiences – the net of *maya* and the law of cause and effect that ties the soul to creation – is all a part of God's plan, all part of his *play*. He himself resolved to put on stage this theatre of the world. In a verse by Soami Ji, the highest Lord says: "I decided to put on this play with full knowledge." It was his inscrutable will that souls should animate the three worlds, and as long as he wants this creation to continue, the souls will be kept here by the play of duality, the interplay of negative and positive powers.

The devil

Concerning the origin of evil in the world, one last important question remains. If there is evil in the world, is there also a devil? In the Christian traditions the answer is an unequivocal "Yes, there is a devil, a Satan, a Diabolus."

According to Jewish and Christian traditions, the tempter first appeared in paradise, where – in the form of a serpent – he seduced Adam and Eve into disobeying the commandment of God that they should not eat from the tree of knowledge. This story in Genesis is an attempt to answer the age-old question about the origin of evil in the world; it is here the devil, in whose existence both Jews and Christians believe, makes his first appearance.

In the Book of Revelations – also called the 'Secret Revelation' or the 'Apocalypse of John' – written at the end of the first Christian century, the devil is described as a renegade angel who rebelled against God and became his antagonist. He is depicted as a great red dragon with seven heads, against which Michael and his angels waged war. The dragon and his followers were thrown down to earth where they persecuted the people of God (the souls).

Although it is not expressly stated in Christian dogma, it is accepted implicitly that the conquered dragon has the power to act as an antagonist against the supreme Lord, to actively combat his plans and to threaten the welfare of souls. This view accepts that there are, in fact, rival powers of good and evil in the world that are fighting for control. According to this way of looking at things, God (who else?) was the creator of a being that was to become his antagonist – a truly blasphemous concept.

The idea that God would have created an entity full of malice and insidiousness who would become his adversary seemed unbearable to me. It therefore became a matter of great importance to me to clarify for myself one of the most confusing misconceptions, or myths, in the Christian teachings. The Sant Mat teachings show that the Lord has not created a being that has become his antagonist and whom one could hold responsible for the evil in the world. This view of the devil is a mental concept, a phantom that can be relegated to the realm of mythology.

How could this disastrous devil myth, which throws such a dark shadow on God's image, ever have developed? This shadow makes it very difficult to believe in the love of God. It also causes many people to lose their faith in God. The Father whom Jesus Christ preached about is all love and mercy. The existence of a devil who according to the Christian theologians is the originator of all evil was for me incompatible with Jesus Christ's message. It is because of this discrepancy that some theologians speak, as does Saint Paul, of the *mysterium iniquitatis* – the mystery of sin and of Satan.

The way people imagine God is a matter of central importance to them, for it determines their relationship with God. How can they have faith in a God and turn to him with love if they have to believe that this God caused them to fall into the hands of a Satan?

Whatever the legends in different cultures and times have contributed to the development of the devil myth, the Masters point out that it is simply a personification of evil in the world that is generated by the perversions of the human mind: lust, anger and hatred, envy and avarice, attachment to the world, egotism, pride and a craving for power and honour. In the final analysis, all the evil in the world can be put down to these perversions. Consequently, temptation to sin does not come from a satanic being – its origin rather lies in the individual human mind that has lost control over the senses because it is no longer ruled by the soul. Through its perversions, the individual mind has become the enemy of the soul – a tempter who himself is tempted.

In some of his parables, Jesus Christ clearly refers to some of the negative tendencies of the human mind. He speaks, for example, of the 'enemy' who, out of envy, sows weeds in his neighbour's field. The Master of Nazareth surely does not speak of the devil himself, but hints at the individual mind of a human being that has become a slave of the senses and under their influence has developed perverse tendencies.

It is also the individual mind that turns the heart of a person into a stony field where the message of the kingdom of heaven cannot take root. It is indeed the mind that makes the thorns grow, which suffocate the seed of the Word. The thorns are the worldly wishes and desires, the temptations by the senses that smother and overgrow the longing of the soul for the kingdom of God. For this reason, Jesus Christ calls the undisciplined individual mind an enemy, as do the Masters of Surat Shabd Yoga.

In Christianity, this negative tendency of the mind, active in all people, was personified and called the devil as though it had an independent existence. Doubtless this mind is very powerful and has developed negative tendencies, but it consists entirely of subtle matter and has no life of its own; it is not an independent entity, but only a mental power that is enlivened by the soul. This personification may partly be based on an all too literal interpretation of the parables of Jesus Christ, in which he adapted his teachings to the level of understanding of his audience by describing the enemy as the personification of evil. This literal interpretation might have contributed to the problematic devil myth.

The cause of suffering and death

The question of the cause of suffering and death in the world had deeply moved me ever since my youth, because my family was helplessly at the mercy of the events of the Second World War, and the death of my father had inflicted much suffering on all of us. Later, in the face of the suffering, misery and death caused by famines, epidemics and wars, I, together with untold others, again asked the question: Who is responsible, when for so many human beings the world they live in is a vale of tears and even a hell?

From the point of view of the Masters, the law of karma, described at the beginning of this chapter, is the cause of suffering in the world; by our actions we trigger reactions in accordance with the law of cause and effect. For instance, if a person kills another person, he may be killed by his victim in another life without either of them being conscious of this karmic mechanism. Time and again, people will be brought together by their fate in order to clear their karmic accounts. The law of karma, however, does not evaluate our actions from an ethical point of view; it knows neither morality nor immorality but reacts in a manner that is entirely neutral. We, however, do not experience the effects of the law of karma as neutral; we feel joy or suffering, pleasure or pain. The law of karma has no feelings; it does not suffer along with anyone to whom fate delivers pain, nor does it feel joy when anyone experiences pleasure. Only we humans go through these experiences, feeling the whole scale of emotions from highest pleasure to deepest suffering, from bodily well-being to extreme physical pain.

Only a living being is capable of experiencing pleasure or suffering. The more highly evolved a creature is, the more its body feels pain and the more its mind experiences psychic suffering. The law of karma yields its effects according to the stage of development of a living being. We humans are the most developed beings on earth, with our level of consciousness distinguishing us from the mammals below us. So taking the life of a human being calls forth, by the law of cause and effect, a much stronger reaction than does the killing of a fly.

The Masters also point out that animals and plants pass through karma as well, yet without creating any new karma. New karma can only be created by human beings, as they perform conscious actions and can think and judge. By virtue of having a sense of discrimination, of being able to distinguish right from wrong, we are responsible for what we do in life.

The section dealing with the law of karma at the beginning of this chapter mentions the rewards and punishments that people will earn for their deeds. But who punishes and who gives the reward? In Sunday school I learnt that God rewards good deeds and punishes bad ones and that committing sins is an offence against God. This view is probably held by all Christians, although the Gospels do not say this. The Lord neither punishes nor rewards anyone, nor can we offend God. Pleasure and pain, good and evil are categories of the domain of the negative power; they are called forth by *maya* and, as we have already seen, the absolute Lord is not touched by it.

What is, however, touched by it, is the Word made flesh, who was sent and continues to be sent to earth for the liberation of souls. In his human form, the Master bears pleasure and pain with his fellow humans. How often the Master of Nazareth refers to the suffering and joys of humankind. With his body and mind, the Christ takes part in everything that we suffer or enjoy. Thus, Maharaj Charan Singh once said, "When you are happy, I am happy too," a statement that moved his listeners deeply.

The cause of death lies in the nature of every living being, because Kal cannot confer immortality on the creatures of his realm; like the whole of the material creation, they are transitory. Therefore, death as such cannot be considered as punishment for any sin; only the form of death is subject to the law of karma.

For most people death involves pain and mental suffering. First, the process of disintegration of the body and the giving up of everything that made up a person's life is painful. Secondly, in the hour of death, people suffer from uncertainty about what is awaiting them after death. We suffer because we have no remembrance of the transition from one form of existence to another and because we cannot anticipate what will happen when we cross the threshold of death.

But is it really unavoidable to live in such a state of uncertainty, or can we become familiar with the experience of dying? If we could do so, then death would lose its sting and we could await it with calmness. Those who have had some experience of death, for instance people who were declared clinically dead but came back to life, assure us that for them death has lost its sting. They say that because of their near-death experiences they are now able to face death with composure or even with joy. However, since they did not really die, they cannot describe the actual process of death.

During the war, I myself tried to take the terror out of death by anticipating it mentally and taking refuge in the bosom of the Father, as described in the first part of this book. But this was only a mental anticipation of crossing the threshold of death – it had not been an actual experience of death.

Disciples of a true living Master can overcome death while still in the body. By raising their consciousness in meditation to a higher level, they can cross the threshold of death and enter the astral world. They leave this body, just as they will at the time of death, but then return to it again at will. This, however, is not a matter for beginners – it can be achieved only in deep meditation, when all mental powers are concentrated at one point. The Masters advise their disciples to 'die to live', because only conquering death in this way will open the door to the higher worlds and the spiritual regions. These regions must be crossed by the soul in order to return to her original home and thereby to gain her liberation.

CHAPTER ELEVEN

The Path of Salvation

THE PRECEDING CHAPTER SHOWED THE FULL extent of the soul's entanglement in the net of *maya* and her imprisonment in the creation in order to show clearly the background to the path of salvation of souls as taught by Sant Mat. Only if one is aware of the hopeless predicament of the soul and fully appreciates her need for salvation is one able to understand this path. The imprisonment of the soul, as described by Soami Ji in his parable, began when the soul let go of the hand of the Father. Her liberation begins with the attempt to take hold of his hand again.

One thing, however, should be quite clear: the initiative does not come from us, but from the Father. The soul has forgotten the Lord and her origin and got lost in the creation. When someone feels the desire to turn to the Lord, it is because the Lord himself has awakened this desire. He never forgets the soul. "You were always part and parcel of me," Soami Ji says, speaking as the Lord. Not only is God close to the soul, but she is – from his point of view – one with him, although in her present condition she is not aware of it.

It is the Father – to remain with the metaphor – who extends his hand to the soul. He does so by coming into the prison in the shape of his Word made flesh in order to release the souls that he has marked to return to his kingdom. In that respect there is total agreement between the Christian teachings and the teachings of the Masters – but not as far as the path of liberation is concerned. Christianity speaks of the *redemption* that Jesus Christ has effected by sacrificing his life on the cross for all who believe in him and who are baptized in his name. Sant Mat speaks of the *liberation of the soul* that is effected by the power of the Word, the Shabd, which again and again takes on human form.

God's plan of salvation

The Father extends his hand to humankind through his Word made flesh, the Christ. Whoever has faith and confidence in the Masters' teachings sees in the true living Master the Word of God, which has taken on a human form so that people may take hold of the saving hand of the Father. According to these teachings, the Master has a fourfold task:

First, by proclaiming the teachings he awakens people to the understanding that their soul is in captivity. In order to illustrate this fact, Maharaj Charan Singh sometimes told the following story: The son of a king had been kidnapped in his childhood and, without knowing about his regal background, had grown up in an alien land. Finally the king was able to find his son and revealed to him that he was a royal prince and invited him to return to the land of his origin. The same idea is mentioned by Jesus Christ in the parable of the prodigal son.

The soul is asleep, and it is the task of the Master to make us aware of this and to give us the desire to wake up from this sleep. As we have heard, deep down in the heart of each one of us, in the depth of our soul, there is a remembrance of the bliss that the soul experienced before descending into the creation.

It is to this remembrance that the Master refers, explaining it and showing the way to again experience true and everlasting bliss and happiness.

Second, when the Master has succeeded in winning the disciple's confidence in him so that the disciple takes shelter with him, the Master will take the disciple into his fold by initiating him and reconnecting the soul with the Shabd, that divine power that effects the liberation of the soul. The Master takes responsibility for the liberation of the disciple's soul, and he stands as surety to Kal that all the karmic debts of this particular soul will be paid. Maharaj Charan Singh assured us of this time and again. Disciples may believe that they themselves chose the Master, but it is the Master who calls each of them onto the path – as Jesus Christ made clear to his disciples: "Ye have not chosen me, but I have chosen you."

In his human form the Master will teach, guide and encourage the disciple to tread the path of liberation of the soul. It is indeed a wonderful experience to be in the presence of the Master, to listen to his words and to hear his answers to the questions of his disciples. Moreover, the disciple is able to see the realization of the Sant Mat teachings in the person of the Master – in his life without blemish, his selfless service, his patience and tolerance, his composure and his perfect love for his own Master and dedication to him.

Third, the Master projects his astral form within the consciousness of his disciples at the time of initiation so that, from that moment, this form is constantly present within them, even if they may not be aware of it. The Master guides his disciples on the inner path and accompanies them in his Shabd form through the transcendental worlds to their eternal goal in the highest realm. Even if the soul has already escaped from the domain of the negative power and shines in her own light, she must still traverse a region of utter darkness that she would not be able to cross unaided. Here, as the Master sometimes explained during the evening satsang, the Master carries the soul of his disciple through the darkness.

Lastly, the hand of the Father is *his plan for the salvation of souls*. The true living Master, the Christ of his own time, has a key position in this plan of salvation, because in his Shabd form he is the redeemer of souls and in his physical form he is the doorway to salvation. Every Christ is the manifested mercy of the Father and the sign of his love for souls in captivity. Of this love, the Masters give testimony through their teachings and by their lives. As Maharaj Charan Singh said on many occasions, "The Masters come to bring love," and it was always a wonderful experience for his audience to hear these words from his own mouth, spoken by the one in whom they had become reality.

Die to live

The Masters do not leave any doubt that the first phase of the way back to the eternal home is a process of dying. This means withdrawing one's consciousness, during meditation, from the body and from everything that makes up our earthly life, in order to cross the threshold of death – to 'die to live'.

The path of the Masters is nothing else but a process of detachment from the world and of the liberation of the soul from the clutches of creation and the negative power. The aim is to overcome the effects of the three *gunas*, to neutralize the pairs of opposites and to purify the individual mind and make it immune to the fascination of the world and indifferent to the enticements of the senses.

At the first stage of the path of the Masters, this process of detachment, including the experience of dying, is doubtless a painful and very lengthy one, as the Masters always stress. Detachment from the creation, however, is not completed even when the disciple has crossed the threshold to the astral world. To regain the original freedom that the soul possessed before descending into the creation, she must shed all the coverings she was furnished with when entering the domain of the negative power – the physical body and the physical mind, the astral body and the astral mind, the causal body and the causal mind.

The shedding of these coverings takes place in deep meditation. When the consciousness leaves the physical world and ascends to the astral world, the practitioner becomes unaware of his body and his environment. When the consciousness ascends to the causal world, the astral coverings of the soul stay behind. When finally the soul leaves the causal region, she leaves behind the causal body and the causal mind. Now she is released from all bondage and attains knowledge of herself. According to the testimony of the Masters, this self-knowledge of the soul is the precondition for the knowledge of God, for the experience of God that she will gain in the highest plane.

The necessity of detachment from the world was always emphasized in Christianity as well. Very early in the history of the Church, the tradition developed of turning one's back on the world in order to attain this detachment. People would withdraw at first to isolated regions and deserts, then later to monasteries or hermitages. This was based on the conviction that in this way it was possible to gain freedom from the world and to come nearer to God. For sixteen years I had followed this way, and it was a time full of grace for me, for which I shall always be grateful to the Lord. But finally it was he who took me out of the 'garden inclosed', because this way of life had fulfilled its purpose and, after the experience of the desert, it had become a hindrance on my spiritual path.

The Masters do not encourage seekers of God and truth to turn their backs on the world, to drop out of life in the world and to dedicate themselves undisturbed to the spiritual life.

The Masters rather advise their disciples to live in the midst of the world, to discharge their responsibilities towards family and society, to earn their living and at the same time to lead a spiritual life – to live in the world, but not to be of the world. The real enemy is not the world, although the world does try in many ways to pull our hearts away from divine matters. The real enemy of our soul here on earth is the human mind. The Masters emphasize that this enemy accompanies us everywhere; it goes with us into monasteries and even into complete solitude, and it is the mind that is to be conquered if the soul wants to escape slavery.

Conquering the mind

The mind is an indispensable instrument for mastering life on earth. Every Master uses his own mind to fulfil his mission on earth. The Master, however, has control over his own mind. Having conquered his own mind, he can help his disciples by showing them the way and providing them with the means to gain control over their own minds. He shows them how to make the mind a friend and finally to take it back to its origin in the causal region.

Sant Mat emphasizes that the human mind is very powerful. To overcome the mind is very difficult. It will not be conquered by running away from the world, nor by mortifying the body, nor by suppressing the cravings of the senses. On the contrary, it may revolt against such methods. As a reaction against suppression, it may break out with redoubled vehemence, seeking happiness through the satisfaction of its desires.

It is the strategy of the Masters to make use of exactly this tendency of the mind to strive for happiness. The Masters explain that to conquer the mind one must offer it something more fascinating than the pleasures of the senses – then it will turn away from them. The key is listening to the Word of God, the divine music. This gives the mind an incomparably greater experience of bliss and happiness than anything this world can offer. As soon as the mind hears the audible life stream, it falls under its spell. It then considers all the pleasures of the senses, which it had hitherto chased after, to be rubbish. In this way, the mind can be won over; then it becomes a friend of the soul that it had enslaved and regains control over the senses.

However, this is a long-term solution to the problem of conquering the mind since the Shabd is rarely heard at the time of initiation or shortly afterwards. The disciple must first develop the capacity to hear with his inner ear in order to perceive the audible Word, but with the help of the Master he will eventually succeed. Meditation is of central importance because by means of concentrated, one-pointed practice of repetition, the doors to the world are closed. Once these doors are closed, the world can no longer intrude into our heart, and the mind can no longer flow out into the world.

Meditation and a life lived according to the Sant Mat teachings sublimate and refine the tendencies of the human mind. The five vices – lust, anger, avarice, attachment and egocentricity – find no more nourishment and in their place come the virtues of chastity, control of the sensual cravings, tolerance and forgiveness. As an antidote to attachment to the world, the disciple cultivates the virtues of contentment and freedom from passion *(vairagya)** as well as discrimination

---

vairagya: detachment from the world and the sense pleasures; indifference to sense objects and to physical or mental pleasures; ceasing to identify oneself with one's possessions, body, spouse and children. *Vairagya* does not mean renunciation, but the gradual relinquishment of one's attachment to the transient things of this world as one becomes attached to the everlasting.

*(viveka).** Egotism and pride are conquered by true humility. Humility, however, is not obtained merely by realizing one's faults and sins, deficiencies and failures, nor is it to be had just by experiencing one's limitations and imperfections; as Maharaj Charan Singh once explained, the realization of one's insignificance is also a very important factor in inducing an attitude of humility. But the strongest means of conquering egotism is the disciples' love and devotion to the Master with whom they have taken refuge.

This love of disciples for their Master, from whom they have received everything, is indeed the most important factor, not only in conquering the mind, but in walking the path of the Masters at all. This is made clear by the advice given by Soami Ji of Agra in *Sar Bachan (Prose)*, when he says:

> Let the mind and the Sat Guru stand before you. If you obey the Guru, you overpower the mind; but if you follow the mind, you turn your face away from the Guru. Whoever has the pain of love will choose to follow the Guru, but one who has no fear (i.e., of offending the Guru) will be carried away by the current of the mind.

"This is a path of love," were the Master's last words at my initiation into Surat Shabd Yoga. It will be the love for the Master that enables his disciples to finally gain victory over their mind.

---

* *viveka*: the faculty of discrimination, especially between *sat* (truth, reality) and *asat* (unreality), between the transient and the non-transient. In the beginning of the spiritual path, *viveka* is a question of the intellect – theoretical knowledge – on the basis of which decisions are made, such as turning towards whatever is true, real, everlasting and good, and turning away from the world of illusion *(maya)*, from all that is transitory and negative. The real discrimination gradually comes on another level of consciousness, when the soul has shed her coverings.

Burning the seeds of karma

Perhaps the strongest chain that binds the soul to creation and to the wheel of reincarnation is the burden of karma that she has accumulated in the course of countless lives on earth. This karma is stored like seeds in the causal mind. Sooner or later, these seeds must sprout and bear fruit that must be harvested in the form of reward or punishment.

Sant Mat distinguishes between three kinds of karma. *Pralabdha karma*, also known as fate karma, is the karma that is allotted to us for the present life. *Kriyamana karma* is the karma that is created in this life. *Sinchit karma* is the balance of unpaid karma from all our past lives that has to be gone through in the next or subsequent lives.

Once during an evening satsang in the Dera, I asked the Master who it is that assigns to each of us that karma that moulds the fate that we have to go through in a lifetime, and who determines the actual course of life of a human being on earth, which is a mixed bag of the most diverse events. Can it be, I asked, that each of us has a guardian angel, as Christians believe, who is responsible for us? Not so, said the Master; the course of each human life is determined by the law of karma. Each of us is born with our life script, our role in life, already in our hands. Among all the various attachments, tendencies and inclinations that were imprinted upon our mental body by our thoughts and actions in previous lives, those that press most for realization combine to form our fate in a new life.

The karmas of each one of us determine the life form in which we can best live out what we have most desired in our previous lives or in which we can best receive whatever rewards and punishments we most urgently need to go through. Thus, we ourselves effectively design and shape the circumstances of our own lives; we choose our native country and our parents, we choose to meet certain people, visit certain places, and so on.

Now the crucial question is: How can the soul free herself from these seeds of karma? Is there any way to get liberation from these unpaid karmic debts? If not, the fate of the souls in creation is sealed because Kal does not allow any soul to leave his domain while the causal mind still carries any seeds of karma in it, for in his realm justice reigns.

It is the Shabd that burns the seed karma. As Sant Mat teaches, the Shabd is the redeeming power; whenever a soul is able to experience the Shabd it liberates the soul from her karma by destroying it. Once this is accomplished, the soul can shake off her last coverings, the causal body and the causal mind, and can leave the sphere of duality and cause and effect accompanied by the Master who connected her with the sound current. Kal cannot keep her back any more.

This shows the greatness and perfect power of a true living Master. He lives in the world like we do, but his true form is the Shabd, the power that liberates the soul, that gives her salvation. This is a truth that human beings can neither grasp with their intellect nor perceive with their senses, but the disciple who is advanced on the path of the Masters can experience it on a higher level of consciousness.

The soul's experience of liberation

The path of liberation as shown by Sant Mat is a slow process of detachment from the world that includes steep ascents and periods of barren dryness. But the reality of liberation can be experienced, at least partly, even before hearing the Shabd inside. For this, however, it is indispensable that disciples attend punctually and regularly to the daily meditation and live according to the Sant Mat principles. In the course of time they will notice that they can go through their fate with much more composure than before and that they can face the future quite calmly. It will become easier to keep an inner balance when going through the ups and downs of life and to meet with indifference the effects of the pairs of opposites that are inherent in creation. Such disciples will be far less affected by feelings of pleasure and pain, sympathy and antipathy, enthusiasm and despondency, and other emotions, because by means of the concentration obtained through meditation they will be able to withdraw to that centre where positive and negative emotions are neutralized.

The disciples of a true living Master will also find that they can free themselves more easily from attachments to people and objects because they gradually gain a certain detachment towards life as a whole. They learn to give precedence to their spiritual life when setting their priorities. In this way they gradually learn to see the people, objects and events of this world in the context of a wider spiritual reality. Since these things are all subject to change, they can never give lasting happiness; the more we become independent from them the more we work instead for that which is eternal and unchanging, the freer we will be.

The above-mentioned experiences are relatively small symptoms of detachment – yet even these are indications of progressive liberation from the world, and they should be consciously recognized as such. They are surely encouraging signs of progress on the spiritual path, where we must leave behind not only our attachments to worldly things and people but also, eventually, our body and our individual mind. Only then will the soul be free to return to the land of her origin, the realm of the Father.

Sometimes the Master was asked during evening satsang whether a soul that has returned to the Lord will ever be sent back into the creation. The Master assured us that this would not happen. Soami Ji deals with this question also in *Sar Bachan (Poetry)*, and from his answer it may be concluded that the return of the soul to her home will be infinitely more beautiful than the life she knew before her descent into the creation. There she will receive an infinitely greater bliss because the highest Lord himself will take her to those regions beyond her land of birth: the indescribable, the inaccessible and the nameless, purely spiritual and divine regions.

The four preceding chapters are a summary of the main aspects of the teachings of the Masters. They go beyond the knowledge and understanding that I had when I was initiated in 1972. They are based on more than thirty-five years of study and practical experience on this path since then. In 1972 I had only a basic knowledge of the teachings and had taken just the first few steps into this new dimension of my spiritual adventure. That basic knowledge would never have been sufficient to step over the threshold to new horizons. It was the Master's inner guidance that removed all the initial uncertainties and doubts. There were moments when the Master bestowed upon me experiences and insights that could not have been transmitted through the intellect.

I am conscious that for those who come into contact with the teachings of the Masters for the first time, reading these chapters will give rise to a number of questions that cannot be answered in the context of this book. Answers to such questions will in general be supplied by the study of the Sant Mat literature (see the list at the end of this book) and conversations with fellow seekers.

With my initiation I had – as it were – reached base camp and could now begin the ascent to heights beyond the highest summits on earth. I still feel today that treading the path of the Masters is like climbing a very high mountain, leading over steep rock faces and precipices. I never felt that after initiation I could afford to rest, even though it was true that my time of searching for the way had come to an end and the goal was clearly in view.

Initiation means the beginning of the first stage of the path of the Masters, which is a preparatory phase. The inner ascent of the soul only begins – the Masters always stress this point – when we take our consciousness across the threshold of the transcendental world. After initiation, it is essential that Sant Mat be lived. Day by day, step by step, the path of the Masters has to be trodden untiringly, without being able to measure the distance already covered and without knowing how much remains before the goal is reached.

CHAPTER TWELVE

Return to Germany

IN THE COURSE OF THIS BOOK I HAVE REPEAT-edly emphasized that I did not know why God had led me to India. The one thing that was clear to me was that the real reason had nothing to do with the many tasks that had been allotted to me. I never saw these tasks as a justification for my stay in India. On the contrary, I was afraid to define for myself the meaning and purpose of my life in India lest I might lose my sensitivity to the impulses of my inner guide as well as my 'eye contact' with him. Yet this one-pointed looking at the Lord was the essence of my spiritual life and I therefore had to live in a state of continuous submission to my utter uncertainty about what God intended to do with my life. Again and again I had to enter anew into my adventure of faith. At the same time, however, I was sure that the Lord would disclose his purpose at the right time.

This time came some days after my initiation. Finally the veil was lifted and God made me realize why he had brought me to this country. For many years this question had been constantly on my mind. I had been waiting for the answer for such a long time and now, suddenly, it stood clearly before my eyes. I saw that the Lord had marked me for the path of the

Masters and that I had come to India to meet my Master and to receive initiation from him.

To be initiated into Sant Mat was, I felt, the single most decisive event, not only in my present life, but in my entire existence as a created being. It was the main reason for the years of walking over the ridge, for leaving the 'house of my fathers' and for going to India. The years preceding initiation had been a phase of development, a necessary preparation for crossing the threshold into a new dimension of spiritual life.

I would probably never have come to this point in my life if I had not left unanswered the question of the purpose of my life in India. Had I prematurely answered this question myself, then in all probability I would have contented myself with the achievement of obvious goals in India. But then the far higher goal, initiation into a practical inner path of self-development, would have remained hidden. At the bottom of my heart I had been conscious of this danger, although I could not have formulated it. My inner guide had prevented my falling victim to that subtle attempt of my own mind to keep me away from the path of the Masters.

There must also have been karmic reasons why I had to come to India; I had to meet certain people, visit certain places and render certain services. But the main reason was, I felt, to come to the path of the Masters. When I became aware of this, the question arose as to what my task in India would be from now on. I was quite sure that I wanted to stay in India – but what good reason did I have for staying?

What I would have liked most of all would have been to stay in the Dera – to be always in the presence of the Master, to think only of Sant Mat and meditation. This would have been the fulfilment of all my dreams. The secretary of the Radha Soami Satsang and other members of the Dera management suggested that I might stay there. They told me that there was lots of work for me in the archives and that somebody was badly needed to supervise the guesthouse for Western visitors. My way seemed to be chalked out.

With these ideas in mind I went one day to see the Master, fully expecting him to consent to this plan. Purely rhetorically, I asked the Master what my task in India would be now, and I added what the secretary and the other members of the Board had told me. I did not remotely think that the Master might perhaps have other plans for my life, but straight away he put a damper on my enthusiasm – he asked me what I would be living on in the Dera. I already knew that all those who lived in the Dera had a pension or some other source of income and worked in the Dera free of charge. Since I did not have an income of my own, I answered that I would work for my living.

The Master did not respond to my argument, but spoke only one sentence that once again was to change the course of my life: "You should think of going back to your country now," he said. Hearing this, my heart nearly skipped a beat and I felt as if the ground was opening before me and I would fall into a bottomless abyss. Unable to utter a single word, I took leave of the Master and went away. For days on end I was incapable of thinking rationally. To leave India, to return to Germany, to live in the world that I had left twenty-five years ago, to take up a job again when I was forty-eight years old? All this seemed unimaginable to me.

When I had finally somehow regained my composure, I decided to make the Master give me a clear order. I wanted at least to hear him say, "You go!" Once more I asked for an interview with the Master and put the question before him, "Do you really want me to go back to Germany?" To this the Master answered, "You should not have anything against it.

One should live in the country where one was born." At this moment it dawned on me that my karma would take me back to Germany. There were so many things I still had to settle there, so many people I still had to meet, so many persons in need of my help, so many family obligations to be fulfilled and *sanskaras** that I did not know of before to be lived out. All this would become obvious in the years to come.

I did not, however, immediately start packing my bags and making arrangements for my return. I wanted to wait and see what events or circumstances would oblige me to leave India. While reflecting on these things, I gradually regained my inner balance. Only much later did I realize how much heartache, pain and tears, even desperation, the Master had saved me from through his advice. Had I not been warned that my karma would one day bring me back to Germany, I would have suffered great anxiety when I realized that after initiation my roots in India had started to wither. Now, thanks to the Master, I was able to watch with some composure how my situation in India gradually changed, because I myself had changed so much. Finally I myself determined the time of my departure – but that time was still one and a half years away.

After this stirring event, I was able to stay in the Dera for four more weeks; then I had to return to the ashram at Paunar in order to apply for the extension of my residence permit for India, which expired on 16th March 1972. The farewells from the Dera extended over the whole of the last day before my departure. First there was the last morning satsang, given by the Master himself. Then I had a farewell interview with the Master, where I could tell him everything that was moving my heart – although words were not needed because all my

---

* *sanskaras*: the good and bad impressions stored in the mind, the inclinations and tendencies of the mind, caused by previous lives, that come to the surface in the present life and influence thought and action.

thoughts were open to him. I spoke of the great transformation
that had taken place in these five months at his feet – how the
darkness had been dispelled and how love for the Lord had
been rekindled in my heart. I had experienced a new birth. I
felt as though my vessel was filled to the brim, unable to take
in more. Now I urgently wanted to put into practice everything
I had received during these five months. This realization made
the departure from the Dera easier for me.

During our farewell interview, the Master also mentioned
my Indian name, which he had called me by so often: Shraddha.
For me as a satsangi, its meaning is faith in the Guru – love and
one-pointed attention on him. I therefore said to the Master,
"The whole of Sant Mat is in my name." Smilingly the Master
answered, "It is not only in your name." This remark made me
decide to keep this name when I went back to Germany and
use it in the circle of satsangis.

In my last evening satsang in the guesthouse, the Master
asked as usual, "What should we read?" Normally, one of the
satsangis living in the Dera who accompanied the Master to
the meeting would read something to us. Since this was my
last opportunity to listen to the Master's voice, I spontaneously
asked the Master, "Please tell us what you said in the morning
satsang." (Since the Master spoke in Punjabi in the morning
satsangs, we were unable to understand him.) The Master in his
kindness complied with this request and while looking at me
he summarized his morning satsang. These were precious and
unforgettable minutes, like a farewell present from the Master.

The roots dry up

When, after nearly one year of absence, I returned to Brahma
Vidya Mandir on 8th March 1972, I was joyfully received by the
ashram community and I had the feeling of being back home. I

told my fellow sisters all about my journey to Europe, especially the keen interest there was in India and in the meeting of religions. I also gave them an account of my experiences at Beas and of my initiation into the path of the Masters. The interest of the sisters in Surat Shabd Yoga, however, was very moderate and some of them felt that it was not proper to have chosen another Master since I belonged to the circle of disciples of Vinoba Bhave. Before leaving for my trip to Germany, I had not spoken to him about my intention to go to Beas and possibly ask for initiation, but he must surely have been informed by the sisters of the ashram.

Vinoba Bhave himself had never spoken to me about the way that I had now taken, but some time after my return to the ashram, a well-known personality from the Dera came to Paunar to see Vinoba Bhave without my knowledge. They spoke about the Dera and Maharaj Charan Singh. Vinoba Bhave was completely in the picture about the Satguru of Beas. He said to his visitor that he had lost a disciple to this Master, but added, "She has done right." To my regret I did not hear about his remark until eighteen years later, when I came for a visit to the Dera and this very same disciple told me about it.

In spite of my happiness at being back home, the new beginning in the ashram was difficult. The noise and lack of silence in the early morning hours posed a problem for my meditation. One fellow sister would sing pious songs as early as four o'clock in the morning. This had not bothered me before, but now my meditation was quite affected by it. I searched the whole ashram for a quiet spot where I could meditate undisturbed, but without success. Finally I spoke to Vinoba Bhave about my problem, because I knew that he used to meditate in the middle of the night. He helped me by stopping the singing in the early morning but this, of course, interfered with the personal religious wishes of my fellow sister. As time passed by,

I learned to concentrate at any place and in any situation and not to get disturbed by noise and talking around me.

I tried to meditate for four hours every day. In order to find the time for meditation, I missed two of the three communal prayer sessions each day, only taking part in the evening session. The sisters knew that I used the other two times for meditation, and they accepted that I did not come to the temple anymore during the day. In this way, of course, I missed an important part of the community life and became somewhat isolated; nevertheless, the sisters did not try to interfere.

These experiences were the beginning of a slow process of detachment from Brahma Vidya Mandir that took on more momentum in the course of time. Gradually I realized that my roots in this country, where I had integrated myself to such an extent that I felt like an Indian, had begun to wither.

Unlike my sisters in the ashram community, my bishop, Monsignor Januarius, was extremely interested in everything that I told him about Beas, the Master and the method of meditation. He saw Surat Shabd Yoga as a new way to come closer to God and to experience him. We had only one talk about the path of the Masters. He never raised the subject again and he allowed me to go my own way.

In the beginning of June 1972, at the express wish of the bishop, I took part in a conference in Bangalore about the integration of elements of Indian culture into the liturgy of the Catholic Church. During the twenty-four hour journey I meditated all day on the train. It was a beautiful experience for me to spend the hours with the Master in this way.

In Bangalore I had a chance to speak about my experiences in Beas with one of my German friends, a Jesuit priest. His reaction was very positive. He showed great interest and repeatedly pointed out what a great task it would be to tread this path as a Catholic nun in India. He thought that it could open a door to the Christian mystic tradition, which had not yet gained a foothold in India. At the same time, a connecting element between the two could be created.

The conference had fifty to sixty participants, most of them priests or members of religious orders. I could not contribute very much to its success, as at that stage of my own spiritual journey I no longer felt able to support this attempt to integrate Indian elements of worship into the liturgy. I had been in favour of it before, though with some reservations. Now the use of rites and ceremonies of any kind whatsoever as an expression of devotion to God felt to me insincere. Through the teachings of the Masters I was beginning to understand that religious ceremonies belong to the realm of the human mind and do not lead to the deeper experiences of God. For this reason, I did not want to encourage anyone to practise such things. I could not reconcile my work for the Church with my conscience, and for the first time I realized that my roots in the Church of India had also begun to wither.

I had a similar experience six months later when I again went to Bangalore at the bishop's request. This time it was for a seminar on prayer in modern India. Since the organizers of this seminar knew about my spiritual path, they were hoping that I could make a major contribution. I was expected to open new perspectives on a deeper life of prayer and show ways to realize this. I tried to point to contemplative prayer and to explain its importance for the life of a Christian and the meaning it has, especially in a country with a mystic tradition of thousands of years.

I spoke from the point of view of Sant Mat, but without mentioning Surat Shabd Yoga. However, my attempts failed. On the one hand, I was unable to make myself sufficiently understood since my terminology differed from the Christian one. On the other hand, there was no great interest in contemplative prayer as such. Finally one of the participants said, "Sister, you have gone ahead too far; you had better stop and wait until we follow."

This remark all of a sudden made clear to me where I stood within the Church of India. I saw that I would not be able to render it any further service – contrary to the view of that Jesuit father to whom I had spoken a few days back. I no longer felt obliged to lead others to vocal prayer, even if the texts were inspiring ones that I had partly formulated myself. Nor was I even capable of it, for it was contrary to my own experience of remaining in the silence before God in order to tread the path leading within.

Here again I had to realize that my roots in India were drying up and that my mental living space in this country was getting smaller and smaller. But I did not try to prevent this since I knew that my time in India was running out. It was a symptom that I noticed with a certain amount of regret. On the other hand it would make it much easier for me to say farewell to India.

In July 1972, six months had passed since my initiation. These six months proved to be quite different from what I had imagined. In the beginning I had progressed quite well in meditation and I had hoped to achieve the breakthrough into the transcendental world during this time; the remarks of some fellow practitioners in the Dera had made me think like this. But my state of health and the circumstances in the ashram had very much tempered my inner urge to cover the way at running speed. I was obliged to realize that nothing can be forced on the spiritual path and that determination and perseverance are important virtues on the inner way.

In the following months at Brahma Vidya Mandir, at the request of Vinoba Bhave, I worked on compiling a German-Hindi dictionary. For this purpose I drew up a table showing the transliteration of German script into Devanagari script, in which Sanskrit and several national languages of India are written.

At the same time, at the request of a German missionary, I translated into English a book about meditation written by my uncle, Dr Klemens Tilmann. Shortly after my return to the ashram, I was given the chance to write an article about Surat Shabd Yoga, the path leading within, which the editor of a German Catholic magazine had asked for. This article gave rise to a range of reactions from the readers. I received enthusiastic letters but also strong criticism from Catholic clergy. Some of the readers found their way to the path of the Masters through reading my article.

In the course of the following months, the reasons for leaving India became more and more pressing. In the first place, it now seemed all but certain that my health would no longer stand the rather extreme climate and the spartan way of living at the ashram. I had already gone through some severe health crises and from time to time there were indications that in the long run I would not be able to stand the living conditions there. But more than anything else, there was no longer any need for me to live in Brahma Vidya Mandir and to put up with the hard life there. In particular, my spiritual life had changed my perspective. Indian philosophy and Vedanta had fulfilled their purpose; they had widened my mental horizons and prepared me for the next step.

It was also clear that sooner or later I would be out of place in the ashram community. I would be living on its periphery because I had outgrown the setting there, just as I had in Kellenried many years before. My roots were starting to dry up in the very ground that had nourished them for so many years. Still, the thought of having to leave was painful enough. I had spent so many fruitful years there, which were among the most beautiful in my life; I still remember them with great joy and gratitude after all this time.

By December 1972 I had not spoken to anybody of my possible return to Germany, except for a hint to one friend of mine in Germany. She had passed on the news to my fellow sisters at Kellenried and now they wanted to know all about it. In this way, my monastery was the first to learn about my plans. At the same time, my mother wrote telling me that my youngest sister and her family would be moving into a house of their own at the end of the following year. They were living with my mother, and when they left she would be alone in her large flat. This led me to prepare my mother for my possible return to Germany in a year's time. I told her that I might want to stay with her, at least for a time, until I was clearer about the next steps.

In this way, I was suddenly confronted with the fact that the time of my departure was fixed by outer circumstances, and it seemed advisable to take them into account. I now had to get used to the idea that this would be my last year in the country where I had wanted to live till the end of my life. My family, my friends and the community of Saint Erentraud at Kellenried did not react very favourably to the prospect of my return to Germany, so I was hardly expecting an enthusiastic reception – but I was confident that with the Master's help I would cope with this new beginning.

In January 1973 the ashram community organized a meeting for Indian ladies and girls who worked in the Sarvodaya Movement (uplift for all), initiated by Vinoba Bhave. One morning a participant approached me and greeted me with the words "Radha Soami", the Dera salutation that is like a "God bless you". Quite surprised to hear the familiar words, I looked at her quizzically. Mrs Kamala Mathur told me that she came from the Dera and that the Master had asked her to see me. I was so happy to speak to a satsangi after such a long time and to hear from the Dera and the Master. I felt a great longing to spend at least a few weeks in the intimacy of the Dera and so I handed Kamala a letter for the Master. Quite soon I received his reply, containing an invitation to spend some time in the Dera. The ashram community understood that I had to see my Master from time to time and they let me go in peace. In this way, I was able to spend the month of February 1973 at the feet of the Master.

Before departing for Beas, I informed Vinoba Bhave of my decision to return to Germany by the end of the year. I gave him my reasons, which he understood and accepted. His letter to me ended with the words: "Let God's will be done." From his mouth, this was no idle phrase. From his youth he had led a life in search of God and he was without doubt an advanced soul, conscious of the fated nature of human life.

On arrival at the Dera, I had an unexpected experience. As I entered the gate, I was surrounded by a wonderful sound. Much to the surprise of those accompanying me, who apparently did not hear anything, I stopped, spellbound, and listened to the sound that seemed to fill the whole atmosphere. This was − I felt − a welcome from the Master.

In the Dera I took up the customary routine; I went to morning satsang, did *seva* and then in the evening sat with the other guests, who came from all four corners of the world, and listened to Master's words. Many questions were asked. The Master kept telling us that he had answered them many times and that all the answers could be found in the books. But then he would add, "It is just an excuse for me to be with you." How much grace the Master poured out over the audience on these occasions was beyond our imagination.

During my stay at the Dera, I was able to speak to the Master about my decision to leave India at the end of the year. The Master advised me to take all the circumstances into account and then decide. Very rarely does the Master give direct advice on how to act in a given situation. He leaves it for his disciples, faced with events, to recognize the fated constellations of their lives – long since predestined – and to decide for themselves how best to deal with them.

In the evening satsangs the Master was often asked how we can recognize the divine will. He always emphasized that, at our present level of consciousness, we cannot know. We should adjust our life to the principles of Sant Mat and shun everything that is not in accordance with them. Through meditation we will develop the sensitivity to know intuitively how to behave or to decide in any given situation.

The Sant Mat teaching about the knowledge and fulfilment of God's will corresponds basically to what I had practised under the guidance of my inner teacher for so many years. This guidance had proved reliable even when difficult decisions had to be taken in the course of my life. However, I found that the teachings of the Masters about this elementary aspect of spiritual life were much clearer and more convincing than anything I had read before. Of great importance to me was the fact that a true living Master administers the karma of his disciple, and the disciple accepts his fate from the hand of his Master. In this way, the disciple recognizes the divine will, and this gives him great inner security and helps him to tackle difficult phases in his life with a composed mind.

Another question that was put before the Master many times was the question of whether we have free will. The Master always pointed out that, seen from the perspective of the Lord, no creature has any free will at all. From the human perspective, however, we have limited free will. But how much free will we have is not important. What Master always stressed is the importance of the motives behind our actions and our acceptance of what fate brings to us.

On 18th March 1973, I returned to the ashram. I only stayed for a few days, because on the twenty-fifth I had to travel to

Bangalore again to attend the seminar on "Prayer in Modern India". On my way south, I visited my bishop to inform him that this would be my last year in India. He was taken aback by this news, but did not make any attempt to change my mind.

Farewell to India

This journey to Bangalore was the beginning of my farewell to India, as I would not be going there again before I left for Germany. I had many friends, particularly in the south of the country, who had often visited me in the ashram and with whom I had established a very intense exchange of ideas over the years, especially about the Indian liturgy. They were all deeply shocked by my decision to leave India and to leave behind everything I had accomplished so far.

I too was overtaken by sadness at the thought of all the years of working together, and especially of all the tokens of friendship I had received. I found it difficult to cut the threads and to realize that everything would soon be over. My decision was respected, but often my friends were unable to understand certain things, particularly because I could not mention the real reason for my decision – the Master's hint that it was my karma to live in Germany. This would have been quite incomprehensible to them. One of them told me that by leaving India I would close a door that nobody else could open again. This was surely an exaggeration, but it shows the importance that people gave to my life in India.

During the following months, I again found myself in Pune, where I seized the opportunity to say farewell to many friends living there in the various seminaries and convents. Over the years I had been a guest there many times, and many of the priests and nuns there had visited me in the ashram. They too were all taken aback on hearing of my decision to leave India, but they also emphasized that many things had been set in motion during the years of our cooperation and that they were grateful for everything that had come out of our meeting each other.

In Pune I had another long talk with Father N., the German Jesuit who had encouraged me to embrace the path of Surat Shabd Yoga. We spoke about the need to interconnect the Christian mystic tradition and Sant Mat. This idea began to occupy my thoughts more and more. During the last year I had been reading Meister Eckhart and I had found many wonderful thoughts in his writings that seemed to speak of the same inner experiences as did the great Indian and Persian mystics. It was important, I felt, that such writings should be given a place in the Sant Mat literature. This was also Maharaj Charan Singh's wish; he spoke about it during my farewell interview in the Dera at the end of 1973.

Finally, my time in Brahma Vidya Mandir had come to an end. Before leaving for Germany I wanted to spend a few months in the Dera, and I had fixed the date for saying my farewells to the ashram for 21st September 1973. Some days before that, I had gone to Balharshah to take leave of Monsignor Januarius, who had received me eight years before with so much understanding and who had followed my path in India with so much interest. Both of us had difficulty knowing what to say, and each of us was having his own thoughts. The pain of parting was eased to some extent only by the fact that we would meet again in Munich in a year's time, as the bishop had planned a trip to Europe.

Then came the hour of my departure from Brahma Vidya Mandir. The whole ashram community had gathered, including the brothers from the nearby Paramdham Ashram. I again explained my reasons for leaving India and spoke about my future in Germany. I emphasized to my fellow sisters and brothers how happy I had been in their midst and how beautiful the years spent together had been. We were filled with sadness by the thought that these eight years had come to an end.

This time of bidding farewell was a kind of death experience for me, and I felt quite numb. It often seemed as if I were a mere spectator of all that happened. Although I had started the whole process myself, it now seemed to be playing out automatically before my eyes; sometimes everything seemed unreal.

On the morning of 21st September 1973, I left Paunar. Half of the ashram community accompanied me to the station, where the farewell scene caused a sensation amongst the travellers in the train. After a thirty-six hour journey I finally reached Beas. During the long journey I had time to reflect on what was now a *fait accompli*. A line had been drawn under eight eventful years and now I was living as if in a kind of void. Although many of my roots in India had already withered away, others were still deeply buried in Indian soil and it was painful to pull them out. The three months at the Dera would help me to gain some distance, to compose myself and to inwardly prepare for the life ahead.

The day after my arrival at the Dera I got the chance to speak to the Master, who received me with great kindness. I wanted to use the time in the Dera to build a deep and firm Sant Mat foundation, to establish a still more intense spiritual relationship with the Master and, above all, to give a lot of my time to meditation. It was a wonderful three months spent in the presence of the Master, with highlights that would stay with me for a long time.

I also wanted to use these three months in the Dera to think about my future life in Germany. The most important decision I had to take concerned the question of whether I should return to my monastery or pursue a spiritual life while living in the world. With my return to Germany the reasons for granting my exclaustration, for living outside the monastery, were no longer valid. If I wanted to remain a nun, I had to return to the monastic community – the convent of Saint Erentraud had made this unequivocally clear on hearing about my plans to come back to my country.

Was it important to me to remain a nun? I had insisted on going to India as a nun because this status had been important for my life in India if I was to carry out my tasks within the Catholic Church there. If I did not return to my monastery but lived in the world instead, I would have to apply to the ecclesiastical authorities in Rome for dispensation from my solemn vows. This would make me a 'runaway nun' and some people would consider me a renegade. This made me feel uneasy, but it was something I would have to live with. I would certainly not let this determine my decision for, in my view, the dedication of my life to God, sealed by the solemn vows when I became a nun, would not be diminished in any way.

Much more momentous was the point that if I were to return to my monastery, then the eight years in India would be seen as a mere episode when I resumed my former life in the monastery. And these eight years had been anything but an episode; they had been an essential phase of my spiritual path. During that time I had passed through a process of development that had inwardly transformed me. It had raised my spiritual life to a new level and opened up new perspectives in my search for God. Consequently, I would return to my community as a different person from the one I was when I left it. Most probably, I would find myself living among my fellow sisters as a stranger, not least because all the reasons that had caused me to leave eight years ago still existed – in fact, they would be even more problematic now than they had been before. The many hours of oral prayer and the celebration of the liturgy, the *opus*

Dei as Saint Benedict called it, would now be an even greater hindrance to my spiritual path than before my departure. If I wanted to have sufficient time for meditation, I would have to ask for a partial dispensation from attending the community prayer, and this would make me very much an outsider in a place where this very *opus Dei* was so central to the way of life. As I thought about all this, it became clearer and clearer to me that there was much weighing against my return to the monastery. However, I put off any final decision until after my meeting with the Mother Abbess and my fellow sisters.

The alternative was a life in the midst of the world – a life that I had left behind twenty-five years ago in the search for God. After twenty-five years of seclusion, the thought of living in the midst of the world made me tremble. Moreover, circumstances in Germany had changed fundamentally since I entered the convent in 1949. During my six months' journey in Europe in 1971, I had seen some alarming evidence of these changes. But trusting in the Master, I gathered all my courage and wrote down some guidelines that would help me to keep my bearings when I returned to Germany and, as was only to be expected, the waves started to break over my head.

The first point in these guidelines was that when difficulties arose I would never look back with regret at my decision to leave India. It was a decision taken following the instructions of my Master and after careful analysis of my situation. It was a part of my adventure of faith, in which I never had to regret any step I had made. I would continue to live my life in search of God. Now I would do it in the midst of the world, testifying by my way of life that it is possible to lead a spiritual life even in the bustle of a big city. I would earn my own living and assist my mother and my brothers and sisters whenever they needed my help. In particular, I would serve the community of satsangis in Germany and contribute to the spread of the

Sant Mat teachings. I would make my future home a centre of spirituality, where seekers of truth would find an open door. I would entrust the care for my life completely to the Master. He would continue to direct my steps as he had already been doing in such a wonderful way. After having written down all these thoughts, I felt much relieved and was sure that, with the Master's help, I would be able to put into practice everything I had set out in these guidelines.

Finally my time in the Dera ran out and I was granted a farewell interview with the Master, who received me with his usual kindness. I sat facing him at his writing table and he looked at me silently for a while. Finally, I asked him for some guidelines for my work for Sant Mat in Germany. He referred me to his representative there and then said, "Give satsang, help the people." He also spoke of the need to integrate the writings of Christian mystics into the literature of Sant Mat, and said that I should write down how I came to the path of the Masters. He also asked me whether I would return to my monastery, and I answered that I was not sure what I should do there, but that I would go first to see my mother in Munich. "Yes," the Master said, "we should look after our parents." These words of the Master were to be a pointer for the future, when I actually would have to nurse my mother.

We also spoke about the fact that, after twenty-five years of living in the 'desert', I would now be returning to the world and, on top of that, to the centre of a big city. The Master looked at me lovingly and said, "Don't be afraid. Do your work with a detached mind and don't get involved in things, but keep your mind above them." Then I said that I did not know whether and when I would be able to come to the Dera again. Hinting at his visit to Germany, planned for 1975, but without telling me about it, the Master said, "If you cannot come to me, I shall come to you."

That would have been the end of the interview, but I wanted to be very close to the Master one last time and so I got up, went around the writing table, kneeled down before the Master and asked for his blessing. The Master put his hand on my shoulder and said, "Be brave." With these words he dismissed me. Outside the Master's room, I was unable to hold back my tears any longer and threw myself sobbing into an armchair in the Master's anteroom. Professor Bhatnagar, who was also in the room, was quite startled. He turned to me and said, "Shraddha, the Master is always with you." After some minutes I had regained my composure sufficiently to go back to my room.

On the day of my departure, I received a last wonderful farewell present from the Master. Because of a strike, all rail and air traffic had been cancelled and I had to go to Delhi by bus, which would get me there late in the evening after a ten-hour journey, not knowing where to spend the night. I awaited this journey with some anxiety, although in the depth of my heart I knew that the Master would be with me whatever the circumstances.

The next morning after satsang, I went as fast as I could to the Master's house, where the foreign guests assembled every day, in order to secure a place directly at the Master's feet. When the Master saw me sitting before him on the floor, he exclaimed, "Shraddha, you are still here! I thought you had left in the early morning with the others." I explained the situation and described the unpleasant things ahead of me. I had hardly finished when a voice came from behind me, "She can go in my car and she can stay in my house." It was Mrs B. R., who had arrived from Delhi by car in the middle of the night; now the car had to be taken back to Delhi by the driver. Triumphantly, the Master looked at me and asked, "What else do you want?" I bent forward and said, "Master, I want you in the car." Everybody laughed, including the Master, who apparently enjoyed the situation because he had a good sense of humour. In this cheerful and happy mood I left the Dera. There was no longer any room for melancholy thoughts – only for joy. The Master really was in the car; although I could not see him I felt his presence strongly.

Many years later, one of the Master's disciples shared with me something that had taken place that morning behind the scenes. He said that he had come to Beas with the intention of giving up Sant Mat and the Master. Mrs B. R. had entered the room just when the Master was asking me about my departure. If she had come only one minute later, things would have taken quite a different turn. This really was precision work! Seeing how the Master had things under such perfect control was enough to make the wavering satsangi take an about-turn of 180°. His faith in the Master was restored by this small 'miracle' that unfolded before his eyes, as he saw the Master's hand in even the smallest detail.

When the aeroplane finally took off, the Master flew with me – at least that was how it felt. It was a blissful flight between heaven and earth, and I clearly sensed that my time in India had run down to the very last minute. More and more I realized that, after these eight years in India, I would return to Germany a totally different person than when I left it. My time in India had changed me completely. Each stage of this journey had left its mark on me. Above all, meeting the Master and learning of the teachings of the Masters had utterly transformed my way of thinking.

While the aeroplane flew westward, India sank behind the horizon. I was leaving behind much that had formerly been of great importance to me – especially the many people who had been near to me. But within me I carried a treasure chest of experiences and knowledge gathered in these years, which would stay with me forever. In particular, I carried with me the precious pearl of Sant Mat, for which the Lord had brought me to India. There were also innumerable memories of India that travelled with me, memories that would remain alive inside me and cause painful homesickness for many years whenever I recalled them.

As the aeroplane approached Europe, the future came to me in ever bigger waves. My thoughts flew ahead of me to Munich, where I would start my new life. The next day – it was Christmas Eve – I set foot on European soil. I was inwardly prepared for what was coming.

Living Sant Mat

THE END OF PART THREE COULD HAVE been the end of this book since, in accordance with the wishes of my Master, I have now told the story of how I came to the path of the Masters. However, the book would be incomplete without some account of how I have lived while treading this path. What is more, my 'adventure of faith' is not yet over – it has only entered a new phase. For these reasons, the fourth part of the book gives an account of the time since my initiation into Surat Shabd Yoga, during which I have tried to live Sant Mat. During this period of more than thirty years, not only has my understanding of the teachings of the Masters widened and deepened, but I have also developed a fuller understanding of my own religion.

While the previous three parts of the book are a chronology of my adventure of faith, this part is arranged according to subjects. It comprises four subject areas that describe my thoughts, discoveries and experiences on the path of the Masters since returning to Germany: a spiritual life lived in the world; the living Master; the mystic dimension of the Christian religion; the realization of the Sant Mat teachings.

CHAPTER ONE

A New Beginning

ON THE FLIGHT FROM INDIA TO GERMANY, I found myself in a kind of mental vacuum. India was now irrevocably in the past and the future was hidden by a dense veil. I gave myself up to the feeling of being outside time and space – it was a short period of grace before reality caught up with me. The moment of landing in Europe would be the moment of truth, like the moment when I had left my monastery eight years earlier. The Master had sent me back to Germany, and now my faith and my trust in his word would be tested. But my gaze was fixed firmly on him and I felt that he was holding my hands, just as he had done two days back in the Dera at the hour of my parting.

When I stepped onto European ground after a nine-hour flight, I felt dazed by the sudden change of scene. My body had covered the distance, but my heart had not yet arrived. It was Christmas Eve when I landed at Amsterdam airport and, during the bus ride into the city, wherever I looked I saw beautifully decorated Christmas trees. I felt completely lost in this big, strange town.

On 3rd January I finally arrived at Munich, the town of my birth and the place where my mother was living. It might have been sensible to go first to my monastery and stay there while I decided what to do next, but I thought it advisable to find some neutral ground where I could think things through calmly. My mother and some of my brothers and sisters welcomed me at the station. They were all very kind and helpful, but they showed a certain reserve. They were not sure what to make of me, so their attitude was one of 'wait and see'. Over the years, they had followed my life in India with interest, and now they were more than a little surprised to see me back in Germany. In the coming months, I had to face many questions from family and friends about the reasons for my return to Germany and my plans for the future. I found it difficult to deal with these questions because I suspected that people would neither understand my reasons nor accept them. I therefore adapted my answers to the understanding of the questioners, but this meant that the reasons I gave, such as health reasons for instance, were not really convincing. They must have been left feeling that I must have other reasons for giving up my life in India.

As we had agreed, my mother gave me a room in her flat, which I furnished in the spartan fashion to which I had become accustomed in the ashram. In the course of the coming years, however, I came to realize that different rules applied when living in the world, and I adapted my style of living accordingly.

From the first day of my return to Germany, I was firmly determined to stand on my own two feet in my new life. In the months before leaving India, I had resolved not to give way to any nostalgic feelings once I stepped onto the ground of my home town. I was determined to face bravely all the demands of this new phase of my life: I would rebuild the bridges that I had burned eight years before when I left for India, and I would weave my life into the German environment in which I now had to live. I even had to get accustomed to my mother tongue again, for after all this time it had become somewhat foreign to me. I also had to get used to the telephone, I had to dress in European style after spending twenty-four years wearing a nun's habit or Indian dress and I had to learn shopping, cooking and housekeeping all over again after years of community catering. The six months I had spent visiting Europe less than two years earlier now proved to be very helpful in this respect. Unbeknown to me, they had served to prepare me for my return to Germany, and the payments I had received for lecturing had enabled me to save some money, which I now needed.

After my arrival in Munich, I allowed myself a few weeks to acclimatize and to adapt to my new circumstances. After that I started to structure my life and, in particular, I began to work out how I would earn my living and secure an old-age pension. I wanted to sort out these things before deciding whether to live in Munich or return to my monastery because I definitely did not want to return to the convent just to secure my livelihood.

While I was busy with these matters, I quite often felt like an actress on a stage who is playing her appointed role – and actually life really is like that, as Master very often explained to us. People are in fact only actors in the play of life, yet few of them realize this. Instead of being just onlookers, they identify with their role – enjoying and suffering, laughing and weeping, according to the script.

Besides settling my life, I was also very anxious to speak with my uncle, Dr Klemens Tilmann, about the complete change of my life circumstances. As mentioned previously, my uncle had been very involved in getting permission from the supreme Church authority for me to go to India as a nun without living in a religious community. His manner now was reserved; he was more than a little disappointed that I had left behind what he called my promising task in India. He made it clear to me that he had not supported me at that time only for me to turn my back on that work.

The talk with my uncle depressed me, because it seemed impossible to explain to him the real reasons for my decision. If I had told him that it was my Master who suggested the return to Germany and that it was my karma to live in Germany, he would never have been able to understand me and we would have been even more estranged from one another. We agreed, however, that I should join a group of meditation teachers that had been formed on his initiative. Years ago he had written the book *Introduction to Meditation* and he expected that the meditation movement within the Church would gain from my involvement.

Regaining a foothold

At the end of January 1974, I began looking for a suitable job. First I applied for work as a bilingual secretary, because there were many positions available. But each time, preference was given to other applicants. I had a good command of English, but my professional career showed considerable gaps because of my sixteen years in the monastery and my eight years in the ashram. My age must also have stopped people from giving me a chance, for I was now fifty years old.

After a thorough analysis of my situation, I decided to return to my former profession as a social worker. I contacted the lady who had once been my superior in the Association for Catholic Social Service for Girls, where I had worked in 1947. They were urgently looking for a headmistress for a girls' hostel in Munich and I was promptly offered the job. It had not been my intention to take on such a responsible post right at the beginning of my professional career but, after some reflection, I agreed. And so my work began with a 'vertical takeoff' in which I had to mobilize all my energies.

These weeks of searching for a suitable job were a unique opportunity for me to surrender to the Master with unconditional trust. My life was in his hands and he would assign to me the place he had chosen. I was therefore calm and confident, having resolved to take from his hand whatever he was planning to give me. He would show me what step to take next, as he had done so often in the past, even before I knew anything about him. While trying to settle my worldly affairs, I had to cope with many banal and mundane things and I often asked myself whether these concerns would allow me to lead a life devoted to God.

This question weighed on my mind more and more: Would I be pulled into the whirlpool of worldly life now that no monastery wall or ashram fence protected me and now that I could no longer live in the seclusion of the Dera in India? The atmosphere in which I now had to live seemed to be completely at odds with a spiritual life, but I remembered the Master's advice to build the Dera *within myself* so as to create an inner place of refuge with an atmosphere conducive to a spiritual life. This was a completely new experience for me after living such a sheltered life for twenty-four years. Now I had to learn how to keep my tiny boat on course in the stormy sea of life. I had to put into practice what had appealed to me and convinced me when I was studying the Sant Mat books and listening to the Master's own words.

Had I not felt the nearness of my Master at every moment, I could hardly have kept my mental balance and overcome the initial difficulties, for the passage from one way of living to another was just too abrupt for me to cope with alone. The invisible presence of the Master kept me afloat. Outwardly, he was far away, yet I was never alone and at any time I could look at him; how often the Master had assured us that he is always close to his disciples. Even so, I would have to work very hard to keep the lamp of my longing for God burning within me and I would have to make great efforts to keep the Master at the centre of my life. What had been so easy in the Dera proved to be much more difficult in my new circumstances. Yet it would all be his grace. Individual effort and the grace of the Lord are the two requirements of success on the inner path – all Masters try to drive this message home to their disciples.

CHAPTER TWO

Monastery or World?

AFTER MY RETURN TO GERMANY, THE REASONS for my exclaustration, my permission to live outside the monastery, no longer applied. If I wanted to remain a Benedictine nun, I ought to have returned directly to my monastery. But I had thought it advisable that I should first stand on neutral ground before making any decisions. For this reason, I had returned first to Munich to inquire about the possibilities of a professional career and to secure there a life in the world.

The final decision about where I would live would depend on the attitude of the monastic community of Kellenried. While I was in India, I had remained in touch with my fellow sisters and during my visit in 1971 had renewed the bonds between us. They had also been able to read my articles in the magazine *Christ in der Gegenwart (The Christian of Today)*, especially the one entitled "The Inner Path". Through these articles, they knew about the spiritual path I now followed. If the community wanted me back because of the spiritual treasures that I had brought with me from India, I could imagine returning to the monastery. It was in order to be clear about their attitude to me that I visited Kellenried in March 1974.

I set out with mixed feelings, having seen how some people were hesitant to accept my decision to leave India. My fellow sisters, however, made our meeting easy for me. Once more they received me with great joy and I immediately felt comfortable amongst them. But at the same time, it was very clear that I did not belong there – I had changed too much. That is why I chose to stay in the abbey's guesthouse, though I had been offered a room within the enclosure.

In my first talk with the Mother Abbess, I found that the convent of Saint Erentraud was aware of the problems that my return to the monastery might cause. I was given the opportunity to speak individually with some of my fellow sisters and to present my thoughts by means of a lecture to the community. In my speech I made clear the conditions under which it would be possible for me to resume the monastic life: I would need their understanding of my chosen path of Sant Mat, and in particular I would need time to meditate in the morning and in the evening, instead of participating in the community prayer. Of course it was clear to me that I could not lay down any conditions, and it was also clear that such conditions could not be accepted. Yet I wanted them to know that I could not simply start from where I had left off eight years back.

In the discussion following my lecture, the position on both sides became completely clear; my fellow sisters spoke frankly about everything. For instance, they asked why I had looked for work and at the same time left open the possibility of returning to the monastery under certain conditions. I answered that I wanted to ensure that the decision to go back to the convent was not motivated by a wish to secure my livelihood; the decision to return to Kellenried or to live in Munich should be based on other considerations. The sisters were able to accept this point of view.

During our personal conversations, some of the sisters openly showed their interest in the path of the Masters and even asked for a photograph of the Master. They really were very open and ready to integrate new aspects of spiritual life into the traditional monastic way. While I was away they had become familiar with the concept of meditation. I was very surprised to learn that a separate meditation room had been provided and that many sisters had followed a course in Zen meditation and were practising it. Some of them now taught meditation to people from outside the convent. Since there was an increasing demand, many contemplative monasteries and convents had begun offering meditation courses. Those sisters who were in favour of my return to the community probably thought that I would teach them my method of meditation, but that was out of the question, because in Surat Shabd Yoga the method of meditation can be imparted only through initiation, which is entirely in the hands of the Master. It is the Master who takes upon himself the responsibility of taking the soul back to its eternal home. This point, however, was not mentioned during our conversations, since nobody asked directly about the possibility of initiation.

Other sisters, by contrast, were of the opinion that if I was to live among them again, I should accept back into my life in particular the whole treasure of the liturgy, which lies at the heart of the Benedictine way of life. In the course of our discussions, it became increasingly clear that, if I returned to the convent, we would probably find it impossible to reconcile our differences. This was a matter of particular concern to our Mother Abbess, who was anxious to maintain peace and harmony in the monastery.

One of the sisters pointed out that within a few years after my leaving, new opportunities for meditation had arisen in our abbey. In her opinion, if I had had a little more patience, it would not have been necessary for me to go away. I explained to her that this development could not have been foreseen and that my departure had been part of God's plan for me – my way led to India in order to meet the Master.

Fulfilment of the monastic vows

Quite a few sisters were of the opinion that I would be obliged to come back to the Convent of Saint Erentraud because of the solemn vows that I had taken in 1954. It filled them with pain that one of their sisters should break – as they saw it – the solemn promise given to God. Yet most of the sisters understood that in the given circumstances these vows could not be a compelling reason to return to the monastery. I was very concerned to show the sisters that in accepting Sant Mat I had not deviated from our common search for God; on the contrary, I would now be in a better position to fulfil my original vows. When I was given the opportunity to give a second lecture, I felt that I was bearing witness to Sant Mat.

The first vow that the founder of the Order of Saint Benedict of Nursia (sixth century) obliged his monks to take was the vow of *stabilitas loci* – the promise to stay for a lifetime at the same monastery. He wanted to prevent the monks from wandering from place to place, as was customary at that time. Even today the monks and nuns of Saint Benedict bind themselves by this vow to the monastery that they first join.

The vow of *stabilitas loci* was designed to protect the disciples of Saint Benedict from worldly temptations, but it is clear that it should also serve to prevent the mind from roaming about in the world. In this connection, I pointed out that other methods are needed to make the mind really steady at one place and stop it roaming around in the world of the senses. I explained that for me the true fulfilment of the vow of *stabilitas loci* lay in making the wandering mind motionless in order to open up the path within us. Only by going within ourselves can we gain access to the true temple of God.

The second vow, the vow of *oboedientia* (obedience), is accorded a very prominent role in monastic life by Saint Benedict. In his view, the obedience given to the abbot is obedience to the Lord, whose place the abbot takes in the monastery. For a monk, obedience is one of the most important preconditions for attaining union with God, because "whoever obeys the abbot obeys God". I explained to my sisters that the Masters of Surat Shabd Yoga also see unconditional surrender to the will of God as an essential condition for the union of the soul with God. These Masters, however, would insist that one can fulfil the will of God only when one knows the universal divine law. The great spiritual leaders, the great teachers and Masters who have lived on earth at all times and are still living here today know this divine law, because they are one with the Lord. By entrusting ourselves to the guidance of such a Master, who can show us the will of God, we are able to fulfil God's will in our lives. I explained to the community that this was my understanding of the vow of obedience, and that I was determined to practise this comprehensive form of obedience. Even if I could not fulfil the vow of obedience literally when living outside the monastery, I would fulfil it in the true sense by unconditional surrender to the will of God, which is an essential part of the spiritual path of Sant Mat.

The third vow taken by disciples of Saint Benedict is the vow of *conversio morum* (conversion of one's moral conduct). This concept is no longer clearly definable nowadays. In my lecture I interpreted it as turning away from the world of the senses, the temptations of *maya* and the power of illusion, which are prevalent not just in this world but in all the three worlds – material, astral and causal. This was in accord with the teachings of Sant Mat. The Masters of Surat Shabd Yoga emphasize that the real turning away from the world of the senses is achieved not by ascetic exercises but by uniting the soul with the Word, the audible life stream. I told them that it was this union of my soul with the Shabd, the Word of the Bible, which I aspired to with all my heart.

I do not know how my points were accepted by the community of Saint Erentraud, because there was no time for discussion afterwards. But my lecture helped me gain a better understanding of my new life outside the monastery. I realized that I would not be abandoning my promise to God, and a great joy filled me, because now I could see clearly how my new life was a continuation of the life of dedication to God that had started when I joined the monastery in 1949.

On the occasion of this visit, no mention was made of dispensation from my monastic vows. It was not until a year later that the community insisted upon settling the matter once and for all. They had probably wanted to give me time to try life in the world and find out whether or not it would be compatible with a spiritual life. Since by then I was sure that I would not return to the convent, I filled an application for dispensation from my monastic vows addressed to the Congregation for Religious in Rome. In that application I explicitly pointed out how important and precious the sixteen years at Kellenried had been, and what a unique foundation for my spiritual life had been laid there. To get dispensation from the vows was only an exterior matter to me – it did not make any difference to the dedication of my whole life to God.

CHAPTER THREE

A Spiritual Life
in the Middle of the World

ON RETURNING TO GERMANY, I FOUND MYSELF
in a very paradoxical situation. When I was young, I had left
the world in search of God and I had expected to find him in
the seclusion of a monastery. For sixteen years I had lived an
enclosed life, remote from the world, dedicated to God. I was
convinced that in this way I could come closer to him. Then the
search for God led me to India and to the ashram community
of Brahma Vidya Mandir. There also I lived separated from
the world and believed that I was on my way to *brahma vidya*
– the knowledge of God. After a total of twenty-four years of
intensive spiritual life, I came to the path of the Masters, the
way for me to meet God. After my initiation into Surat Shabd
Yoga, I found that I had to continue my spiritual life while
living out in the world.

As long as I was in search of the way to union with God,
I was allowed to live in a 'garden inclosed'. But when I found
the way, the Master sent me back into the world in order to
pass through the fate that was assigned to me for this life.
Outwardly I had to adjust to a worldly life, while inwardly I

had to continue with a life of devotion to God. At first, this seemed to be a great contradiction and it was not easy to regain my inner balance.

Most practitioners of the path of the Masters come to the path while leading a very normal worldly life. They have families and professions, take holidays and have their hobbies. Of course they have to try to integrate their life fully into Sant Mat, yet their circumstances of life as a whole do not essentially change when they become initiates. I, however, had to get accustomed to a way of living that was quite strange to me.

Yet my twenty-four years of living first in a convent and then in an ashram had laid a firm foundation on which I could now build. In those years I had tried to put into practice the rule of *soli Dei quaerere* (search only for God) from the *Rule of Saint Benedict*, and my life had been shaped by the *opus Dei* (the work for God, the life of prayer throughout the day), "to which nothing should be given preference". The 'experience of the desert' had put an end to the phase of external worship, and it had been replaced by the path leading within, which from now on was to take first place in my daily routine. How often had I heard the Master say that our meditation should be our main concern.

I was actually well prepared for life as a God-seeker in the midst of the world. Moreover, I felt sure that the Master would never allow my spiritual life to suffer because I had entered into the adventure of faith and obeyed his instruction to return to Germany. My confidence in the Master's guidance was confirmed again and again in the years to come, for I experienced his help at all times in my spiritual as well as in my worldly life.

While I was trying to integrate into my profession as a social worker and to adapt to my new place in life, at the same time my greatest concern was to progress on the spiritual path, to turn to God with all my strength and to follow the path leading within by meditation. The Master was always telling us that meditation cannot be replaced by anything – neither by *seva* (service to the Master), nor by good deeds, nor by reading holy scriptures. When I was a child, much emphasis had been put on good intentions – doing things to honour God or out of love for him. But these things cannot replace the inner worship of God, nor can they bring us face to face with God. Only a true spiritual way can take us to God; this is what all the great saints and mystics tell us, whatever their religious background.

When he was asked whether there is any short cut that we can take on this slow and tiresome way of meditation, Maharaj Charan Singh used to say that a great and overwhelming love of God can pull the attention inside with irresistible power. But then he would always add that such love is found in very few seekers of God. Ultimately, this very love would lead the disciple of a living true Master to the vision of his inner form and to the experience of the Word of God within.

In 1971, during my first stay at the Dera, when I was not yet initiated, I once asked the Master how one could attain such a love. "By meditation," the Master answered. Therefore the time of meditation is the most precious time of the day for the disciple – even if he is not always aware of it – because, as a gift of grace, it awakens the love within us and makes it grow. It is the time that a disciple spends with his Master or, at least, in awaiting his coming. Once the Master confided to us the secret – his secret – of successful meditation: it is the repetition of the holy words, done with love and devotion. The Master said, "One has to put one's whole being into the words. One should not think of anything else, but just give oneself to the Master through the repetition."

Like the author of that very valuable book *The Cloud of Unknowing*, the Master's advice is that during meditation we should stop all reflective thinking; we should not even think about God, his qualities and his grace, or about the work of redemption done by Jesus Christ. We should give ourselves entirely to the impulse of love and unconditional, single-minded devotion to the pure essence of God.

When the Masters point to this love as the great and high goal of the practice of meditation, which gives us access to the worlds beyond and to the final union with the Lord, they do not hide the fact that the path leading there is a long and arduous one, not meant for cowards and weaklings. It calls for the bravery of a warrior, because to meditate two and a half hours daily demands not only determination but also the renunciation of many things that other people consider important. I soon realized this when I began living in Munich and discovered many new fields of interest and talents that I would have liked to pursue. Consequently, I had to set priorities, because under no circumstances did I want to neglect my meditation. I had to learn to fulfil my worldly obligations and give time to activities that interested me while also treading the spiritual path. This was not easy at times. In the monastery and in the ashram, I had had so many hours free for God; now I had to learn to free myself for him during my day-to-day life.

As the weeks and months passed, I was assailed by countless impressions and demands. Sometimes my professional life was quite turbulent, but I remembered Maharaj Charan Singh's advice, which I had heard so often during the evening satsangs at the Dera: "We have to build a fence or a wall around our meditation." He told us that we need to do this because our own mind, the enemy of our spiritual life, is always on the lookout for opportunities to sow weeds in the field of our heart. As the Master of Nazareth says in his parable: "The kingdom of heaven is likened unto a man which sowed good seed in his field: But while men slept, his enemy came and sowed tares among the wheat." The best way to protect our spiritual life, as Maharaj Charan Singh said time and again, is to win over our mind as a friend so that, instead of putting obstacles in our path, it will urge us on to perform the most important task of our life – our spiritual exercises.

Two strong 'bricks' in the wall protecting the field of meditation are participation in satsang (a gathering of seekers where a talk on Sant Mat is given) and reading Sant Mat books, through which the Masters speak to us. These books have always been a source of inspiration to me; quite often, reading just a few words or sentences is enough to feel the effect of their inherent spiritual energy.

I found that preparing talks to give at satsangs was another effective means of protecting the field of spirituality because, in doing so, I had to go deeply into the teachings of Sant Mat. Preparing these lectures was invaluable, especially at times of heavy professional demands or during stressful periods. In this way I quite often received the support for my spiritual life that I needed at a particular time. Yet the greatest help of all was to remember all the beautiful moments with the Master at the Dera and the many signs of his grace that I had experienced when I was there with him, learning about the path and seeing him every day.

One other means of protecting our field of meditation that the Master often recommended was to repeat inwardly the words of meditation during the day, whenever the attention is free – an exercise that I was already familiar with through the Jesus Prayer. This exercise runs like a bright thread through the day and keeps alive the atmosphere of meditation. Out of love for the Master, the disciple seeks contact with him in this way and frequently thinks about him during the day. Eventually there comes a time when the words repeat themselves within automatically, without any effort. Yet this is not in the hands of the disciple; it cannot be brought about by any amount of individual effort, however hard we try. I found this out for myself after initiation, when I tried too hard to make the words of meditation automatic and in so doing gave myself a severe headache.

Now I know from experience that it takes years to grow into the life of a disciple, learning how to tread the spiritual path out in the world. On every page of their books the Masters caution against expecting quick results and against making our continued efforts dependent on experiencing tangible success. It is a slow process to still our mind and lead it inside. After all, for millions of lives it has been accustomed to going out into the visible creation and succumbing to every lure of the senses. With every warning, however, the Masters also offer words of encouragement to help us persevere on a way that is long and can often enough be stony and steep. I had to go through some difficult phases in which the goal seemed not just far away but altogether out of reach. Sometimes, however, the Master gave me an inkling of what was to come on the path. These moments of encouragement, which come to every seeker on this path, are more inspiring than even the most beautiful descriptions of inner experiences – they give wings to the disciple.

At the focal point of social problems

On 1st March 1974, when I started work, an entirely new phase of my life began. In October 1973, I had had my fiftieth birthday, and through my work at the girls' home I saw myself confronted with a situation I had never experienced before. I had not seen this generation of girls grow up, and now I found myself having to deal with them, but without understanding their way of life. Their values, ethics and moral views were quite strange to me. Moreover, since making personal contacts was not easy for me, I often had to overcome my own limitations during this work.

I only realized this when I started my job as a social worker. Twenty-five years earlier, I had taken the professional training in social work not out of inclination but in order to escape from office work. At that time I was already sure that I would not practise this profession, for I was set on taking the veil.

The beginning of my professional work was a kind of vertical take-off. In order to cope with the manifold tasks, I had to work fourteen hours a day. I got up early in the morning for meditation, which I did not want to miss under any circumstances, although that left me with hardly four hours of sleep. Only a few weeks passed before I realized that I would not stay in this post for long – the work to be done required two persons at least. I therefore soon started to look for another job. Through an advertisement in the newspaper I learned of a headmistress in a similar position, who was looking for a leading assistant. I applied for the job and was accepted. Although the big gaps in my professional career were mentioned during the interview, it was obviously felt that I would stand up to the challenges of that job.

My new post, which I took up on 1st July 1974, was a focal point of social problems. It was a residential home with eighty-three apartments, which took in battered women and young single mothers with small children. It was my task to give them advice and to support them in their many difficulties. Quite a few of them had found themselves in an awkward situation through the birth of a child – usually unwanted. As a result, some had had to leave their parents' house, some had lost their work, and some were let down by the father of the child or had chosen to leave him. Many of these women had no professional training and hardly any chance of getting a job. Some had been badly brought up and were not accustomed to a regular way of living. Most of them had no perspective in life and lacked the most basic prerequisite skills for raising a child.

In most cases the women came to see me when they were completely at a loss as to what to do; they had reached the point where they had no money to buy food for their child or felt altogether incapable of coping with their situation. Consequently, for a greater part of each day, I was busy trying to think of solutions for their problems. Sometimes they seemed to be their own worst enemies. It was as if they were magically attracted by the next trap and would do everything they could to fall into it. Then they would cry for help. In dealing with these women, I developed a capacity for solving other people's problems. Working with them was a varied and interesting experience. Yet, in spite of a certain sense of achievement, it was often depressing and frustrating, because many of these women had no interest in changing their plight. I was especially shocked by those cases where it was obvious that one day the child was going to go astray, because the mother was unable to cope with her task.

Altogether I worked for thirteen years in that institution and every day I was confronted with problems that were beyond my experience and to which I had to adapt. Sometimes I wondered what whim of fate had put me in this particular place. In reality, though, it was no whim of fate, but a part of the role that was assigned to me for this life. The reasons for this were unknown to me – I only knew that it was part of my karma to be brought into contact with so many people to whom I still owed some assistance. This conviction helped me to discharge my duties with devotion and all the personal engagement that was needed. Possibly I had to go through this kind of life experience and tackle situations that were quite new to me in order to learn how to integrate them into my life.

During all these years of professional work, I was allowed to feel the nearness of the Master who was, albeit invisibly, always at my side. When I looked up at him, I received the strength and the courage to cope with the demands of my profession. Sometimes I thought I saw him smile at me, when I had once again solved a difficult situation in that house. I was working, as it were, in his name, and I trusted that he would accept my service to those people as a *seva* to him. In this way, the professional routine connected me with the Master in a very special way, and at the same time it saved me from seeing this work as just another worldly activity. In 1987, when I had reached the age of sixty-three, I was able to end this phase of my life and retire, but only to soon take up another task – that of nursing my aged mother.

Companions on the path

With the change of scene that took place on my return to Germany, I sometimes felt I could hardly breathe. With the help of my intellect and my will power, I was somehow able to cope with the situation, but my soul still dwelt in India, in the ashram and in the Dera, and often I was overwhelmed by a deep homesickness. Every colourful sunset reopened the old wounds and even the cooing of the pigeons in the city was like a stab in my heart, because it reminded me of India, where I had experienced so many spectacular sunsets and had heard the pigeons cooing all the time. Even years later, my tears would flow for days on end whenever I received a letter from the ashram. For a long time I felt uprooted, like a stranger in my own country, but I knew for certain that for me there was to be no return to India.

In that situation, it was a great consolation and help to me to have a group of fellow disciples in Munich who met regularly. At first, I felt as though I was amongst foreigners, because I knew Sant Mat and satsang only from the Dera. I even found it difficult to listen to the teachings of Sant Mat in

German, because up to now I had heard them only in English. After some time, though, I felt at home with the group and I soon realized the importance of participating in the satsang meetings. We were all living in the diaspora as far as Sant Mat was concerned, and we needed the togetherness that was a source of inspiration and encouragement for each one of us on the path of the Masters. I longed to immerse myself time and again in the atmosphere of Sant Mat, to have my companions around me and to spend some hours with them in the name of the Master. We remembered with gratitude the words of the Master of Nazareth, who had promised his disciples: "For where two or three are gathered together in my name, there am I in the midst of them."

At that time, the group had approximately twenty-five members. Our satsang meetings were never social gatherings. In accord with the expressed wishes of the Master, they were devoted exclusively to listening to the Sant Mat teachings and to spending some hours in a spiritual atmosphere. Mentally, we assembled around the Master and we were happy and grateful to be able to spend some time sitting at his feet. Over the years the group became bigger and it was always a great joy to us when seekers came and, after a certain period of probation, were accepted as disciples and received initiation into the path of the Masters.

For some, however, these regular monthly meetings were not enough. So in Munich and many other places, weekly home satsangs were established. For sixteen years, there were satsangs at my home in Munich, where a small group of us read many Sant Mat books together and received much inspiration and encouragement from the Master's words.

When I came back to Germany, only a few Sant Mat books had been published in our language. Therefore it was a great concern to the Master's representative for Germany, Rudolf

Walberg, to be able to offer more books in German, and he asked me to help with the translation. One of the first books I was asked to translate was *Spiritual Discourses* by Maharaj Charan Singh. I particularly loved this book by my own Master, because it contains the satsangs he gave at various places all over the world. When reading this book, I seemed to hear the familiar voice of the Master and therefore it was a great joy to me to translate it page by page into my native tongue in order to make his message accessible to German-speaking people. Other books followed in the course of the years and then I began compiling a small *Lexicon of Surat Shabd Yoga*, comprising important Sanskrit, Hindi and Punjabi terms used in the Sant Mat literature. Many of these terms are key words in the Sant Mat teachings, but they can be difficult to translate into another language. This work took me four years, after which Mr Walberg entrusted me with the translation of *Sar Bachan (Prose)* by the saint of Agra, Soami Ji. Maharaj Charan Singh once said of this book that it is "pure gold".

At the time of my return to Germany, only one and a half years had passed since my initiation, so I was still a 'young' disciple who was just beginning to acquire a rudimentary knowledge of Sant Mat. Translating these books helped me to go deeper and deeper into the teachings. Over the years I – like many others – found that the study of the Sant Mat books opens up ever new dimensions of the teachings, once the disciple begins putting them into practice and is making progress on the path. The deepest dimensions of the teachings are unfathomable to anyone who has not yet reached the inner worlds of which the Masters speak, because they speak from the fullness of their own experience and point to dimensions that are inaccessible to the human mind.

The reading of Sant Mat books can be a great help for those in search of God and the truth, because it can fill our minds with enthusiasm for the path of the Masters. Nevertheless, a Sufi saint, Abyat-i Noori, once exclaimed: "Throw in the fire the hundreds of books and sheets of papers you read." Baba Gurinder Singh, the present Master of Beas, appointed by our beloved Maharaj Charan Singh before his passing in 1990, voiced the same idea and pointed out that even Sant Mat books can be a danger if the disciple succumbs to the temptation of thinking that intellectual knowledge about the path can be a substitute for spiritual practice. The reading of books must lead to the performance of the spiritual exercises, to meditation, because only this can open up the way leading within.

Therefore the most important thing for me was that I should not only understand the path of the Masters intellectually, but that I should put it into practice by meditating for at least two and a half hours every day, while at the same time fulfilling my professional and social obligations. Admittedly, this was not always an easy task. For a long time, severe headaches interfered with my meditation and there were phases of great stress in my professional work. But I found that when times were difficult I was allowed to experience the nearness of the Master more than during times of success and ease. During all these years – with the Master's help – I tried to take charge of my life, to cope with the daily demands while at the same time walking the spiritual path.

The way is the goal

One year after having taken up my professional work, I was confronted with the fact that I was entitled to a six-week holiday; this was the beginning of my career as a mountaineer. Ever since my youth, mountains had fascinated me, for in Munich they stood, as it were, on our doorstep. Although twenty-five years had passed since I had last stood on a mountain peak, this did not discourage me from taking it up again. I soon realized that there are many parallels between mountaineering and treading the path of the Masters and that climbing could have advantages for my spiritual life.

The motto of the Summit Club of the German Alpine Society is: "The way is the goal." Although this saying does not apply to the path of the Masters, it is certainly true that the journey along the spiritual way is just as essential for a disciple of Sant Mat as is the ascent of a mountain for the mountaineer; it is something that both have to do before they can reach their respective goals. There is indeed a deep spiritual symbolism in climbing a mountain. Every step brings the wanderer closer to his goal and increases the distance from the lowlands of the world below. Climbing was to me not only a way of keeping fit, but also a source of mental strength. I felt my mental powers increasing whenever, often with great effort, I aimed for a mountain peak. Every successful ascent trained and strengthened my endurance, not only for the worldly but also for the spiritual life. As I undertook bigger and more demanding mountain tours, I gained greater courage in facing life and enhanced my ability to cope with difficult situations.

There was one occasion, during my basic training in rock and ice climbing that took place in the midst of the glacial world of the Ötztal Alps, when I reached the very limits of my physical strength. Even this proved to be a useful experience, because I learned that by attaining the utmost concentration, it is possible to overcome such limits. Thus, what was initially a very critical situation turned into a positive experience, even from the Sant Mat perspective.

Climbing steep slopes and passing over ridges always reminded me of the 'sharp edge of a sword' over which I had passed on my way to God during my life in the monastery. Time and again I went through such phases on my spiritual path, but in my Master I had an experienced guide at my side, whom I could trust implicitly.

Standing on a mountain peak has always been a special experience for me, but at this point, the similarity between mountaineering and treading the path of the Masters ends. After conquering the summit, the mountaineer has to descend again into the valley, but on the path of the Masters there is no descending. The disciple may sometimes have the impression of not progressing on the path or even of falling back, but the Masters assure their disciples that – however discouraged they may sometimes feel – there are no failures in Sant Mat. What counts is not immediate success but sincere effort. Success will come at the correct time. Quite often I heard the Master say at the evening satsang at the Dera that under the guidance of the Master, we will always progress on the path. Ascending into the higher regions of the creation, however, will not be a matter of days or weeks, nor even of years. The pilgrim on the spiritual path must take this into account.

Maharaj Sawan Singh once said, in answering a disciple who had enthusiastically written to him about his experiences in the mountains, that he could well understand this enthusiasm, because during his work as an engineer in the army he was mostly stationed in the mountains. But he went on to point out that the beauty of the mountains is merely a shadow of the splendour of the inner worlds and that the disciple should strive to reach there.

Though I gained much in many ways from my mountain walks and my tours of the high peaks, I sometimes wondered when I was making my way through this beautiful mountain world whether I might be wasting precious time. Would it not be better to withdraw into solitude in order to devote this time exclusively to Sant Mat and to meditation? From time to time during my holidays, when I felt this conflict, I would remember

Sardar Bahadur Jagat Singh, who, after completing his lectures at the university, would immediately withdraw to his house in order to meditate. But he was a very advanced disciple who would later become the third Master of Beas. Could I really take him as my model? Finally I told myself that I could seek leisure and relaxation with a clear conscience, for it would help me to keep the balance between my worldly life and my spiritual endeavours, in accordance with the Master's advice. The disciple should be wary of going to extremes on the path of meditation, because this is rarely inspired by a true longing for God; usually, striving for success is based for the most part on ego, even on the spiritual path. Maharaj Charan Singh used to explain that when a disciple progresses on the path, he will reach a point where he is quite unable to resist the "pull inside". When this time comes, his only wish will be to meditate, and even his own mind will urge him to do so.

And so, I still go into the mountains, enjoying their beauty, and time and again looking at the Master who – although invisible – is at my side; he seems to enjoy it as well. "Your happiness is my happiness," he used to say. Often I remember the words of Soami Ji in *Sar Bachan (Prose)*: "But those who hold on to the hand of a living Satguru make the most of this world, and attain *parmarth* (spiritual benefit) too."

During all my excursions in the mountains, I always made sure that there was sufficient time for meditation and that there were no compromises regarding the vegetarian diet when I was staying in mountain huts. Sometimes my friends tease me about my "mountain goat *sanskaras*", my impressions from former lives that still turn up every once in a while.

CHAPTER FOUR

Setting Out towards Reality

IN THE SUMMER OF 1974, SIX MONTHS AFTER
I had returned to Germany and had my first experience of living a spiritual life in the midst of the world, I was offered the
chance of participating in the fifth International Congress of
Imago Mundi (image of the world). Imago Mundi is a forum
that deals with the areas on the borders of science, such as near-
death experiences, spiritual healing, clairvoyance, sixth sense
and so forth.

Participating in this Congress was my first break after my
turbulent new beginning in Munich; it was not only a breathing
space during this period of vertical takeoff in my new profession, but it was also a crucial opportunity to integrate into the
Western world to which I had returned as a stranger. Among
the many interesting topics taken up during the Congress, the
one that especially appealed to me and deeply impressed me
was the epoch-making lecture of Burkhart Heim, Director of
the Institute of Power Field Physics and General Cosmology,
about the experience of cosmic space.

The speaker depicted to his audience a six-dimensional
image of the world, which he wrote in mathematical formulas on

the blackboard. He called our widely accepted four-dimensional world a limited depiction of reality. He pointed out that as a scientist he felt compelled to postulate two more dimensions. The fifth dimension was the spirit, the evolving, shaping, structuring and controlling power of creation. The sixth dimension was the origin of all that exists, a supreme divine Being. Burkhart Heim also pointed out that the reality of the additional dimensions of which he spoke became more real as the distance from time and space, the peripheral form of existence, became greater.

At the end of his two-hour lecture, to which the audience had listened in a breathless silence, the speaker arrived at a conclusion quite unusual for a scientist and mathematician. He said that the highest task of human beings is to extend their consciousness into those dimensions to which the human senses and intellect have no access. As long as they are not capable of doing this, even people of the age of atomic physics and space travel are bound to consider themselves in no better a state than a blind worm crawling around on the ground. In the truest sense of the word, they eke out a life unworthy of humankind because – fascinated by their four-dimensional world – they remain imprisoned in it.

In his lecture Burkhart Heim emphasized time and again that this world on which we stand – which we can see and touch and which is the scene of countless destinies and tragedies – is not real. Coming from the mouth of a scientist, this all sounds strange enough, but it corresponds exactly to what the great rishis of ancient India and the great spiritual Masters of our time, as well as the prophets of Israel and the mystics of all religions, knew then and know now: that the ephemeral world is *maya* – a deceptive reality, actually a non-reality *(asat)*, a mirage, a nothing. As is written for instance in Ecclesiastes: "Vanity of vanities. All is vanity!"

The vision of reality that Burkhart Heim had set out before his audience, using both the methods of a scientist and the intuition of an ingenious thinker, seemed to me to sketch out an image of the world that corresponds surprisingly well to that of the Masters of Surat Shabd Yoga. The Masters' image of the world is, however, not a speculative or intuitive vision but their presentation of a reality that they experience directly. While I was listening to the speaker's words with fascination, I saw in my mind's eye, parallel to them, the description of those supernatural and purely spiritual worlds that I had read in the Sant Mat books. Mr Heim surely had no knowledge of the Masters' descriptions, but after his lecture I was at least able to point out to him the fact that his vision seemed to correspond with the image of the world presented by the Masters, and he appeared happy to learn this.

The fifth dimension postulated by Burkhart Heim, the spirit, could be seen, according to Sant Mat, as the universal mind, whose origin is the causal region (Trikuti). It is the formative and controlling force in the causal, astral and physical worlds.

The sixth dimension postulated by this ingenious scientist would then be the ultimate creative power of God, the Word of God, the Shabd, called by Soami Ji the "unique current of transcendent power", which is a manifestation of the absolute One, the eternal, limitless ocean of divine Being. The Shabd created the purely spiritual regions and the three material worlds and sustains them. In this sixth dimension lies the origin of the entire creation, of all life and all existence. The whole creation is an emanation of that highest divine entity, a reflection of his Being. The causal and astral, and especially the physical worlds, are only a pale reflection of the splendour and the grandeur of their Creator. What we perceive with our physical senses is only the remotest, shadow-like periphery of reality and it can hardly be called real in comparison to the purely spiritual divine reality. According to Sant Mat, to experience this reality is not only the highest task of human beings, as Burkhart Heim said, it is also our birthright.

Developing one's spiritual nature

In his lecture Burkhart Heim did not explain how this 'setting out towards reality' that he was calling for should be realized. He did not speak about methods of expanding one's con- sciousness, but he and his audience were surely aware that the experience of the ultimate reality has nothing to do with the intellectual comprehension of that dimension. It can only be perceived with the powers of the soul, powers that are dormant in most people. In order to awaken the soul from her deathlike sleep, we must develop our spiritual nature. This is, the Masters emphasize, our most important task in life, the task for which we have received the human body.

More than thirty years have elapsed since Burkhart Heim's lecture at Innsbruck. The phrase 'developing our spiritual nature' was one that I discovered in the booklet *A Spiritual Primer*, published by the Dera in 1997. With a sudden intuition I realized that this is one of the key phrases of the spiritual path taught by Sant Mat. At the same time, it became clear to me that making these words a reality means fulfilling Burkhart Heim's postulate that human beings have to expand their consciousness into the fifth and sixth dimensions, and that this is our supreme task. The subject fascinated me since it showed me an aspect of the path of the Masters that I had not been fully aware of till then.

According to the teachings of Sant Mat, all receptors needed for the perception of the transcendental reality are present within the human body. However, only a few people are aware of the unique potential that we carry within our- selves and that can enable us to overcome all limitations of our physical and mental nature and rise to the purely spiritual divine region. Before this can happen, we must awaken and develop the 'points of contact' with these higher worlds that are situated above the third eye. This will be accomplished with the help of the technique of meditation that is imparted to the aspirant at the time of initiation into Surat Shabd Yoga.

Under the guidance of the Master, disciples can activate these centres above the third eye and from there take the consciousness higher. Thus they can gradually gain access to all the worlds beyond and perceive them with the eye and ear of the soul. In what Heim calls the fifth dimension and Sant Mat calls Trikuti, the region of the universal mind, the individual mind will merge in the universal mind and the soul will be freed from her last shackle. Guided by the Master, she will then continue her way up to her true home, from where she emerged at the moment of her birth.

This process of setting out towards reality surely cannot be undertaken out of scientific interest. Nor is scientific interest a precondition for following the path of the Masters, which is a path of liberation of the soul from the four-dimensional world and also from the fifth dimension of Burkhart Heim. Even so, the path of Surat Shabd Yoga is described as the science of the soul by the Masters, and they insist that under the guidance of a competent teacher each of us can carry out the experiment in the laboratory of our own body. An advanced initiated disciple can systematically investigate the regions of the worlds beyond, and the results of this research will be the same for each 'spiritual scientist'.

It should, however, be made very clear that gaining experience of the transcendental worlds is not an important aim on the path of the Masters; the essential aim is the return of the soul to its origin. The path is a way of liberation on which the soul passes through these worlds – not so much in order to experience them, but rather to cross them and leave them behind so that she can experience first her own real nature and finally the divine reality.

To the disciple this means recognizing, with the help of meditation, that the disciple's real self is the soul, which is born of God and is a pure spiritual being that God has created after his own image and which has never lost her likeness to God. Therefore our present Master, Baba Gurinder Singh Ji, points out that we are spiritual beings passing through the experience of a human existence and not human beings seeking spiritual experiences.

On her descent from her place of origin the soul has lost the knowledge of her god-likeness. As already mentioned, the Masters speak of a sleep of death in which the soul has been caught ever since she was covered by her mental, astral and material bodies. When she was enveloped in these coverings, she lost all knowledge of herself, and the individual ego came to dominate the soul.

Sant Mat teaches that the soul, in order to gain self-knowledge, must first cast off all her coverings – the three bodies and the three minds, with which she was furnished when she entered into the domain of the negative power. The individual mind with all its capacities is not an instrument of self-realization of the soul, still less of God-realization. Although the human mind can erect the most admirable theological edifices, such intellectualizing about God is a very great hindrance to the soul's gaining knowledge of herself and of God because the mind's capacity is limited to the material and mental creation – it has no access to the purely spiritual worlds.

In order for the soul to attain self-realization and God-realization, the individual mind must be conquered. One may, with its help, gain a certain degree of intellectual conviction about the existence of transcendental worlds and an absolute

Being, but it is necessary to realize that no amount of philosophical or theological study, however intense it may be, nor
any amount of participation in external worship, rites and
ceremonies, nor any number of visits to so-called holy places,
nor asceticism and good deeds, can contribute to the realization of our spiritual nature. All these things may help to purify
the mind to some extent, but such purification is merely
provisional in nature and is, at best, a preparation for the real
spiritual path. My own experience of the deeper dimension of
spiritual life and my experience of the desert have played an
essential part in bringing me to this understanding.

If people feel an irresistible desire to find the meaning of
life and to experience God, the first thing they must do is bat-
tle with their own mind. When, with the help of the spiritual
exercises, they have reached that level of deep concentration
and have crossed the threshold to a higher consciousness,
their soul will awaken from her existential sleep and become
conscious of the transcendental worlds and, finally, of herself.
The soul's inner eye will open and she will perceive again the
supernatural divine light within, and with her inner ear she will
hear the divine harmonies of the Word, which she experienced
before descending into the three worlds.

The Masters don't leave any doubt that this first phase
in the development of our spiritual nature will require much
effort from disciples of Surat Shabd Yoga, and that this will
often extend over many years, possibly over a whole lifetime. I
had to realize as well that on the spiritual path nothing can be
forced. But I had often heard the Master say that progress on
the path does not lie in the hands of the disciple and that we
do not need to succeed in order to please our Master. All that
is expected from us is our sincere effort – not success.

But again and again I realized that the process of striving
to develop one's spiritual nature in itself has its effect on our

life and our thinking. For instance, one notices that it becomes possible to meet the ups and downs of life with a much more composed mind if one identifies with one's spiritual nature – even if, for the time being, this is only a matter of theory. It becomes easier to put oneself at a distance from events, and one is no longer exposed to the effects of the sense perceptions and the emotions without any protection. This makes it easier to regain one's inner balance when adverse circumstances agitate the feelings, or when sensual pleasures flood the emotions. One will become, as it were, a bystander, still having to play one's allotted role, but having gained a certain measure of indifference in the face of the vicissitudes of life.

In the course of the years, my efforts to develop my spiritual nature made me sometimes feel like a stranger in the world; they detached me from the world so that I could experience its beauty and grandeur, only with a certain reserve. More and more I became conscious of the shadowy, provisional and transitory nature of the visible world in which I am living. Sometimes this experience evokes feelings of fear and insecurity, but the more intense the striving for spiritual development becomes, the more fearless and invulnerable one will become.

On the other hand, that great teacher of spirituality, Soami Ji, emphasizes that one who is united with God – who holds the hand of the Father – can enjoy the creation and at the same time can lead a spiritual life. This pertains especially to the Masters, who are able to recognize the Lord as the instigating, moving and guiding power in every creature. For this reason, Soami Ji emphasizes that they "can enjoy the show of this world as nobody else can".

So when we strive for spiritual development, this initiates a process of transformation of our thinking, feeling and acting; but we will experience our true nature only when, during meditation, we have crossed the threshold towards a higher level of consciousness. That is the moment when we will awaken from the dream condition of our earthly existence to a new, much more comprehensive consciousness, one that is frequently described in the Sant Mat literature.

However, the theoretical knowledge of what the advanced disciple on the path will one day experience, together with the daily attempt to develop his spiritual nature through meditation, will give every satsangi a deep inner peace and a small taste of that bliss that the soul will experience when she has reached her eternal goal, the true land.

CHAPTER FIVE

The Living Master

THIS CHAPTER IS COMPRISED OF FIVE SEC-
tions covering the second subject area of this part of the
book – my experience of the living Master after my return to
Germany. In many chapters – beginning with my first meeting
with Maharaj Charan Singh – I have given an account of how I
found my way to the Master. It had begun with the realization
that it was essential for me to find a spiritual teacher. The first
steps had not been easy, since I had considerable difficulties
accepting a living Master in the Sant Mat sense.

In those chapters I described how the Master guided me
from inside until I finally became his convinced disciple; with
the Bible in my hand I discovered, through the self-testimony
of the teacher of Nazareth, the greatness of a contemporary
Christ who is the teacher of wisdom sent by God – simultaneously divine and human – and who is the fountain of life for
his disciples. Finally the Master revealed himself to me as the
same inner guide who had called me in my youth, who had laid
his hand upon me, and whose gaze had rested on me when I
walked over the ridge.

All these experiences not only deeply imprinted themselves
on my memory, they also transformed me inwardly and made

the Master the centre of my life in a way I never could have imagined. In his human form, he was as near to me as my Christ – he spoke to me, answered my questions and counselled me. At the time of initiation, he took his abode within me in his astral form and in this form he is nearer to me than I could ever have wished. His invisible presence shines over my life, draws my gaze to him and fills me with deep joy and great inner security. On 24th December 1973, I returned to Germany with the blissful knowledge of his physical existence and with some knowledge, albeit mostly theoretical, of his true nature. I returned also consoled by the Master's promise to visit my country someday.

Seeing the Master again

Much earlier than I could ever have hoped, the Master made good his promise to come to Germany and we were able to meet him there as early as June 1975 in Königsstein (Taunus). It was with great joy that we looked forward to the Master's visit. During the two days of his stay I especially wanted to revive my memories of all the meetings with him at the Dera, which had already begun to fade behind all the new impressions and experiences I had had since my return to Germany.

After the Master's first satsang we were allowed to meet him for some minutes in small groups. As I had been secretly wishing, it so happened that I was the first person in my group to enter the room in which the Master was waiting for us. He was sitting on a chair, looking towards us. Unable to keep back my feelings, I ran towards him, fell down on my knees before him and folded my hands in the accustomed manner to greet him. The Master was full of kindness and understanding about my spontaneous reaction.

Following this interview with the Master, I had to give a lecture, which was open to seekers, family members and friends of initiates. I was still so full of enthusiasm after my first meeting with the Master after one and a half years that my lecture turned out to be quite emotional. The satsangis might have understood this, but others in the audience may have found my words somewhat exaggerated. In any case, some remarks were made after the lecture. During my speech I had not thought about the impression my words would make on others, but had spontaneously expressed my feelings. At the beginning of the lecture, however, I had pointed out that I wanted to address the initiates in the audience and that the other participants would be witnesses of what we found so moving in those days – witnesses of our happiness, our gratefulness and our love for the Master. I added that, like us, they would also be witnesses to his kindness, his radiance and his perfect humanity.

The Master knew about the feelings of his disciples because he himself had been a disciple of his Master, to whom he was especially close and whom he loved more than all else. Sometimes in the Dera I was able to witness the intensity of love and attachment with which the Master spoke about his own Master, Maharaj Sawan Singh. He was unable to hold back his tears when asked about his relationship with his own Master, who had left this world decades before. "I would give my life to see him again in his human form," he said. But he also pointed out that feelings of love are unstable, and that true and unshakeable love for the Master can only develop if one sees him inside in his inner form. To a disciple, this remark of the Master is very important. He should not expect to be constantly on an emotional high and should be wary of trying to evoke strong feelings in himself. This leads to self-deception.

On the other hand, abandoning oneself to feelings of resignation and indifference is deadly for the spiritual life. I could not avoid going through such phases time and again, when I felt at least the temptation to give way to such feelings.

The Masters address the problem very frankly, but they also mention the antidote, which is *sharan* – taking shelter with the Master. Only the weak, the helpless, the fallen seek shelter with a stronger person. How often in the course of my life as a satsangi I would realize that on the path of the Masters each failure and each shortcoming can be transformed into a gain for the spiritual life by taking shelter with the Master. He does not reject disciples who are full of faults but takes them in hand, just like the Master of Nazareth describes it in the stirring parable of the lost sheep, where the good shepherd carries it on his shoulders back to the fold.* How often Jesus Christ had shown this mercy towards sinners, as every true living Master does.

It was very hard for us to bid farewell to our beloved Master after two days. In his presence we had forgotten time and space, because when the Master is there one can think only of him and is unable to turn one's gaze away. During those precious moments that disciples are able to spend with their Master, no room is left for anything else in their thinking. Now I had to face my daily routine again. I was still in the first stages of my professional work and quite often felt unhappy because the memories of India were catching up with me again and again and my homesickness for that beautiful time was still very much present. But being with the Master had been a great solace for me and had filled me anew with confidence.

The Master's journeys to foreign countries do not serve any missionary purposes. He undertakes these journeys in order to give initiates and people interested in the teachings of the Masters a chance to see him. Publicizing his visit was not

---

*"What man of you, having an hundred sheep, if he lose one of them, doth not leave the ninety and nine in the wilderness, and go after that which is lost, until he find it? And when he hath found it, he layeth it on his shoulders, rejoicing." *Luke* 15:4–5

permitted, but disciples were allowed to invite family members and interested people to attend the Master's discourses. Also, the Master didn't give initiation abroad anymore, as many seekers might have wished. When a seeker is accepted by the Master for initiation, his respective representative in each country imparts the method of meditation to him. It is always stressed that only a person authorized by the Master is allowed to give the instructions for initiation; otherwise, seekers would receive the technique of meditation, but nobody would assist and guide them on the spiritual path. The same pertains to those who learn the method of meditation from books. The path of the Masters is more than practising meditation; it is a path of salvation that cannot be walked without a true living Master. This is the essential difference in comparison with the various meditation techniques people may choose for reasons of their own.

In 1979 we welcomed the Master once again in Germany. Meanwhile, the German sangat (community of disciples) had grown and satsangis and seekers of neighbouring countries also wanted to participate in his visit, so the meeting with the Master took place in a bigger setting at the Congress Hall of Wiesbaden.

We waited in our seats in the large hall, disciples and guests, silent and full of expectation. Inwardly we prepared ourselves for the coming of our Master. As is the custom in the Dera, many had come an hour or more in advance to get a seat in the first row. Although the Master frequently pointed out that physical nearness is not essential and would certainly not convey more grace, most disciples make a special effort to be nearer to the Master in order to try to catch his eye, and are happy when the Master looks at them. Whenever we asked him about this subject, the Master explained that a disciple should yearn for inward *drishti*, the gracious look of the Master that a disciple experiences, rather than physical proximity.

In his own incomparable way the Master spoke to us about Sant Mat. It was always a wonderful experience to listen to him as he presented the Sant Mat teachings with so much authority, power of conviction and fascinating eloquence. Although he always pointed out that he was not saying anything new, and although we might already be very familiar with what he had to say, his way of explaining it was always a revelation to us.

In his discourses the Master spoke about the purpose of human life, saying that it is an invaluable gift bestowed on us in order to attain true God-realization and the union of the soul with God. The Master further spoke about the return of the soul to her true home and told us that the only means of salvation for us was through the union of the soul with the divine sound current, the Word. He also pointed out that no one can find the way back to the Lord without the help of a Satguru, a true living Master. With great urgency the Master also stressed the importance of daily meditation, saying that it is indispensable and irreplaceable. He encouraged us to persevere on the path and to walk it with confidence. After the satsang the Master offered us a chance to ask questions, and many of those present made use of this opportunity, so that long queues formed at the microphones.

Somebody asked what benefit we could derive from the Master's visit and from meeting him. He answered that this would depend on our inner disposition and our receptivity. He emphasized that the Master does not withhold his grace, and he illustrated the point with a strikingly impressive simile: the Niagara Falls, he said, carries water in abundance, yet someone who comes with a thimble receives only a few drops. If someone comes with a cup or a big bowl, he will get proportionately more. But anyone who puts a bucket under the falls can draw water abundantly. When asked how we can increase our receptivity to the overflowing grace of the Lord, the Master answered, "Open your heart." By regular meditation, by love and devotion to the Lord, by trust and perseverance on the path, our capacity would grow.

After his last satsang the Master walked through the adjoining rooms in the Congress Hall, where we were waiting for him in groups. When he came to the German group he saw me and exclaimed, "Shraddha, you are in European dress!" I was so happy that the Master still recognized me and I took the opportunity to complain about still not having received an invitation to the Dera; I asked the Master for permission to visit the Dera again after being away for so many years. The capacity of the guesthouse in the Dera was limited, and all the foreign satsangis who wanted to spend a few weeks there with the Master had to obtain prior permission from the management. I had already applied several times, but my request was always rejected. To my great joy, the Master immediately gave his permission, and so in the spring of 1980, six years after my return to Germany, I was at last able to travel to India again.

The days we were able to spend with our Master in Wiesbaden were a time full of grace. It seemed as if the Master had assembled us in an oasis of peace and bliss so that we could refresh ourselves from a fountain of living water after a long journey through the desert. His presence gave us new strength and his words inspired us and gave a fresh impetus to our spiritual journey.

The Master's guidance

The experience of having an inner guide runs through my life like a bright thread. As described at the beginning of the book, he entered my life in the form of inner light and spoke to me from within, giving my life a decisive turn. Since then, this invisible power, which I called 'my Lord and God', has moved my heart and guided my steps. Over the years, the claim of this inner guide on my life has become more and more irresistible and absolute. First he led me into the 'garden inclosed' and opened to me the fountain of living water, then he led me into the 'desert' and made me experience for myself the truth that 'God alone suffices'. Finally he led me over the ridge into my promised land, where he awaited me in the form of the living Master.

Many years, however, were still to pass before I was ready to meet the living Master. As an oft-quoted saying states, "When the disciple is ready, the Master appears." Although I was of course not aware of it at that time, the inner guide was preparing the future disciple of a living Master step by step for the moment of meeting him. When the time was right, he evoked within me the longing for a living guide and led me to his feet. And even when I was able to sit before the living Master, listen to his words and speak to him, it was still mainly the inner guide who helped me to overcome the hurdles in my way and to learn the lessons I still needed to learn, until the time came for him to reveal his identity to me.

It was a moment of indescribable bliss when I realized that I stood before my inner guide in human form, and realized that it was his 'gaze' that had saved me on the ridge from falling into the abyss, that it was he who had made me persevere in the darkness. Even now, I am unable to fathom the greatness and the mystery of that moment, in which the gaze of the inner guide and that of the living Master merged and I was granted the certainty that he had always stood by my side and had always been the guide whom I followed.

Through this experience I also became aware of the continuity of my spiritual path. I saw that although its various phases were outwardly quite different, the direction had always remained the same. It was very important to me to be able to see that setting foot on the path of the Masters was a continuation of my inner way to God and not a breaking away, for this gave me the security that I had made every step on the spiritual path under the guidance of the inner Master. It was the inner Master who had brought me to the feet of the living Master, because God's plan of salvation is such that only in the physical form can he show the soul the way back to the land of her origin.

After initiation it had been my greatest wish to be near the Master in his human form, to live in the Dera and to follow the inner path right under his eyes. This would have been the fulfilment of my most beautiful dream, but instead the Master sent me back to Germany and, as a disciple of a living Master, I now had to learn to seek the nearness within by learning to direct my inner gaze at him, just as I had formerly directed my gaze at my inner guide. I now had to learn how to establish eye contact with Master inside, just as I had practised looking at him without interruption in his physical presence.

Although I could often experience the invisible presence of the Master, and although he always granted me his inner guidance, the fact that I could not be near the Master in his physical form caused me deep pain for years, and I longed very much to sit once more at his feet. When I finally returned to the Dera again after a six-year absence, I found that much had changed: two big guesthouses had been built and I now had to share the Master with hundreds of international guests.

Some years later, due to the terrorism in the Punjab, no foreigners were allowed to come to the Dera. Instead we were allowed to attend the Master's satsangs in Mumbai and Delhi. More than a thousand visitors from abroad had assembled, along with hundreds of thousands of Indian disciples and seekers, amongst whom I was just one disciple. In those days I shed bitter tears about losing the nearness to the Master that I had experienced during my first stay in the Dera, when we sometimes had been no more than twelve guests. The desire to have the Master all to oneself might seem egocentric and emotional, but on the path of devotion it is natural. True longing in the disciple is the very foundation of the inner way and is fulfilled at increasingly higher levels of consciousness as the disciple grows in love and awareness.

It is certainly an overwhelming experience to meet the 'Word made flesh' eye to eye, to listen to his message and to realize that he has become one of us. But once initiated, disciples can cross the threshold into a new dimension of their spiritual life – the path leading within. Certainly the Master will continue to answer questions, and to have the *darshan* of the living Master will always remain a blissful experience for the disciple – but the Masters never tire of pointing out that most of all it is the inner *darshan* of the Master that a disciple should long for. Like every disciple of a true living Master, I now had to learn this lesson.

However, for most disciples there is a long way to go before meeting the Master's astral form and getting his inner *darshan*. It is necessary first to go through a long process of detachment and purification, during which the inner guidance of the Master is essential. The Masters have given various answers to the frequently asked question: how can a disciple experience this guidance? Maharaj Sawan Singh, for instance, says in *Spiritual Gems* that the very fact that a person finds his way to the Master and is initiated by him shows that he was guided by him. At first, this can only be a theoretical concept for the disciple, and one must have a certain measure of faith and confidence in the Master in order to be able to take the first steps on the path of the Masters. In his letter, Maharaj Sawan Singh says that when a person begins feeling an aversion to a life turned completely towards the world and becomes a seeker of God, it is an unmistakable sign of inner guidance. Mostly there are no spectacular signs of the Master's inner guidance;

rather, the Master's grace accompanies the disciple secretly but none the less ceaselessly.

The more diligently disciples practise their spiritual exercises and the more they advance on the path, the greater their sensitivity to the inner guidance of the Master will become and the more readily they will follow the inner impulses and inspiration, which they will perceive more clearly, more frequently and irresistibly. They will experience the 'pull within' more strongly and the invisible presence of their Master will become ever more perceptible to them. Their longing for meditation will intensify and their need for worldly things will lessen.

Maharaj Sawan Singh also points out that a true living Master is more than just a teacher, for he is always close to his disciples in his radiant inner form; this is the greatness and the effectiveness of his grace. As mentioned often before, at the moment of initiation the Master in his astral form takes his abode in the third eye of his disciple, from where he is always keeping watch. The Master lets his disciples experience his help on the spiritual path and extends to them his protection against the powers of seduction of Kal, the power of negativity, and *maya*, the illusion of the world.

In spite of the Master's promise to be always by the side of his disciples, probably all satsangis go through phases when they feel lonely or abandoned by their Master. At any rate, all the Masters deal with this issue in an attempt to give their disciples some solace. In *Divine Light* Maharaj Charan Singh writes to a disciple:

> After initiation, the question of our Master's leaving us does not arise. As long as he has not seen us to our home and made us stand face to face with our Father, he does not leave us. He is not only with us in this life but this companionship goes on even after death. He does not

become carefree after initiating us, but has taken on the responsibility of taking us back to our original home.

On this promise – of this I am convinced – every satsangi can rely, even if sometimes they feel far away from their Master. At any time they can turn to him and take hold of his hand, whatever their reason might have been for letting it go.

What a Master does for his disciples every moment, how he leads them step by step on the way to the final goal, is something disciples will only realize when they raise their consciousness to a higher level and meet their Master in his inner astral form. From then on disciples will consciously experience the Master's guidance and they will be able to speak to him inside.

Next to faith, trust and surrender, the prayer of the disciple for guidance and protection is an important factor on the spiritual path, and Maharaj Charan Singh explicitly points this out in many of his letters. The inner Master will never turn a deaf ear to a sincere and fervent prayer from his disciple, but will rush to answer any plea for help on the spiritual path that comes from a pure and loving heart. I have become convinced of this through personal experience on many occasions. The secret of this is that it is the Master himself who puts the longing into the heart of his disciple in order to fulfil it – as Maharaj Charan Singh says in *Die to Live*.

By far the most important task of a true living Master on earth is to free souls from all the bonds tying them to the creation. He frees them from the net of *maya*, leads them out of the realm of the negative power and brings them back to their eternal home. However, he also helps his disciples to cope with their worldly affairs. He does not simply leave them to go through their karma for this life. On the contrary, his protecting hand is there even in worldly matters. Maharaj Charan

Singh repeatedly assured us of this, and over the years I have often experienced it for myself.

The search for a Master

Since I had been following the inner guide for so many years, accepting a living Master was difficult for me at first. But when I did finally realize how necessary it was to have a living spiritual guide, there was no need for me to search for him, for through my acquaintance, Mr H. Singh of Nagpur, I had already known about him for a number of years.

Many seekers of truth, however, are not so fortunate. The search for a spiritual guide is often a hard and tedious process. Whoever searches in esoteric literature will find a great confusion of Gurus and Masters, and will find it difficult to make a choice. We may however rest assured that everybody will find the spiritual guide he needs at the time. Those who want to develop supernatural powers or lift the veil of the future or contact disembodied beings or try to change their karma will be drawn to a suitable teacher. Those who want to enter into the secrets of the transcendental worlds and their gods, of which the holy scriptures of the East speak, will turn to an adept who is able to teach them the method of going there. But if a person feels an irresistible desire to tread the mystical path of union with God, then that person will find a Master of spirituality.

Seekers can be sure that their future Master has already chosen them, even before they have recognized him, for as the Master of Nazareth assured his disciples: "Ye have not chosen me, but I have chosen you."

As I experienced myself, the Master prepares his future disciples in manifold ways for meeting him. This preparation can extend over many years and may be a painful and dark phase of life, especially because, as Madame Blavatsky writes, one very often cannot be sure of ever finding the Master. Certainty is only achieved when one has reached the feet of the Master. Only then will one become aware of the fact that it was not the disciple who found the Master, but the Master who found his disciple.

But how can seekers know whether they have found a true Master? This is a question that was often asked, especially during meetings with the Master in Europe and other parts of the West. The answer was given by Baba Gurinder Singh, the Master at Radha Soami Satsang Beas since June 1990, when he spent three days in Germany in August 1999. He said that we cannot know for sure. He gave a startling illustration of our dilemma when he said that if we want to find out for sure whether someone is a true Master, then we are like a first-year pupil who wants to test his teacher to see whether he is qualified to teach him.

Still, there are a number of objective criteria by which a sincere seeker can be guided in making a choice. One of the most important criteria is that a true Master does not charge for his teachings. He lives on his own income and never takes a single cent or even the smallest gift from anybody. All great Masters of the past have followed this principle, even if they lived in poverty and kings and princesses were amongst their disciples. A true Master dedicates his entire life, all his time and strength, to the service of those souls for whom he has taken responsibility. It is indeed deeply moving to witness the selflessness and the self-denial of the Masters in discharging this service.

There is another important sign by which to ascertain whether someone is a true Master – he must teach the supreme importance of the audible Shabd or Word. In addition, Soami Ji insists that a true living Master must abstain from drawing attention to himself by performing miracles or displaying his supernatural powers in any way. Certainly, miracles do happen in the life of a true Master, but he does not want people to speak about them, and they never should be a reason to believe in a Master.

A true Master does not aim at a position of power in the world, nor at wealth or honour, for as Jesus Christ said to his judge when he was asked about his kingdom: "My kingdom is not of this world." A true Master is interested only in spiritual matters – the kingdom of God and the salvation of souls assigned to him by God. He does not promise his disciples material advantages or worldly success. He is more concerned with their spiritual welfare than with the fulfilment of their worldly ambitions or their desires for material welfare and worldly riches. Rather, a true Master considers it his task to free his disciples from all these attachments and bonds.

The trustworthiness of a Master is also based on the fact that he himself practises what he teaches. He leads a flawless life and is an example to all his disciples. From the life of his Master, the disciple can deduce how a life dedicated to the search for God should be lived. The present Master, Baba Gurinder Singh, expresses the same point when he says that our actions should reflect our desire for God-realization.

There is another token of a true Master, which we often experience when listening to a Master's discourses. Although they speak a simple language, which even uneducated people can understand, at the same time their words possess such a wonderful power of conviction and clarity that hardly anybody can escape their impact. One feels that here is someone who teaches with authority, as must the people of Jesus Christ's home town have marvelled at his words.* The power of conviction of a

---

* "For he taught them as one having authority, and not as the scribes." *Matthew* 7:29

true Master's words rests in the fact that he knows about God and creation from his own experience. Another unmistakable indication of a true Master is that he never makes any claims for himself – he never claims to be a true Master.

When a seeker, whether after careful consideration or possibly through unusual experiences, has come to the conviction that he has found the right Master and that he should apply for initiation, he should have as much faith and confidence in the Master as is necessary to take the first steps on the path of the Masters. In due course he will receive so much evidence of the Master's inner guidance and of the Master's care for his entire life that his faith will grow ever stronger and steadier. Faith may waver initially, but if one gets the chance to see the Master in person and to listen to his satsangs, then this wavering faith in the Master will mature into conviction. A certain measure of faith in the path of the Masters is needed to begin with, until one has experiences on the way inside. Until there is personal inner experience, faith may be shaky, as Maharaj Charan Singh sometimes pointed out. As long as we are unable to see him face to face, we are not safe from doubts; if we are not vigilant, our intellect may come up with counter-arguments at any time.

During the evening meetings with the Master in the Dera, the question of the necessity of a living Master was also frequently asked. It is worth looking at how the Master frequently answered this question. He pointed out that from our early childhood we need living teachers who convey to us the knowledge necessary for our development and prepare us for our future life. Books alone would not be enough to do this. In the same way, when we are sick, we need a living physician for diagnosis and to prescribe medicine. A deceased physician, be he ever so famous, cannot help the sick today. Equally, if one plans a dangerous expedition or a long journey, one will look out for a competent guide and not rely only on a description of the route.

The Masters of bygone times have returned to the Father, as Sant Mat teaches. Since they are no longer in the human form, they can no longer initiate people onto the spiritual path. Their words can still inspire us, but initiation must be imparted by a contemporary Master who lives on our human level and who, at the same time, in his capacity as a Son of God, can enter the kingdom of God. Only such a one can lead souls to that kingdom.

A day like the end of the world

This event took place many years ago, but it was of such a great significance in my life and in that of every satsangi and seeker of that time that it is important to describe it here: the passing away of Maharaj Charan Singh and the formal investiture of his successor, Baba Gurinder Singh.

On the first of June 1990 the news of the departure of our beloved Maharaj Charan Singh spread with lightning speed all over the world and came as a great shock to all his disciples. My first reaction was: unthinkable! Such feelings were shared by all the disciples of the Master. The Master's representative in South Africa, Sam Busa, wrote in a memorial pamphlet what all of us had felt when the news of Master's passing away reached us: "It never entered my mind at any stage in my life on the path that Maharaj Ji would leave his body, let alone leave it before my time came to depart this life."

The shocking news came to me in a phone call when I had guests in my home, so that I had to maintain my composure outwardly. When I was alone at last, I let my tears flow freely. It felt like the end of the world and I had no idea how I would live on after my Master's death. After the first eruption of pain and sorrow it became clear to me, as it did to many others, that nothing had really changed for us with Master's passing away. In his astral form he is present in each of his initiated disciples and they can meet him inside as soon as their consciousness has reached that threshold where he is waiting for them. Although we would never be able to see him again in his human form – and this is a thought that is painful to every one of his disciples even after many years – the Master had not left us. We therefore dried our tears and vowed to strive with all our strength for his inner *darshan*.

Two days later, many of the satsangis from Munich spontaneously travelled to Salzburg for the satsang that routinely took place on that Sunday. First the Master's representative in Austria, Hansjörg Hammerer, spoke to us, and then we read together our Master's words of farewell, which were spoken to his disciples many years earlier when he commented on Saint John's Gospel and were later printed in the book *Light on Saint John*. Some of us had been in the Dera at that time, but we never could have imagined that these words would one day be his legacy to us.

In his commentary on this Gospel, Master discussed Jesus's speeches of farewell before his arrest. I, too, had been in the Dera when the Master took the Bible and explained to us the real meaning of the Gospel of Saint John. Therefore, while reading out this text at the satsang I felt the Master's presence intensely. Now his words, spoken so long ago, were as real and relevant to us as if they had been spoken especially for this hour.

The Master tried to console us. He admonished us to cope with the situation and to submit lovingly to the will of God. He advised us how to behave after he had left this world. First there were the words of consolation that Jesus had spoken to his disciples and that the Master quoted for us:

Let not your heart be troubled.... In my Father's house are many mansions.... I go to prepare a place for you. And if I go and prepare a place for you, I will come again, and receive you unto myself; that where I am, there ye may be also.

Then the Master continued explaining Jesus Christ's words, saying: "You will never be orphaned, Christ tells his disciples. I will always be with you to comfort and to guide you if you turn to me for guidance." The Master continued with "the world seeth me no more", and then commented:

He (Jesus) says: The world will not see me when I leave this body, but you will still see me because I am not going to leave you. Where will you see me? Within yourself. I will always be with you in my radiant form so for you I do not die.... The Master never leaves, he never dies.

And so we continued to read, page after page, until we came to the passage where Jesus says to his disciples: "It is expedient for you that I go away." Of this the Master said, "He (Jesus) says: When I leave you it will be in your interest.... How can it be in the interest of a disciple that the Master leave him physically?" The Master explained it by saying that disciples must connect with the Holy Spirit, the Shabd within, if they want to return to the Father. To run after the Master in his human form day and night will not lead us inside. But if the Master leaves his physical body, his disciples have no other choice than to seek him within.

Those hours in Salzburg brought us very close to the Master and they were a great consolation for us, because they so clearly and unmistakably pointed the way: meditation would lead us to the Master – at first in darkness, but one day the light would shine within us and we would meet him in his inner form. In spite of all the pain caused by the death of our Master, we were also very anxious to know whether he had nominated a successor. Every satsangi trembled at the idea that with the death of Maharaj Charan Singh all might end at Beas, all the more so because the Master had sometimes dropped hints to us that the line of the Masters would come to an end some day. But we received the answer to our question while we were still in Salzburg. One brother was in telephone contact with satsangis in India and they conveyed to us the news from the Dera: Maharaj Charan Singh had appointed his successor by executing a will on 30th May 1990.

The successor was Sardar Gurinder Singh Dhillon, who had been given all the powers – spiritual and temporal – of a Sant Satguru, as well as inheriting the role of Patron of the Radha Soami Satsang Beas with the authority to give initiation. In spite of our grief over the departure of our Master, we felt great consolation, joy and gratitude that we would not be without a Master in the human form, who would be in charge at the Dera and who would give initiation and guidance. We would extend to the new Master our love and our faith, because he was for us the embodiment of the love and the care of our own Master, of whom he too had been a disciple.

Eighteen years have passed since the death of my Master. I have always tried to treasure in my memory the precious moments of my personal meetings with him. But I have had to go through the painful experience of my recollections fading away more and more as the years passed. It is especially difficult to recall emotionally the blissful experiences of the past. In the course of time I realized that I was given all this to engender love and devotion to the Master. I recognized that memory alone cannot maintain the direct and living contact with the Master. The desire to be in his presence and to experience his nearness cannot be fulfilled merely by recalling beautiful experiences. This can only be done by a constant effort to turn to him, to keep one's attention at the eye focus with him and to carry on making him the centre of one's life. Daily meditation, practised with zeal and the longing of love, is the strongest means of doing all this, but it depends above all else on the grace of the Lord. This is something one realizes more and more in the course of a long life as a disciple. What every disciple was able to experience after the death of our Master was, first and foremost, the fact that the inner guidance of the Master had not diminished in any way, now that he was no longer with us in his human form.

The pledge of his love

After our Master's passing away, there was at first 'radio silence' between Beas and Germany – only very scant information reached us. But some Indian satsangis living in Austria had travelled to Beas and reported from there. On the tenth of June 1990, the installation ceremony of the new Master had taken place – a ceremony that is the outer sign of the succession. The authority of the new Satguru is exclusively based on his nomination by the preceding Master and does not in any way depend on the ceremony, but the ceremony provides some consolation and assurance to disciples and seekers who need it.

Later we learned from the publications of the Dera that the transition from one Master to the next had taken place without any break or problems. In his inauguration speech the new Master said that Maharaj Ji had been very exact in his planning; he had thought about every detail.

From the first day, Baba Gurinder Singh took over all the tasks that his Master had discharged up to his death, with just one exception – he made it clear, when asked, that he would not give initiation until his Master ordered him to do so. This answer touched me profoundly, because it made us feel the deep and immediate contact of the new Master with his own Master.

In autumn 1990, when the Dera opened again for foreign guests, some satsangis from the Munich sangat travelled to Beas. I still could not bring myself to accompany them, knowing that I would not find my Master there; the memory of all my meetings with him was too vivid. Everything would remind me of him – every corner where we had waited for him, every tree under which he had spoken to us. Even seeing the fields that had been cultivated under his supervision would make me burst into tears – let alone the pain of not having the Master's *darshan* any more.

The visitors returned from the Dera consoled and full of joy. They brought a photograph of the new Master, whom they described as a young, dynamic and worldly-wise man, who was married and had two children. In May 1990 he had wanted to come to the Dera in order to spend his holidays there, but his fate caught up with him and he came to succeed his beloved Master. Deeply impressed, those returning from the Dera told us about the evening satsangs with the Master – which questions were asked and how the Master had answered them. These were the first words of guidance from the new Master and we received them eagerly. One sentence engraved itself deeply in my mind: we should not build Sant Mat around our lives but our lives around Sant Mat. To make Sant Mat the centre of our lives – this was what the Master was calling us to do. All our thinking should revolve around the Master and the path. From the very beginning, all those who could observe the new Master in the Dera felt that every word he uttered was based firmly on his own actions and experience. 'Do it' was, and still is, one of his favourite instructions to us disciples.

In October 1991 I too travelled with other satsangis from Munich to the Dera. The two weeks with the youthful Master were a wonderful experience. His vigour, his alertness, his kindness and his charming personality captivated us all. Our visit was still overshadowed by the death of our Master and we were not as happy as in previous years, but all of us realized with great gratitude that the new Master was the greatest and most valuable pledge of our Master's love for us.

Around that time, I had completed my small *Lexicon of Surat Shabd Yoga* in German and asked for an interview with the Master to get his instructions concerning its publication. The Master welcomed me in the room where I had received initiation twenty years ago and I mentioned this to him. These moments spent in the Master's presence were very moving and they contributed greatly to deepening my feelings of familiarity and attachment towards him.

During my stay at the Dera, I realized more and more that one of the greatest mysteries of human existence was taking place before our eyes: the complete transformation of a human being into a divine one – the metamorphosis of a man, who until now had been one of us, into the Son of God – the incarnation of the divine Word that now lives amongst us. We felt that we were witnesses of that *mysterium tremendum* – awe-inspiring mystery – and this filled us with deep reverence and admiration. One should not let oneself be deceived by the Master's outward appearance into seeing in him only a human being charged with the tremendous task of administering the affairs of the Dera and all the satsang centres around the world. In truth, the Satguru is much more than that – he is the saviour of the souls assigned to him by God, their redeemer from the hands of the negative power.

After the passing away of Maharaj Charan Singh, all his disciples had to deal with the question of their future relationship with his successor. In reality, our Master had not left us alone. He would continue to stand at our side and he would keep his promise to take us to our eternal goal. As his disciples, did we need a living Master? I searched in the Sant Mat literature for the answer, but actually I already knew it, because our Master had touched on this subject more than once: as long as a disciple is unable to communicate with his Master on the astral level, the successor of the Master stands by his side. The disciple can turn to him whenever he needs advice and help on the spiritual path. The second task of the successor of a Master is to teach Sant Mat to all disciples and seekers of truth. He is the guarantor that Sant Mat will be taught unadulterated and he is the only one who can explain the writings of past Masters with absolute authority.

Another important feature of the living Master for disciples of his predecessor is that he is a unique example of a perfect disciple. In the evening satsangs with the new Master, it became clear over and over again that for him, his Master is the guiding principle. Time and again he advised us: Always ask how your Master would think, how he would act. He confided to us that he would not even be able to discharge his responsibilities as Patron of the Dera if his Master was not with him at all times. The immediacy with which the new Master made us partake of his experiences impressed us deeply. He is giving us a living example of perfect obedience towards the Master, of complete self-surrender. We, for our part, can still hesitate to practise such obedience – at least that is what we think – but he had no alternative.

I intuitively felt that Baba Gurinder Singh was for us a standard-bearer who walks ahead of us. He proves to us that the path is practicable and that returning to our origin is possible with the help of the Master. In the beginning I found it difficult to look at the new Master because I missed the sight of my own Master so badly, but my understanding of his role helped me to give myself without reservation to the *darshan* of the Master sitting before us. I saw that this would not in any way diminish the love and devotion I felt for my own Master, as some disciples feared.

The fact that the Masters in their true form, which is the Shabd, are all one was a consolation that helped quite a few disciples to overcome the pain of separation from their own Master. But this idea, that all Masters are one, remains a theory for us until we are able to experience the truth of it for ourselves, and I drew little comfort from it. I received more consolation from the knowledge that the Master is with me in his astral form even after leaving his physical form.

The German sangat has had the great pleasure of being visited several times by our new Master. Each time he has spoken forcefully about the path of the Masters and answered the questions directed to him in detail and very patiently. One suggestion he made to us in Bamberg in 1999 has particularly imprinted itself in my memory: our actions should reflect our desire for God-realization. This short sentence could be the leitmotif for a disciple's whole life. Whenever I have the opportunity to listen to our Master, I am fascinated again and again by the conciseness, comprehensiveness and depth of his words, which impressed me from the very beginning.

At the time of this writing, Baba Gurinder Singh, referred to by his disciples as Baba Ji,* has been the Satguru of Beas for eighteen years and already has initiated hundreds of thousands of seekers into Surat Shabd Yoga. The power of a living true Master has no limits, yet Baba Ji insists that he still is the same as he was before he was appointed Master. Maharaj Charan Singh always used to explain the reality of a living Master by reminding us that the true Master is the Shabd, just as the real disciple is the soul and not mere flesh and blood. This is a great mystery that will only unveil itself when one has progressed on the path.

---

*'Baba' means a father, a respected senior or an ascetic; 'Ji' is a term of reverence and endearment.

CHAPTER SIX

The Universal Christ

WITH THIS CHAPTER BEGINS THE THIRD SUB-
ject area of Part Four: the Christian perspective on the teachings of the Masters and the Sant Mat dimension of Jesus
Christ's teachings. Some parallels between the teachings of
the Master of Nazareth and Sant Mat were pointed out earlier
in the book. While I was preparing for my initiation, it was
important to me to gain insights into the similarities and possible differences between the two teachings. But during the
course of the years and decades after my return to Germany,
new perspectives of understanding have opened, and I would
like to present to the reader my new insights, for I found them
to be truly fascinating and inspiring.

One of the starting points for the growth in my understanding was the key term 'universal Christ'.* This concept

---

*The term 'Christ' (from Latin *Christus* – the anointed one) is frequently
used in the Bible. In the Old Testament (as it is called in Christianity)
this term often appears as its Hebrew equivalent, 'Messiah' – and refers
to a king, or to God's representative who takes the place of God on earth.
It is only by being anointed that the chosen one becomes ordained,
becomes king. In the New Testament, the Epistle to the Hebrews uses
this expression no less than 258 times. A Christ is the one sent by God as
an intermediary or saviour.

was introduced by the philosopher Justin Martyr (d. CE 165). When the Christian churches during the 1960s aimed at a dialogue among religions, theologians reintroduced, amongst other concepts, the idea of the universal Christ or the cosmic Christ, which Teilhard de Chardin (1881–1955) had already used in his writings. The term 'universal Christ' seems particularly suited to casting new light on one of the central points of the Sant Mat teachings. According to Sant Mat, the Masters of the highest order, true Masters like Jesus Christ, are incarnations of the one Word. In this way each Master is universal. To me as a Christian and disciple of a true living Master, the question of the relationship between true Masters in the Sant Mat sense and the historical Jesus of Nazareth was thus of primary importance.

The definition of this term in Christian theology opened up for me a new perspective on this relationship. Of particular significance was the statement of Christian theologians that the universal Christ is transhistorical and pre-existent to his incarnation as Jesus of Nazareth. This pre-existence refers not only to his eternal being as the Word of God, but also to his position as a Christ, the anointed one. The universal Christ is the Word inasmuch as it is sent to earth by God to liberate the souls from the negative power and to show them the way back to the house of the Father. As Jesus spoke of himself: "In my Father's house are many mansions.... I go to prepare a place for you.... I will come again, and receive you unto myself; that where I am, there ye may be also."

In many of his self-testimonies, Jesus Christ transcends his earthly personage, indicating the mystery of his timeless existence, as for instance when he says to the Jews: "Verily, verily, I say unto you, Before Abraham was, I am." The Jews must have considered this as blasphemy and they reportedly picked up stones and threw them at him. In his conversation with the Jewish councillor and Pharisee Nicodemus, Jesus revealed himself as the one pre-existent to his birth, as the one who descended from heaven:

> Verily, verily, I say unto thee, We speak that we do know, and testify that we have seen; and ye receive not our witness. If I have told you earthly things, and ye believe not, how shall ye believe, if I tell you of heavenly things? And no man hath ascended up to heaven, but he that came down from heaven, even the Son of man which is in heaven.

On many pages of *The Gospel According to Saint John*, we can read similar self-testimonies of Jesus Christ. His most important statement is probably: "I and my Father are one." In another instance Jesus says: "No man knoweth the Son, but the Father; neither knoweth any man the Father, save the Son." Even in the face of death, Jesus still testifies that he was in the glory of the Father, which he had with him "before the world was".

The existence of a true Master beyond time is also a component of the Sant Mat teachings. An Indian mystic of the sixteenth century, Guru Arjun Dev, himself a Master of the highest order, describes the greatness of his own Master in the following words: "How could one describe the greatness of a Guru? He is an ocean of wisdom and truth: he was from the beginning, from aeons to aeons."

According to Christian theologians, the concept of the universal Christ relates exclusively to the person of Jesus of Nazareth, concerning his existence beyond time. In the Sant Mat teachings, however, the universal Christ is transpersonal, an aspect of the Word, of the Shabd, in relation to his manifestation in the human form as a saviour of the souls. The concept of the universal Christ – according to the teachings of the Masters – includes all incarnations of the divine Word that have taken place in history. There is, however, no synonym for 'universal Christ' in Sant Mat. This term then would be a contribution of Christian theology to Sant Mat, whilst on the other hand, the teachings of the Masters add a new dimension to the concept of the universal Christ.

In the universal Christ, all Masters, all historic Christs, are one. On the basis of the above-mentioned considerations, I can agree with this statement as a Christian and as a disciple of a true living Master, and my conviction is based not just on intellectual insights but on my experience. Nevertheless, such ideas fascinate the intellect and are therefore a valuable encouragement to attaining the experience of this truth on a higher level of consciousness by means of spiritual exercises.

A second aspect of the universal Christ of the theologians relates to Jesus Christ after his life on earth. After having completed the work of liberation of those souls that were assigned to him by the Father, he returned to the throne of God, from where he had come. From that point on, the Christian teachings speak of him as the elevated Lord, whom the author of the Epistle to the Hebrews describes with these enthusiastic words:

> Who being the brightness of his glory,
> And the express image of his person,
> And upholding all things by the word of his power,
> When he had by himself purged our sins,
> Sat down on the right hand of the Majesty on high.

In his Epistles, the apostle Paul often expresses similar thoughts about the elevated Lord, the universal Christ, even if the text does not use this word. However, the term 'elevated Christ', used in the Epistle to the Hebrews, does not refer just to the time after the death of Jesus Christ, because as God-man he already had this status while living on earth. Jesus Christ had access to the throne of the Most High even during his lifetime. He himself testified that "All power is given unto me in heaven and in earth," and on another occasion he calls himself "Son of man sitting on the right hand of power". In fact, it was this statement that provoked his death sentence.

In the Sant Mat literature, there exist many statements about the true Masters similar to those in the Epistle to the Hebrews. Thus Kabir, the great Indian mystic (1398–1518) who is considered a true Master, writes: "I have ascended to the throne of the Most High," and there is a hymn by Guru Arjun Dev (sixteenth century) that puts the following words into the mouth of a true Master:

> My temple is the highest of all temples,
> My country is limitless and inaccessible,
> My kingdom exists since eternity.
> Boundless and everlasting are my treasures
> And my glory radiates from aeons to aeons.

The living Christ

This section about the universal Christ deals with a central theme of the teachings of the Masters: the necessity of a contemporary true Master for the liberation of the soul, already mentioned earlier.

In sending out his Word in the human form as a Christ, God meets the needs of human nature. Since human beings are unable to perceive the metaphysical and purely spiritual worlds with their senses or to grasp God with their intellect, they are – so to speak – beyond the reach of God as well. God therefore needs a mediator who establishes contact between him and humankind. This mediator is the God-man, the Christ. As a person, he can be seen, heard and touched, and as such he is familiar to those amongst whom he lives. He shares their lives, knows their worries and needs, their longings and disappointments, and he also knows about their sins, as the Master of Nazareth has repeatedly shown and as every disciple of a true living Master can experience. The writings of the Masters abound with references to this fact.

A Christ, while being human and at the same time one with God, is therefore able to reveal to human beings the divine mysteries and to bring them the message of the Father. He is a bridge between God and humanity. Being an incarnation of the Word, the Shabd, he can – in carrying out his divine assignment – put people back in contact with its music. Although the sound current pervades the entire creation, it does not carry the soul back to her origin unless she is able to make contact with it, hearing it with her inner ear.*

But if, in order to save souls, it was necessary once that God should send us a messenger – the incarnation of the divine Word – then it will always be necessary. This is what Sant Mat teaches and this is what Jesus Christ referred to when he said: "As long as I am in the world, I am the light of the world." Time and again, Maharaj Charan Singh assured us that such messengers of God, the true Masters, have always lived on earth and that this world would have been consumed by fire long ago if those messengers of divine grace were not always living in it.

---

*In his book *Philosophy of the Masters*, Maharaj Sawan Singh uses the familiar example of electricity to illustrate this point: "The formless Lord pervades everywhere, but in spite of this, unless we become directly connected with him, we do not receive any virtue from him. Electricity is present everywhere, but we cannot derive any light or other benefits from it unless we know the location of the switch."

The Masters also emphasize that these messengers of God, on the highest level of consciousness, are all one – they are the Word. Equally, the Masters insist that all the Masters of the highest order teach the same truth,

When I came in contact with the teachings of the Masters, the idea that the Word comes to earth again and again in the human form and that there is always a Christ living on earth was completely strange to me. It was very difficult to accept this essential point of the Sant Mat teachings. Only after I had received a direct intimation of this truth did my doubts dissolve into thin air.

Up to the present day the Master Jesus of Nazareth moves the hearts of untold numbers of people and calls forth in them a deep love for God. His teachings still fascinate people, even if they do not belong to any Christian church and even if they are not Christians, as for instance Mahatma Gandhi. But Jesus Christ had fulfilled his task on earth when he left the world and returned to the Father. This he clearly testified in his prayer to the Father on the eve of his capture: "I have glorified thee on the earth: I have finished the work which thou gavest me to do." He has merged into the Father and in his divine form he no longer r establishes contact with us. It is more than two thousand years since he spoke to us and dwelt among us.

According to the teachings of the Masters, since the death of Jesus Christ many other incarnations of the divine Word have come down to contact the souls in this creation and to be instruments of the supreme Lord's mercy, just as they did before Jesus. God sends all these saviours to earth to manifest his divine love for humankind.

CHAPTER SEVEN

The Mystic Dimension
of Jesus Christ's Teaching

EVER SINCE THE GERMAN JESUIT KARL RAHNER
(1904–1984) made the thought-provoking statement: "The pious
one of the future will be a mystic or he will be nothing," Christian theologians and exegetes (experts in the interpretation of
the Bible) have been discussing the question of whether Jesus
Christ was a mystic and whether his teachings – apart from
their religious, ethical, moral and educational aspects – also have
a mystic dimension. Christian theologians have not yet come to
an agreement on this question, but the subject is being seriously
discussed and is given great importance, as is evidenced by the
extensive literature that it has generated – at least in Germany.

From the point of view of Sant Mat, there is no doubt
that the Master of Nazareth, as a Christ, was a mystic who
possessed the *cognitio Dei experimentalis** to the highest degree.

---

* According to the definition of the great mediaeval theologian and Doctor of the Church, Thomas Aquinas, a mystic is someone who possesses
the *cognitio Dei experimentalis* – the knowledge of God by experience. The
existence of God will not only be believed in and philosophically and theo-
logically asserted, but by inner experience it will be known for certain.

He himself testifies that he knows the Father and the Father knows him and that he is one with the Father. These two statements do not relate to any intellectual knowledge of God but to the mystic experience of God.

If Jesus Christ was a mystic, his teachings doubtless have a mystic dimension,* originating from an immediate vision of God in which the mysteries of God were revealed to him. This aspect, indeed, runs through the entire message of the Master of Nazareth – but it is visible only to the eyes of one who knows. I had never asked myself about the mystic dimension of the teachings of Jesus Christ, but when I came into contact with the teachings of the Masters, I started to reflect on it, because there I found many statements about God and the way to reach him, the like of which I had never read in the Gospels. It was only through Maharaj Charan Singh's commentaries on the Gospels, *Light on Saint John* and *Light on Saint Matthew*, that I gained access to the mystic dimension of Jesus Christ's message. Through meeting a living Master, the familiar texts of the Gospels took on a new meaning, based on a reality that had been unknown to me before.

In Christianity there has never been any lack of Biblical scholars, often mystics themselves, who gave mystical interpretations of the Gospels and other books of the Bible, ranging from Origen (c.185–254), Gregory of Nyssa (c.333–c.394) and Augustine (354–430), to Bernard of Clairvaux (1090–1153) and others. But their writings are mostly allegorical interpretations of Christ's teachings or of texts from the Old Testament, rather than explanations of their mystical meaning. Moreover, they are often very difficult to understand.

---

*The term 'mystic dimension' refers to the transcendent, spiritual and divine truths that can be experienced through the soul's powers of perception.

The difficulty in comprehending the mystical significance of Jesus Christ's teachings is compounded by the fact that the Master of Nazareth himself kept it concealed. He preached his message to the people in similes and parables so that the deeper meaning of his words remained hidden to most of his audience. When his disciples mentioned this to him, he told them that it was given only to them to understand the mysteries of the kingdom of God.* Clearly therefore, behind the message that Jesus preached to the people, there is another mystical dimension that was meant only for his disciples. There are some passages in the Gospels indicating that Jesus took his disciples to the mountains or into the wilderness in order to be alone with them. There he confided in them, speaking privately to them about his real spiritual teachings.

Another problem that arises when trying to recognize the mystical dimension of Christ's teachings is the fact – frankly conceded today – that although the substance of his message has been handed down to us, the Gospels contain few of Jesus's authentic words. There are various reasons for this. In the first place, Jesus Christ gave his message only by word of mouth; he wrote nothing himself. Not only that, but in addition none of his words were written down during his lifetime. It is therefore reasonable to assume not only that what has come down to us is incomplete, but also that legends were added to it and that Christ's person was mythologized. These problems are compounded by the problems inherent in translation. Being translated into so many languages, the Gospels unavoidably suffered changes and distortions; there would inevitably have

---

*"And the disciples came and said unto him, Why speakest thou unto them in parables? He answered and said unto them, Because it is given unto you to know the mysteries of the kingdom of heaven, but to them it is not given." *Matthew* 13:10–11

been errors in translation, errors in copying manuscripts by hand, and perhaps even deliberate falsification on occasion.

Today, we cannot ask the Master of Nazareth for the exact wording of his teachings. Such clarification would be of importance to theologians and exegetes, but it is not needed in order to understand the mystical significance of the texts; such understanding is open to all those who have 'eyes to see and ears to hear'.* A person with understanding of spiritual matters based on their own inner experience can look beyond the words of the Gospels and grasp their deeper meaning. Christ's message has come down to us only in a fragmentary form, but a real knower will sift out the mystic content of the teachings and will be able to explain it to others.

It was important for me to make these preliminary observations before looking at two central aspects of the mystical message of Jesus Christ and showing how they connect with the teachings of the Masters. These two themes cast light on the intimate relationship between Jesus's teachings and the teachings of Sant Mat about the mystical path and the union of the soul with God.

The kingdom of God

One of the great themes in the teachings of Jesus Christ was that of the kingdom of God or the kingdom of heaven. In Jesus Christ's message, this term had no political significance, whereas for the Jews of his time – in terms of their own history – it had the established meaning of a kingdom of God on earth. Jesus Christ did not speak of the kingdom of God in terms of the great visionary pictures expounded by the prophets

---

* "Yet the Lord hath not given you an heart to perceive, and eyes to see, and ears to hear, unto this day." *Deuteronomy*, 29:4

of Israel, which were familiar to the Jewish people and fuelled their hopes for a theocratic yet worldly kingdom. When the Master of Nazareth talked about a 'kingdom of God' he had in mind a very different sort of kingdom, a kingdom "not of this world". This kingdom was not to be found anywhere on earth; it could be found only in man. As Jesus said: "the kingdom of God is within you." Not only is this statement of key importance in understanding Jesus's teachings about the kingdom of God, but it is also one of the fundamental themes of the Sant Mat teachings. But the Gospels tell us nothing about the nature of this kingdom of God, what it looks like and how it can be experienced. This was part of the secret, mystical message of Jesus Christ, which he imparted only to his chosen disciples.

It was in the teachings of the Masters that I found the answer to my questions about the nature of this kingdom of God. According to those teachings, the kingdom of God is the *inner spiritual world* that the mystic experiences within himself. It is the everlasting and unchangeable reality, the divine realm so eloquently described by various Masters, especially by Soami Ji, mentioned earlier. When, during meditation, a disciple of a true living Master crosses the threshold to these worlds with his consciousness, he has made the first step into the kingdom of God. Supernatural light will engulf him and he will hear the voice of God, the audible Word. From there he will, under the guidance of his Master, ascend from region to region, leaving behind the astral and causal worlds and finally entering the purely spiritual worlds, the birthplace of the soul, the kingdom of God.

The food of the soul on the long journey through the metaphysical and spiritual worlds is the bread of life and the spring of living water, which Jesus promises to all who believe in him. It is the divine light and heavenly sound that feed the soul on her way back to the kingdom of God. This is an experience to which mystics of all religions bear testimony. In this way, the Christ himself becomes that food and that drink, as Jesus Christ said to his people: "I am the bread of life: he that cometh to me shall never hunger," and "whosoever drinketh of the water that I shall give him shall never thirst; but the water that I shall give him shall be in him a well of water springing up into everlasting life."

Jesus Christ spoke in numerous parables about the kingdom of God. I would like to take up two of them from *The Gospel According to Saint Matthew*, because they are of great mystic significance. Jesus likens the kingdom of heaven to a treasure that is hidden in a field and is then discovered by someone. Full of joy he goes away, sells all his possessions and buys the field. In the second parable Jesus compares the kingdom of heaven with a precious pearl. In order to acquire this pearl the merchant sells everything he owns.

The field, as Maharaj Charan Singh explains in his commentary on Saint Matthew's Gospel, is the human body, in which the Shabd – the divine light and the sound – is hidden like a treasure or like a pearl of incomparable value. If this treasure is to be gained, the seeker of God must abandon all his possessions. This is what Jesus asked of the rich young man who wanted to follow him. But Jesus is not referring to the man's worldly possessions, although that is how it is interpreted in the Christian tradition and that is how it was understood and practised by some Christian saints such as Saint Francis of Assisi. What is meant, as the Masters of Surat Shabd Yoga explain, is that a seeker of God must, through spiritual practice, mentally leave behind everything that draws the attention away from the path leading within. The seekers must leave behind all desires and attachments, forgetting their environment and even their body, emptying the mind completely of all 'I' and 'mine'. When, during her ascent to the final goal, the soul of the seeker of God passes beyond time, duality and the worlds of the negative power and enters the pure spiritual regions, she leaves behind even her own individual mind, her individuality as a mental being. This is the only way the soul can acquire the treasure that is God himself.

The entrance into the kingdom of God

Christ leaves no doubt that the way to the kingdom of God is not a broad and comfortable road. He said: "Enter ye in at the strait gate...Because strait is the gate, and narrow is the way, which leadeth unto life, and few there be that find it." Jesus Christ makes clear how narrow that entrance into the kingdom of God is. After the rich young man, who was not prepared to give up everything he possessed, had gone away, Jesus said:

> Verily I say unto you, That a rich man shall hardly enter into the kingdom of heaven. And again I say unto you, It is easier for a camel to go through the eye of a needle, than for a rich man to enter into the kingdom of God.*

This metaphor of the eye of a needle has a mystic dimension as well. With the expression 'eye of a needle', Jesus refers to the point that in the Indian spiritual literature is called the third eye. It is above the root of the nose, between the two eyebrows, but has nothing to do with the physical body – it is rather a centre in the astral body. As the Masters explain, this

---

*Biblical scholars are still not sure about the meaning of the word translated as "eye of a needle". It may also relate to the narrow gates of the city walls of Jerusalem through which only an unloaded camel could pass. Other exegetes point out that the Aramaic word for 'camel' may also mean a thick woollen thread that can hardly pass through the eye of a needle.

third eye is the seat of the soul and of the individual mind in the body. From here the attention flows out into the visible world and so the view of the transcendent, incorporeal and spiritual worlds is blocked. Through this eye of a needle, the camel – the entire attention of the disciple – must pass during meditation, before his consciousness can ascend to the astral regions and from there to the other higher worlds, in order to finally reach the kingdom of God.

In Saint Matthew's Gospel, there is still another instance where the Master of Nazareth refers to the third eye and in so doing gives a clear indication of the mystical dimension of his teachings. There Jesus says: "The light of the body is the eye: if therefore thine eye be single, thy whole body shall be full of light."

With these words, Jesus Christ refers to the perfect concentration of the attention at the above-mentioned point, which is the entrance to the transcendent worlds. When a person has become 'single-eyed' and his consciousness has crossed this threshold to another level, his first experience will be of a flame of light. When his consciousness rises still higher, the transcendent light will appear to extend throughout his whole body, filling it completely. This supernatural light changes in quality and intensity from region to region, until in the highest plane the soul merges completely into the divine light. At the time of initiation, the Master describes these experiences, as well as the various sounds of the Shabd that the soul will perceive while ascending through the higher worlds.

Mystic union with God

A second central aspect of Jesus Christ's teachings is the soul's union with God. Jesus himself had experienced the mystic union of his soul with God in the most perfect way, so that he could say of himself: "I and my Father are one." The union of his disciples with him was one of his great concerns, as expressed in the prayer to his Father on the eve of his arrest: "That they all may be one; as thou, Father, art in me, and I in thee, that they also may be one in us." How his disciples could attain this union with him he demonstrated by the parables of the door and of the vine. In these two similes, the mystic dimension of his teachings is made especially clear.

In his parable of the good shepherd, Jesus calls himself a door: "Verily, verily, I say unto you, I am the door of the sheep.... By me, if any man enter in, he shall be saved." Thus the Master of Nazareth indicates his central role as a mediator between God and man. Whoever longs to meet God must enter through that door – the Christ is the entrance into the kingdom of God.

In what respect Jesus Christ is the door to the Father, and how the passing through this door is to take place, is something about which *The Gospel According to Saint John* gives no hint. This again is fully understood only by a mystic who can relate it to his own mystic experience. It was from the true living Master that I gained a deeper understanding of Christ's parable.

Jesus Christ points clearly to the necessity of a living Master, because only a human being can serve as an instrument of mediation between God and other human beings. The Christ in his human form is the first door through which a seeker of God must pass. This takes place at the moment of initiation into the spiritual path – through the baptism in the Holy Spirit of which John the Baptist spoke, saying that Jesus would administer it.* The living Master reconnects the soul of

---

*"He that sent me to baptize with water, the same said unto me, Upon whom thou shalt see the Spirit descending, and remaining on him, the same is he which baptizeth with the Holy Ghost." *John* 1:33

his disciple with the Holy Spirit, the audible Word or Shabd. Thus the disciple passes through the first door.*

The union of the soul with God, however, requires a long process of purification in order to remove the immeasurable amount of karmas that a person has collected during countless existences on earth. It is also essential to go through a process of becoming completely detached from creation. On the way to the throne of God, to the final union of the soul with God, many doors are to be passed through – and the door through which the seeker for God must go is always the Christ.

After passing through the first door (meaning when they are put on the path by the living Master), the seekers will be guided by their shepherd to the threshold of the next door, the third eye. This is pointed out by Maharaj Charan Singh in his commentary on the Gospel of Saint John, where he explains the parable of the good shepherd. The door that will then open before them is the inner form of the Christ, the living Master, who had accepted the disciples into his fold.

The disciples will then contemplate on this inner Shabd form of the Master until they merge into it. The heavenly music, emerging from the radiant form of the Master, opens one by one the doors to all the mansions in the Father's house.†
It will lead the pilgrims through all the spiritual worlds until their souls merge completely into the sound of the voice of God and become one with it. This will be the moment when Jesus Christ's words to his Father come true: "And the glory

---

*The teachings of all true Masters are the same, because there is only one divine truth. The methods, however, through which the Masters open the entrance into the kingdom of God to their disciples can differ – they are in the hands of the Master; he can open the door according to his will. Even a single graceful glance of the Master on his disciple *(drishti)* can open the door to the transcendental worlds. The Masters choose the way they deem most fitting for seekers of God at that time.

†"In my Father's house are many mansions." *John* 14:2

which thou gavest me I have given them, that they may be one, even as we are one: I in them, and thou in me."

After all that has been said, the mystic significance of Jesus Christ's statement: "I am the way, the truth, and the life: no man cometh unto the Father, but by me" becomes clear. His words do not refer exclusively to the Master of Nazareth, but to every Christ whom God has sent and will send into the world in order to lead souls into his kingdom and to the final union with him. In the parable of the good shepherd, who is the door, the dynamics of the way to union with God become visible, whilst we find that in the second parable, that of the vine and the branches, emphasis is placed on the life-giving power of the Word, through which the union of the soul with God will be attained.

It was in his farewell speech before his capture that Jesus spoke to his disciples about the mystery of their union with their beloved Master: "Abide in me, and I in you. As the branch cannot bear fruit of itself, except it abide in the vine; no more can ye, except ye abide in me. I am the vine, ye are the branches: He that abideth in me, and I in him, the same bringeth forth much fruit."

Here Jesus points out very clearly that the living contact, meaning the experience of the intimate relationship with his Master, is of vital importance for the disciple's soul. The Master establishes this contact at the moment of initiation, but in order to bear fruit the branch must feed on the vine. In the first phase of the way to the perfect union of the disciple with his Christ, this is accomplished through meditation and love and devotion to the Master. For most disciples, this phase is long and arduous and it is shrouded in darkness. It will end when the supernatural light shines within the disciple and the divine music begins resounding within him. From then on, that divine light and the voice of God will be food for the soul, as discussed above. According to the words of Jesus Christ, the rich fruit that the branch will bear is eternal life and the union of the soul with God.

With this second parable it becomes clear that a seeker of God who yearns for union with him must first be attached to the true vine that bears life in itself, because, as Jesus Christ says: "without me ye can do nothing." According to the teachings of Sant Mat, this connection consists in the experience of the sound of the Shabd within.

I am aware that in the chapters about the universal Christ and the mystic dimension of Jesus Christ's teachings I have gone far beyond the Christian Church's interpretation of the Bible. I have endeavoured to show the parallels between the teachings of the Master of Nazareth and the teachings of the Masters, in particular the mystic dimensions of both teachings. When differences become apparent in these comparisons, it is my understanding that they arise not from the teachings of Christ but from the teachings of the Christian Churches as they have evolved in the course of their historical development.

As a Christian and a disciple of a living true Master, I felt the need to explore the unfathomable wealth of Jesus Christ's teachings with the aid of Sant Mat. In the framework of this book, however, I can give only a general idea of the immeasurable wealth of mystic wisdom that is found in the Gospels. Much can be read only between the lines, and many interconnections are not pointed out here. Some readers may also see a certain risk of syncretism in my search for a synthesis of the two teachings. Such suspicions on the part of the followers of different religions are understandable, because it concerns the content of their beliefs; but the central point is that these beliefs are replaced by the experience of truth. In their beliefs, religions may differ – but not in the experience of truth taught by the Word of God in human form.

CHAPTER EIGHT

The Mystic Dimension
of the Christian Feasts

To conclude this subject about the mutual relation between the teachings of Jesus Christ and the teachings of the Masters, I would like to discuss the mystic dimension of the three great Christian feasts: Christmas, Easter and Pentecost. Every time these feasts are celebrated in the course of the year, I feel the need to delve into their hidden meaning in order to recognize their significance for the spiritual path.

These feasts are in the first place days of remembrance of remote events in the life of Jesus Christ. However, the Christian Churches, especially the Catholic Church, are convinced that the liturgical celebration 'actualizes' these events; in other words, those who participate in the liturgy receive the same grace from Jesus Christ as was received by his contemporaries through his birth and death. As mentioned before, I could no longer believe this, but at the same time I felt unable to let these holy days pass without bringing them into my spiritual life as a satsangi, because my roots are Christian and their celebration, with right understanding, nourishes my heart.

In order to prepare inwardly for these feasts, I turned to the familiar texts of the liturgy, searched in the writings of Christian mystics for explanations of the mysteries of these days, read the commentary of Maharaj Charan Singh on the Gospels of Saint John and Saint Matthew and went through other Sant Mat books. In this way, I became aware of the mystic dimension of these feasts – a discovery I would like to share with my fellow travellers on the path of the Masters and all those who wish to fathom more profoundly the mystery of those days.

Christmas

Whilst the Synoptic Gospels of Matthew, Mark and Luke report the historical event of the birth of Jesus in detail, thus making it into the legend with which we are familiar in Christian cultures, it is the prologue to the Gospel of Saint John that reveals the true mystery and significance of the birth of this child. In concentrated language, the author of this fourth Gospel speaks of the greatest mystery in the history of humankind when he speaks of how the eternal Word, the Logos, takes human form: "In the beginning was the Word, and the Word was with God, and the Word was God." In the next sentence, the author states that this Word is the creative power of God: "All things were made by him; and without him was not any thing made that was made." Later, the Gospel writer reveals that "the Word was made flesh and dwelt among us." The name of the newborn child is not mentioned at this place, but a few verses later the author of the Gospel refers to Jesus Christ as "the only begotten Son, which is in the bosom of the Father".

One of the mystical messages of Christmas is that the Word has taken human form so that human beings can become children of God. On this point Christianity and Sant Mat are in full accord. But Sant Mat goes beyond this when it teaches that the birth of the divine Word through Jesus Christ is not a unique event in the history of humankind. On the contrary, this Word descends again and again to earth; it has lived, and is still living, among the peoples of the earth. This is a central point in the teachings of the Masters to which I have referred several times in the course of this book.

This fundamental point in the Sant Mat teaching took on a unique relevance for me when I was in the Dera at Christmas in 1998. As was the tradition, the international guests had organized a Christmas celebration and our Master, Baba Gurinder Singh, agreed to attend. A group of German satsangis had rehearsed a Christmas carol that we sang during the programme: "A ship comes to us, loaded to the highest board." The important words are in the third verse of the song: "The anchor touches the ground, the ship docks on land: The Word becomes flesh – the Son was sent to us." I was quite overwhelmed by the thought that the Son of God, about whom the song speaks, was sitting before us and celebrating with us this event of times long gone, which becomes a reality again and again in each Christ, in each true living Master.

The birth of the Son from the Father, mentioned in the prologue of *The Gospel According to Saint John*, is one of the inscrutable mysteries of God. Referring to this birth of the divine Word from the bosom of the Father, Saint Augustine asks: "Of what benefit is it to me, that this birth continuously takes place, but not in me? That it happens in me, this only matters."

Another great mystery is the incarnation of this Son of God in time and space, which is proclaimed in so few words in Saint John's Gospel. On this point, the German mystic Johannes Scheffler, who lived in the seventeenth century and who is known by the *nom de plume* Angelus Silesius (Angel of Silesia), makes the thought-provoking statement in his

Cherubic Wanderer: "Were Christ to be born a thousand times in Bethlehem and not in you – you would be lost forever."

Though I didn't know these two quotations at the time, the ideas that they express had moved me profoundly in my monastery at Christmas time. The very same questions had arisen in my mind and I had suppressed them.

The birth of God in the soul

The mystery of the birth of God in the soul takes place when the soul is united with the divine Word. A person becomes a 'son of God" when his soul becomes one with the Word of God. In order to make this birth of the Word in the soul possible, God sends his Son into the world. The mystics express this in paradoxical words: God became man so that man may become God.

An arcane sentence in the Christmas liturgy points to the mystic dimension of Christmas, to the birth of God in the soul. Whenever I heard it during the Christmas celebration in the monastery, I was fascinated by this sentence: "When peaceful silence lay over all, and night had run the half of her swift course, down from the heavens, from the royal throne, leapt your all-powerful Word." In the ecclesiastical Christmas celebration, this text refers to the incarnation of the Word of God in Jesus Christ; but it also relates to the mystery of the birth of God in the soul.

No other Christian mystic mentions this birth of God in the soul as often as Meister Eckhart (1260–1328). On one Christmas day Meister Eckhart gave an entire sermon on this subject, which was his life's theme, permeating all his sermons. He quotes the above-stated passage from the Christmas liturgy,

---

*"But as many as received him, to them gave he power to become the sons of God, even to them that believe on his name." *John* 1:12

changing it slightly and says: "Out of silence a secret word was spoken to me."

Meister Eckhart then asks what this silence is and where this place is, into which this Word will be spoken. He answers by saying:

> It is in the purest element of a soul, in the soul's most exalted place, in the core of the soul, i.e., the most hidden part of the soul; where the medium is silent, because here no creature, no image can enter, the soul neither thinks or acts, nor entertains she any idea either of herself or of anything else.... Here only peace and the celebration of this birth and of this work prevail, so that God the Father may speak his Word there: Because it is by nature receptive to nothing else but solely to this divine Being, without any medium.... Here God enters the soul through its core and nothing touches this core of the soul except God himself. No creature can enter this core – it must stay outside...and therefore, you must of necessity get into this being and into this core and remain there: there God must touch you with his single Being, without the interposition of any image.

Then Meister Eckhart asks a fundamental question: What should people do to prepare themselves for and to deserve this birth of the Word in them? He says: "Perhaps by imagining God visually and contemplating on this image, or by reflecting about the wisdom, the omnipotence or the eternity of God and the like, or perhaps by giving up every thought, every word and every work and becoming empty and receptive inwardly?" He gives the answer saying: "The best and most noble thing one can attain in this life is to keep silent and let God work and speak. Where all powers are withdrawn from all one's works and pictures, there the Word will be spoken."

To me, as a disciple of a living Master, Meister Eckhart's words sound very familiar – as also his sentence: "So a man should keep away from all his senses and turn all his powers inside and achieve obliviousness of all things and even of himself." The Masters of the East do not demand any less of their disciples than the eloquent medieval magister of theology, Meister Eckhart. In Surat Shabd Yoga, all that matters is to make the mind completely motionless so that the powers of perception of the soul can develop, and her inner eye and her inner ear can open in order to prepare herself for the birth of the Word. To experience this birth of the Word, seekers of God must leave behind during their meditation not only the consciousness of their own body and their environment, but finally even their individual mind. Asked for the symptoms of this birth of God in the soul, Meister Eckhart answered that it may be compared to a flash of lightning and that the 'face' of the soul is turned wholly to this birth.

Sant Mat has opened my eyes to the mystic dimension of Christmas, and everything this feast implied according to Christian traditions I have been able to understand within the framework of the teachings of the Masters. It was very important to me to see clearly that initiation into Surat Shabd Yoga does not involve any rupture with my own religion; on the contrary, I have gained a deeper understanding of the central mysteries of Christianity.

Easter

At Easter the Christian Churches celebrate the remembrance of the death of Jesus Christ on the cross and his resurrection – two events that traditionally are considered to be historical facts. Moreover, Easter is, according to the Christian faith, celebrated as the feast of the redemption through Jesus Christ's death on the cross. As already mentioned, in the course of time, serious questions concerning the teaching of the Church on salvation had risen in me, so that as a Christian and as a disciple of Sant Mat, I felt the need to trace out the mystic dimension of Easter that lies hidden behind the celebration of the historical events and their theological interpretation. This venture extended over many years, during which I came to a very surprising understanding of the origin of the Christian salvation doctrine, as well as gaining important and thrilling insights concerning the nature of salvation as taught by Jesus Christ.

In the course of my study of the liturgical texts and the Bible, I came to realize more and more that access to the mystic dimension of Easter is overlaid and obscured by the partly legendary account in the Gospels of the events at Golgotha and at Jesus's burial place, as well as by their interpretation by the apostles. In particular, the interpretation of Jesus's death on the cross as an expiatory sacrifice for the sins of the world was to have far-reaching consequences for the development of the Christian faith, in which it was given a position of central importance. Saint Paul in particular, but also other apostles, repeatedly expressed this view in their Epistles. In the first Epistle of Saint John for instance, we read that "he is the propitiation for our sins" and Saint Peter writes in his first Epistle to the Christian communities at Pontus, Galatia, Cappadocia, Asia and Bithynia that the elected ones "were not redeemed with corruptible things...but with the precious blood of Christ."

Although I had read such and similar phrases frequently and heard them often during the Easter liturgy in the monastery, I had never realized that the concept of salvation of Jesus Christ's apostles is based on the Jewish tradition of sacrifice and atonement. To the recipients of the Epistles of the apostles, many of them belonging to the Jewish religion, the idea of an expiatory sacrifice was very familiar. Animals were still sacrificed in the temple of Jerusalem in order to appease God; this was believed to be what God had once ordained on Mount Sinai. Although the Jews, unlike other tribes in their part of the world, did not sacrifice human beings to God, the death of Jesus on the cross was considered by his apostles as a death of atonement for the sins of the world. In their eyes, Jesus Christ was the sacrificial lamb of God, this metaphor being much used, especially in the Book of Revelations.

In his Epistles to the young Christian communities, the apostle Paul repeatedly expresses the idea that God has demanded expiation for the sins of men: "He that spared not his own Son, but delivered him up for us all." In the same Epistle he also says: "God commendeth his love toward us, in that, while we were yet sinners, Christ died for us." But is it not a terrifying thought that a father demands the death of his son to pay for the sins of humankind? And to whom is the payment made?

I searched the four Gospels thoroughly in search of statements of the Master of Nazareth to justify this view and I finally arrived at the conclusion that the interpretation of the death on the cross as an expiatory sacrifice, based on the Old Testament, has no foundation in Jesus Christ's message in the New Testament. This realization was a shock for me, because it concerns a fundamental element of the Christian faith. Jesus Christ knew that he would end on the cross and he predicted it on several occasions to his disciples, but he never said that his death would be an expiatory sacrifice for the sins of humankind and a means of salvation.

There is, however, one passage in the Gospel of Saint Matthew, where Jesus says: "Even as the Son of man came not to be ministered unto, but to minister ..." After saying this, the author of the Gospel continues with the following words of Jesus: "and to give his life (as) a ransom for many." Some modern exegetes and theologians suggest that this fragment is out of context, and may have been added at a later time, either by the author or by another editor. This addition reflected the views of the early Church, which in the beginning consisted mainly of Jewish Christians, yet it is still considered by Christianity to be the authentic words of Jesus.

The same is true of the words Jesus spoke to his disciples during the Last Supper when he gave them the unleavened bread and the cup of wine: "Take, eat; this is my body.... Drink ye all of it; For this is my blood of the new testament, which is shed for many for the remission of sins." This is nowadays considered by some exegetes not to be the authentic words of Christ, but were rather added on after the tradition of the memorial Last Supper had developed in the early Christian communities.

I do not doubt that Jesus Christ redeemed the souls of those who were given to him by the Father. But what does this redemption consist of and how was it attained? Because the Christian theologians I consulted were unable to answer such questions, I put them – figuratively speaking – before the Master of Nazareth himself, searching for an answer in the Gospels. To my great surprise, I first discovered that Jesus Christ never used the term 'redemption' for his work of salvation, nor did he ever call himself a saviour. Instead, the Master of Nazareth spoke of the life that he would give to his own. By his own account, he saw the purpose of his coming into the world, his real mission, as bestowing life. Along with the proclamation of the kingdom of God, this is one of the great themes of his teachings, which Jesus Christ took up frequently.

Seen in the light of Sant Mat, these words were a revelation to me and they offered me access to the mystical dimension of Easter. This mystical dimension is not related to the historical events Christianity celebrates at Easter, for Jesus Christ did not redeem the souls of his disciples by his death on the cross, but by his life on earth. This is shown very clearly by his own words.

Abundance of life

"I am come that they might have life, and that they might have it more abundantly." With these words the Master of Nazareth testifies to his mission on earth. And during the feast of the dedication of the temple at Jerusalem, he says: "I give unto them eternal life." The apostle John testifies at the end of the prologue to his Gospel that Christ's disciples had experienced the fulfilment of their Master's words "And of his fullness have all we received, and grace for grace."

Time and again, in his metaphors and parables, Jesus Christ refers to his role as a mediator who gives life to the souls entrusted to him. To the Samaritan woman at Jacob's well he reveals himself as the 'fountain of life': "Whosoever drinketh of the water that I shall give him shall never thirst," he promises her, and then continues: "But the water that I shall give him shall be in him a well of water springing up into everlasting life." On another occasion he calls himself the 'bread of God' that has come down from heaven and gives life to the world. According to the teachings of the Masters, the water of life and the bread of life is a spiritual power, the divine light and sound, the Word, the Shabd.

Jesus Christ did not take upon himself the giving of life – it was the Father who appointed him to proclaim his commandment, which is eternal life. It is the Father who gave him the power to give eternal life to all he had entrusted to him, as Jesus Christ himself says in his prayer to the Father. And then he adds a very important sentence showing the meaning of his statement: "And this is life eternal, that they might know thee the only true God." This knowledge of God is synonymous with the vision of God, the experience of God. It has nothing to do with any intellectual knowledge of God. It is the knowledge of God that is gained by the soul's contact with the divine life current, the Shabd, as has frequently been pointed out in this book.

Jesus Christ could transmit life to his disciples because he carried it in himself, for, as he testified of himself, he was 'life'. In his message he proclaims this truth again and again: "For as the Father hath life in himself; so hath he given to the Son to have life in himself." Whoever wants to have eternal life must turn to a Christ who is the "resurrection and the life".

When – as the Master of Nazareth emphasizes – it was his mission to give life in abundance to the souls entrusted to him by the Father, this implies that they are dead. However, this death cannot refer to the physical body, for Jesus is talking to living people. Moreover, physical death comes to all human beings, just as death ends the existence of every living creature. It was not the task of Jesus Christ to confer bodily immortality or to resurrect those already deceased. His mission was, in his own words, to rescue the souls of his disciples from eternal death and to give them everlasting life.

The immortal soul, that drop of the eternal divine Being, is actually bound with the chains of death during her life in the realm of the negative power. The law of cause and effect, the law of karma, ties her down in an endless circle of birth and death. Together with the various physical and mental bodies in which the soul is imprisoned, she suffers constantly recurring death, for in her present condition she is unable to return to the fountain of life, to her Creator. Although the soul is alive and infuses life into her various bodies, just as she also sustains her individual mind, these same coverings prevent her from being conscious of her own existence, for she identifies with her physical body and her mind. Seen in this light, the soul is, as it were, unconscious and sleeping a sleep of death, as the Masters put it. And, painful and full of suffering as physical death may be for a human being, the sleep of death of the soul is incomparably more excruciating. While alive she is dead and lives in darkness and the shadow of death. Her liberation and resurrection through the Son of God, the Word made flesh, consists in her awakening from the sleep of death and attaining life eternal.

Resurrection and new birth

The second event in the life of Jesus Christ that Christianity remembers at Easter is his resurrection from death. Belief in the physical resurrection of Jesus Christ is one of the fundamental elements of the Christian faith. On it rests the hope of Christians for their own resurrection at the end of time. Whether Jesus's physical resurrection from death as related in the Gospels is a historical fact must, however, be doubted. The partly contradictory accounts of the evangelists must be deemed to be legendary – they were meant to illustrate in a popular way the apostles' conviction that Jesus was still living, in the sense that he had, as it were, risen from death.

Some of Jesus Christ's apostles and disciples may have seen their Master after his death in his radiant form, in his astral body, just as Peter, John and Jacob saw him in his transfigured body on a high mountain. Still, the record of the evangelists clearly speaks of a bodily resurrection. This could indicate that Jesus Christ did not die on the cross but survived crucifixion in a coma-like condition, before being put into a burial chamber and called back to life by physicians – a theory that is advocated by a number of theologians and which some people believe is supported by the Turin Shroud.

The Masters of Surat Shabd Yoga do not speak directly about the Christian belief in the bodily resurrection of Jesus Christ, but they do point out that every Christ, after having discharged his task on earth, returns to the Father. His body remains on earth, like the body of every other deceased creature, while his mind merges with the universal mind in the causal region and his soul, being one with the divine Word, returns to the bosom of the Father. Meanwhile, the memory of the earthly personality of a Christ and the memory of his teachings remains with us on earth, where it continues to exercise its effect on people, inspiring them, lifting up their hearts to God and filling them with love for him.

The faith of the apostles and disciples of Jesus in his resurrection from death was not typically or exclusively Christian; it was taken over by the early Church from the Jewish tradition. The majority of the Jews in Jesus's time believed in physical resurrection, although their ideas about what this entailed were foggy. For this reason, the apostle Paul writes in his first Epistle to the community at Corinth that resurrection refers not to the physical body but to the spiritual body. He says: "It is sown in corruption; it is raised in incorruption." Saint Paul's faith in Jesus's resurrection was not based on an empty tomb but on his visionary meeting with Jesus after his death, to which he refers in the same Epistle to the Corinthians.*

Paradoxically, Saint Paul gives great importance to the physical resurrection of Jesus Christ and makes it the foundation of the Christian faith. In the first Epistle to the Corinthians he writes: "And that he was buried, and that he rose again the third day according to the scriptures.... But if there be no resurrection of the dead, then is Christ not risen: And if Christ

---

*"And last of all he was seen of me also, as of one born out of due time."
1 Corinthians 15:8

be not risen, then is our preaching vain, and your faith is also vain." But the true resurrection of a soul, her rising up from the sleep of death, will be caused not by any historical event in the life of a saviour but by the bestowal of divine life through a Christ, a true living Master, as Sant Mat teaches.

The mystic dimension of the faith in resurrection, in the liberation of the soul from the power of darkness and death and her entering into eternal life, is based on the fact that every Christ bears life in himself. As the teacher of Nazareth testifies: "I am the resurrection, and the life." And he passes this life on to his disciples. This resurrection is synonymous with the new birth of which Jesus Christ said to Nicodemus: "Verily, verily, I say unto thee, except a man be born again, he cannot see the kingdom of God.... Except a man be born of water and of the Spirit, he cannot enter into the kingdom of God."

What exactly this new birth in the spirit, this resurrection to life, consists of and how Jesus Christ has conferred it on his disciples, is a matter on which the Gospels remain silent. For myself, I found the answer to this question, which concerns the essence of salvation, in the teachings of the Masters. There the mystical meaning of Jesus's words became clear to me, because a true Master not only knows the mystery of this new birth, but he has – as Sant Mat teaches – the power to cause it. A Master bestows, as did the Master of Nazareth, the spiritual baptism with the Holy Spirit, the Shabd, on his disciples, and in so doing resurrects their souls from the sleep of death.

Resurrection from death and new birth into eternal life consist in the soul first gaining consciousness of herself, and then in attaining true knowledge of God – the experience of God. According to the testimony of Jesus Christ, he who has this knowledge of God has eternal life. If Jesus spoke of the abundance of life that he would give to his disciples, his meaning was that with baptism in the Holy Spirit he would give them this knowledge. Through such perfect knowledge of God, the soul's sleep of death is overcome and she enters eternal, never-ending life. This is her resurrection from death, from the permanent cycle of birth and death in which she is caught. The teachings of the Masters say that resurrection from death and new birth unto eternal life is a progressive process of awakening the soul of a disciple.

As Sant Mat teaches, the true living Master, a living Christ, reconnects the soul through initiation, the baptism in the Holy Spirit, with the fountain of life, the Word, the Shabd. It is by an act of volition – not by a ceremony – that the Master during this baptism ignites a spark of divine light in the disciple's heart. Through the grace of the Master, this spark will develop into a bright shining light of mystical knowledge of God. In the liturgy of Easter Eve in which, during the first Christian centuries, baptism was administered, the Church refers in the rapturous words of the Exultet to this light that is symbolized by the Easter candle: "Rejoice, earth, irradiated by heavenly light, and feel, illumined by the bright light of the eternal king, how the darkness has receded from you." These words, often attributed to the great Doctor of the Church, Saint Augustine of Hippo, are sung at the consecration of the Easter candle.

It is my intention in sharing my understanding of my own Christian experience to present a perspective to those searching for the mystic dimension of Easter. I myself have found it in the light of Sant Mat and I am convinced that it was my initiation into the path of the Masters that enabled me to become a truer Christian. It is my firm belief that on this path I shall find the fulfilment of my faith in the mysteries of Easter, the resurrection from death and a new birth in the spirit.

Pentecost

At Pentecost, Christianity commemorates an event that – according to the Acts of the Apostles – took place fifty days after Jesus's resurrection in Jerusalem on the Jewish feast of Shavuot. That day, it is said, saw the descent of the Holy Spirit upon the apostles and upon a large number of other disciples of the Master of Nazareth.

For me, Pentecost had always been the feast of the 'unknown God'. Although at my baptism a priest had called down upon me the Holy Spirit, and at the occasion of my confirmation the bishop had put his hands on my head and again called down upon me the Holy Spirit with its seven gifts, I was unable to say who this spirit of God was and in which way he was working in me.

I felt the same even after I joined the Abbey of Saint Erentraud, where my fellow sisters and I fervently celebrated Pentecost every year. On our knees we implored the Holy Spirit to descend upon us, believing and hoping that our entreaty would be answered in one way or another. Even so, he remained an unknown God to me. I believed in his existence, but his nature and his working were still covered by a dense veil. The nature of the Holy Spirit and the true meaning of Pentecost remained hidden from me for many years and I became reconciled to the idea that the Holy Spirit would remain an unfathomable mystery. As a disciple of a true living Master, however, it became my greatest concern to fathom the nature of the Holy Spirit and the mystic dimension of Pentecost – even if, for the time being, it would be no more than an intellectual understanding.

When preparing for the feast of Pentecost, I would have the liturgical texts of that day to hand and would read the account in the Acts of the Apostles of the descent of the Holy Spirit. But what had actually happened on this day of Pentecost in Jerusalem more than two thousand years ago? Whether the spirit of God really had come down like a raging storm and like fiery tongues upon those hundred and twenty men gathered in a room, and whether they had really spoken to the crowd in 'other tongues' afterwards, is something that will probably remain a mystery forever. The author of the Acts is Luke, the same Luke to whom one of the Gospels is attributed, in which he narrates in legendary language the birth of Jesus Christ. We may assume that in the Acts, Luke is figuratively describing the inner experiences granted to the apostles and disciples of Jesus Christ. Whether it was a collective ecstasy of people filled by the spirit, in the way that Luke describes it, is now doubted by many exegetes of the Bible.

Still it must be remembered that before his crucifixion Jesus Christ had predicted the descent of the Holy Spirit. In his farewell speech to his apostles he had said: "And I will pray the Father, and he shall give you another Comforter, that he may abide with you for ever; even the spirit of truth, whom the world cannot receive.... But the Comforter, which is the Holy Ghost, whom the Father will send in my name, he shall teach you all things."

Thus the Master of Nazareth promised to his disciples that the Holy Spirit, the spirit of truth, would descend upon them and would reveal to them the mysteries of God he had spoken about. By this he surely did not mean an intellectual knowledge of God, but the experience of God on a higher level of consciousness. Aided by the divine spirit, the Shabd or Word, his disciples were to ascend to the transcendent worlds, where God's truth and reality were to be unveiled to them before their inner eye. Jesus Christ's words also suggest that his disciples had not come to the highest experience of God while he was still amongst them. Under the inner guidance of the Comforter, they still had to pass through a process of maturing before they would be able not only to realize the mysteries of God but to merge into them.

Detailed information about the nature of this spirit cannot be found in the Gospels. To those listening to Jesus's words, the term 'spirit' or 'spirit of God' was not unknown. The account of the creation in *Genesis*, for instance, tells us that this spirit of God "moved upon the face of the waters" and in *Wisdom* we read that "the spirit of the Lord, indeed, fills the whole world." Since the time of King David, who is considered the author of the psalms, the Jews prayed to God: "Thou sendest forth thy spirit, they are created: and thou renewest the face of the earth." In the book of the prophet Joel, God also promises to pour out his spirit on all people when he says: "And it shall come to pass afterward, that I will pour out my spirit upon all flesh; and your sons and your daughters shall prophesy." And Ezekiel prophesies in the name of God: "A new spirit will I put within you."

Parts of these texts were integrated into the Pentecost liturgy, as also was a hymn written by the Archbishop of Canterbury, Stephen Langton (d.1228), in which this theologian expresses his faith in the attributes and the working of the Holy Spirit:

> Come, Holy Spirit, come!
> And from Your clear celestial home,
> Shed a ray of light divine!
>
> Come, Father of the poor!
> Come, source of all our store!
> Come, within our being shine!
>
> You, of comforters the best;
> You, our soul's most welcome guest;
> Sweet refreshment here below.

In our labour, rest most sweet;
Grateful coolness in the heat;
Solace in the midst of woe.

O most blessed Light divine,
Shine within these hearts of Thine,
And our inmost being fill!

Where You are not, we have naught,
Nothing good in deed or thought,
Nothing free from taint of ill.

Heal our wounds, our strength renew;
On our dryness pour Your dew;
Wash the stains of guilt away.

Bend the stubborn heart and will;
Melt the frozen, warm the chill;
Guide the steps that go astray.

On the faithful, who adore
And confess You, evermore
In Your many gifts descend.

Give us virtue's sure reward;
Give us Your salvation, Lord;
Give us joys that never end.

The blowing of the wind

In his conversation with the Jewish councillor Nicodemus, about the spirit out of which a person has to be born anew, Jesus compares this spirit to the blowing of the wind: "The wind bloweth where it listeth, and thou hearest the sound thereof, but canst not tell whence it cometh, and whither it goeth: so is every one that is born of the spirit." According to the teachings of the Masters, these words indicate the mystic dimension of Pentecost: the experience of the Holy Spirit in the form of various sounds, such as for instance the sound of the wind blowing. In Greek and Hebrew the word 'wind' is synonymous with spirit. For this reason, the blowing of the wind in this passage may well stand for the sounding of the spirit of God, the Shabd, which can be heard within by those who have received the baptism in the Holy Spirit. This blowing of the wind has no physical origin and whoever can hear it does not know whence it comes.

There does not seem to be any indication in the Gospels that the spirit of God manifests itself within as the sound. This is an objection many Christians make when they first come across the teachings of the Masters and I too felt the same. On this question, Maharaj Charan Singh points to a fact that has escaped the Christian exegetes. Jesus Christ frequently indicates that his word gives life, as for instance:

Verily, verily, I say unto you, he that heareth my word, and believeth on him that sent me, hath everlasting life, and shall not come into condemnation, but is passed from death unto life. Verily, verily, I say unto you, the hour is coming, and now is, when the dead shall hear the voice of the Son of God; and they that hear shall live.

And to the tempter in the desert who tried to induce him to change stones into bread, Jesus answers: "It is written, man shall not live by bread alone, but by every word that proceedeth out of the mouth of God." Similarly, in Jesus's parable of the good shepherd, the shepherd says: "My sheep hear my voice, and I know them, and they follow me: And I give unto them eternal life." All of these statements can be interpreted as references to the Shabd. The Master explained that they can all be best understood as references to the Word of God, to the resounding audible life stream, because ordinary, spoken words cannot have the effects described by Jesus Christ.

The nature of the Holy Spirit

In Christian dogma, the Holy Spirit is referred to as the third divine 'person' – the first and second being the Father and the Son. The doctrine of the Church speaks of a triune God and every Christian professes, in the Apostles' Creed: "I believe in the one God, the almighty Father, creator of heaven and earth…and in the one Lord Jesus Christ, his only begotten Son…(this is the wording used by the Catholic Church) of one nature with the Father…. I believe in the Holy Spirit, the Lord and giver of life, who emerges from the Father and the Son."*

In the course of the years following my initiation onto the path of the Masters, I realized more and more that the Word of God and the spirit of God, the Holy Spirit of Christian dogma, are identical. This is clearly expressed in the prologue of Saint John's Gospel. It begins with the words: "In the beginning was the Word…. All things were made by him…. That was the true

---

*The distinction between the Word of God and spirit of God or Holy Spirit does not go back to the Gospels. The dogma of the one God in three persons was not formulated until the second Ecumenical Council of Constantinople in CE 382, when the Council added the word *'filioque'* (and the Son), saying that the Holy Spirit emerges from the Father and the Son. The instruction given by Jesus to his disciples to baptize "in the name of the Father and the Son and the Holy Spirit", as recorded in *The Gospel According to Saint Matthew* (28:19), is apparently an addition, reflecting the practice of baptism in later times.

light, which lighteth every man that cometh into the world."
Although the text speaks of the Word, the concepts of the
Creator and the light are doubtlessly attributes of the spirit of
God – the Holy Spirit.

Sant Mat speaks of the creative power of God that manifests
itself as light and sound as the Word, the Shabd. Therefore, the
Holy Spirit of the Christian dogma would be identical with the
divine Word, emerging from the Most High. According to this
perspective, the Son referred to in the Creed is the *incarnate*
Word of God. In a very surprising way, Jesus Christ confirms
this identity of the Word with the spirit of God when he says:
"I am come a light into the world, that whosoever believeth on
me should not abide in darkness."

The New Testament likens the manifestation of the Holy
Spirit not just to light, but also to fire. According to the Acts of
the Apostles, the Holy Spirit descended in the form of tongues
of fire upon the apostles and the disciples of Jesus Christ.* John
the Baptist also had prophesied that Jesus would baptize with
the Holy Spirit and with fire.† Later, the Master of Nazareth
indirectly confirmed these words of John the Baptist when he
said: "I am come to send fire on the earth." This fire is the Holy
Spirit that Jesus Christ ignited in the hearts of those whom
the Father had entrusted to him. As the disciple of a true living Master advances on the path, this flame or light, together
with the sound, all emanating from the Word, show the way
through the inner regions up to the soul's place of origin.

According to the Sant Mat teachings, only a contemporary
Christ, a living true Master, can bestow baptism into the Holy
Spirit – the 'baptism with fire' that John the Baptist speaks

---

* "And there appeared unto them cloven tongues like as of fire, and it sat
upon each of them." *Acts* 2:3
† "He that cometh after me…shall baptize you with the Holy Ghost, and
with fire." *Matthew* 3:11

about. This is also my firm conviction. Only one who is the Word made flesh, who carries the divine light and fire in himself, can kindle it in human beings and can awaken their soul to this new life. This baptism cannot be effected by rites and ceremonies, but only by a direct act of volition of a light-bearer, a living Christ.

The Christian mystics' experience of the Holy Spirit

In my attempt to discover the mystic dimension of Pentecost, I also consulted the writings of Christian mystics. There I found out that they had experienced the spirit of God in various ways in the form of light and sound.

In particular, I searched the writings of Hildegard of Bingen (1098–1179), called even during her lifetime the Prophetissa Teutonica. In a letter to the monk Volmar, her spiritual guide, she writes about how from early childhood she was surrounded by a supernatural light that accompanied her throughout her life. Hildegard also often mentions in her visionary writings the experience of heavenly sounds, of a heavenly music or the music of the spheres. While beholding stupendous symbolic pictures within, she hears at the same time wonderful sounds. Thus, she writes:

> From the roaring vibrations of the ether above, by which the firmament revolves, a lovely and glorious sound of the elements emanates. Sweetly it sounds in its liveliness, like the sweet sounding voice of the human mind. Each element has – as ordained by God – its own sound. All together, they sound like the music of stringed instruments and of the zither, united in harmony.

In the *Vita*, her biographers quote Hildegard as saying:

In a mystical vision and in the light of love I saw and heard these words about the wisdom that never perishes: five sounds of righteousness sent by God resound in all people. On them the salvation and the redemption of the faithful rest. And these five sounds are superior to all human works, because all works of humankind are sustained by them.

In her main work, *Scivias (Know the Ways)*, Hildegard writes that heavenly music resounded when the Son of God led the redeemed ones to their heavenly abode:

By his redeeming touch and full of mercy he brought them back to their inheritance.... As they were returning to their inheritance, heavenly timbales and harps, every kind of strain of music resounded in indescribable harmony and beauty, because man, who had lain in perdition, stood up in blessedness.

In her book *Liber Divinorum Operum (Book of Divine Works)*, Hildegard speaks of the resounding cosmos and also of the music of the spheres. The description of the sound current, the Word that called the world into being, has an exciting vivid concreteness in the account of the Prophetess of Mount Saint Rupert, as she is sometimes called – after the name of her cloister. She describes the firmament as constantly revolving, while this revolving movement causes "wonderful sounds". In this sound the whole creation takes place: "As the Word of God resounded, there this Word appeared in every creature and this sound was the life in every creature."

To me as a follower of Surat Shabd Yoga it was interesting that Hildegard of Bingen mentions five sounds. According to the Sant Mat teachings, the Shabd, the audible life stream, manifests differently in each of the five transcendental worlds or regions. Soami Ji of Agra depicts his experience with the five sounds in his teachings compiled in *Sar Bachan (Poetry)*, comparing them with the sounds of different musical instruments.

> The reverberating melodies
> of bell and conch resound
> With the enchanting music of *veena* and flute.
> The *kingri* is played to the beat of the *mridang*,
> The *dholak* and the *pakhawaj* play on and on.
> The nectar streams in through a thousand channels
> While the sky revolves like a spinning wheel.

In his *Spiritual Canticle*, John of the Cross (1542–1591) describes the experience of the divine spirit in a different way. In this poem he speaks of the meeting of the soul with God as that of bride and bridegroom, saying that this encounter takes place in the form of a "roaring flow of torrents" and like a "whistling of the love-stirring breeze". In his commentary on these two lines, John of the Cross writes: "These sounds have three qualities... they inundate in their rush everything that they encounter... they fill up every depth and emptiness they meet... they muffle and suppress every other sound." Further on he continues: "What the soul experiences in this roaring flow of her Beloved is the sound of a spiritual clamour and outcry louder than all the sounds, a voice that enfeebles all other voices, a sound that exceeds all sounds of the world." Then he explains:

> This clamour, this roaring of the torrents, is such an abun-
> dant outpouring, such a forceful taking possession of her,
> and it appears to the soul not merely as the sound of
> cascades, but also as a roaring thunder. Yet this voice is a
> spiritual one that does not contain these other material

sounds.... It brings greatness and power, strength, delight and glory.... This voice is infinite, because it is God who communicates himself by producing this voice.

One of the great German women mystics, Gertrude of Helfta (1256–1302), in a prayer in which she thanks God for the great grace she had received, speaks of a "sweet-sounding melody of spiritual music, gentle and melting". And one of her fellow sisters in the same convent, Mechthild of Magdeburg (1210–c.1285), describes in her book *Flowing Light of the Godhead* how "the Holy Spirit plays the harps of heaven so that all strings resound".

I also remembered a poem by Bernard of Clairvaux (1090–1153) that I once heard during my noviciate in the monastery:

> O Lord, it is a ceaseless dying,
>   if one wants to gain You.
> O Lord, it is a ceaseless letting go,
>   if one wants to seize You.
> O Lord, it is like death to the senses,
>   if one wants to obtain You.
> Yet it is the rejoicing sound of a thousand violins,
>   when You become my own.

These are some of the testimonies of Christian mystics to their experience of the Word of God as supernatural sound. In the fourth volume of his *Philosophy of the Masters*, Maharaj Sawan Singh explains in detail that the Shabd, the audible Word, is an experience to which people have borne testimony in many ways. The Vedas and Upanishads speak of the great variety of sounds that are audible within and which the yogis can perceive if, through their spiritual practice, they have turned their attention inside. The Masters of Surat Shabd

Yoga speak of the *anahada* Shabd, sound not produced by any instrument, which can be heard by the inner ear. Zoroaster, the great Persian Master, speaks of Sraosha, the power of God that can be heard. Pythagoras spoke of the 'music of the spheres', an experience also shared by the German poet Joseph von Eichendorff (1788–1857) in one of his poems:

> A song sleeps in all things,
> A song that sounds and sounds.
> And the world starts singing
> If you only catch the magic word.

The Masters of Surat Shabd Yoga, however, point out that without a Master of the highest order to guide one, the experience of the music of the spheres, the singing of the angels, the hearing of bells and sounds within of which the mystics speak, cannot liberate the soul. They may lift up the consciousness of people to the astral and in rare cases to the causal regions, but there the soul is still in the domain of the negative power. She remains tied to her individual mind, with which she identifies. Only when a living true Master initiates his disciple into the secret of the audible Word that reaches to the highest realm, will the disciple be able to tread the ultimate path of salvation. Without a spiritual guide of the highest order at one's side, the ascent will come to an end before the region of true spirit is reached.

I found that in the course of writing this chapter on the mystic dimension of the Christian feasts, the teachings of the great and beloved Master of Nazareth and those of Sant Mat became unified within me, in just the same way as the gaze of my inner guide and that of my Master were united long ago. I recognized that these teachings spring from the same source: the divine Word, which time and again brings down to earth in human form the messenger of the kingdom of God. The reason for the parallels between the teachings of Jesus Christ and those of all true Masters lies in the fact that it is not his own teaching that each individual Master proclaims, but – as testified by the Master of Nazareth – it is the teaching of the Supreme Father: "The word which ye hear is not mine, but the Father's which sent me."

However, I was only able to experience this unity when I had become as familiar with the teachings of the Masters as I was with the teachings of Jesus Christ. Up to that stage, I always felt a certain inner restlessness, subconsciously at least, especially during the Christian feasts. But now I had come full circle: my faith in Jesus Christ's teachings and in those of the Masters had become one – an exceedingly blissful experience for a Christian disciple of Sant Mat. I am convinced that on this path, everything that the great Christian feasts promise will eventually come true in my life and in the life of every disciple of a true living Master: the awakening of the soul in God, her resurrection from countless deaths to eternal life, and the experience of the divine light and music of the Shabd, the Word. These are only different aspects of the salvation of souls through the incarnate Word.

CHAPTER NINE

On the Path of the Masters

WITH THIS CHAPTER BEGINS THE LAST PART of this book, treading the path of the Masters. While earlier chapters present the theoretical aspects of the spiritual path, this chapter deals with four fundamental elements of its practice: meditation, *sharan* (surrender and devotion), nourishing the flame of spirituality, and cultivating intense longing for meeting the Lord.

In our time, acquiring theoretical knowledge about the path of the Masters is important for most seekers of truth and God. But Maharaj Charan Singh, like all Masters, repeatedly explained that the Sant Mat teachings should not remain a mere theory; disciples must also practise it in their lives. The Master insisted time and again: Sant Mat is a way of life. To walk this path demands from disciples far more than daily meditation; they must tread it twenty-four hours a day. Therefore, as our present Master insists, Sant Mat should not merely be a part of our life; it must envelop, permeate and shape it completely.

The way of meditation

Surat Shabd Yoga is a spiritual path that leads the disciple of a true living Master to the mystic experience of God and to the union of the soul with her Creator. Initiation into the path of the Masters gives the disciple access to the transcendent, mystic dimension of spiritual life. The Master furnishes his disciples with the required equipment – the method of meditation – by which they can cover the first phase of the way, opening the third eye.

The meditation technique consists of the repetition of five names of God, which are imparted by the Master at the time of initiation and are filled by him with his spiritual power. He gives to the words the centripetal power that acts like a magnet to the disciple's mind. If repeated continuously, one-pointedly and with full concentration at a specific place within the forehead, they pull the attention inside. Some disciples experience the magnetic pulling power of these words at the time of initiation or shortly afterwards. Most, however, must first go through a long period of preparation. How long this first phase of meditation lasts will depend on the inner disposition of the disciple. Someone who has already followed a spiritual path in a previous life will perhaps proceed faster on the path of the Masters, while someone who is treading it for the first time in this life may make only slow progress; but this should not worry the disciple, for the Master will ensure that the disciple reaches the eternal goal.

Every soul has the capacity to experience the transcendent reality and God himself. This mystic potential lies within every human being. Some people are born with a leaning towards mysticism, while in others a strong desire for spirituality awakens only in later life. The first group are, as it were, born mystics, whose mystic potential was activated and developed in a previous life. Some of them, such as Hildegard of Bingen, were able to see the transcendent light from childhood, while for others this experience came later. Quite a few can also hear the audible Shabd, as shown in the chapter on Pentecost. Others begin their search for the truth and for God later in life, when the urge for mystic experience of God is awakened in them.

During the years I call the 'phase of remembrance' I went through a kind of initial mystic experience, to which I contributed nothing myself. When this phase ended, I fervently wanted to learn a method of meditation by which I could continue my spiritual path. The Lord's grace led me to the path of the Masters, the mystic path of the experience of the transcendental reality and God-realization. In *Spiritual Gems* Maharaj Sawan Singh assures his disciples that the sincere and irresistible longing to tread the spiritual path can be considered a sign that the Creator is calling back a soul after having sent her into creation, where she has been since time immemorial. Soami Ji says in *Sar Bachan (Poetry)*: "Radha Soami calls out to the soul to come and take possession of its home." When a disciple of Surat Shabd Yoga, under the guidance of his Master, dedicates himself to the practice of meditation, he can be sure of being on his way home.

To enable a soul to return to her eternal home, God sends his Word into the world. The Word of God become man is, as Jesus Christ testifies of himself, the way back to the house of the Father: "I am the way." The Master of Nazareth's statement reveals the unique position of a true living Master, the contemporaneous Christ, without whom the soul cannot make the journey back to her home. The realization of this fact is of great importance for the spiritual path, especially for meditation. Since the true living Master plays a central part in the salvation of a soul, he also stands at the centre of meditation. The disciple carries out the practice of concentration as instructed by the Master – and with his invisible presence. Once the first stage has been achieved and the practitioner's attention is collected at the third eye, the disciple's consciousness enters the transcendental worlds. There the disciple meets the Master in his radiant Shabd form. It is the Master who accompanies his disciple all the way back, and when the goal is reached the disciple realizes that the Master and the Lord are one.

On one occasion Maharaj Charan Singh indirectly indicated the Master's central position in meditation, when with great urgency he explained what inner attitude the disciple should take in performing his daily spiritual exercise, the repetition of the five holy words: he should put his whole self into the repetition of the names of God. He should put himself into the words. He should not think of anything else but to surrender to the Master by repeating the holy words. In this instruction the Master reveals the secret – his secret – of successful meditation. It shows the ideal that a disciple on the path of the Masters should keep in mind when starting his meditation. It is love for the Master that will finally generate the attention and concentration on the holy words by which the inner eye is opened.

Do your best

After my initiation into Surat Shabd Yoga in February 1972 I had only one desire: to make haste on the path of the Masters, to cover the first stage on the way as quickly as possible. Meditation dominated my whole thinking – that was why I had asked for initiation in the first place. Because I could begin on the path of the Masters at the Dera, where I was in daily contact with my Master, I had had a good start and I thought I could calculate how much time it would take me to cover the first stage on the path and to reach the threshold to the transcendental worlds. But a year and a half later, fate brought me back to Germany, where the circumstances of my life changed fundamentally. I soon had to realize that not only is the path steep and full of obstacles, but the journey might take much longer than I had anticipated. This is something all the Masters never tire of pointing out in their satsangs and letters to their disciples, but I had paid little attention to it. Now I was confronted with it every day.

In this new phase of my life, practising meditation proved to be a difficult exercise. Since the vertical take-off in my professional activity demanded all my strength, I either felt sleepy during meditation or had to struggle against a flood of thoughts that my mind ceaselessly produced. As soon as I sat down for meditation, closed my eyes and began repeating the five names, the film would start – the events and experiences of the previous day passed before me and countless impressions and remembrances flooded my brain. The problems of my professional work and so many other things that occupied my mind during the day did not allow me to come to rest inwardly. To make body and mind motionless and to turn my attention solely to the repetition of the meditation words seemed impossible. "No way!" was a thought that crept into my mind quite often. Moreover, I had to ask myself again and again whether and to what extent I was myself to blame for not progressing in my meditation. Why was there no tangible success? Had my zeal diminished? Did I have too many other hobbies and interests besides my daily duties? Was I really doing the best I could?

I could find the answers to my questions in the Sant Mat books, especially in *Die to Live* by Maharaj Charan Singh, because these were problems that other disciples faced as well, and they frequently put them before the Masters. All the Masters remind their disciples that for millions of years their souls have been in the creation and that they are bound to it with thousands of shackles. To untie these bonds is a very long, drawn-out process. The Masters also emphasize that the soul's way back to the highest realm, from where she once descended, is immeasurably long. Sometimes the Masters use the image of a tunnel that the disciple has to dig through a mountain in order to reach the transcendental world. They also point out that during its innumerable existences on earth each soul has accumulated an immense load of karmas. Meditation is the most powerful way to reduce this load and to purify the mind, they say. However, they also explain to their disciples that treading this path is a strenuous and lengthy affair and that quick results are not to be expected.

The biggest problem, the Masters point out, is to conquer the mind during meditation. It is the mind's nature to wander into the world of the senses, never to keep still at all and to move constantly from one thing to the next. Since the human mind has grown accustomed over millions of earthly existences to pouring forth into the creation, it takes a maximum of effort to turn it inside. Moreover, the soul is inescapably ensnared in the extremely fine-meshed net of *maya*; to dissolve this net also needs effort and unending patience.

The Masters have many ways of encouraging their disciples to persevere on the path of meditation. This is one of their great and important tasks, to which they dedicate themselves with great love and patience. They are untiring in reminding their disciples that the Master is standing by their side and that he has taken upon himself the responsibility of ensuring that they reach their goal, that there are no failures on the path of the Masters and that every minute of meditation counts. Often Maharaj Charan Singh encouraged his disciples, saying, "You simply do your duty and leave the results to the Master." Sometimes he also said, "When the time has come, the disciple will experience that inner pull."

The Masters also point out that as we progress on the way inside, meditation will become easier. In the beginning, they say, the disciple is like an ant trying to crawl up a vertical wall. Time and again the ant will fall down, but again and again it will start anew, and finally it will reach the top. Once the disciple has stilled his mind in meditation and the first success in the practice of concentration has been achieved, he can be compared to a spider that can effortlessly move up and down its self-spun thread.

When a disciple has made even more progress, he can move on the spiritual path like a fish that can not only swim against the current but also jump up waterfalls. When he has advanced still further, he finally is like a bird that can become airborne by a single beat of his wings. So perfectly does he control his mind that he can move from one level of consciousness to another in a flash. Then he has attained mastery on the spiritual path.

Reflecting on the Masters' answers, I kept wavering between discouragement and confidence, between doubt and trust, between disappointment and gratitude, but by the Master's grace I never gave up. In the depth of my heart I was happy and grateful for being on the path of the Masters. Many years ago I had set out on my adventure of faith and entrusted myself to the guidance of my inner Master. It had been a long and laborious way, at the same time both painful and deeply blissful, and it had led me to the feet of a living Master. But having reached there, I had to acknowledge that the actual way to God had just started and that every day I had to set out anew. This is an experience that has been beautifully put into words by a Christian mystic, Gregory of Nyssa (c.335–c.394):

> To find God
> Means always to search for him.
> And indeed, searching and finding are the same.
> Because the reward of the seeker is
> To search on and on.
> The longing of the soul is fulfilled
> In remaining insatiable,
> Because to really behold God
> Means not to tire in one's longing for him.

For a disciple on the path of the Masters, the hours of meditation are a time of awaiting the advent of the Lord, the coming of the Master in his radiant presence. In the monastery, the four weeks before the celebration of the birth of Jesus Christ, called Advent, was a time of fervent waiting for his coming. Now every day is a day of Advent for me. Mira Bai, an Indian princess (1498–1563), has expressed her longing for the coming of her beloved Master in moving words:

> Come, pray come, O Lord of mine,
> I await Thee. I long and pine.
> Oh come to my mansion, come, I pray;
> I stand with my eyes glued on Thy way.

In their satsangs the Masters often emphasize that for disciples on the path, the hours of meditation are the most precious time of the day. Even if they cannot yet experience the presence of their Master and the purifying and transforming effect of meditation, they may be sure it is working inside. They can trust that the moment will come when they will consciously realize everything that secretly has taken place within them. Then they will be able to look back on the way behind them and be able to continue and complete the way ahead in the light and sound of the Shabd. Until then, they must walk in darkness and trust the word of their Master.

Meditation is the most important task of disciples on the mystic path of the Masters. It is the first and central pillar of their spiritual life. The longer we are on the way, the more clearly we recognize that we can practise meditation only when our whole thinking and acting are directed towards God-realization. Above all, we become increasingly aware that we cannot do anything without the Master, as Jesus Christ emphasized when he said: "Without me ye can do nothing." Disciples therefore make every effort to place the Master at the centre of their lives. We may have realized theoretically the significance of the true living Master in our lives – but now we must try to transform this insight into action. And every disciple can rest assured that for every step taken towards the Master, the Master will take ten steps to meet him – something that I was allowed to experience time and again.

Sharan – taking shelter, surrender

The second pillar of a disciple's spiritual life, in my experience, is devotion to God and surrender to his will. From my early youth, this was what my adventure of faith meant to me. God taught me this in many ways: when he demanded my undivided heart; when he called me into the garden inclosed and then led me into the desert; when he made me walk on the ridge and the tightrope, and finally when he made me step over the threshold into a new dimension of my spiritual life. In this way, devotion to God and obedience to his inner guidance had become the guideline in my life. In the same way, *sharan* – taking shelter in God and surrendering to the divine will – plays a central role on the path of the Masters. *Sharan* is a Sanskrit word that has two meanings: to take shelter and to submit unconditionally.

In the Indian spiritual tradition, especially in the Upanishads, *sharan* is of fundamental importance. In Buddhism, it is a key element of the practice, and the religion of the prophet Muhammad has taken *sharan* in its Arabic form – *islam* – as its name. The Christian spiritual tradition also gives great importance to the unconditional surrender to God's will and devotion to him; it is considered the most important precondition for the union of the soul with God. Père de Caussade deals with this subject at length in his book *Abandonment to Divine Providence*.

The first aspect of *sharan* – taking shelter – is a basic element of human life. Whenever we experience our helplessness and defencelessness or the hopelessness of our situation, we look for someone to help us. The reason may be a difficult phase in our life, such as a stroke of fate, when the ground under our feet seems to be shaking; or we may fear for the future when faced with the vicissitudes of life; or we may be unable to find an answer to the pressing questions of life. To take shelter with someone stronger, from whom one hopes to receive help and protection, implies surrender to him or, expressed positively, loving submission to this stronger being. This is the second aspect of *sharan*. Taking shelter with God means a submission to the will of the Creator that is at the same time both conscious and willing; it is not for us to make conditions.

In the context of Sant Mat, *sharan* means taking shelter with a Master. The concept of *sharan* runs like a thread through the teachings of the Masters, and all the Masters underline the importance of *sharan* for a disciple of Surat Shabd Yoga. Whoever takes shelter with a Master submits himself unconditionally. But surrender and loving submission relate not to the human person of the Master as such, but to the divine Word that has taken human form in him. According to Sant Mat, the will of God and the will of the Master are one and the same. Maharaj Sawan Singh says in *Philosophy of the Masters*: "The Master is the Lord's will personified." While obeying the instructions of the Master, a disciple recognizes the will of God and becomes its executor. Whatever the disciple does, he does in the name of the Lord, and the Lord works through the disciple.

Surrender to the Master is a gradual process. A certain measure of faith and confidence in the Master is necessary to take the first, perhaps hesitant steps on the way of surrender and devotion. As disciples progress on the spiritual path, willingly and sincerely devoting themselves to the Master's spiritual guidance and surrendering to him, their faith and confidence in the Master becomes deeper. The more perfect the disciple's loving submission to the Master becomes, the more his faith turns into certainty. Every disciple on the path of the Masters can learn from experience that sincere surrender saves much suffering and helps to avoid many mistakes, whereas each attempt to push through one's own will always ends in disappointment and pain.

Sharan is the disciple's conscious 'Yes!' to the divine will that manifests itself in the circumstances of his life, in daily events and situations. It has been my experience that every attempt to observe the teachings and principles of Sant Mat, every 'Yes' of surrender and submission to God, brings 'eye contact' with him. Thus, the many daily acts of submission to the Master are moments of grace during which the disciple can meet the Master. The more the disciple makes use of such opportunities, the more the Master will become the centre of the disciple's life.

This being said, the Masters point out explicitly that *sharan* is not the surrender of a servant to his master, but the loving submission of a child to his father. If the child – as mentioned by Soami Ji in *Sar Bachan (Prose)* – lets go of the hand of his father in the excitement of the fair, he takes hold of it again by taking refuge with him and submitting to him. From now on, it is not the disciple's will that is the motivating force behind his actions, but the will of the Lord, through the Master.

The will of God, the divine law

Surrender to the will of God is of fundamental importance on the spiritual path. Guru Nanak says that the Lord cannot be realized by any other method except that of obeying and following his will. This being so, the central question is: What is the will of God and how can one recognize it? Maharaj Sawan Singh discusses this question in his book *Philosophy of the Masters*.

Maharaj Sawan Singh speaks of two aspects of the will of God: the will of the Lord that causes the creation to come into being and the divine law that emanates from this divine will. Both are actually the same, as the Master explains. The divine law executes the creative will of God. This law is the stage direction of the Creator for his 'play', the creation. It is this law that gives structure to the whole creation and governs its development and expansion. By its dynamic force the plurality of beings and the multiplicity of forms are brought about. The divine law is the basic origin of all the laws of nature, including the laws of physics and of biology. The laws of nature are not themselves the divine law, but are its manifestation.

Maharaj Sawan Singh emphasizes that it is very difficult for us to understand the nature and functions of this law. Human intellect can comprehend it only within a very small scope. Only the innermost self, the soul, can truly experience the divine law. Up to a certain point, however, we can recognize and investigate with our intellect how this divine law works in the creation, at least within our own small world.

In our day-to-day life we experience, for instance, the law of polarity prevailing in creation. This law is the basis of the pairs of opposites such as light and darkness, heat and cold, growth and decline, birth and death, pleasure and pain, love and hatred, and so forth. It is the cause and effect that we experience in our lives, which is also known as the law of karma. The whole of creation is subject to this law. No creature can escape its effects or resist its influence. Its principles determine and shape the animate and inanimate; no event in the life of any creature stands outside this law and nothing in any life happens by chance. Everything we see, everything that happens, is ultimately a consequence of the working of this law. Everyone's fate, down to the smallest detail, is determined by the law of cause and effect. Jesus Christ pointed to this fact when he said to his disciples that no sparrow falls to the ground without the Father's knowledge, and that even the hairs on our head are numbered.*

Of all the laws inherent in creation, the law of cause and effect has the deepest, most comprehensive and lasting effect on the life of all creatures. It applies not only to the physical and mental levels of their existence, but it also determines the fate of the souls in the creation, for it is this law that ties souls down to the creation.

Originating at the highest level of creation, the divine law is not merely a collection of dos and don'ts. It is the force that permeates and governs the whole of creation. Seen from this perspective, the question of a creature's recognizing and fulfilling the divine law does not arise. Nevertheless, being aware of this law is of prime importance for human beings; indeed, it takes a central position on the spiritual path. The attempt to recognize the will of God and to consciously and willingly submit to it, to practise *sharan*, is for a seeker of God one of the most effective means of living in the divine presence and finally becoming one with God.

For me it was an overwhelming and blissful experience to have received, through Sant Mat teachings, at least the beginning of an understanding of the divine law and its workings in creation and in the life of each individual creature. Our whole existence is completely integrated into its network – no matter whether we know it or not. The divine law surrounds, permeates and shapes the entire creation and our individual life, and in accepting it consciously and submitting to it, we are connected with our Creator.

Asked about the possibility of recognizing the will of God in our life, Maharaj Charan Singh pointed out – as all

---

*"Are not two sparrows sold for a farthing? and one of them shall not fall on the ground without your Father." *Matthew* 10:29. "But even the very hairs of your head are all numbered." *Luke* 12:7

Masters do – that on our level of consciousness we are unable to recognize the divine will with certainty. Nevertheless, the Master added, there are certain indications that may help us: everything that comes to us as fate, all that is inevitable and happens without our interference, we are to consider as the unalterable will of God for us. All the circumstances of our life, our family obligations, our professional and social duties – in Indian tradition called *dharma* – belong to this category.

For a disciple on the path of the Masters, the second aid to recognizing the will of God is the Sant Mat teachings, including the moral and ethical principles for our way of life given by the Masters. These help to adjust the whole life of a disciple, every thought and every act, to serve the supreme task of treading the path of liberation of the soul and attaining union with God. As a general rule the Masters advise their disciples that we should do whatever helps us on the path of God-realization, while what is obstructive and detrimental should be avoided.

Although the course and the circumstances of each person's life are determined in every detail by the law of karma, we are regularly confronted with the necessity of taking bigger and smaller decisions, both in worldly life and on the spiritual path itself. Can it be concluded from this that we have free will and, if so, then how can we bring it in line with the will of God?

Each of us has, the Masters assure us, a very limited free will – beyond that we are bound. To illustrate this, Maharaj Sawan Singh used the example of a boy flying a kite. His father has given him a string of a hundred or two hundred yards, and he can fly the kite only as high as the length of the string. To fly the kite means to decide and act according to our strength, our capacity and our intellect. This margin we can regard as our free will.

The Masters, however, declare that within this margin, wrong subjective decisions on our part might happen. But the law of cause and effect regulates our decisions automatically so that we cannot do anything that is not in accordance with our karma. The string is, as it were, pulled in. It follows that, objectively speaking, there can be no wrong decisions. Detours caused by our mistakes are also part of our karma. They serve to clear certain karmic conditions and to teach lessons that cannot be learnt otherwise. The effects of such wrong decisions are to be seen as consequences of one's individual karma, because everybody will – according to the law of karma – be called to account for every decision, meaning that we have to bear the consequences of our actions and of our motives in acting in a particular way.

If someone sincerely endeavours to recognize the will of God, then there is another, extremely subtle way in which that person may become conscious of the divine will. It is that particular capacity of the human mind that we call conscience, which acts as a channel for receiving impulses of divine guidance. To cultivate receptiveness to inner guidance – to make one's conscience sensitive and obey its hints – is one of the important conditions for progressing on the spiritual path.

From my early youth, it had been these inner impulses that led me on my way, especially during the ridge walk, when I had no other compass with which to find my way. When I met my Master, my submission to the inner guide gained a concrete and recognizable focus, whereas previously it was directed at an invisible being.

It is in this way that the disciple of a living Master can experience the Master's inner guidance. Intuitively, he can perceive the Master's instructions or suggestions both about daily life and more and especially about the spiritual path. It is, above all, by attending to meditation that disciples on this path become sensitive and receptive to these mostly gentle and subtle impulses of the inner Master, which speak to the mind and heart.

Although it is natural in the life of every human being that from early childhood we have to submit in many ways to others, those living in Western societies, where there is a strong traditional emphasis on individuality and independence, have great reservations about submitting their will to a Master. To surrender one's whole being to someone causes fear in many people. But according to Sant Mat, *sharan*, taking refuge with a Master, means to surrender to God and to submit oneself lovingly to him as a way of life. By virtue of his universal law, God rules over his creatures anyway; his will happens with or without their consent, nay, even without their knowing or recognizing it. Some might consider this a passive fulfilment of the will of God – that this passivity has a fatalistic tone and they react to their fate with dull, hopeless resignation. Conscious surrender to the divine will is, on the other hand, active participation in the fulfilment of God's plan for oneself.

Benefits of sharan

To conclude these considerations on *sharan*, there is one last question: What is the result or outcome of surrendering to the will of one's Creator, of submitting one's whole being to him? What is the benefit of *sharan*? Every time this question was asked, Maharaj Charan Singh answered spontaneously: One who loves does not calculate the reward for his love. This question does not exist for him. A lover of God does not calculate: so much surrender and love I give – so much protection, grace and love I shall receive.

On the other hand, the Masters do speak in their satsangs and books in detail about the numerous positive effects of *sharan*. For them, *sharan* is not a theory, not an intellectual or rational affair – they have travelled this path and have harvested the fruits of *sharan* in their own life. Therefore they can guide their disciples on the way of *sharan* and are able to make clear statements about its marvellous effects.

In *Philosophy of the Masters*, Maharaj Sawan Singh begins his comments on the effects of *sharan* by emphasizing that a disciple who has taken shelter with a Master can feel as carefree and happy as a child in his mother's lap. All Masters emphasize that *sharan* frees a disciple from all worries and anxieties and gives him an inner security he cannot gain through any other means. As paradoxical as it may sound, anyone who surrenders confidently to God attains the greatest safety in life.

Jesus Christ also urges his disciples to have this implicit trust in their Father in heaven, who knows the needs of each one of us. This trust, which comprises unconditional submission to the Creator, is an elementary part of his message.

In a parable the Master of Nazareth refers to the birds of the sky that eat without having sown, and to the lilies in the fields that do not spin but wear a more beautiful garment than King Solomon. "Are ye not much better than they?" Jesus asks. "Therefore take no thought, saying, 'What shall we eat?' or, 'What shall we drink?' or, 'Wherewithal shall we be clothed?'... Your heavenly Father knoweth that ye have need of all these things." Then, with a single sentence Jesus Christ names the condition for attaining this carefree state: "But seek ye first the kingdom of God, and his righteousness; and all these things shall be added unto you."

To believe in the care of the Creator and to trust that his creatures will receive everything needed, however, does not mean that what the Creator gives will be identical with our own ideas of what we need. Secretly, we hope that the Creator will give us what we think is best for us. True faith in the Father who knows what we need must be unconditional.

In one of his letters Maharaj Charan Singh mentions still another aspect of the effects of *sharan*. He points out that by *sharan* a disciple throws the whole burden of karma onto the Master and that the effects of bad karma will be essentially mitigated thereby so that one will feel their impact far less.

In *Philosophy of the Masters*, Maharaj Sawan Singh then addresses the question of the fruits of *sharan* for the disciple's spiritual life. *Sharan* removes the darkness of ignorance *(avidya)* about our true nature and the nature of God, and with *sharan* the light of truth will shine in us. *Sharan* gives us knowledge about the creation, the Creator and ourselves. Perfect submission to the will of God liberates us from the imprisonment of creation. *Sharan* is the key that opens the gate of the prison of birth and death and gives wings to the soul so that she can cross the immeasurable regions of the transcendent worlds and return to her eternal home. *Sharan*, the Master explains, transforms the whole being of a disciple and gives access to the treasures and mysteries of the spiritual worlds – to the kingdom of God.

The Masters also point out that by surrendering our own will and by submitting to the will of God, we only seemingly abandon ourselves. In reality, *sharan* bestows the highest freedom we can attain, because by submission of our own will we acquire perfect harmony with the divine law. Whoever gives up the ego and submits it to the Creator will find instead not only his own real self but also God, into whom the self will merge. With impressive words the Master of Nazareth speaks of the necessity of giving up one's ego when he says: "Verily, verily, I say unto you, except a corn of wheat fall into the ground and die, it abideth alone; but if it die, it bringeth forth much fruit. He that loveth his life shall lose it; and he that hateth his life in this world shall keep it unto life eternal."

One of the greatest and most important experiences in the disciples' spiritual life comes when they realize that through *sharan* their Master will become more and more the centre of their life, and that in this way they will experience his presence in meditation more distinctly, even if they are not yet able to see his radiant form.

On these pages, I have presented the ideal of *sharan* according to the teachings of the Masters, but the Masters emphasize that a disciple can achieve real surrender of the ego only after attaining control over the mind. "One can only give what one owns," as Maharaj Charan Singh used to say when asked about perfect surrender. But even a beginner on the path can experience something of that bliss and deep inner peace that *sharan* confers. A seeker of God is content with what the Creator grants. It is important to be modest and undemanding if one wants to keep inner contentment and balance, especially in this age, which is completely directed towards the acquisition and consumption of worldly goods.

Nourishing the flame

The third aspect of walking the path of the Masters to which the disciple must give full attention is nourishing the flame of spirituality. This requires constant alertness, firm resolve and perseverance. The disciple must always guard against the attacks of his individual mind, which is his worst enemy and which constantly threatens this flame. The disciple should always gaze fixedly at the highest goal – the return of his soul to her eternal home – and go towards it with firm determination and endurance.

After my return to Germany, I soon realized that continuing on my spiritual path would now demand all my strength. Up to then I had been driven by a strong inner urge. There had been obstacles, but they were different from those I had to conquer now. In Germany I found so many things assailing me, and I found too that the strong inner urge lessened and that I no longer felt that irresistible urge to meditate that had been there after my initial experience of the deeper layers of the spiritual life, and especially after my initiation into Surat Shabd

Yoga. Under completely changed living conditions, I was trying to cover – figuratively speaking – the required metres of
altitude on the path, or rather to crawl just a few millimetres,
often stumbling, sometimes falling, not infrequently feeling
listless and tired. I would often recall those blissful moments
when I seemed to rush forward on the path and imagined I was
not far from completing the first stage of my journey.

This was a profoundly disturbing experience for me and at
the same time the beginning of a new phase on my spiritual
path. From now on, what counted was to nourish the flame
that God had kindled in me, which had seemed to burn all
by itself, as it were, and to see to it that the lamp I held in my
hands was not extinguished. Often I remembered the fate of
the five wise and the five foolish virgins, of whom Jesus speaks
so impressively in his parable. The wise virgins had taken oil in
their vessels in order to keep their lamps burning while waiting
for the coming of the bridegroom. When he finally arrived in
the middle of the night, they were prepared and could enter
the wedding hall with him. The foolish virgins, however, had
no surplus oil and the flame in their lamps threatened to die. In
order to buy oil, they had to go away, and when the bridegroom
arrived, they were not there. When they finally returned, the
doors were closed and they were not admitted to the wedding.

This parable of the Master of Nazareth startlingly explains
how indispensable it is for each seeker of God and for each
disciple on the path of the Masters to keep oil in readiness, in
order to nourish the flame of his or her spiritual life. Those who
are not admitted to the wedding have missed the meaning and
the aim of human life.

There is oil for the lamp in abundance. There are so many
sources for the disciple to draw from and so many ways to
make use of them. First there is food for the intellect, copiously
available in spiritual literature and meetings with fellow seekers

of God. Time and again we can satisfy our intellect with this food and can get inspiration for our spiritual life. Indeed, it is always fascinating for me to delve into the wealth of spiritual books available to a seeker and to discover new aspects of the teachings that had hitherto escaped my attention.

As valuable and often indispensable as such food for the intellect may be, I had to realize that this alone is not sufficient to nourish the flame. Though all the different aspects of the Sant Mat teachings interested me, the knowledge that I gained by reading the books was only theoretical, and the goal shown in the books was no more than imaginary. A much stronger motivation was needed to generate sufficient will power within me for walking the spiritual path day after day.

For me, the strongest motive of all for nourishing the flame is the Master himself – love and devotion for him, the ceaseless endeavour to be aware of his presence, to be conscious of his nearness and to behold a glimpse of his face. It was for him that I wanted to keep the lamp burning. Therefore I often tried to recall the wonderful meetings with my Master that had been bestowed upon me in the course of the years and to revive the emotions that had moved me on those occasions. In that way I also tried to experience anew the Master's love – his everlasting, timeless presence – even if the outer signs of this love were now part of the past. But I found that I was no longer able to revive these blissful moments, and this experience was very painful. Remembering these experiences was indeed oil for the lamp, but it could nourish the flame only for a short while, and in the end I had to recognize that the only way to reach the Master was the way that leads inside.

The encounter with the Master in his physical form is a starting aid for following the way inside in order to behold the Master there in his Shabd form. How often Maharaj Charan Singh emphasized the point that instead of trying to revive the past the disciple should turn inside. One important preparation for this consists in turning the heart towards the Master in the present moment, under the present circumstances. Food for the flame of spirituality is the living connection with the Master that must be kept alive all the time. The relationship with the Beloved must be nourished, lest it die; time and again our Master stresses this point.

So it is with photographs of the Master; these also cannot create a living connection with him. Rather, gazing at a photograph creates a kind of veil, covering his face. Photos of the Master can even constitute a serious obstacle if one wants to direct the inner gaze at him, as I once experienced for myself.* The use of photos during meditation is recommended in some meditation methods, but it is not advised in Surat Shabd Yoga.

The Masters themselves show their disciples how best to nourish the flame. Soami Ji, for instance, indicates a very effective method in his book *Sar Bachan (Prose).* "It is very necessary", he says, "to please him (the Master)."

This advice is the key that opens an inexhaustible source of oil for the spiritual lamp. It makes the lamp burn brightly, frees the disciple from his mediocrity and indifference and awakens in him true spiritual zeal. And how many ways there are to please the Master in the course of a day. Maharaj Sawan Singh names them in *Spiritual Gems,* from his own experience: there is first and foremost *sharan,* submission to the divine will; then come faith, trust and gratitude; then sincerity, perseverance and

---

*When I returned to Brahma Vidya Mandir after my initiation, I put a small photograph of my Master on my desk, which I used to look at while I was working. After a while I noticed that during meditation my attention was permanently drawn towards this photo, which made concentration in the eye centre impossible. I was most concerned about this and I removed the photograph from the desk, but it took many days until my attention could again focus at the point indicated by the meditation technique.

humility on the spiritual path. Last but not least there is love for the Master and the wish to be near him.

The most important way to please the Master, as Maharaj Sawan Singh mentions, is the daily meditation practice, even if often it is no more than an attempt to meditate. In many of his letters, collected in *Spiritual Gems*, he assures us time and again that no effort remains unnoticed, but that, on the contrary, the disciple's unsuccessful attempts to meditate attract the Lord's grace upon us. Oil for the lamp is also provided by repeating the meditation words during the day, whenever the mind is free. These words are like a magnet, attracting the attention of the Master. Disciples may feel that their vain attempts, their failures, their weaknesses, their inabilities and apparent defeats on the spiritual path are like water poured on a flame; but whenever a disciple brings these attempts to the Master, the grace of the Master transforms the water into oil for the lamp. How often did I find that even sorrowful circumstances in the life of a disciple, difficulties and adversities of all kinds, can be oil for the lamp of spirituality, provided the disciple practises *sharan* and confidently surrenders his fate into the hands of the Master.

There is one thing, however, that the Masters never cease to emphasize. They stress that it is the Lord himself who plants the desire to nourish the flame in the disciple's heart. He awakens the desire in the disciple, only to fulfil it himself, as Maharaj Charan Singh points out in his book *Die to Live*:

> He has created that desire in us to meditate. He wouldn't create that desire in us to meditate if he were not anxious to give to us.... That shows he is very desirous to pull us to his own level. Otherwise he wouldn't put that instinct in us to meditate. He wouldn't give us the facilities, opportunities and environment to meditate if he were not anxious to pull us out of the creation.

Nourishing the flame is a lifelong task for disciples on the path of the Masters, demanding all their resolve and perseverance. But all those who dedicate themselves unswervingly to it will receive rich recompense: within them will shine the unearthly flame that heralds the end of the first difficult and steep stage of his spiritual journey and that will one day change into the eternal divine light.

Cultivating intense longing

These then, are the three essential elements of a disciple's daily efforts on the path of the Masters: to walk the path within through meditation, to submit to the will of the Lord with loving devotion, and to persistently nourish the flame of spirituality. These are indeed, in my experience, the three pillars supporting the spiritual life of a disciple on this path. These three pillars stand on a foundation that is of the greatest importance on the spiritual path – *intense longing for meeting God.*

To long to meet God and to foster this longing is an essential quality of a seeker of God – the whole of a seeker's life is marked by it. The intense longing to meet God helps all seekers to persevere on the spiritual path. It saves them, too, from feelings of disappointment if tangible results are not quickly forthcoming from spiritual practice. Above all, intense longing saves a seeker of God from indifference and half-heartedness, which are among the greatest dangers on the spiritual path.

I shall never forget the moment when Baba Ji, during an evening satsang, gave us a fresh reminder of this foundation. At the request of a friend, a lady guest had put the question before the Master: "I have such a great longing to come to the Dera and to see the Master, but I am unable to come. What sense does it make to keep this longing awake, if it cannot be fulfilled?" Our answer to this question would perhaps have been a few words of consolation and the recommendation to have patience, but the Master's answer was quite unforeseen: Sister, longing is the foundation of spirituality.

Intense longing is a theme that runs like a thread through all of the Sant Mat literature – all Masters speak of its importance with great urgency and I was well acquainted with these texts – even so, those words of the Master at that particular moment came like a revelation to me.

In the following weeks I pondered about the Master's words and attempted to fathom their profound significance. I looked in *Philosophy of the Masters*, where Maharaj Sawan Singh dedicates a whole chapter to the subject of intense longing *(birah* or *bireh)*. There I found the reason for Baba Ji's answer to the disciple's question. Maharaj Sawan Singh writes: "In order to meet the Beloved, intense longing comes first, in the same manner as flowers bud and bloom on a fruit tree before it can bear fruit. Where there are no flowers, there can be no fruit. Similarly, where there is no *bireh* there can be no meeting with the Beloved."

In this chapter, Maharaj Sawan Singh brings us page after page of testimony from great mystics and saints who, with deeply moving words, tearfully express their burning desire to meet their Lord. Even up to this very day, it moves me deeply to read these quotations. These are the words of revered and learned adepts, who were not ashamed to speak of their unbearable pain of separation and their tears of longing for their Beloved.

Thus, for instance, Jalaluddin Rumi, the great Sufi mystic (1207–1273) exclaims:

> O friend, if you wish to reach the home of God,
> You should go by way of an ocean of tears,
> For it is only in that way
> That you will be able to reach him.

A poem that Jalaluddin Rumi wrote under the inspiration of his beloved Master, Shams-i Tabriz (1206–1248), attaches great importance to tears of longing:

> Those eyes which are weeping
> For the sight of the Beloved
> Will one day surely behold him.
> In love, weeping acts as a ladder.
> When you make a ladder of your eyes,
> Then you will automatically be speeding
> Towards the sky.

The Indian Rajput princess Mira also teaches us about intense longing for meeting the Beloved. In one of her most beautiful poems, she describes how the gaze of her Beloved, her Master, hit her like an arrow in the middle of her heart. Now she is incessantly longing for a glimpse of his face. With burning pain her eyes watch for him and she fears she will die if the Master will not grant her his *darshan*.

On the path of the Masters, this longing of a disciple to behold the Beloved refers to both forms of the Master – to the outer *darshan* of his human form and to the inner *darshan* of his Shabd form. For a disciple on the path, the longing to meet God is fulfilled in meeting the Master, the Word made flesh, the contemporary Christ. As the Master of Nazareth assured his disciples, "He that hath seen me hath seen the Father." The love for the Son whom the Father has sent into the world to proclaim the kingdom of God does not differ from the love for the Father, with whom the Son is one.

In the intense longing to meet God there is no difference between the experiences of the mystics of the various religions. The great Christian mystics expressed their intense longing with the same beautiful words as do the above-quoted Sufi mystics and Mira. From the great treasury of the Christian mystic tradition, I have selected the poem of the Scottish Augustinian prior, Richard of Saint Victor (d.1173), in which he expresses his longing for God:

> May our burning desire
> Spread the wings of our heart
> In expectation of the manifestation of God,
> Every hour – any time,
> So that our soul – when the moment has come
> In which the divine breath has driven away
> The clouds of our mind
> And showed us the rays of the true sun –
> Ascends without delay on these wings
> And advances towards this light
> And fixes her gaze on it.
> We should keep our soul, burning with desire,
> In such an attitude.

What causes this longing in us? With our senses and our intellect we turn towards the visible world in which we live and of which we are part. We seek to explore and enjoy it, but at the same time we get ensnared in it. Our restless minds ceaselessly crave for new experiences and new insights into this world, often longing insatiably for the possession of worldly goods or the satisfaction of sensual cravings. The Masters point out, however, that there is also an inner urge in us to experience God. It is the natural tendency of the soul to return to her origin. Some people feel that urge very strongly, while in others it is buried under a load of worldly ambitions and desires. Quite often, the awakening longing will be misled by the human mind, which seeks happiness in mundane things. But neither worldly happiness nor fulfilment of worldly wishes and cravings can satisfy the longing of the soul, as countless seekers of God have experienced for themselves: only God suffices.

All Masters of spirituality emphasize that it is God himself who puts the longing for union with him into the human heart. It is *he* who touches our hearts and places there the spark of desire. Very often it is a soft yet irresistible impulse that stirs within us. Sometimes it is a supernatural light that shines inside us or a streak of lightning that strikes us inside and turns our gaze inevitably towards God. One of the great Indian Masters of spirituality, Kabir, personifies this longing, saying that God sends out 'longing' to enliven the hearts of seekers of God. Its purpose is to search for souls that are restless for God and bring them back to him.

In her book *Herald of the Divine Love*, the German mystic, Gertrude of Helfta (1256–1302), also personifies that yearning. The soul sends 'longing' to go out and look for the Beloved.

> There longing hurriedly went
> And came to the height and exclaimed:
> "Great Lord, open and let me come in!"
> Then the Lord said: "What do you want
> That you are pressing so much?"
> "Lord, I tell You
> That my mistress can no longer live like this.
> She is like a fish
> That can no longer drift in the sand and live on."
> "So go and bring the hungry soul to me:
> For her I long above all."
> When the messenger returned
> And the soul learnt of the Lord's will,
> O what bliss flooded her!
> And flying she soared up.

While saints and mystics express their intolerable pain of separation from the Beloved with glowing words, they also describe the fulfilment of their longing for God with exuberant words, frequently using the simile of bride and bridegroom. In a deeply moving poem Kabir, for instance, has the soul say:

> After endless days of separation
> I have met my Beloved
> Within my own home.
> My temple is flooded with light,
> And in bliss I lie with my Beloved
> In the deep trance of his loving embrace.
> He himself has come to me
> Within my own home,
> And boundless is the bliss
> Of our union.

Blessed is the person in whose heart the Lord has put such ardent longing for union with him. Whoever reads the words of the mystics about their intense longing may heave a deep sigh and confess to not feeling such a strong desire for God within themselves. But the moving and inspiring words of the mystics can create a painful awareness that this desire is lacking. This deep pain is precisely the precondition for stepping onto the spiritual path, because it creates in the seeker's heart that empty space in which the Lord can kindle the spark of true longing for him.

To nourish this desire for the longing for God within and not seek consolation in worldly things is essential for walking the spiritual path. Seekers of God can trust that the Lord will kindle a spark of longing for him in their hearts and that, if it is nourished, this spark will develop into a blazing fire of love.

In this chapter I have described my understanding of the ideal of living Sant Mat. Nevertheless, a disciple on the path of the Masters will often wonder whether it is not altogether utopian to strive for such an ideal. In the evening satsangs in the Dera, this subject was frequently touched upon. Many were those who confessed that they were falling well short of the fulfilment of this ideal and felt incapable of realizing it in their lives. It is an experience I am confronted with time and again.

To such confessions from his disciples, Baba Ji regularly replies with the advice that we should be realistic and should bear in mind that Sant Mat shows us the ideal towards which we should work. On no account should we be discouraged when we feel far away from this ideal, or when we meet with many obstacles on the way. All the Masters emphasize that the disciple's role is to go forward unwaveringly on the path and to strive untiringly to come closer to the goal step by step. However, the Masters say that attaining the goal is not in the disciple's hands; it is a gift of grace from the Most High, from the One who calls us to return home to the land of our origin.

In the first stage on the path of the Masters, progress is mainly a question of perseverance, even if the years pass by without being able to measure the distance covered since initiation. This has been my own experience in the course of the more than thirty-five years that have passed since I stepped onto the path. Failing to acknowledge this here could amount to misrepresenting the experience of disciples on the spiritual path. The description of the shining ideal in this chapter is therefore followed by an account of day-to-day life on the path of the Masters, characterized by tireless endeavour, constant effort and a determined struggle against the ever-present enemy of spiritual life, one's individual mind. In their instructions the Masters do not leave any doubt about this aspect of the spiritual path.

CHAPTER TEN

As the Years Pass By

WHEN, AFTER MY RETURN TO GERMANY IN 1974, I tried to continue my spiritual life and to live Sant Mat, I was soon forced to realize that my striving was threatened by dangers that I had to fight against continuously. Firstly, there was my very active temperament, which led me to take an interest in many things and to realize talents I had not even been conscious of before. Quite often this brought about an inner restlessness, which meant that the most important task of my life, the search for God, was sometimes pushed into the background. Then there were times in which my spiritual life was threatened by the monotony of the daily routine. During these phases, I felt a certain aversion to meditation and I would have preferred to drift in the current of habits and chance events.

The third threat to my spiritual life was a sense of discouragement that sometimes crept up when the years were passing and there was no discernible progress on the way within – no seeing any inner light, no hearing the audible Word or beholding the Master's radiant form. The Masters, however, constantly point out that on the path of the Masters it is rare for a disciple to meet with quick progress and that for most disciples the way leading within is a lifelong journey. As the years were passing,

I had to remind myself of this fact again and again. To get discouraged is a sign of impatience and lack of confidence – a very characteristic feature of the human mind.

Long is the way

The Masters mention three reasons why a disciple on the spiritual path generally advances only very slowly. First, the path of the Masters is – as explained above – a way of liberation of the soul from the realm of the negative power, whose task is, amongst others, to keep the souls in this creation. The extent to which souls are imprisoned in creation, ensnared in the net of *maya* and dominated by the mind has been described in detail earlier. One of the strongest bonds by which the negative power ties souls to the creation is the individual mind, to which the soul is firmly tied. In order to release herself from these fetters and to return to her true home, the soul has to detach herself from the net of *maya*, control her individual mind, overcome it and finally untie the knot between herself and the mind.

In the first stage of the spiritual way, the most important means of reaching that goal is meditation, the repetition of the holy names. By way of meditation, the disciple stills the mind and finally makes it motionless so that the attention turns inside and comes in contact with the Shabd. The Shabd or sound current will release all the fetters that tie the soul to creation and will carry her back to the place of her origin, her eternal home.

Since it is the task of the mind to draw our attention to the world and to keep it there, it continuously pulls it outside. The Masters warn us that to counteract this tendency of the mind by the spiritual practice, and finally to overcome it, can be an extremely lengthy process. They point out that for countless earthly existences the mind has been accustomed to running out into the creation and to seeking satisfaction there. In order to change the mind's habitual course, there is a need not only for great effort and determination, but also for untiring patience and perseverance. I therefore had to tell myself time and again that it is natural for the path to drag on sometimes, and that tangible success may only come at the end of a long spiritual pilgrimage.

The Masters say that there is another reason why the first phase of the spiritual way usually extends over many years; this is the extreme difficulty most people face in doing the repetition practice of meditation with undivided attention. Quite often I had to realize that I did not have the strength for such a degree of concentration. My restless mind not only produced thousands of thoughts of all sorts, but also flooded my consciousness with the remembrance of countless impressions and experiences that it had received in the course of my life. Until one is able to eliminate this upsurge of thoughts and remembrances, the mind cannot experience the power of the holy names. Only when the entire attention is concentrated on the repetition of the words and they finally revolve automatically can one experience their centripetal effect. Only then will the consciousness withdraw from the body and collect in the third eye. As soon as the repetition of the holy words becomes automatic, they will be present in the disciple's consciousness even when the disciple is not meditating. The repetition will be going on within, even while the disciple is attending to other things. When that happens, the disciple is a mere witness of it.

It is not difficult to understand that it can be a tiresome and tedious matter to attain such intense concentration. Every fibre of our mind and body is exposed to the impressions and influences of the world around us. The world flows ceaselessly through the gates of our senses into our consciousness, whereas the worlds beyond are for most people at best a mental concept that has only little attraction for our mind. Much patience and perseverance is needed to walk this path, as well as great courage and unswerving determination. Most important, however, is a faithful confidence in the path of the Masters and love for the Master. This, however, cannot be forced – it is a gift of grace, as Maharaj Charan Singh often pointed out.

He also reminded us more than once that success in meditation is not the concern of the disciple – his task is only to make the effort. Whenever lack of success in meditation was mentioned during the evening satsangs in the Dera, the Master advised us to do our best and leave the rest to the Master. To do one's best, he explained, means investing just as much effort in meditation as we invest in our worldly life when we want to achieve a certain result. This only happens, the Master said, when we have love and devotion for the Lord.

Our load of karma is the third reason given by the Masters to explain why the way is so long before any success in meditation is attained. This immeasurable load has accumulated since the soul's descent from her place of origin. As long as this load is not cleared, as long as the seeds of karma have not been – figuratively speaking – burnt, the soul cannot get rid of her mind coverings and return to her eternal home. On the spiritual path meditation is the most important means of clearing a part of the karma that weighs on our mind. As soon as the mind and soul of the disciple come in contact with the sound of the Shabd, the burning of the seeds of karma begins. To attain this goal, every minute in meditation counts, as Maharaj Charan Singh used to say. Our part is to persevere on the path while trusting in the Master, and to surrender to the process of purification we have to go through.

Carpe diem

With the passing of the years, one of the biggest dangers on the spiritual path arises when disciples resign themselves to the idea that apparently nothing can be gained through meditation and let their spiritual life drift along. When the path seems to be dragging on, it is hard for disciples to maintain the enthusiasm of the first hour. The chances are that they will give up the struggle against the restless mind as they perform their daily meditation merely as a matter of duty. Sometimes indifference towards Sant Mat and the Master may creep in and doubts concerning the path of the Masters may arise – this possibility was sometimes mentioned by Maharaj Charan Singh. It may even happen that disciples temporarily turn away from Sant Mat or leave the path altogether. However, initiation means that the Master has taken upon himself the responsibility to bring back the soul of each of his disciples to her eternal home, and he will not abandon any of them, but will bring them all back to the path some day. The Master reassured us on this point many times.

Walking the path of the Masters often seems to me like trekking through jagged mountains where one has to climb steep rock faces and go over ridges without seeing the peak. It is still an adventure of faith for me to tread this path, even though I have at my side the guide who prompted me to set out long ago, long before I knew of any Master actually living on earth.

On this journey, turning to the Master and looking up at him is extremely important, but it is not always easy to keep this 'eye contact' with the Master when one is feeling dejected or guilty on account of one's lack of zeal and love. But Maharaj Sawan Singh encouraged his disciples to take even their weaknesses and failures to him; with nothing but their shortcomings in their hands, they could and should come to him. Therefore, in Sant Mat, those who feel that they have failed have every reason to go to their Master instead of covering their faces in shame as if to hide from him. Similarly, the Master of Nazareth once encouraged his disciples to come to him with their entire labour and heavy load, saying that he would give them rest.*

Even if tangible success in meditation is a long time in coming, the years that a disciple spends trying to walk the path of the Masters are not spent in vain. "Every minute in meditation is important," Maharaj Charan Singh once assured me. Not a single minute is lost, not even the time spent in seemingly unsuccessful meditation. Walking on the path transforms the disciple slowly but steadily. Every satsangi will be able to confirm this. When he looks back at the time before initiation he will become aware how much Sant Mat has changed him and how the Sant Mat teachings also help him to master his worldly life. Many a disciple have confessed to me that without Sant Mat and the Master they could not have coped with life.

With the passing of the years, it was no longer important to me to know how long it would take me to reach the next stage on my spiritual path. The only thing that mattered was making use of every day as well as I could, in order to come closer to the Master. *Carpe diem* (seize the day – *make good use of* the day), as the Masters continuously and urgently exhort their disciples. I cannot say that I have always made the best use of my time in this sense. Again and again I found that the enemy, my own mind, called to me its own *carpe diem – enjoy the day*. The mind very shrewdly puts before us a fascinating and inexhaustible array of sensual pleasures. All too easily it diverts us from using our time in the best possible way for the benefit of our spiritual life. Once I asked Baba Ji whether the negative power can harm a disciple on his spiritual path. The Master exclaimed: Sister, we are surrounded by *maya*!

---

*"Come unto me, all ye that labour and are heavy laden, and I will give you rest." *Matthew* 11:28

Maya, as has been explained, is the power of illusion in this creation that makes us consider the visible world to be reality. It is ceaselessly invading us, and our mind and our senses are only too eager to open themselves to its influence. As the Master of Nazareth also admonished his disciples: Be vigilant. At any moment death can put an end to *carpe diem*. But even if manifold dangers are lying in wait for him on the spiritual way, as the years on the path passed by I was also allowed to realize that a disciple gains inner security and confidence in the Master.

Time and again I found that the Master led me to an oasis and made me feel his nearness. These moments, hours or days of inner bliss largely made up for the times of trouble, struggle and even tears. Such experiences give us a presentiment of what awaits us when we have gone through the most difficult phase on the path of the Masters, when our consciousness has made the breakthrough to the next stage of our ascent to God, to the astral world, and we meet our Master in his inner form and hear the resounding Shabd.

As the years passed by I was also granted the experience of how a disciple becomes ever more receptive to the inner guidance of the Master. The more we surrender to the Master, the more we feel the Master's guiding hand and the more we trust in him like a child holding the hand of his father. And then we know no fear. This experience gives a beautiful inner peace and a security that envelops one's whole life.

Sometimes I wondered what my life would be like without Sant Mat and the Master. Deeply moved, I realized that without Sant Mat I would never have been able to make any sense of my life or of all my spiritual longing and striving. I would never have known who the inner guide was, who led me from my youth, who took me into the desert and who made me walk over the ridge. Without the Master, I would never have known whose gaze had supported me when – figuratively speaking – I had to go over the sharp edge of a sword. Without Sant Mat, the mystery of the universal Christ and of God's plan for the salvation of souls would not have been revealed to me. Without the teachings of the Masters, the mystic dimension of the teachings of Jesus Christ would not have been disclosed to me. Without initiation into the path of the Masters I would never be able to experience, one day, the highest aspirations of my religion: the awakening of the soul in God, the true resurrection from death to eternal life and the union of my soul with the Holy Spirit, the audible Word.

It is with the utmost gratitude that I express my conviction that through Sant Mat and the Master, not only my present life but also my entire existence as a spiritual being has taken a decisive turn towards liberation from the realm of the negative power and the eventual return of my soul to the land of her origin.

Keeping a promise

As the years went by, the moment also came for putting into action the instruction that Maharaj Charan Singh had given me at a farewell interview in December 1973. He had advised me to look after my mother, because "we should take care of our parents". Throughout the years I had kept the Master's words in my memory; they were like a promise that I had given to myself. Sometimes the Master had reminded us in his satsangs that we are so indebted to our parents that we can hardly repay them. We had often been deeply moved when we witnessed the love and reverence the Master showed to his aged mother.

In November 1987, my mother had turned eighty-eight and was still keeping quite well. On the first of May of the same year, at the age of sixty-three, I had myself retired and we could sometimes go for extended trips or walks. But shortly after her eighty-ninth birthday, my mother fractured a femur and for a while lost her mobility and independence. From then on there was a long series of accidents. My mother was increasingly dependent on my help, but she always recovered to some extent. I much admired her courage in trying to master these mishaps. She never showed the slightest impatience or discontent with her situation, but adapted uncomplainingly to the changing circumstances.

In this way, she was able to still spend seven years in relative sprightliness, until in 1995 other serious health problems made her more and more frail. I had never had much to do with nursing or caring for elderly people and was therefore virtually unable to cope with this task I was now facing. My mother's condition was sometimes life threatening and often I felt helpless. Since she needed my help even in the night, I was no longer getting enough sleep, and I reached a state of overtiredness and exhaustion from which there was no escape. In every respect, it was a difficult time. Quite often I felt as if I were hanging from a rock wall that rose above me like the famous Eiger north face. In this situation, preparing satsangs for the Munich sangat was very helpful. Working out a subject for satsang was like hammering in a hook on which I could secure myself and climb another length of rope.

My mother was a devoted Catholic and her entire life was marked by love of God and unconditional surrender to his will. Her favourite prayer, formulated by Nicholas of Flüe (1417–1487), which she had made her own, was:

> My Lord and my God,
> Give me everything that leads me to Thee.
> My Lord and my God,
> Take everything from me
> That keeps me away from Thee.

My Lord and my God,
Take me away from me and give me to Thee.

To my great regret, I never could speak to my mother
about Sant Mat, because she was afraid of my 'other faith', as
it appeared to her, and I did not want to shake her faith. But
my mother's unreserved surrender to God would have been an
example for every satsangi, and I trusted in the Master's words
when he said that the family members of a disciple are also
protected by him.

Shortly after her ninety-eighth birthday in November
1997, my mother had another serious fall and suffered another
fracture of the femur. She never recovered from this shock and
became utterly helpless. The last six months before her death
were one long stretch of suffering and her only wish was to be
allowed to leave the world. Needing so much nursing depressed
her and the thought that this burden lay almost exclusively on
my shoulders was an added worry for her. Sometimes she said,
"When I am no more, you will have it good." My mother's
miserable condition broke my heart and I did everything I
could to make life easier for her. I wanted at all cost to avoid
having to admit her into a home for the aged, which for me
would not have been a solution. I wanted her to end her life in
familiar surroundings, and for this I was prepared to sacrifice
everything. All her life she had selflessly served her big family,
and now I considered it my duty of love to make her last years
as comfortable as possible in the home where she had lived
since 1938.

On 5th August 1998 the life span of my mother ended.
Five days earlier I had returned from Malaga in Spain, where
we had spent some days with Baba Ji. The Master shaped the
circumstances of my mother's death in the most wonderful
way. She was able to die in my arms and I felt the Master's

presence in a very special way. I was confident that she was in good hands and this thought greatly consoled me.

Nonetheless, my mother's death hit me very hard. I had never imagined that losing her would shake me so deeply. After my return from India in 1974, we had lived together for twenty-five years, and nursing her for so many years had created a strong bond between us. Now I felt as if I had died with her. This put me in a condition where I perceived my environment as through a veil, and grief enclosed me like a suit of armour that took my breath away. I lost all *joie de vivre* and felt forlorn in the world as never before.

But then it dawned on me that for a satsangi the experience of death is actually a positive one. A sense of detachment from the world, an awareness of its transitory and shadowy nature, as well as the immediate realization that we are only guests on earth constituted an important lesson for me, for it led me to admit the pain that my mother's death had caused and to make it part of my life. This death experience marked me profoundly, even when with time it slowly lost its intensity.

After some time, my life returned to normal to some extent, and it then became clear to me that my pain of separation was based mainly on ego – suddenly *I* no longer had anyone to relate to, *I* had lost my partner in conversation, the one with whom *I* could share my experiences. Now, for the first time in my life, *I* was alone. It was a sobering realization and at the same time a salutary lesson. From the Sant Mat point of view, the situation looked quite different – my mother's death had created a vacuum that could now be occupied by the Master, and since I no longer had any family obligations I would now be able to meditate for more than the regular time. I would build up within myself a new identity, shaped exclusively by Sant Mat, and I would free myself from the identity of a bereaved person that had all but paralysed me. These thoughts filled me with confidence and encouragement, and with this perspective I started the next stage of my life.

Again a new beginning

I began planning my next steps just a few weeks after my mother's death. This was the best way to combat a certain lethargy that was threatening to take hold of me. To gain some distance from the painful events of the past weeks and to overcome my chronic overtiredness, I decided to take a health cure. Not wanting to stay any more in the big flat in Munich, where everything reminded me of my mother, I decided I would search for a new place to live before taking the health cure. Then, at the beginning of December, I wanted to go to the Dera to regain my inner balance.

I had never worried about searching for a place to live, since that problem would only arise after my mother's death, and I was sure that the Master would take the matter into his own hands. And when the time came, that's exactly how it was – at least, that is what I felt. Even before I began to search seriously for a flat, it was already there, lying at my feet, beautiful and perfectly suited to my needs. It was much nicer than I could ever have imagined, and I now live in it with the feeling that my Master has assigned it to me. I was happy and grateful, remembering the words of the Bible: "Seek ye first the kingdom of God, and his righteousness; and all these things shall be added unto you."

When the time came for moving house I was still in a traumatized state of mind and mourning for my mother, whose death still weighed heavily on me, but I hoped to get over it in the peaceful and spiritual atmosphere of the Dera. I travelled there four weeks later, and after only a few days the heavy, suffocating iron band of pain around my chest vanished and I could breathe freely once more.

For my visit to the Dera I had taken along my diaries of the happy five months I had spent there in 1971–1972. In these diaries I had written down the whole process of becoming a disciple at the feet of the Master. Now these notes would remind me of everything that had happened then and would help me to make a new beginning after the difficult years lying behind me. Rereading these notes, I came across my Master's advice to write down the story of how I found my way to the path of the Masters. Since then twenty-five years had passed. During the years of professional work and nursing my mother, there had been no time to write and I had more or less forgotten the Master's wish. Now it seemed the time had come to fulfil it. I presented to Baba Ji my Master's advice that was given to me so many years back and now Baba Ji in his turn assigned to me the task of writing the book, and he promised to take the matter into his hands.

After returning from the Dera in January 1999, I immediately started working on the book. But many years would pass before it took its present shape. Writing down my adventure of faith became an adventure in itself, which continually kept me on my toes, and sometimes I was close to giving up. But that was exactly what I could not do, for it was a service to the Master that I was bound to perform. Despite all the difficulties, I was granted the Master's help and encouragement in many ways – sometimes during a personal interview and frequently through what seemed like inspiration, through which he accompanied me throughout the years of writing the book. In the course of the years I was surprised to see how the book developed its own dynamic, how unexpected perspectives opened and new aspects appeared that extended far beyond my original concept.

It was altogether a wonderful experience to see my adventure of faith that had begun nearly seventy years ago passing before me once more, and to realize anew the grace and guidance of the Master. Only now, while writing them down and reflecting on them, was I able to fit together and to understand the various phases of my spiritual path and so many of the events on this journey. These were always blissful moments, which alone would have made it worthwhile to write the book. What other purpose the book is to fulfil, I do not know; the effect it will have on its readers is not in my hands, but entirely in the hands of the one according to whose wishes it was written.

CHAPTER ELEVEN

Completing Life

SEVENTY-FIVE YEARS HAVE PASSED SINCE I became involved in my adventure of faith as a young girl. My whole life has been shaped and moulded by this experience, which set my path on an irreversible course and predestined me for a religious and spiritual life. Before I could make my own decisions about my life, God claimed it and I knew – as young as I was then – that I could not refuse him.

After that experience I have been following my inner guide, who entered my life in such an unforeseen manner so many years ago. I did not know who he was, yet I called him my Lord and my God. When I finally met a living true Master, I experienced the joy and security of encountering my inner guide in human form. For thirty-five years I have been a disciple of this Master.

Of all the roles I have played in this life, the role of disciple of a living Master was and still is the most beautiful one. How many marvellous scenes have occurred in this play in which the Master is, so to say, my 'co-actor'! This play, however, will not come to an end when the curtain of my present life falls, because the Master's role ends only when he has taken the soul of his disciple to her eternal goal, when her existence as a spiritual being is fulfilled. This book will conclude with a look at the transcendent phase of this play, the path of the soul through the inner regions.

When the number of years of life assigned to me by fate have expired, when all the breaths to which I am entitled are exhausted and the last hour approaches, my earthly life will be completed. At that time I will have gone through everything that on account of my karma I had to receive, to give and to do – all the pleasures of life that had to be enjoyed and all the adversities that were to be endured. My karma will have brought me to all the places I had to go and led me to all the countries I had to enter. All the people I was to meet will have crossed my way and I will have played all the roles I had to play in the world-theatre of the Lord, even though I have not always been conscious of this fact.

Completed also in this last hour of my life will be that phase I call my adventure of faith. All the steps that I had to make on the path of this adventure, which had become my way to God, will be behind me. All the ridges that I had to cross will have been crossed, while every fall into the abyss and each instance of being caught in the Lord's arms will have been accomplished. Completed shall be all the hours and days and years of searching and finding, of doubts and certainty, of waiting for the Lord and of his coming. Completed shall be the degree of transformation that I had to undergo on my spiritual path and the measure of grace and bliss that I was to receive. At the hour of the completion of my life, my heart will be full of joy and gratitude for all the experiences that I was granted. All these experiences on my spiritual path have engraved themselves deeply in my memory, and my soul will take them with her to the other shore.

Quite often the Master has been asked about the completion of a disciple's life at the hour of his physical death. In his book *Die to Live*, Maharaj Charan Singh points out that every meditation is a preparation for the final crossing of the threshold of consciousness at the hour of separation of body and soul. The Masters teach their disciples at the time of initiation how to die while living, how to cross with their consciousness during meditation the threshold into the world beyond. When the soul of a disciple who has already crossed this threshold separates from the body at the time of physical death, this will be an experience that he has already made during his life. Surely, every disciple longs to have this experience while still living – yet to grant it, that lies in the hands of the Master.

When once asked about the passing away of dedicated disciples who have not been able to die while living, the Master replied that these disciples should look forward to their last hour with joy, because then they will receive what they have desired all their life. For this reason, death for a satsangi is a moment of deep happiness. This answer is deeply encouraging for all disciples who have not had the experience of transcending to another level of consciousness during their life.

When the life of a devoted disciple nears the end, the Master will be at his side. Having the sight of his Master's radiant form, the disciple will be so deeply enthralled that no pain of separation and no attachment to the world or to beloved relatives will divert his attention from the crossing to the world beyond. He will rather turn his love to the Master and will direct all his thoughts to the other shore.

Then the Master will tell him, "Now come," and the disciple will follow with all his heart. Immediately he will inwardly let go of everything that up to now had been his life. His Master will receive him and lead him across the 'bridge to the beyond'. The soul of the disciple has crossed this bridge uncountable times in his previous lives, although he cannot remember this. The repeated incarnations in new bodies have been to the spiritual being only short transitory phases in her existence on earth. The Masters of Surat Shabd Yoga point out that we should see our present life in this perspective. In the context of the immeasurable period of time the spiritual being has spent in creation, the duration of our present life is extremely short.

Whether the soul of a disciple has to reincarnate again after crossing the bridge to the beyond depends on his karma. For instance, if there is still karma that can be cleared only in a human body, the soul will have to be born again. The disciple's wish not to be born again has no influence on that. Full of confidence he should leave this to his Master, just as he should entrust the circumstances of his final days and death to his Master as well.

In crossing to the beyond, whether in meditation or at the time of death, the spiritual being takes a significant step on her way back to her origin, although the turning point of her existence in creation had already been reached at the time of initiation in the path of the Masters. When the soul leaves her physical body, she leaves behind an instrument that she needs in the material world, but which is at the same time a grave obstacle to experiencing her spiritual nature and God-realization.

Leaving behind the physical body is, however, only the beginning of the soul's liberation from all the material and mental coverings that prevent the spiritual being from ascending to the throne of the Lord. She is at first still enwrapped in her astral and causal bodies and her individual mind, in which an immeasurable store of karma of previous lives is piled up. The soul has to be rid of these coverings, and all the seeds of karma have to be destroyed before the spiritual being can leave the realm of the negative power and proceed to her eternal goal.

After leading his disciples over the bridge to the beyond, the Master remains at their side and accompanies them on their way back to their eternal home.

The journey of the soul through the transcendent worlds, however, is not a sightseeing tour through the spiritual regions. The Masters always emphasize this. It is rather the way of her liberation from the domain of the negative power. The Master who accompanies the soul will protect her from being tempted by the indescribable beauty of these regions and staying there. The task of the soul is solely to listen to the Sound Current, which will burn the immense store of seed-karma so that she can regain the consciousness of her divine nature.

When the disciple has covered the most difficult phase of the spiritual path and reached the third eye, the ascent of his soul through the worlds beyond will be full of glory. This experience the apostle Paul has described in his first Epistle to the Christian community of Corinth: "Eye hath not seen, nor ear heard, neither have entered into the heart of man, the things which God hath prepared for them that love him."

Just as the soul discards her physical body when leaving the material world, she will shed her astral body when leaving the astral region, and when crossing the border of the causal region to the pure spiritual regions she will be rid of her causal body. There she will also leave behind her individual mind, which has been her strongest enemy on the spiritual path. Free of all her coverings, the soul will then realize that she is a spiritual, divine being. With indescribable bliss she will speed through the two regions still lying before her, carried by the sound of the heavenly music, into which she will merge when she reaches her true home. The drop will become one with the divine ocean. Thus the existence of that spiritual being will be fulfilled.

The Masters assure us that after the soul reaches her land of birth, from where she descended eons ago, she will never again have to return to the creation. The writer believes with all her heart that the way that she has described above will – by the grace of the Lord – also be her way.

With this look at the completion of the disciple's human life and the soul's final journey, the last cycle of the adventure of faith described in this book is fulfilled. The reader has accompanied the author on her long pilgrimage, and I hope he has gained some insight into the teachings of the Masters and a life lived according to the path of the Masters. He might also have gained a perspective on the mystery of Jesus Christ and the mystic dimension of his teachings. And I hope that *Adventure of Faith* may also have encouraged some readers to get involved in the adventure with God – the adventure of God's beloved creatures with Divine Love.

Adi Granth   Literally, primal (*aadi*) book or scripture (*granth*); also
called the Granth Sahib; the scripture that brings together the
poetry of the first five Gurus and the ninth Guru in the line of
Guru Nanak, as well as numerous saints from India. The Adi
Granth is a mosaic of esoteric poetry by saints from various
religious, cultural, vocational and geographic backgrounds whose
teachings emphasize the oneness of God, the path of the Word,
the equality of all people and the pursuit of truth. The Adi Granth
was compiled by Guru Arjun, the fifth Guru, and completed in
1604. The hymns of Guru Tegh Bahadur, the ninth Guru, were
added by Guru Gobind Singh, the tenth Guru. The followers of
the teachings of the Gurus have adopted the Adi Granth as their
most sacred scripture.

Agnes, Saint (291–304)   Saint Agnes, also known as Agnes of Rome
and Saint Ines (Santa Ynez), was a virgin martyr, executed at age
twelve or thirteen for refusing, it is said, to worship pagan gods
or to marry the son of a Roman nobleman. Decades later, Saint
Ambrose wrote that she chose persecution, including attempted
rape and death, rather than marry, saying, "He who chose me first
for Himself shall receive me." In *The Golden Legend* (1275), Jacobus
de Voragine, Archbishop of Genoa, attributed to her the words
"He has imprinted his seal on my forehead, so that I would not
admit another lover."

Angelus Silesius (1624–1677)   Angelus Silesius is the monastic name
of Johannes Scheffler, a German mystic poet born in Breslau,
Silesia. His growing mysticism led to his conversion to Catholicism, at which time he took the name Angelus. He was ordained a

priest and retired to a monastic life in Breslau. He was the author of several books, the most notable being *The Cherubic Pilgrim*, a collection of over sixteen hundred rhymed couplets, and *The Soul's Spiritual Delight*, a collection of over two hundred hymns, several of which are still sung in Catholic and Protestant churches.

Arjun, Guru (1563–1606)   Guru Arjun Dev, son of Guru Ram Das, was the fifth Guru in the line of Guru Nanak. Born in Goindwal, Punjab, India, he became the Guru at eighteen. He was tortured and died in Lahore. He designed and supervised the building of the Harmandir Sahib (Golden Temple) in Amritsar. Guru Arjun Dev collected, classified and arranged the writings of the Adi Granth, including hymns of the first four Gurus and over two thousand of his own hymns along with those of Muslim and Hindu saints from all over India and neighbouring countries. These writings emphasized the oneness of God, the equality of all people and the pursuit of truth.

Augustine of Hippo (354–430)   Born in Tagaste (now Souk-Ahras), Algeria, Saint Augustine served as Bishop of Hippo from 396 until his death and led a monastic community life which became the foundation for the Augustinian Order in the thirteenth century. In 1298 he was named one of the four original Doctors of the Church, a title given to a saint whose writings benefit the whole of Christianity. His most well-known work, the *Confessions*, is still widely read around the world.

Benedict, Saint (c.480–547)   Born in Nursia, Umbria, Italy, Saint Benedict is considered the founder of Western monasticism. His religious beliefs led him to found twelve monasteries, including one at Monte Cassino which became one of the most famous in Italy. He is the author of the *Rule of Saint Benedict*, also known as the *Regula*, which contained precepts for his monks based on balance and moderation. The *Regula* was ultimately adopted by most monasteries founded in the Middle Ages and is still used today.

Bernard of Clairvaux (1090–1153)   Saint Bernard was a French abbot born in Fontaines to a noble family. He was responsible for the rapid spread of the Cistercian monastic order, which was founded as a reform of the Benedictine Order. The Cistercian Order is known for austerity, manual labour, a focus on personal faith and the importance of the Virgin Mary. Seen as the voice of conscience, he was a dominating figure in the Catholic Church from 1125 to 1153. He was a prolific writer of sermons, letters and several books still in print, including *On Loving God*, *Sermons on the Song of Songs*, and *On Grace and Free Choice*.

Bhagavad Gita   Literally, sung *(gita)* by the Lord *(bhagavad)*; a Sanskrit text probably written some time between the fifth century BCE and the second century CE. The Bhagavad Gita embodies the teachings of Lord Krishna and is written as a dialogue between Krishna, an incarnation of the deity Vishnu, and Arjuna on the battlefield of Mahabharata. The Bhagavad Gita is one of the most popular books of Hindu philosophy.

Bhave, Vinoba (1895–1982)   Vinayak Narahari Bhave was born into a pious family in Gagode, Maharashtra in India. He became inspired after reading the Bhagavad Gita as a child, participated with Gandhi in the independence movement and is considered Gandhi's spiritual successor. He was a social reformer, seen in his *sarvodaya* (awakening of all potentials) and *bhoodan* (land gift) movements, and advocated non-violence and compassion, including not slaughtering cows. He was a scholar, fluent in many languages, writer of numerous books and introductions to religious scriptures, and translator from Sanskrit of many religious works.

Bible   The term Bible refers to the sacred scriptures of Judaism and of Christianity. The Jewish Bible, written mostly in Hebrew, is divided into the Torah (five books traditionally ascribed to Moses), Prophets and Writings. It recounts the story of humankind from the time of the Creation, the lives of the Patriarchs and early Israelites and the teachings of their prophets and holy men. The Christian Bible includes the Old Testament, which contains the Torah of the Jewish Bible, as well as the New Testament, which consists of writings pertaining to the life and teachings of Jesus Christ and his disciples. It contains the four Gospels, the Epistles, the Acts of the Apostles, and the Book of Revelations (also known as the Apocalypse).

Boros, Ladislaus (1927–1981)   Born in Budapest, Hungary, Boros was ordained a priest in Belgium, worked for the Jesuit publication *Orientation* and taught religious studies. After leaving the Jesuits, he worked as a freelance writer. Boros developed the 'decision-making hypothesis', which says that at the moment of death the individual's acts in life result in one moving towards or away from God. He was a prolific writer whose works include *The Mystery of Death, Breaking Through to God, God is With Us* and *You Can Always Begin Again.*

Bourignon, Antoinette (1616–1680)   A Flemish mystic, Antoinette Bourignon de la Porte was born in Lille, France to a rich Catholic family. While living in Amsterdam, she published her ideas. Her religious enthusiasm, individuality of views and disregard of all sects drew both zealous persecutors and warm adherents. After inheriting an island, she moved there and started a commune, set up a printing press and continued her controversial writing until her press was confiscated by the local government. Her works include *Light of the World, A Treatise of Solid Virtue* and *The Restoration of the Gospel Spirit.*

Brahma Sutra   Also called Vedanta Sutra, the Brahma Sutra is one of the three canons of Vedantic scriptures, along with the Upanishads and the Bhagavad Gita. It is attributed to Sri Badarayana and is the authoritative exposition of the teachings of Vedanta. Composed of 555 terse aphorisms or sutras that are open to interpretation, it has been the subject of numerous commentaries. The Brahma Sutra discusses, in a systematic and logical order, the teachings of the Upanishads and the Bhagavad Gita, including the nature of the ultimate reality and the way of liberation of the soul.

Buddha (c.563–483 BCE)   Prince Siddhartha Gautama of the Shakya clan in India was a great sage whose teachings formed the foundation of Buddhism. Born into the family of a minor king in the foothills of the Himalayas, he renounced his family and future kingdom to set out in pursuit of spiritual truth. It is said that he sat for meditation under a peepul tree in Gaya in Bihar, where he experienced the 'Great Awakening' when he was thirty-five. He taught the 'Four Noble Truths' and the 'Eightfold Path'.

Caussade, Jean-Pierre de (1675–1751)   Born in Cahors, Lot, France, de Caussade became a Jesuit teacher of Greek and Latin. His books *Abandonment to Divine Providence* and *The Sacrament of the Present Moment* lay out his belief that the present moment is a gift from God and abandoning oneself to it is a holy state. His books and his posthumously published letters of instruction to the Nuns of the Visitation in the French city of Nancy are considered spiritual classics.

Charan Singh, Maharaj (1916–1990)   Born in Moga, Punjab, India, Maharaj Charan Singh was a disciple of Maharaj Sawan Singh of Radha Soami Satsang Beas. He was a lawyer by profession. In 1951 Maharaj Jagat Singh made him his successor, and for the next four decades he travelled throughout India and the world, giving discourses and initiating seekers. Teaching about the Word, he stressed looking beyond differences of race, culture and religion. He published many books on Sant Mat, including several volumes of questions and answers, discourses and letters to seekers and disciples. Before his death in 1990, he appointed Baba Gurinder Singh as his successor.

Cloud of Unknowing, The   *The Cloud of Unknowing* is a practical spiritual guidebook thought to have been written in the latter half of the fourteenth century by an anonymous English monk who counsels a young student to seek God not through knowledge but through love. The same author wrote a follow-up book, *The Book of Privy Counselling*, and is believed to have authored several other spiritual treatises and translations. He urges his student to "go after experience rather than knowledge.... Knowledge is full of labour, but love, full of rest."

Eckhart, Meister (c.1260–c.1328)   Also known as Eckhart von Hochheim, Meister Eckhart, born in the region of Thuringia, Germany, was a Dominican theologian, philosopher and mystic who taught religion in Paris and later in Cologne. He left a large body of work that is still popular. Religious scholars have compared him to eastern mystics. His works include *The Sermons*, which contains a commentary on the Bible, *From Whom God Hid Nothing* and

Way of Paradox. Central themes were the presence of God in the individual soul, the value of detachment and contemplation, and the goodness of God. "The Eye with which I see God is the same Eye with which God sees me" is one of his most famous quotes.

Eichendorff, Joseph von (1788–1857)   Joseph Freiherr von Eichendorff was born in Upper Silesia (Poland). He became a lawyer, then an administrator in various capacities in the Prussian government. He is considered one of the greatest of the German Romantic lyric poets. His guiding theme was that people should find happiness in full absorption of the beauties and changing moods of nature. His poems have been set to music by many composers. His most famous work is *Life of a Good-for-Nothing*.

Evagrios the Solitary (345–399)   Born in Ibora, Italy, Evagrios Ponticos was a Christian monk and ascetic known as an accomplished writer and speaker. After becoming archdeacon in Constantinople, he moved to Jerusalem and later Egypt. There he began recording and systematizing the oral teachings of the monks known as the Desert Fathers, and eventually became known as one of these teachers. His writings were incorporated into the compendium of teachings of the Desert Fathers known as the *Philokalia*. He taught to the level of understanding of his students and is especially known for his description of eight negative thought patterns from which all sinful behaviour springs.

Frossard, André (1915–1995)   Born in Colombier-Châtelot, Doubs, France, Frossard was a journalist and essayist known for his comic wit and direct, personal observations. He wrote a popular column in "Le Figaro" for thirty years. Raised an atheist, he converted to Roman Catholicism at age twenty following a mystical experience. This is described in his famous work *God Exists: I Have Met Him*, which became a bestseller. He wrote: "I was as surprised to find myself a Catholic when I left the chapel as I would have been to find myself a giraffe when I left the zoo."

Gandhi (1869–1948)   Mohandas Karamchand Gandhi, known also as Mahatma ('great soul'), was born in Porbandar in the present-day state of Gujarat in India. He was a major political and spiritual leader of India and the Indian independence movement and is officially honoured as the Father of the Nation. He pioneered *satyagraha*, resistance to tyranny through mass non-violent civil disobedience. His organization and determination were a major factor in helping India achieve independence from British rule in 1947. His ideas influenced freedom fighters around the world. He wrote *An Autobiography*, and many compilations of his speeches and writings have been published. He said, "My life is my message".

Gertrude of Helfta (1256–1302)   Gertrude of Helfta, also known as Saint Gertrude the Great, was born in Germany of unknown parentage and so was likely an orphan. She was raised in the Benedictine nunnery at Helfta, Eisleben, Saxony, from the age of five. She was known as a bright student and a gentle person. Legend has it that she became too enamoured with philosophy and received a vision of Jesus, who reproached her. From then on she studied the Bible and the works of the Church Fathers. Her many visions formed the basis of her mystical writings. Her book, *Herald of Divine Love*, is still popular today.

Gregory of Nyssa (c.335–after 394)   Born in Caesarea, Asia Minor (now Turkey), Saint Gregory was appointed bishop of Nyssa in 372 by his brother, Basil of Caesarea. They, along with Gregory of Nanzianus, became known as the Cappadocian Fathers and made many contributions to Christian theology, including the concept of the infinity of God and the doctrine of the Trinity. Gregory's later works became more mystically oriented as he argued that knowledge must be transcended in order to commune with God. He wrote a mystical commentary on the *Song of Songs*, as well as *The Life of Moses*, interpreting the journey of Moses as an allegory of the soul's progress toward a vision of God.

Hesychios of Sinai (c.8th–9th century)   Very little is known about Hesychios of Sinai, also known as Hesychios the Priest, other than the fact that he was abbot of the Monastery of the Mother of God of the Burning Bush (Vatos) on Mount Sinai. Many works attributed to others of the same name, particularly Hesychios of Jerusalem, should probably be ascribed to him. Today it is universally accepted that Hesychios of Sinai is the author of the collection of maxims *On Watchfulness and Holiness* included in the *Philokalia*.

Hildegard of Bingen (1098–1179) Hildegard of Bingen was born in Bockelheim on the Nahe, Germany to noble parents. Though most famous as a mystic who had visions starting in childhood, she was an accomplished artist, author, composer, linguist, naturalist, herbalist, scientific writer and founder of two Catholic monasteries. She travelled widely on preaching tours, the only woman known to have done so during the Middle Ages. She interpreted her visions in three books: *Know the Way*, *Book of Life's Merits* and *Book of Divine Works*.

Ignatius of Loyola (1491–1556) Originally known as Iñigo Oñaz Lopez de Loyola, Saint Ignatius was born in the Basque province of Guipúzcoa, Spain. He became a soldier, was wounded, and while convalescing read commentaries on the lives of Christ and the saints, which changed his life. His subsequent pilgrimages and studies led to the founding of the Society of Jesus, a religious order of the Catholic Church known as the Jesuits. He is the author of *A Pilgrim's Journey* and *Powers of Imagining* as well as *Spiritual Exercises*, a set of meditations and prayers, which is still used in training Jesuits.

Isaiah (c.8th century BCE) Isaiah, son of Amoz, is the main figure in the Biblical Book of Isaiah and is traditionally considered to be its author. A citizen of Jerusalem, Isaiah was a prophet and advisor to four kings of Judah over four decades. He warned people to turn to God, who was God of the whole world, not just particular nations. God, he said, had called Judah and Israel his covenant people in order to teach the world about Him. But the covenant could not protect them if they worshipped idols and acted injustly or with cruelty.

Jagat Singh, Maharaj (1884–1951) Born in the village Nussi, not far from Jalandhar, Punjab in India, Maharaj Jagat Singh was initiated when he was twenty-six years old by Maharaj Sawan Singh. Sardar Bahadur Maharaj Ji, as he was affectionately known, was

considered by his colleagues and fellow disciples alike to be excep-
tionally devoted. He was chemistry professor, then vice-principal
of the Punjab Agricultural College. Following his retirement in
1943, he spent the remainder of his life in his master's service at
Beas. In 1948 his master appointed him to be his successor. During his three years as master, he attracted followers from all over
the world. *Science of the Soul*, a compilation of his discourses and
excerpts from his letters to seekers and disciples, was published
after his death.

Jaimal Singh, Baba (1839–1903)   Born into an agricultural family
in Ghuman, Punjab, India, Baba Jaimal Singh, widely known
as Baba Ji Maharaj, was initiated by Soami Ji Maharaj of Agra
and directed by him to propagate the Sant Mat teachings in the
Punjab. After retiring from military service, he chose a secluded
place on the west bank of the Beas River to pursue uninterrupted meditation. Soon seekers started visiting him, laying the
foundation for organized satsang at Beas. Several months before
his death in 1903, he appointed Maharaj Sawan Singh as his successor. It was the latter who named the place Dera Baba Jaimal
Singh in honour of his master's memory. Baba Ji Maharaj's letters
to Maharaj Sawan Singh have been published in the form of a
book entitled *Spiritual Letters*.

Jesus (c.6 BCE–30 CE)   The teachings of Jesus of Nazareth, which
became the basis of Christianity, are known only through accounts
chronicled in the Gospels and in Christian tradition. Raised in
the Jewish religion, he was baptized by John the Baptist and
was considered the Messiah by his disciples. He taught that the
relationship of the soul to God is one of love, that the kingdom
of God is within and that one should love one's enemies and love
one's neighbour as oneself. Shortly before his death, Jesus passed
the spiritual mantle to his disciple Peter.

John of the Cross (1542–1591)   Saint John of the Cross was a Spanish mystic and poet. Born Juan de Yepis y Alvarez in Fontiveros,
Spain, he became a Carmelite monk in 1563 and was ordained as
a priest in 1567. In 1568 he, Saint Teresa of Ávila and Anthony of
Jesus founded the first convent of Discalced Carmelite Brethren.

John's attempts at monastic reform led to his imprisonment, and it was there that he began to compose some of his finest work, including the poems *Spiritual Canticle* and *Living Flame of Love*. In his best-known lyric, *Dark Night of the Soul*, he described the soul's progress in seeking and finally attaining union with God through an experience similar to Christ's crucifixion and glory.

John the Baptist (c.6 BCE–c.27 CE)   A cousin of Jesus and son of Elizabeth and Zacharias, John baptized Jesus and named him as his successor. It is believed that John may have received training from the Essenes, a sect of Jewish mystics who practised from the second century BCE through the second century CE. He taught in the wilderness of southern Judaea and in the Jordan valley. John was imprisoned and later beheaded for denouncing the marriage of Herod Antipas, a political figure of the time.

Johnson, Julian P. (d.1938)   Dr Johnson, author of the spiritual classic *The Path of the Masters*, was a theologian, surgeon, pilot and artist. At the height of his worldly success, he abandoned all his activities except for his search for spiritual truth and found a spiritual master in Maharaj Sawan Singh, the Satguru at the Radha Soami Satsang in Beas, India. Once initiated, he meticulously carried out the spiritual discipline taught to him by his Master and shared his experiences and knowledge gained at the feet of his Master with seekers in the West. He also wrote *The Unquenchable Flame* and *With a Great Master in India*, as well as *The Call of the East*.

Kabir (1398–1518)   Born in Kashi (Banaras or Varanasi), India, Kabir Sahib was a contemporary of Guru Nanak and Guru Ravidas. He travelled throughout India teaching the practice of the Word. In Kashi, one of the main centres of Hindu orthodoxy, he eked out a living by weaving cloth. His teachings about the inner Word attracted a large following of disciples from various religious backgrounds, but his outspoken condemnation of rituals and religious observances drew unrelenting opposition from the priestly class. Many of his poems were incorporated into the Adi Granth and are widely quoted in daily life throughout India today, attesting to their versatility and power.

Katha Upanishad *See* Upanishads.

Le Saux, Henri (1910–1973) Born in Saint Briac, Brittany, France, Le Saux entered 'minor seminary' at the age of eleven, becoming a Benedictine novice in 1930. In 1948 he moved to India, immersing himself in *advaita* philosophy. Two years later he founded an ashram, Shantivanam, and took the name Swami Abhishiktananda. In his latter years he was drawn to solitude, spending much time in the hermit caves at Arunachala. He remained a Christian, becoming a bridge between Christian and Hindu spirituality. His writings have been compiled in *Swami Abhishiktananda: Essential Writings.*

Mahatma Gandhi *See* Gandhi.

Maulana Rum *See* Rumi.

Mechthild of Magdeburg (c.1210–c.1285) Mechthild was born to a noble family in Saxony. At age twelve, she had her first visions of mystical union. In 1230, she left home to become a member of the Beguine sisterhood and to continue her spiritual development under the guidance of the Dominicans there. Shortly after 1270, she joined the Cistercian nuns at Helfta, where she spent the remaining years of her life. The record of her manifold visions is published in *The Flowing Light of the Godhead.*

Merton, Thomas (1915–1968) One of the most influential Catholic authors of the twentieth century, Thomas Merton was born in Prades, France, moved to the United States as an infant, attended school in London and Paris and graduated from Columbia University, where he first embraced Catholicism. Merton later entered the Abbey of Gethsemani, a community of Trappist monks in Kentucky, where he became a priest in 1949. He was a prolific writer, poet, student of comparative religion, social activist and author of numerous works on spirituality. His books include *The Seven Storey Mountain, No Man Is an Island, The New Man, Seeds of Contemplation* and *Contemplative Prayer.*

Mira (1498–1563) Mira Bai was a Rajput princess and a devotee of Lord Krishna until she met her Guru, Saint Ravidas, and was initiated by him. Persecuted by her family for following a cobbler saint, Mira eventually left her home and wealth and travelled widely. Her songs of devotion and longing are still popular today.

Nicholas of Cusa (1401–1464)   Nicholas of Cusa, also known as Cusanus, was born to a German merchant family. He became a lawyer, travelled widely as a papal envoy and was made a Cardinal of the Roman Catholic Church around 1448. On one of his envoy journeys he had an experience that led thereafter to deeply mystical writings, including the possibility of knowing God through 'learned ignorance'. He is considered one of the fifteenth-century geniuses in mathematics and astrology. His *On the Peace of Faith* envisions a summit meeting in heaven of representatives of all the world's religions. He also wrote *Sifting the Koran*, a commentary on the Qur'an.

Nicholas of Flüe (1417–1487)   Nicholas of Flüe, born in the Swiss canton of Unterwalden, was a hermit and ascetic who is the patron saint of Switzerland. He was a distinguished farmer, soldier, councillor and judge until receiving a mystical vision indicating that the cares of his worldly life were swallowing his spiritual life. He abandoned his worldly life to become a hermit in the Ranft valley in Switzerland. He became known as 'Brother Klaus' and visitors from all over Europe sought his council. He is credited with averting a civil war between the cantons. A short prayer of his is cited in the Catechism of the Catholic Church.

Pascal, Blaise (1623–1662)   A child prodigy educated by his father, Pascal was born in Clermont, France. He was a mathematician, physicist and religious philosopher. His ideas and inventions contributed significantly to the natural and applied sciences, economics and social science, and he is regarded as one of the most important authors of the French Classical Period. Following his conversion to Catholic Jansenism in 1646, he had a mystical experience in 1654, abandoned his scientific work and devoted himself to philosophy and theology. His two most famous religious works are *Provincial Letters* and *Thoughts on Religion and Other Subjects*.

Paul the Apostle (c.10–c.67) Saint Paul was born to a Jewish family from Tarsus. Named Saul at birth, by virtue of his Roman citizenship he also bore the Latin name of Paul. He first opposed the followers of Jesus but was converted into a fervent believer by an inner experience. Following his baptism, he travelled throughout the Middle East on apostolic missions. He died of uncertain causes in Rome. Known as the Apostle of the Gentiles, Saint Paul was the second most prolific contributor to the New Testament.

Philokalia The *Philokalia* ('Love of the Beautiful') is a collection of texts written between the fourth and fifteenth centuries by spiritual masters of the Eastern Orthodox Christian tradition. It focuses on the disciplines of Christian prayer and a life dedicated to remembrance of God. Compiled by Saint Nikodemos of the Holy Mountain and Saint Makarios of Corinth, it was first published in 1782 and is featured prominently in the book *The Way of the Pilgrim*.

Rahner, Karl (1904–1984) Born in Freiburg, Germany, Karl Rahner was one of the most influential Roman Catholic theologians of the twentieth century. His theology influenced the Second Vatican Council and was ground-breaking for the development of what is generally seen as the modern understanding of Catholicism. He is the author of numerous essays including those in his book *Foundations of Christian Faith*.

Regula See *Rule of Saint Benedict*.

Richard of Saint Victor (d.1173) Born in Scotland, Richard was one of the most important mystical theologians of twelfth century Paris. He was prior of the Augustinian Abbey of Saint Victor in Paris from 1162 until his death. His writings on mystical contemplation earned him the title Magnus Contemplator, the 'Great Contemplator'. He had great influence on Saint Bonaventure and the Franciscan mystics. He is mentioned in Dante's *Paradise*. His most important work was *On the Trinity*.

Rule of Saint Benedict The *Regula*, written by Saint Benedict of Nursia, is a book of precepts for those living in monastic communities under the authority of an abbot or abbess. Pope Gregory the Great, the first biographer of Saint Benedict, characterized the Rule with these brief but significant words: "He (Benedict) wrote a rule for monks outstanding in its wisdom and illuminating in its presentation." The Rule was established to insure a balance between the needs of the individual monks and the requirements of the monastic community. The motto of the Benedictine Order, *"ora et labora"* (pray and work), summarizes the spirit of the *Regula*.

Rumi (1207–1273)   Jalaluddin Rumi, known respectfully as Maulana Rum in India, was born in Balkh in present-day Afghanistan. He moved to Konya, Turkey, where he became a religious teacher. There he met Shams-i Tabriz and became his disciple. He rose to become a powerful spiritual influence not only in the Persian-speaking world, including Afghanistan and Central Asia, but also in India and Turkey. He wrote the *Masnavi* and *Diwan-i Shams-i Tabriz*, both of which have contributed to his contemporary status as one of the most well-known Sufi mystics, popular in both the East and the West.

Sawan Singh, Maharaj (1858–1948)   Affectionately known as the Great Master, Maharaj Sawan Singh was born in India in the village of Jatana, Punjab. He was initiated by Baba Jaimal Singh, who appointed him as his successor in 1903. Thereafter, for forty-five years, Great Master assiduously served as the Master at the Radha Soami Satsang Beas, spreading the teachings of Sant Mat in India and abroad. His books include *Philosophy of the Masters*, an encyclopaedia of the teachings of the saints, as well as two volumes of letters written to Western disciples, and a volume of his discourses. He appointed Maharaj Jagat Singh as his successor.

Seth Shiv Dayal Singh   *See* Soami Ji.

Shankaracharya (788–820)   Considered one of the greatest philosophers of India, Shankaracharya was the main exponent of Advaita Vedanta. He displayed such wisdom and holiness that he was considered to be an incarnation of Lord Shiva, whose ardent devotee he was. In the short span of his life he composed numerous works, the most important being his commentaries on the Brahma Sutra, the Bhagavad Gita and the ten main Upanishads.

Soami Ji (1818–1878) Seth Shiv Dayal Singh, referred to as Soami Ji Maharaj by his followers, was born in Agra, India. He was associated with Tulsi Sahib of Hathras right from his birth, as his parents were Tulsi Sahib's disciples. After about seventeen years of intense meditation, he started teaching the way of the Word in 1861 and gave out the universal teachings of the saints in unveiled, simple language. His teachings are set forth in *Sar Bachan Poetry* and *Sar Bachan Prose*.

Teilhard de Chardin, Pierre (1881–1955) Born in Orcines, France, Pierre Teilhard de Chardin was a Jesuit priest and philosopher who worked, taught and published as a palaeontologist and geologist. He spent most of twenty-five years in China and took part in the discovery of Peking Man. His primary book, *The Phenomenon of Man*, published posthumously, set forth a sweeping account of the unfolding of the cosmos. He postulated that the universe was evolving in the direction of more complex arrangements and a higher consciousness rather than randomly or by survival of the fittest. His superiors denied publication of his spiritual and mystical works during his lifetime due to his views on evolution and original sin.

Teresa of Ávila (1515–1582) Teresa de Cepeda y Ahumada was born in Ávila, Spain. Known also as Teresa de Jesús, Saint Teresa was a Catholic mystic, writer, monastic founder and reformer. She entered a Carmelite convent in 1532 and in 1562 re-established the Carmelite rule, which included additional observances. Her memoirs have been translated into English and preserved in several books. In *The Interior Castle*, she describes the seven concentric groups of mansions within the soul that lead the spirit to the central court and a spiritual 'marriage' to God, which she says can be reached during one's life. Other well-known works include *The Way of Perfection*, *Life* and *Meditations on the Song of Songs*.

Teresa, Mother (1910–1997)   Born Agnes Gonxha Bojaxhiu in Skopje, Macedonia, Mother Teresa was a Roman Catholic nun and noted humanitarian. From 1931 to 1948 she taught school in Kolkata, but was so moved by the suffering and poverty around her that in 1950, she founded the Missionaries of Charity to minister to the needs of the helpless and dying. Her ministry grew to include the poor, sick and orphaned and soon spread to other countries. She won the Nobel Peace Prize in 1979. She wrote or co-wrote thirteen books, including *In My Own Words*, *A Simple Path*, *No Greater Love*, *Total Surrender* and *Reaching Out in Love*.

Thérèse of Lisieux (1873–1897)   Also known as Saint Thérèse of the Child Jesus or The Little Flower of Jesus, Saint Thérèse was born in Aleçon, France, to religious parents. She tried to become a Carmelite nun starting at age nine, was accepted at sixteen and died of tuberculosis at twenty-four. Her spiritual memoir, *Story of a Soul*, along with letters, prayers, poems and plays she wrote have been published and widely read. She is known for her 'Little Way', showing love for God by simple loving actions. She described prayer as "a surge of the heart…a cry of recognition and of love which enlarges my soul and unites it to God".

Thomas Aquinas (c.1225–1274)   Also known as Thomas of Aquin or Aquino, Saint Thomas Aquinas was an Italian Catholic Dominican priest, philosopher and theologian. He was born in the castle of Roccasecca of the family of the Counts of Aquino and educated by the Benedictines of Monte Cassino. He is considered by many Catholics to be the Church's greatest theologian. Over three decades he wrote numerous essays and books, the most famous of which is *Summa Theologica*, in which he summarized the reasons for all of the main theological teachings of his time, quoting from Aristotle, Augustine and many others.

Upanishads   The last section of the Vedas, the Upanishads contain philosophical and mystical teachings. Upanishad literally means 'to sit near or close'. These instructions were so named because their esoteric secrets and mysteries are personally imparted to the disciple by the teacher. The Upanishads are concerned with the nature of the indescribable Reality and the way to realize the oneness of the soul with that Reality through meditation.

Vedas   Literally, knowledge; revealed knowledge as embodied in the four early Hindu scriptures (Rig Veda, Sam Veda, Yajur Veda, Atharva Veda). The Vedas deal with spiritual matters, the divine powers of gods, sacred formulas (mantras) and the problems of life in the world. The Vedas reveal that some of their authors knew about the Word of God, which they called *naad* (Sound) or *vaak* (Word). The term also refers to Vedic literature in general, including the Upanishads and various interpretive texts.

Yoga Sutra   The Yoga Sutra (*yoga* – union, *sutra* – thread or aphorism) is a foundational text of yoga, a collection of 196 sutras or aphorisms often attributed to Patanjali and thought to have been written around the second century BCE. The sutras describe an eight-step system designed to free the body and mind from restlessness and impurity and to direct bodily and psychic energy towards higher consciousness and liberation. The Yoga Sutra is used by many schools of yogic thought because of the thoroughness, succinctness and consistency with which it clarifies many important concepts common to all traditions of Indian thought.

NOTE: 'Bible' refers to *The Holy Bible*, Authorized King James Version. 'Jerusalem Bible' refers to *The Jerusalem Bible*. Unless an English-language book is noted as the source, the quotation referenced is generally the author's own translation, at times rendered, summarized or extracted from the original.

INTRODUCTION

1   **God always remains an adventure...** Ladislaus Boros, *Im Leben Gott erfahren*, p.118. See *The Moment of Truth: Mysterium Mortis*, tr. Gregory Bainbridge, p.175.

PART ONE: Called by Name

CHAPTER ONE: When God Becomes Fate

8   **I have called thee by thy name...** Bible, *Isaiah* 43:1.

8   **Nobody knows what God will make...** Ignatius of Loyola, recollection of the author. See *Powers of Imagining: Ignatius de Loyola: A Philosophical Hermeneutic of Imagining through the Collected Works of Ignatius de Loyola*, tr. Antonio T. de Nicolás, p.330.

9   **God always remains an adventure...** Ladislaus Boros, *Im Leben Gott erfahren*, p.118. See *The Moment of Truth: Mysterium Mortis*, tr. Gregory Bainbridge, p.175.

10   **But seek ye first the kingdom of God...** Bible, *Matthew* 6:33.

11   **Since I did not have...** Teresa of Avila, *Sämtliche Schriften der heiligen Theresia von Avila*, vol.1, p.2. See *The Life of Saint Teresa of Ávila by Herself*, tr. J. M. Cohen, p.86.

12 He beholds me... Johannes Marie Vianny, recollection of the author. See Alfred Monninx, *Life of the Cure d'Ars*, p.242.

13 But I would have you without carefulness... Bible, *1 Corinthians* 7:32–35.

CHAPTER TWO: Living in the Face of Death

16 Only by praying can we divert... Reinhold Schneider, *Die Sonette von Leben und Zeit, dem Glauben und der Geschichte*, Sonnet 86.

17 Seek first his kingdom... Bible, *Luke* 12:31.

CHAPTER THREE: In Search of the Way

21 We, who are all Christians... Author unknown. See Charles M.A. de Brandt et al, *Contemplations and Meditations on the Passion and Death, and on the Glorious Life of Our Lord Jesus Christ: according to the Method of St. Ignatius*, p.100–101.

CHAPTER FOUR: Leaving the World

24 restlessness for God... Saint Augustine, *Bekenntnisse*, tr. Joseph Bernhart, chap.1. See *The Confessions of Saint Augustine*, tr. Edward Bouverie Pusey, p.1.

CHAPTER FIVE: The 'Garden Inclosed'

27 Listen, my son... Saint Benedict, *Benediktusregel (Regula)*, p.5. See *The Rule of Saint Benedict: Insights for the Ages*, tr. Joan Chittister, p.19.

27 nothing should take priority... Saint Benedict, *Benediktusregel (Regula)*, Rule 43. See *The Rule of Saint Benedict*, tr. Abbot Parry, p.71.

27 Now ye are the body of Christ... Bible, *1 Corinthians* 12:27.

28 Make thy face to shine upon thy servant... Bible, *Psalms* 31:16.

28 My soul thirsteth for God... Bible, *Psalms* 42:2.

29 He has imprinted His seal... Saint Agnes, *Ritus der Jung-frauenweihe*. Quoted in Louise André-Delastre, *Saint Agnes*, tr. Rosemary Sheed, p.54.

30 Thy love is better than wine... Bible, *Song of Solomon* 1:2–4.

31 Rise up, my love, my fair one... Bible, *Song of Solomon* 2:13.

31 Let me see thy countenance... Bible, *Song of Solomon* 2:14.

31 By night on my bed I sought him ... Bible, *Song of Solomon* 3:1–4.

31 Thou hast ravished my heart... Bible, *Song of Solomon* 4:9–10, 12.

32 I am my beloved's... Bible, *Song of Solomon* 6:3.

32 Set me as a seal upon thine heart... Bible, *Song of Solomon* 8:6–7.

32 I rejoice in loving him... Mechthild of Magdeburg, *Das fließende Licht der Gottheit*, vol.2, p.85. See *The Revelations of Mechthild of Magdeburg (1210–1297)* or, *The Flowing Light of the Godhead*, tr. Lucy Menzies, p.16.

CHAPTER SIX: In the Sign of Fire

37 On 23rd November, in the year of grace 1654... Blaise Pascal quoted in *Vermächtnis eines großen Herzens*, vol.2, p.85. See *The Thoughts of Blaise Pascal: Tr. from the Text of M. Auguste Molinier*, tr. Charles Kegan Paul, p.2.

40 The comprehensive and solid foundation... Jean-Pierre de Caussade, *Hingabe an Gottes Vorsehung*, vol.2, p.116. See *Abandonment to Divine Providence*, tr. John Beevers, p.72.

CHAPTER SEVEN: On a Pilgrimage to God

41 The present moment is like... Jean-Pierre de Caussade, *Hingabe an Gottes Vorsehung*, I:2:10. See *Abandonment to Divine Providence*, tr. John Beevers, p.38.

41 Man's unconditional submission... Jean-Pierre de Caussade, *Hingabe an Gottes Vorsehung*, I:2:10. See *Abandonment to Divine Providence*, tr. John Beevers, p.66.

42   **You desire to see the face of the Father...** Evagrios the Solitary in *Kleine Philokalie*, p.44. See *The Philokalia: The Complete Text*, tr. G.E.H. Palmer, vol.1, p.68.

42   **Man therefore should not...** Meister Eckhart, *Deutsche Predigten und Traktate*, ed. Josef Quint, Sermon 7. See *Selected Writings*, tr. Oliver Davies, p.10.

43   **I am no longer able...** Saint Thomas Aquinas, quoted by Joseph Bernhart in the introduction to *Summe der Theologie*. See *Albert & Thomas: Selected Writings*, tr. Simon Tugwell, p.266.

43   **speed up the way...** Saint Benedict, *Benediktusregel (Regula)*, chap.11. See *The Rule of Saint Benedict: Insights for the Ages*, tr. Joan Chittister, p.25.

44   **Jerusalem, rise up...** *Schott-Messbuch (Missale Romanum)*, 2nd Sunday of Advent. See Sylvester P. Juergens, *The New Marian Missal for Daily Mass*, p.59, and Jerusalem Bible, *Baruch* 5:5.

44   **Were Christ to be born...** Angelus Silesius, *Der Cherubinische Wandersmann*, vol.1, no.1, p.61. See *Selections from The Cherubinic Wanderer*, tr. J. E. Crawford Flitch, p.139.

45   **O happy sin that has deserved...** *Schott-Messbuch (Missale Romanum)*. See *Missal*, Easter Eve liturgy, "The Exultet".

45   **fills the whole world...** Jerusalem Bible, *Wisdom* 1:7.

46   **Come, Holy Spirit...** *Schott-Messbuch (Missale Romanum)*, Pentecost Hymn. See Sylvester P. Juergens, *The New Marian Missal for Daily Mass*, p.479.

46   **follow the guidance of the Holy Spirit...** Jean-Pierre de Caussade, *Hingabe an Gottes Vorsehung*. See *Abandonment to Divine Providence*, tr. John Beevers, p.193.

CHAPTER EIGHT: God Alone Suffices

48   **Teresa of Avila eloquently depicts...** Teresa of Avila, *Sämtliche Schriften der heiligen Theresia von Avila*, chap.8–9. See *The Life of Saint Teresa of Ávila by Herself*, tr. J. M. Cohen, p.66–67.

48   **One day, when I went to the oratory...** Teresa of Avila, *Sämtliche Schriften der heiligen Theresia von Avila*, chap.8–9.

See *The Life of Saint Teresa of Ávila by Herself,* tr. J. M. Cohen, p.66–67.

51 **Todo se pasa... sólo Dios basta...** Teresa of Avila, *Obras Completas de Santa Teresa de Jesus.* See *The Way of Ecstasy: Praying with Teresa of Avila,* p.24.

CHAPTER NINE: Incessant Prayer

54 **Jesus, Son of David, have mercy on me...** Bible, *Mark* 10:47.

54 **In my opinion the first step of wakefulness...** Hesychios of Sinai, in *Kleine Philokalie,* p.185. See *The Philokalia: The Complete Text,* vol.1, tr. G.E.H. Palmer et al, p.164–165.

55 **Be patient...** Evagrios the Solitary, in *Kleine Philokalie,* p.137. See *The Philokalia: The Complete Text,* vol.1, tr. E.H. Palmer et al, p.58.

55 **Teach your mind...** Evagrios the Solitary, in *Kleine Philokalie,* p.32. See *The Philokalia: The Complete Text,* vol.1, tr. G.E.H. Palmer et al, p.63.

55 **This incessant prayer...** Recollection of the author. See Patrick Laude, *Pray without Ceasing: The Way of the Invocation in World Religions,* p.126–127.

55 **Sit with lowered head...** Gregory of Sinai, in *Kleine Philokalie,* p.34. See *The Philokalia: The Complete Text,* vol.4, tr. G.E.H. Palmer et al, p.264.

CHAPTER TEN: The Call into the Desert

60 **fashion of this world passeth away...** Bible, *1 Corinthians* 7:31.

60 **nakedness of the Absolute...** Meister Eckhart, *Deutsche Predigten und Traktate,* ed. Josef Quint, Sermon 34. See *Wandering Joy: Meister Eckhart's Mystical Philosophy,* tr. Reiner Schürmann, p.165.

60 **Meister Eckhart speaks...about this desert...** Meister Eckhart, *Deutsche Predigten und Traktate,* ed. Josef Quint, Sermon 13, p.213 and Sermon 34, p.312. See *Meister Eckhart: Sermons & Treatises,* vol.2, tr. M.O'C. Walshe, Sermon 57 (Quint 13), p.83 and Sermon 60 (Quint 34), p.105.

61   O Lord, what must I do... Antoinette Bourignon, "An Apology for Mrs. Antoinette Bourignan" [sic], p.269–270, quoted in Evelyn Underhill, *Mystik*, p.280. See Evelyn Underhill, *Mysticism* (1995), p. 213.

61   Only in the nakedness and bareness... René Voillaume, recollection of the author.

63   Who once has found the desert... Author unknown, recollection of the author.

CHAPTER ELEVEN: The Ridge Walk

67   O Lord, it is a constant dying... Bernard of Clairvaux, *Die sieben Kehren*, quoted in Johannes Schuck, *Geschichte des hl. Bernhard von Clairvaux*, p.26.

67   The path to God... *Katha Upanishad* 1:3:14

71   You will only find peace... René Voillaume, personal letter.

CHAPTER TWELVE: Who Are You, O Lord?

75   When will I have the vision of God... Quoted by Swami Chidbhavananda in his commentary on *The Bhagavad Gita*, p.319.

CHAPTER THIRTEEN: To the Promised Land

76   When God gives himself as a guide... Jean-Pierre de Caussade, *Hingabe an Gottes Vorsehung*, vol.2, p.7. See *Abandonment to Divine Providence*, tr. John Beevers, p.83.

81   Nothing weakens a person more... René Voillaume, recollection of the author.

82   Whoever accepts the possibility... Recollection of the author.

84   Said I not unto thee... Bible, *John* 11:40.

CHAPTER FOURTEEN: Recognising the Will of God

90   the one lesson God himself... Ignatius of Loyola. See *Ignatius of Loyola: The Spiritual Exercises and Selected Works*, edited by George E. Ganss, p.336.

PART TWO: In the Promised Land

CHAPTER ONE: On Hold

95 Get thee out of thy country... Bible, *Genesis* 12:1.
102 If thou wouldest believe... Bible, *John* 11:40.

CHAPTER TWO: House of the Knowledge of God

106 And blessed is she... Bible, *Luke* 1:45.
108 Whosoever can do without... Meister Eckhart, *Deutsche Predigten und Traktate*, ed. Josef Quint, Talk of Instruction 23, p.97. See *Selected Writings*, tr. Oliver Davies, p.48.
109 meek and lowly in heart... Bible, *Matthew* 11:29.
109 Yea, yea; Nay, nay... Bible, *Matthew* 5:37.
110 This is my commandment... Bible, *John* 15:12.
112 All this, whatever moves... Ishavsya Upanishad 1, 4–5.
112 Those who are devoted to a-vidya... Ishavsya Upanishad 9.
113 The face of Truth is covered... Ishavsya Upanishad 15.
113 Through Thy grace... Ishavsya Upanishad 16.
114 This is fullness... Ishavsya Upanishad, prologue.
115 I and my Father are one... Bible, *John* 10:30.
115 That they all may be one... Bible, *John* 17:21.
115 Therefore, when I am... Meister Eckhart, *Deutsche Predigten und Traktate*, ed. Josef Quint, Sermon 7. See *Meister Eckhart: Sermons & Treatises*, tr. M. O'C. Walshe, vol.2, Sermon 65 (Quint 7), p.135–136.

CHAPTER THREE: With the Blessings of the Church

126 If thou wouldest believe... Bible, *John* 11:40.

CHAPTER FOUR: Meeting Mother Teresa

131 But whom say ye that I am?... Bible, *Matthew* 16:15.
131 Jesus is my only love... Mother Teresa, quoted in Kathryn Spink, *Mutter Teresa*, p.342. See *No Greater Love*, tr. Becky Benenate and Joseph Durepos, p.89.
131 inasmuch as ye have done it... Bible, *Matthew* 25:40.

CHAPTER FIVE: In the World of Vedanta

139   Now, therefore, the desire to know Brahman... Brahma Sutra 1:1:1.

141   Brahman cannot be known... Recollection of the author. See Mundaka Upanishad III:1:8.

141   There is no return for the released souls... Brahma Sutra 4:4:22.

144   verses of the Bhagavad Gita... Bhagavad Gita 2:54–69.

144   How does a man behave... Bhagavad Gita 2:54.

144   A man of steadfast wisdom will... Bhagavad Gita 2:56.

145   Again, the kingdom of heaven... Bible, *Matthew* 13:44–46.

144   Krishna describes... Bhagavad Gita 2:60–68.

145   That which is night... Bhagavad Gita 2:69.

147   The knowing Self... See Katha Upanishad 1:2:18–24.

149   I have learned so much from God... Daniel Ladinsky, *The Gift*, p.32.

CHAPTER SIX: Sachchidananda Community

154   Your face, my dear... Chandogya Upanishad 4:14:2.

CHAPTER SEVEN: Life between Christ and Krishna

162   Yours is a country... Pope Paul VI, recollection of the author. See Kuncheria Pathil, *Mission in India Today: The Task of St. Thomas Christians*, p.53.

162   From the unreal lead me to the real... Brihadaranyaka Upanishad 1:3:28

163   the true worshippers shall worship the Father... Bible, *John* 4:23.

165   Let your life speak to us... Gandhi, recollection of the author. See Mahatma Gandhi and Anand T. Hingorani, *The Message of Jesus Christ*, p.71.

165   Love one another as I have loved you... Bible, *John* 13:34.

166   And if any man will sue thee at the law... Bible, *Matthew* 5:40–41.

167   Take, eat; this is my body... Bible, *Matthew* 26:26–28.
170   And this is life eternal... Bible, *John* 17:3.
170   My mind is restless... Guru Ram Das, *Adi Granth*, p.861.
170   The pious one of the future... Karl Rahner, *Schriften zur Theologie*, vol.7, p.22. See *Philip Endean, Karl Rahner and Ignatian Spirituality*, p.63.

CHAPTER NINE: Monastic Perspectives

180   A soul that belongs to God... Etienne de St. Marie, *Conversation avec Dieu*, recollection of the author.
182   I believe that I know and I have seen... Thomas Merton, quoted in *Christ in der Gegenwart*, June, 1983. See *Thomas Merton, Spiritual Master: The Essential Writings*, p.226.

CHAPTER TEN: On the Threshold of a New Horizon

189   dark contemplation... John of the Cross, *Des heiligen Johannes vom Kreuz Dunkle Nacht*, tr. Aloysius Alkofer and P. Ambrosius a. S. Theresia, p.47. See *Dark Night of the Soul*, tr. E. Allison Peers, p.55.
198   except a man be born of water and of the Spirit... Bible, *John* 3:5.

CHAPTER ELEVEN: Dialogue between Religions

205   it would require personal experience of God... Thomas Aquinas, *Summe der Theologie (Summa Theologica)*, 1:3:3. See *Summa Theologica of St. Thomas Aquinas*, tr. Fathers of the English Dominican Province, p.2, 454, 480.
205   Man should not be content... Meister Eckhart, *Deutsche Predigten und Traktate*. ed. Josef Quint, Talk of Instruction 6. See *Selected Writings*, tr. Oliver Davies, p.10.
206   Brahman cannot be known... Recollection of the author. See Mundaka Upanishad III:1:8.
209   Know ye not, that so many of us as were baptized... Bible, *Romans* 6:3–4.

Part Three: The Path of the Masters

Chapter One: On the Threshold

232   the Word was made flesh... Bible, *John* 1:14.

219   As long as I am in the world, I am the light of the world... Bible, *John* 9:5.

219   I am not sent but unto the lost sheep... Bible, *Matthew* 15:24.

Chapter Two: Taking Hurdles

223   cognitio Dei experimentalis... Thomas Aquinas, *Summe der Theologie (Summa Theologica)*, 1:3:3. See *Summa Theologica of St. Thomas Aquinas*, tr. Fathers of the English Dominican Province, p.2, 454, 480.

228   Marana tha – Come, O Lord... Bible, *1 Corinthians* 16:22–23.

Chapter Three: The Master in the Light of the Gospel

230   I have manifested thy name... Bible, *John* 17:6.

231   In the beginning was the Word... Bible, *John* 1:1.

231   And the Word was made flesh... Bible, *John* 1:14.

231   only begotten Son... Bible, *John* 4:9.

232   Your father Abraham rejoiced to see... Bible, *John* 8:56.

232   Before Abraham was, I am... Bible, *John* 8:58.

232   lovedst me before... Bible, *John* 17:24.

232   Believe me that I am in the Father... Bible, *John* 14:11.

233   For as the Father hath life in himself... Bible, *John* 5:26.

233   But whosoever drinketh of the water... Bible, *John* 4:14.

234   Moses gave you not that bread... Bible, *John* 6:32–35.

234   the stature of the fullness of Christ... Bible, *Ephesians* 4:13.

234   the light of men... Bible, *John* 1:4.

234   I am the light of the world... Bible, *John* 8:12.

235   Him that sent me... Bible, *John* 5:37.

235   he that receiveth me... Bible, *Matthew* 10:40.

235   he gave his only begotten Son... Bible, *John* 3:16–17.

236 But now I go my way... Bible, *John* 16:5.
236 For this I have come to the world... Bible, *John* 18:37.
236 I am the way and the truth... Bible, *John* 14:6.
236 taught them as one having authority... Bible, *Matthew* 7:29.
236 Whence hath this man this wisdom... Bible, *Matthew* 13:54–56.
237 We speak that we do know... Bible, *John* 3:11.

CHAPTER FOUR: It Had Been His Gaze

244 the measure of the stature... Bible, *Ephesians* 4:13.

CHAPTER FIVE: Towards Initiation

248 I am the good shepherd... Bible, *John* 10:14.
249 except a man be born again... Bible, *John* 3:3.
252 Siddhis are supernatural powers... Patanjali, Yoga Sutra 3:37–51.

CHAPTER SIX: Looking Back

257 I am the way, the truth, and the life... Bible, *John* 14:6.
257 The words that I speak unto you... Bible, *John* 6:63.
261 my Father's house... Bible, *John* 14:2.
262 No man cometh unto the Father... Bible, *John* 14:6.

CHAPTER EIGHT: Surat Shabd Yoga

271 Narrow indeed is the path of true love... Kabir, *Kabir Sakhi Sangrah*, 44:10. See V.K. Sethi, Kabir, *The Weaver of God's Name*, p.580.
271 Except a corn of wheat fall into the ground... Bible, *John* 12:24.
272 The radiant form catches our attention... Maharaj Charan Singh, *Die to Live*, no. 204, p.179.
274 The reverberating melodies... Soami Ji, *Sar Bachan Poetry (Selections)* 6:5:16–17.

275   He is omnipresent... Maharaj Sawan Singh, *Philosophy of the Masters*, vol.4, p.18.

276   For the bread of God... Bible, *John* 6:33.

276   he that eateth of this bread... Bible, *John* 6:58.

276   temple of the living God... Bible, *2 Corinthians* 6:16.

CHAPTER NINE: God and Creation

278   The best answer that I can give... Maharaj Sawan Singh quoted in Daryai Lal Kapur, *Call of the Great Master*, p.50.

279   the Lord gave the souls to Kal... Soami Ji, *Sar Bachan Poetry (Selections)* 26:1:2:39–41.

279   The human soul, jiva, was sent... Soami Ji, *Sar Bachan (Prose)*, p.62:2:42.

280   First the supreme Lord created... Soami Ji, *Sar Bachan Poetry (Selections)* 26:1:1:22–25.

280   These three worlds were created... Soami Ji, *Sar Bachan Poetry (Selections)* 26:1:1:27, 30–31.

280   When fullness is taken from fullness... *Ishavasya Upanishad*, prologue.

280   None can fully grasp the secret... Soami Ji, *Sar Bachan Poetry (Selections)* 26:1:1:37.

281   the architect of the multiplicity... John Davidson, *A Treasury of Mystic Terms*, vol.4, p.243.

281   Many suns and moons... Soami Ji, *Sar Bachan Chhand Bandh* 26:2:12, 14–15. See Lekh Raj Puri, *Radha Soami Teachings*, p.186–187.

282   the reverberating sound of the beating... Soami Ji, *Sar Bachan Chhand Bandh* 26:2:2:10. See Lekh Raj Puri, *Radha Soami Teachings*, p.186.

282   the oval shape of that region... Hildegard of Bingen, *Scivias*, tr. Maura Böckeler, book 1, p.109. See *Hildegard of Bingen: Scivias*, tr. Columba Hart and Jane Bishop, p.93–94.

284   Spirit of the Lord shall rest... Bible, *Isaiah* 11:2.

285   The wolf also shall dwell with the lamb... Bible, *Isaiah* 11:6–8.

285   divine law... Maharaj Sawan Singh, *Philosophy of the Masters* vol.4, p.103–104.

CHAPTER TEN: The Souls in the Creation

287   The human soul was sent... Soami Ji, *Sar Bachan (Prose)*, p.62:2:42.

289   the reason for this longing is... Saint Augustine, *Bekenntnisse*, book 10, chap.20. See *The Confessions of St. Augustine*, tr. Edward B. Pusey, X:20.

290   fundamental properties of the gunas... Bhagavad Gita 14:5–8.

291   Know that it is a compounded creation... Soami Ji, *Sar Bachan Poetry (Selections)* 26:1:1:46.

291   coincidentia oppositorum... Nicholas of Cusa, *De docta ignorantia, Die belehrte Unwissenheit.* See Steven M. Wasserstrom, *Religion after Religion: Gershom Scholem, Mircea Eliade, and Henry Corbin at Eranos*, p.5.

296   for whatsoever a man soweth... Bible, *Galatians* 6:7.

299   tree of the knowledge of good and evil... Bible, *Genesis* 2:17.

300   Wherefore, as by one man sin... Bible, *Romans* 5:12.

301   I decided to put on this play... Soami Ji, *Sar Bachan Poetry (Selections)* 26:2:76.

301   the devil is described as a renegade angel... Bible, *Revelation* 12:1–9.

302   mysterium iniquitatis – the mystery of sin and of Satan... Bible, *2 Thessalonians* 2:7.

303   the 'enemy' who, out of envy, sows weeds... Bible, *Matthew* 13:24–30.

303   the mind that makes the thorns grow... Bible, *Matthew* 13:3–8.

CHAPTER ELEVEN: The Path of Salvation

308   You were always part... Soami Ji, *Sar Bachan Poetry (Selections)* 26:1:2:38.

309   Christianity speaks of the redemption... Bible, *Mark* 16:16.

309   the parable of the prodigal son... Bible, *Luke* 15:11–32.

310   Ye have not chosen me... Bible, *John* 15:16.

315   Let the mind and the Sat Guru... Soami Ji, *Sar Bachan (Prose)*, p.56:2:22.

319   Soami Ji deals with this question... Soami Ji, *Sar Bachan Poetry (Selections)*, 26:2:2.

PART FOUR: Living Sant Mat

CHAPTER TWO: Monastery or World?

354   The first vow that the founder... Saint Benedict, *Benediktusregel (Regula)*. See *The Rule of Saint Benedict*, tr. Abbot Parry, p.94.

355   Whoever obeys the abbot obeys God... Saint Benedict, *Benediktusregel (Regula)*, chap.5. See *The Rule of Saint Benedict (Regula)*, tr. Leonard J. Doyle, p.5.

CHAPTER THREE:
A Spiritual Life in the Middle of the World

358   to which nothing should be given preference... Saint Benedict, *Benediktusregel (Regula)*, chap.43. See *The Rule of Saint Benedict*, tr. Abbot Parry, p.71.

358   Our meditation should be our main concern... Maharaj Charan Singh. See *Quest for Light*, p.34:75.

360   The kingdom of heaven is likened... Bible, Matthew 13:24–25.

366   For where two or three are gathered... Bible, *Matthew* 18:20.

368   Throw in the fire the hundreds... Abyat-i Noori, in *Kitab al-Bai'at of Hakim Gulam Jeelani Shah*, quoted in *My Submission*, p.79.

371   But those who hold on to the hand... Soami Ji, *Sar Bachan (Prose)*, p.62:2:42.

CHAPTER FOUR: Setting out towards Reality

373   Vanity of vanities. All is vanity... Bible, *Ecclesiastes* 1:2.

374   unique current of transcendent power... Soami Ji, *Sar Bachan Poetry (Selections)* 26:1:1:21.

379   who holds the hand of the Father... Soami Ji, *Sar Bachan (Prose)*, p.62:2:42.

379   can enjoy the show of this world... Soami Ji, *Sar Bachan (Prose)*, p.69:2:76.

CHAPTER FIVE: The Living Master

388   God alone suffices... Teresa of Avila, quoted in Peter Tyler, *The Way of Ecstasy: Praying with Teresa of Avila*, p.24.

388   When the disciple is ready... Proverb of unknown origin, quoted by H.P. Blavatsky. See *The Theosophist Part Six 1884 to 1885*.

390   that the very fact that a person finds... Maharaj Sawan Singh, *Spiritual Gems*, letter 28.

391   After initiation, the question of our Master's leaving us... Maharaj Charan Singh, *Divine Light*, letter 191.

393   Ye have not chosen me... Bible, *John* 15:16.

394   a true living Master must abstain from... Soami Ji, *Sar Bachan (Prose)*, p.83:2:132.

395   My kingdom is not of this world... Bible, *John* 18:36.

397   It never entered my mind... Sam Busa, "A Prisoner of Love," *Science of the Soul*, 28:3, p.9.

398   In his commentary on this Gospel... Maharaj Charan Singh, *Light on Saint John*, chap.14.

399   Let not your heart be troubled... Bible, *John* 14:1–3.

399   You will never be orphaned... Maharaj Charan Singh, *Light on Saint John*, p.207.

399   the world seeth me no more... Bible, *John* 14:19.

399   It is expedient for you that I go away... Bible, *John* 16:7.

401   Maharaj Ji had been very exact in his planning... Baba Gurinder Singh, quoted in Shanti Sethi, *Treasure Beyond Measure*, p.291.

CHAPTER SIX: The Universal Christ

406   universal Christ... Teilhard de Chardin, recollection of the author. See David Grumett, *Teilhard de Chardin: Theology, Humanity and Cosmos*, p.99

534

407 dialogue among religions... David Grumett, *Teilhard de Chardin: Theology, Humanity and Cosmos*, p.75, 99.

407 In my Father's house are many mansions... Bible, *John* 14:2–3.

407 Before Abraham was, I am... Bible, *John* 8:58.

408 We speak that we do know, and testify... Bible, *John* 3:11–13.

408 I and my Father are one... Bible, *John* 10:30.

408 No man knoweth the Son, but the Father... Bible, *Matthew* 11:27.

408 before the world was... Bible, *John* 17:5.

408 How could one describe... Guru Arjun, Adi Granth, p.397.

409 Who being the brightness of his glory... Bible, *Hebrews* 1:3.

410 All power is given unto me... Bible, *Matthew* 28:18.

410 Son of man sitting on the right hand of power... Bible, *Matthew* 26:64.

410 I have ascended to the throne... Kabir, Adi Granth, p.969.

410 My temple is the highest... Guru Arjun, Adi Granth, p.1141.

411 The formless Lord pervades... Maharaj Sawan Singh, *Philosophy of the Masters*, vol.5, p.82.

411 As long as I am in the world... Bible, *John* 9:5.

412 I have glorified thee on the earth... Bible, *John* 17:4.

CHAPTER SEVEN:
The Mystic Dimension of Jesus Christ's Teachings

413 The pious one of the future... Karl Rahner, *Schriften zur Theologie*, vol.7, p.22. See Philip Endean, *Karl Rahner and Ignatian Spirituality*, p.63.

413 cognitio Dei experimentalis... Thomas Aquinas, *Summe der Theologie (Summa Theologica)*, 1:3:3. See *Summa Theologica of St. Thomas Aquinas*, tr. Fathers of the English Dominican Province, p.2.

415 Jesus took his disciples to the mountains... Bible, *Mark* 3:13, *Matthew* 24:3, *John* 11:54.

415 There he confided in them... Bible, *Mark* 4:10–23, *Luke* 9:18–23, 11:1–4.

417   kingdom of God...not of this world... Bible, *John* 18:36.
417   the kingdom of God is within you... Bible, *Luke* 17:21.
418   I am the bread of life... Bible, *John* 6:35.
418   whosoever drinketh of the water... Bible, *John* 4:14.
418   Jesus likens the kingdom of heaven to a treasure... Bible, *Matthew* 13:44.
418   Jesus compares the kingdom of heaven... Bible, *Matthew* 13:45–46.
418   The field, as Maharaj Charan Singh explains... *Light on Saint Matthew*, p.182.
419   Enter ye in at the strait gate... Bible, *Matthew* 7:13–14.
419   That a rich man shall hardly enter... Bible, *Matthew* 19:23–24.
419   eye of a needle... Bible, *Matthew* 19:24, *Mark* 10:25, *Luke* 18:25.
420   The light of the body is the eye... Bible, *Matthew* 6:22.
421   I and my Father are one... Bible, *John* 10:30.
421   That they all may be one... Bible, *John* 17:21.
421   parable of the good shepherd... Maharaj Charan Singh, *Light on Saint John*, p.161–164.
421   I am the door of the sheep.... Bible, *John* 10:7, 9.
422   And the glory which thou gavest me... Bible, *John* 17:22–23.
423   I am the way, the truth, and the life... Bible, *John* 14:6.
423   Abide in me, and I in you... Bible, *John* 15:4–5.
424   without me ye can do nothing... Bible, *John* 15:5.

CHAPTER EIGHT:
The Mystic Dimension of the Christian Feasts

426   In the beginning was the Word... Bible, *John* 1:1.
426   All things were made by him... Bible, *John* 1:3.
426   the Word was made flesh... Bible, *John* 1:14.
426   the only begotten Son... Bible, *John* 1:18.
427   A ship comes to us... Johannes Tauler in *Weihnachts-Singbuch (Songbook of Christmas Carols)*.

427 Of what benefit is it... Saint Augustine, quoted in Meister Eckhart, *Deutsche Predigten und Traktate*, ed. Josef Quint, Sermon 57. See *Meister Eckhart: Sermons & Treatises*, vol.1, tr. M.O'C. Walshe, Sermon 1, (Quint 57), p.1.

428 Were Christ to be born... Angelus Silesius, *Der cherubinischer Wandersmann*, vol.1, p.61. See *Selections from The Cherubinic Wanderer*, tr. J. E. Crawford Flitch, p.139.

428 When peaceful silence lay over all... Jerusalem Bible, *Wisdom* 18:14.

429 Out of silence... Meister Eckhart, *Deutsche Predigten und Traktate*, ed. Josef Quint, Sermon 57, p.145. See *Meister Eckhart: Sermons & Treatises*, vol.1, tr. M. O'C. Walshe, Sermon 1 (Quint 57), p.3.

429 It is in the purest element.... Meister Eckhart, *Deutsche Predigten und Traktate*, ed. Josef Quint, Sermon 57, p.414–415. See *Meister Eckhart: Sermons & Treatises*, vol.1, tr. M.O'C. Walshe, Sermon 1 (Quint 57), p.1–4.

429 Perhaps by imagining God... Meister Eckhart, *Deutsche Predigten und Traktate*, ed. Josef Quint, Sermon 57, p.414. See *Meister Eckhart: Sermons & Treatises*, vol.1, tr. M. O'C. Walshe, Sermon 1 (Quint 57), p.2.

429 the best and most noble thing... Meister Eckhart, *Deutsche Predigten und Traktate*, ed. Josef Quint, Sermon 57, p.415. See *Meister Eckhart: Sermons & Treatises*, vol.1, tr. M.O'C. Walshe, Sermon 1, (Quint 57), p. 6–7.

429 Asked for the symptoms... Meister Eckhart, *Deutsche Predigten und Traktate*, ed. Josef Quint, Sermon 59, p.437. See *Meister Eckhart: Sermons & Treatises*, vol.1, tr. M. O'C. Walshe, Sermon 4 (Quint 59), p.44–45.

430 he is the propitiation for our sins... Bible, *1 John* 2:2.

431 were not redeemed with corruptible things... Bible, *1 Peter* 1:18–19.

432 what God had once ordained... Bible, *Exodus* 20:24.

432 He that spared not his own Son... Bible, *Romans* 8:32.

432 God commendeth his love toward us... Bible, *Romans* 5:8.

432   Even as the Son of man came not to be ministered... Bible, *Matthew* 20:28.

433   Take, eat; this is my body... Bible, *Matthew* 26:26–28.

434   I am come that they might have life... Bible, *John* 10:10.

434   I give unto them eternal life... Bible, *John* 10:28.

434   And of his fullness have all we received... Bible, *John* 1:16.

434   Whosoever drinketh of the water... Bible, *John* 4:14.

434   bread of God... Bible, *John* 6:33, 35.

434   Jesus Christ did not take upon himself... Bible, *John* 12:49–50.

434   Jesus Christ himself says... Bible, *John* 17:2.

434   And this is life eternal... Bible, *John* 17:3.

435   For as the Father hath life in himself... Bible, *John* 5:26.

435   resurrection and the life... Bible, *John* 11:25.

436   Peter, John and Jacob saw him... Bible, *Matthew* 17:1–2.

437   It is sown in corruption... Bible, *1 Corinthians* 15:42.

437   Saint Paul's faith in Jesus's resurrection... Bible, *1 Corinthians* 15:8.

437   But if there be no resurrection of the dead... Bible, *1 Corinthians* 15:4, 13–14.

438   I am the resurrection, and the life... Bible, *John* 11:25.

438   except a man be born again... Bible, *John* 3:3.

438   Except a man be born of water... Bible, *John* 3:5.

438   he who has this knowledge of God... Bible, *John* 17:3.

439   Rejoice, earth, irradiated... Saint Augustine of Hippo, in *Schott-Messbuch (Missale Romanum), Karsamstagsliturgie.* See Easter Eve liturgy, Exultet.

441   And I will pray the Father... Bible, *John* 14:16–17.

441   But the Comforter, which is the Holy Ghost... Bible, *John* 14:26.

442   moved upon the face of the waters... Bible, *Genesis* 1:2.

442   The spirit of the Lord, indeed... Jerusalem Bible, *Wisdom* 1:7.

442   Thou sendest forth thy spirit... Bible, *Psalms* 104:30.

442   And it shall come to pass afterward... Bible, *Joel* 2:28.

442   **A new spirit will I put within you...** Bible, *Ezekiel* 36:27.

442   **Come, Holy Spirit, come...** Stephen Langton in *Schott-Messbuch (Missale Romanum)*, Pentecost liturgy. See Sylvester P. Juergens, *The New Marian Missal for Daily Mass*, p.479.

444   **The wind bloweth where it listeth...** Bible, *John* 3:8.

444   **he that heareth my word...** Bible, *John* 5:24–25.

444   **It is written, man shall not live by bread...** Bible, *Matthew* 4:4.

444   **My sheep hear my voice...** Bible, *John* 10:27–28.

445   **I believe in the one God...** *Apostolisches Glaubensbekenntnis.* See *Catechism of the Catholic Church*, Apostolic Confession of Faith: The Credo, p.49.

445   **In the beginning was the Word...** Bible, *John* 1:1.

445   **All things were made by him...** Bible, *John* 1:3.

445   **That was the true Light...** Bible, *John* 1:9.

446   **I am come a light into the world...** Bible, *John* 12:46.

446   **I am come to send fire on the earth...** Bible, *Luke* 12:49.

447   **From the roaring vibrations...** Hildegard of Bingen in *Migne Patrologia Latina, Triginta octo quaestionum solutione*, answer 27, p.197. See Andrew Weeks, *German Mysticism from Hildegard von Bingen to Ludwig Wittgenstein: A Literary and Intellectual History*, p.65.

448   **In a mystical vision...** Hildegard of Bingen in Adelgundis Fuhrkötter, *Das Leben der heiligen Hildegard von Bingen*, vol.2, chap.2. See *Hildegard of Bingen: Scivias*, tr. Columba Hart and Jane Bishop, p.152.

448   **By his redeeming touch...** Hildegard of Bingen, *Scivias*, part 2, p.111, vision 1, no.13. See *Hildegard of Bingen: Scivias*, tr. Columba Hart and Jane Bishop, p.154–55.

448   **As the Word of God resounded...** Hildegard of Bingen, *Liber Divinorum Operum*, vol.1, "And the word was with God". See Andrew Weeks, *German Mysticism from Hildegard von Bingen to Ludwig Wittgenstein: A Literary and Intellectual History*, p.55.

449   **The reverberating melodies of bell...** Soami Ji, *Sar Bachan Poetry (Selections)* 6:5:16–17.

449   roaring flow of torrents... John of the Cross, *Sämtliche Werke des heiligen Johannes vom Kreuz*, vol.4, stanzas 14–15, commentaries 9–10. See *A Spiritual Canticle of the Soul and the Bridegroom of Christ*, tr. David Lewis, p.32, 110.

450   sweet-sounding melody... Gertrude of Helfta, *Gesandter der göttlichen Liebe*, vol.2, chap.9. See *The Herald of Divine Love*, tr. Margaret Winkworth, p.107.

450   the Holy Spirit plays the harps... Mechthild of Magdeburg, *Das fließende Licht der Gottheit*, vol.2, chap.3. See *The Revelations of Mechthild of Magdeburg (1210–1297)* or, *The Flowing Light of the Godhead*, tr. Lucy Menzies, p.118.

450   O Lord, it is a ceaseless dying... Bernhard of Clairvaux, *Die sieben Kehren*, quoted in Johannes Schuck, *Geschichte des hl. Bernhard von Clairvaux*, p.26.

450   the Shabd, the audible Word, is an experience... Maharaj Sawan Singh, *Philosophy of the Masters*, vol.4, p.127–130.

451   A song sleeps in all things... Joseph von Eichendorff, "Schläft ein Lied in allen Dingen", *Gedichte*, compiled by Joseph Kiermeier-Debre. See Lawrence Radner, *Eichendorff: the Spiritual Geometer*, p.164.

452   The word which ye hear is not mine... Bible, *John* 14:24.

CHAPTER NINE: On the Path of the Masters

455   Maharaj Sawan Singh assures... Maharaj Sawan Singh, *Spiritual Gems*, letter 28.

455   Radha Soami calls out to the soul... Soami Ji, *Sar Bachan Poetry (Selections)* 30:20:16.

455   I am the way... Bible, *John* 14:6.

458   You simply do your duty... Maharaj Charan Singh, *Divine Light*, p.213.

459   To find God means always to search... Gregory of Nyssa, *Des heiligen Bischofs Gregor von Nyssa ausgewählte Schriften*. See *From Glory to Glory: Texts from Gregory of Nyssa's Mystical Writings*, tr. Herbert Musurillo, p.26.

460   **Come, pray come...** Mira, *Mira Sudha Sindhu*, p.207. See *Mira: The Divine Lover*, tr. V.K. Sethi, p.131.

460   **Without me ye can do nothing...** Bible, *John* 15:5.

462   **The Master is the Lord's will personified...** Maharaj Sawan Singh, *Philosophy of the Masters*, vol.4, p.88.

463   **If the child...lets go of the hand of his father...** Soami Ji, *Sar Bachan (Prose)*, p. 62:2:42.

463   **The Lord cannot be realized...** Guru Nanak, Adi Granth, p.1. Quoted in *Philosophy of the Masters*, vol.4, p.81.

463   **What is the will of God...** Maharaj Sawan Singh, *Philosophy of the Masters*, vol.4, p.80–82, 87–89.

464   **two aspects of the will of God...** Maharaj Sawan Singh, *Philosophy of the Masters*, vol.4, p.103–105.

464   **that it is very difficult...** Maharaj Sawan Singh, *Philosophy of the Masters*, vol.4, p.106–110.

466   **example of a boy flying a kite...** Maharaj Sawan Singh, *Philosophy of the Masters*, vol.4, p.86.

469   **disciple who has taken shelter...** Maharaj Sawan Singh, *Philosophy of the Masters*, vol.5, p.203.

469   **Are ye not much better than they?...** Bible, *Matthew* 6:26.

469   **Therefore take no thought...** Bible, *Matthew* 6:31.

469   **But seek ye first the kingdom of God...** Bible, *Matthew* 6:33.

469   **by sharan a disciple throws...** Maharaj Charan Singh, *Light on Sant Mat*, letter 81.

470   **question of the fruits of sharan...** Maharaj Sawan Singh, *Philosophy of the Masters*, vol.5, p.202–207.

470   **except a corn of wheat fall...** Bible, *John* 12:24–25.

472   **five wise and the five foolish virgins...** Bible, *Matthew* 25:1–12.

474   **It is very necessary...** Soami Ji, *Sar Bachan (Prose)* p.104:2:182.

475   **He has created that desire in us...** Maharaj Charan Singh, *Die to Live*, p.271.

477   **In order to meet the Beloved...** Maharaj Sawan Singh, *Philosophy of the Masters*, vol.2, p.76.

477   **O friend, if you wish to reach...** Rumi, quoted in Maharaj Sawan Singh, *Philosophy of the Masters*, vol.2, p.86.

478 Those eyes which are weeping... Rumi, quoted in Maharaj Sawan Singh, *Philosophy of the Masters*, vol.2, p.86.

478 Mira also teaches us about intense longing... Mira, *Mira: The Divine Lover*, tr. V.K. Sethi, p.187.

478 He that hath seen me... Bible, *John* 14:9.

479 May our burning desire... Richard of Saint Victor, recollection of the author. See *The Twelve Patriarchs; The Mystical Ark; Book Three of the Trinity*, tr. Grover A. Zinn, p.273.

480 One of the great Indian Masters... Kabir, *Kabir: The Weaver of God's Name*, tr. V.K. Sethi, p.713–714.

480 There longing hurriedly... Mechthild of Magdeburg, *Das fließende Licht der Gottheit*, vol.3, p.123. See *Flowing Light of the Godhead*, tr. Frank Tobin, p.101.

481 After endless days... Kabir, *Kabir: The Weaver of God's Name*, tr. V.K. Sethi, p.451–452.

CHAPTER TEN: As the Years Pass By

491 My Lord and my God... Nicholas of Flüe, quoted in Werner T. Huber, *Bruder Klaus*, p.197. See *Compendium of the Catechism of the Catholic Church*, part 1, section 2:IV:1, and *Married Saints and Blesseds*, tr. Michael J. Miller, p.287.

494 Seek ye first the kingdom of God... Bible, *Matthew* 6:33.

CHAPTER ELEVEN: Completing Life

499 Every meditation is a preparation... Maharaj Charan Singh, *Die to Live*, p.137.

499 bridge to the beyond... See Peter Dinzelbacher, Die Jenseitsbrücke im Mittelalter, PhD dissertation, University of Wien, 1973

501 Eye hath not seen... Bible, *1 Corinthians* 2:9.

English and Indian Books

Abyat-i Noori. *Kitab al-Bai'at of Hakim Gulam Jeelani Shah.* Jalandhar: Mian Karim Bakhsh Barkatullah, Tajran-e Kutub, 1939.

Adi Granth. *Sri Guru Granth Sahib.* 2 vols. Amritsar: Shiromani Gurdwara Prabandhak Committee, 1952.

———. *Sri Guru Granth Sahib.* 8 vols. 2ⁿᵈ ed. Translated by Manmohan Singh. Amritsar: Shiromani Gurdwara Parbandhak Committee, 1996.

Agnes, Saint. Quoted in Louise André-Delastre. *Saint Agnes.* Translated by Rosemary Sheed. New York: Macmillan, 1962.

Angelus Silesius. *Selections from The Cherubinic Wanderer.* Translated with an introduction by J. E. Crawford Flitch. London: G. Allen and Unwin, 1932.

Augustine, Saint, Bishop of Hippo. *The Confessions of St. Augustine.* Translated by Edward B. Pusey. New York: Kessinger Publishing, 1949.

Benedict, Saint, Abbot of Monte Cassino. *The Rule of Saint Benedict (Regula).* Translated by Leonard J. Doyle. Collegeville, Minnesota: The Liturgical Press, 2001.

———. *The Rule of Saint Benedict: Insights for the Ages.* Translated by Joan Chittister. New York: The Crossroad Publishing Company, 1995.

———. *The Rule of Saint Benedict.* Translated by Abbot Parry. Leominster: Gracewing Publishing, 1990.

Bhagavad Gita. *The Bhagavad Gita*. Translation and commentary by Swami Chidbhavananda. Tirupparaitturai: Tapovanam Publishing House, 1967.

―――. *The Bhagavadgita*. Translated by Sarvepalli Radhakrishnan: HarperCollins, 1994.

Bible. *The Holy Bible*. Authorized King James Version of 1611. London: Oxford University Press, n.d.

―――. *The Jerusalem Bible Reader's Edition*. Garden City, New York: Doubleday, 1968.

Bhave, Vinoba and Kalindi. *Moved by Love: The Memoirs of Vinoba Bhave*. Translated by Marjorie Sykes. Foxhole, Devon: Resurgence, 1994.

Blavatsky, H.P. *The Theosophist Part Six 1884 to 1885*. Whitefish, Montana: Kessinger Publishing, 2004.

Boros, Ladislaus. *The Moment of Truth: Mysterium Mortis*. Translated by Gregory Bainbridge. Montreal: Palm Publishers, 1965.

Bourignon, Antoinette. In Anonymous, "An Apology for Mrs. Antoinette Bourignan [sic]". London: 1699. Quoted in Evelyn Underhill, *Mysticism: The Development of Humankind's Spiritual Consciousness*. 14th ed. London: Bracken Books, 1995.

Brahma Sutra. *Brahma Sutra: The Philosophy of Spiritual Life*. Translation and commentary by S. Radhakrishnan. London: George Allen & Unwin, 1960.

―――. *Brahma-Sutra-Bhasya of Sri Sankaracarya*. 3rd ed. Translation by Swami Gambhirananda. Mayavati. Pithoragarh: Swami Vandanananda, Advaita Ashrama, 1977.

Brandt, Charles Michel Alexandre de. *Contemplations and Meditations on the Passion and Death, and on the Glorious Life of Our Lord Jesus Christ, According to the Method of St. Ignatius*. Revised by W. H. Eyre. London: Burns & Oates, 1901.

Brihadaranyaka Upanishad. See *Upanishads*.

Busa, Sam. "A Prisoner of Love". *Science of the Soul*. 28:3 (September 1990). Johannesburg, South Africa: Radha Soami Satsang Beas.

Catechism of the Catholic Church. Mahwah, New Jersey: Paulist Press, 1994.

Caussade, Jean-Pierre de. *Abandonment to Divine Providence*. Translated by John Beevers. Garden City, New York: Doubleday, 1975.

Charan Singh, Maharaj. *Die to Live*. (1st ed. 1979) 7th ed. Beas, Punjab: Radha Soami Satsang Beas, 1999.

———. *Divine Light*. (1st ed. 1967) 7th ed. Beas, Punjab: Radha Soami Satsang Beas, 2002.

———. *Light on Saint John*. (1st ed. 1967) 8th ed. Beas, Punjab: Radha Soami Satsang Beas, 2007.

———. *Light on Saint Matthew*. (1st ed. 1978) 5th ed. Beas, Punjab: Radha Soami Satsang Beas, 2000.

———. *Light on Sant Mat*. (1st ed. 1958) 9th ed. Beas, Punjab: Radha Soami Satsang Beas, 1997.

———. *Quest for Light*. (1st ed. 1972) 6th ed. Beas, Punjab: Radha Soami Satsang Beas, 2002.

Chandogaya Upanishad. See *Upanishads*.

The Cloud of Unknowing. Translation and commentary by Ira Progoff. London: Rider, 1959.

Davidson, John. *Treasury of Mystic Terms*. Vol.4. New Delhi: Science of the Soul Research Centre, 2003.

Eckhart, Meister. *Meister Eckhart: Sermons & Treatises*. Vol.1–4. Translated and edited by M. O'C. Walshe. Shaftesbury, Dorset: Element Press, 1979.

———. *Selected Writings*. Translated and edited by Oliver Davies. New York: Penguin, 1994.

———. *Wandering Joy: Meister Eckhart's Mystical Philosophy*. Translated by Reiner Schürmann. Great Barrington, Massachusetts: Lindisfarne Books, 2001.

————. *The Works of Meister Eckhart.* Translated and edited by Franz Pfeiffer. Whitefish, Montana: Kessinger Publishing Co., 1992.

Eichendorff, Joseph von. Quoted in Lawrence Radner, *Eichendorff: The Spiritual Geometer.* Purdue, Indiana: Purdue University Studies, 1970.

Frossard, André. *God Exists: I Have Met Him.* Translated by Marjorie Villiers. New York: Herder and Herder, 1971.

Gandhi, Mahatma and Anand T. Hingorani. *The Message of Jesus Christ.* Bombay: Bharatiya Vidya Bhavan, 1963.

Gertrude of Helfta, Saint. *The Herald of Divine Love.* Translated and edited by Margaret Winkworth. New York: Paulist Press, 1993.

Gregory of Nyssa, Saint. *From Glory to Glory: Texts from Gregory of Nyssa's Mystical Writings.* Translated and edited by Herbert Musurillo. Selected and with an introduction by Jean Daniélou. Crestwood, New York: St. Vladimir's Seminary Press, 1979.

Hildegard of Bingen, Saint. *Hildegard of Bingen: Scivias.* Translated by Columba Hart & Jane Bishop. Translation, introduction, and commentary by Barbara Newman. Mahwah, New Jersey: Paulist Press, 1990.

————. *Hildegard of Bingen: A Spiritual Reader.* Edited by Carmen Acevedo Butcher. Brewster, Massachusetts: Paraclete Press, 2007.

————. *Hildegard of Bingen's Book of Divine Works with Letters and Songs.* Edited by Matthew Fox. Santa Fe, New Mexico: Bear & Company, 1987.

————. *Selected Writings: Hildegard of Bingen.* Translated and edited by Mark Atherton. New York: Penguin, 2001.

————. *Symphonia: A Critical Edition of the Symphonia Armonie Celestium Revelationum.* Translation, introduction, and commentary by Barbara Newman. Ithaca, New York: Cornell University Press, 1988.

———. Quoted in Andrew Weeks, *German Mysticism from Hildegard of Bingen to Ludwig Wittgenstein: A Literary and Intellectual History*. Albany, New York: State University of New York Press, 1993.

Ignatius of Loyola, Saint. *Ignatius of Loyola: The Spiritual Exercises and Selected Works*. Edited by George E. Ganss. New York: Paulist Press, 1991.

———. *Powers of Imagining: Ignatius de Loyola: A Philosophical Hermeneutic of Imagining through the Collected Works of Ignatius de Loyola*. Translated by Antonio T. de Nicolás. Albany, New York: State University of New York Press, 1986.

Ishavasya Upanishad. See *Upanishads*.

John of the Cross, Saint. *The Collected Works of Saint John of the Cross*. Translated by Kieran Kavanaugh and Otilio Rodriguez. Washington, DC: Institute of Carmelite Studies, 1991.

———. *Dark Night of the Soul*. Translated by E. Allison Peers. New York: Dover Publications, 2003.

———. *The Spiritual Canticle*. Translated and edited by E. Allison Peers. Garden City, New York: Doubleday Image Books, 1961.

———. *A Spiritual Canticle of the Soul and Bridegroom of Christ*. Translated by David Lewis. Corrections and introduction by Benedict Zimmerman. Whitefish, Montana: Kessinger Publishing, 1997.

Johnson, Julian P. *The Path of the Masters*. (1st ed. 1939) 16th ed. Beas, Punjab: Radha Soami Satsang Beas, 1997.

Kabir. *Kabir: The Great Mystic*. Translated and edited by Isaac A. Ezekiel. (1st ed. 1966) 6th ed. Beas, Punjab: Radha Soami Satsang Beas, 2003.

———. *Kabir Sakhi Sangrah*. c.1902. Reprint, Allahabad: Belvedere Printing Works, 1996.

———. *Kabir: The Weaver of God's Name*. Translated and edited by V.K. Sethi. (1st ed. 1984) 3rd ed. Beas, Punjab: Radha Soami Satsang Beas, 1998.

Kapur, Daryai Lal. *Call of the Great Master.* (1st ed. 1964) 11th ed. Beas, Punjab: Radha Soami Satsang Beas, 2004.

Katha Upanishad. See *Upanishads.*

Ladinsky, Daniel. *The Gift.* New York: Penguin Compass, 1999.

Laude, Patrick. *Pray Without Ceasing: The Way of the Invocation in World Religions.* Bloomington, Indiana: World Wisdom Inc., 2006.

Mechthild of Magdeburg. *Flowing Light of the Godhead.* Translated by Frank Tobin. New York: Paulist Press, 1998.

———. *The Revelations of Mechthild of Magdeburg (1210–1297) or, The Flowing Light of the Godhead.* Translated by Lucy Menzies. London: Longmans, Green, 1953.

Merton, Thomas. *The Seven Storey Mountain.* London: Sheldon Press, 1975.

———. *Thomas Merton, Spiritual Master: The Essential Writings.* Edited by Lawrence S. Cunningham. Mahwah, New Jersey: Paulist Press, 1992.

Mira Bai. *Mira: The Divine Lover.* Translated and edited by V.K. Sethi. (1st ed. 1979) 3rd ed. Beas, Punjab: Radha Soami Satsang Beas, 1996.

———. *Mira Sudha Sindhu.* Edited by Anand Swarup. Bhilwada: Shri Mira Prakashan Samiti, 1957.

Missal. Sylvester P. Juergens, S.M. *The New Marian Missal for Daily Mass.* New York: Regina Press, 1958.

Nicholas of Cusa (Cusanus). Quoted in Steven M. Wasserstrom, *Religion After Religion: Gershom Scholem, Mircea Eliade, and Henry Corbin at Eranos.* Princeton, New Jersey: Princeton University Press, 1999.

Nicholas of Flüe. Quoted in Ferdinand Holböck. *Married Saints and Blesseds: Through the Centuries.* Translated by Michael J. Miller. San Francisco: Ignatius Press, 2002.

Otto, Rudolph. *Mysticism East and West: A Comparative Analysis of the Nature of Mysticism.* Translated by Bertha L. Bracey and Richenda C. Payne. London: Theosophical Press, 1987.

Pascal, Blaise. *The Thoughts of Blaise Pascal: Tr. from the Text of M. Auguste Molinier.* Translated by Charles Kegan Paul. London: G. Bell and Sons, 1905.

Paul VI, Pope. Quoted in Kuncheria Pathil, *Mission in India Today: The Task of St. Thomas Christians.* Bangalore: Dharmaram Publications, 1988.

Philokalia. *The Philokalia: The Complete Text; Compiled by St. Nikodimos of the Holy Mountain and St. Markarios of Corinth.* Vol. 1–4. Translated by G.E.H. Palmer et al. London: Faber and Faber, 1979.

———. *Writings from the Philokalia on Prayer of the Heart.* Translated by E. Kadloubovsky and G.E.H. Palmer. London: Faber and Faber, 1951.

Puri, Lekh Raj. *Radha Soami Teachings.* (1st ed. 1965) 7th ed. Beas, Punjab: Radha Soami Satsang Beas, 2007.

Rahner, Karl. Quoted in Philip Endean, *Karl Rahner and Ignatian Spirituality.* Oxford: Oxford University Press, 2001.

Richard of Saint Victor. *The Twelve Patriarchs; The Mystical Ark; Book Three of the Trinity.* Translation and introduction by Grover A. Zinn. London: SPCK, 1979.

Sawan Singh, Maharaj. *My Submission.* (1st ed. 1959) 5th ed. Beas, Punjab: Radha Soami Satsang Beas, 2004.

———. *Philosophy of the Masters.* Vols. 2, 4, 5. (1st ed. 1964–1967) 5th–6th ed. Beas, Punjab: Radha Soami Satsang Beas, 1997–2000.

———. *Spiritual Gems.* (1st ed. 1965) 9th ed. Beas, Punjab: Radha Soami Satsang Beas, 1996.

Sethi, Shanti. *Treasure Beyond Measure.* (1st ed. 1990) 2nd ed. Beas, Punjab: Radha Soami Satsang Beas, 1991.

Soami Ji [Shiv Dayal Singh]. *Sar Bachan Chhand Bandh.* (1st ed. c. 1902) 15th ed. Beas, Punjab: Radha Soami Satsang Beas, 1997.

———. *Sar Bachan Poetry (Selections).* 1st ed. Beas, Punjab: Radha Soami Satsang Beas, 2002.

———. *Sar Bachan (Prose).* (1st ed. 1955) 10th ed. Beas, Punjab: Radha Soami Satsang Beas, 1999.

Teilhard de Chardin. Quoted in David Grumett, *Teilhard de Chardin: Theology, Humanity and Cosmos.* Leuven, Belgium: Peeters, 2005.

Teresa of Avila, Saint. *The Collected Works of St. Teresa of Avila.* Translated by Kieran Kavanaugh and Otilio Rodriguez. Washington, D.C.: Institute of Carmelite Studies, 1976.

———. *Life of Saint Teresa.* Translated by John Dalton. Philadelphia, Pennsylvania: P.F. Cunningham, 1870.

———. *The Life of Saint Teresa of Avila by Herself.* Translated with an introduction by J.M. Cohen. London: Penguin Books, 1957.

———. Quoted in Peter Tyler, *The Way of Ecstasy: Praying with Teresa of Avila.* Harrisburg, Pennsylvania: Morehouse Publishing, 1997.

Teresa, Mother. *No Greater Love.* Translated and edited by Becky Benenate and Joseph Durepos. Novato, California: New World Library, 1989.

———. Quoted in Kathryn Spink, *Mother Teresa: A Complete Authorized Biography.* New York: HarperCollins, 1997.

Thérèse of Lisieux, Saint. *The Autobiography of Saint Therese of Lisieux: The Story of a Soul.* Translated by John Beevers. New York: Doubleday, 1957.

Thomas Aquinas, Saint. *Albert & Thomas: Selected Writings.* Translated and edited by Simon Tugwell. New York: Paulist Press, 1988.

———. *The Summa Theologica of St. Thomas Aquinas.* Vol.1. Translated by the Fathers of the English Dominican Province. New York: Benzinger Brothers, 1947.

Underhill, Evelyn. *An Anthology of the Love of God, from the Writings of Evelyn Underhill.* Edited by Lumsden Barkway and Lucy Menzies. London: A.R. Mowbray, 1961.

————. *The Life of the Spirit and the Life of Today.* San Francisco: Harper & Row, 1986.

————. *Mysticism: The Development of Humankind's Spiritual Consciousness.* 14th ed. London: Bracken Books, 1995.

————. *Mysticism: A Study in the Nature and Development of Man's Spiritual Consciousness.* New York: Noonday Press, 1955.

Upanishads. *The Principal Upanishads.* Translation, introduction, and editing by S. Radhakrishnan. London: G. Allen & Unwin, 1953.

Yoga Sutra. *How to Know God: Yoga Aphorisms of Patanjali.* Translated by Swami Prabhavananda and Christopher Isherwood. London: George Allen & Unwin Ltd., 1953.

German, French and Spanish Books

Angelus, Silesius. *Der cherubinische Wandersmann: Mit einem Anhang Heilige Seelenlust oder Geistliche Hirtenlieder.* Herausgegeben und eingeleitet von Charles Waldemar. München: Wilhelm Goldmann Verlag, 1960.

Augustinus, Aurelius (Augustinus von Hippo). *Bekenntnisse.* Eingeleitet, übersetzt und erläutert von Joseph Bernhart. Frankfurt am Main: Insel Verlag, 1987.

Benedikt von Nursia. *Die Benediktusregel (Regula), lateinisch und deutsch.* Herausgegeben von Basilius Steidel OSB. Beuron: Beuroner Kunstverlag, 1963.

Bernhard von Clairvaux. *Die sieben Kehren.* Zitiert in *Geschichte des hl. Bernhard von Clairvaux,* von Johannes Schuck. München: Verlag Ars Sacra, Josef Müller, 1925.

Bhagavad Gita. *Bhagavadgita: Sanskrit text mit Einleitung und Kommentar von S. Radhakrishnan.* Deutsch von Siegfried Lienhard. Baden-Baden: Holle Verlag, 1958.

Bhave, Vinoba. *Struktur und Technik des inneren Friedens*. Bellnhausen: Verlag Hinder & Deelmann, 1971.

Bibel. *Deutsche Luther-Bibel*. Stuttgart: Deutsche Bibelgesellschaft, 1984.

———. *Die Bibel: Die heilige Schrift des Alten und Neuen Bundes*. deutsche Ausgabe mit den Erläuterungen der Jerusalemer Bibel. 2. Auflage. Freiburg, Basel, Wien: Herder, 1969.

Boros, Ladislaus. *Im Leben Gott erfahren*. Olten/Freiburg: Walter-Verlag, 1976.

Canisius, Petrus. *Gebete des heiligen Nikolaus von der Flue*. Publication information not available.

Caussade, Jean-Pierre de. *Hingabe an Gottes Vorsehung*. Aus dem Französischen übertragen von Peter Alto. 4. Auflage. Einsiedeln: Verlagsanstalt Benziger, 1952.

Dinzelbacher, Peter. Die Jenseitsbrücke im Mittelalter. PhD dissertation. University of Wien, 1973.

Eckehart, Meister. *Deutsche Predigten und Traktate*. Herausgegeben und übersetzt von Josef Quint. Zürich: Diogenes Verlag, 1979.

Eichendorff, Joseph von. *Schläft ein Lied in allen Dingen, Gedichte*. Herausgegeben von Joseph Kiermeier-Debre. München: Deutscher Taschenbuch Verlag, 2007.

Etienne de St. Marie, *Conversation avec Dieu*. N.p.: Du Carmel, 1998.

Frossard, André. *Gott existiert: Ich bin ihm begegnet*. Freiburg im Breisgau: Verlag Herder, 1970.

Gertrud von Helfta. *Gesandter der göttlichen Liebe*. Herausgegeben von Johannes Weißbrodt. 11. Auflage. Freiburg im Breisgau: Herder & Co, Verlagsbuchhandlung, 1939.

Gnosis: Das Buch der verborgenen Evangelien. Herausgegeben und übersetzt von Werner Hörmann. München: Pattloch Verlag, 1989.

Gregor von Nyssa. *Des heiligen Bischofs Gregor von Nyssa ausgewählte Schriften*. Bibliothek der Kirchenväter. Bd.56. Aus dem Griechischem übersetzt von Karl Weiss. Einleitung von Joseph Stiglmayr. Kempten/München: N.p.,1927

Heim, Burkhart. *Der kosmische Erlebnisraum des Menschen*. Imago Mundi. Bd. 5 (Schriftenreihe für Ausbau und Vertiefung des christlichen Welt-und Menschenbildes). Innsbruck: Resch Verlag, 1975.

Horaz (Quintus Horatius Flaccus). *Die Oden und Epoden des Horaz*. Übersetzt von Hermann Menge. 6. Auflage. Berlin SW: Langenscheidtsche Verlagsbuchhandlung, 1910.

Hildegard von Bingen. *Scivias (Wisse die Wege): Eine Schau von Gott und Mensch in Schöpfung und Zeit*. Übersetzt und herausgegeben von Walburga Storch OSB. München: Pattloch Verlag, 1990.

―――. *Scivias (Wisse die Wege)*. Übersetzt von Maura Böckeler. Salzburg: Otto Müller Verlag, 1954.

―――. *Briefwechsel*. Nach den ältesten Schriften übersetzt und nach den Quellen erläutert von Adelgundis Führkötter OSB. Salzburg: Otto Müller Verlag, 1965.

―――. *Liber Divinorum Operum, das Buch „De operatione Dei", Welt und Mensch*. Aus dem Genter Kodex übersetzt und erläutert von Heinrich Schipperges. Salzburg: Otto Müller Verlag, 1965.

―――. *Triginta octo questionum solutiones* in *Patrologia Latina*. Vol.197. Editiert von Migne. Paris: N.p., 1949.

―――. Zitiert in *Das Leben der heiligen Hildegard von Bingen, verfasst von den Mönchen Gottfried und Theoderich*. Adelgundis Führkötter. Düsseldorf: Patmos-Verlag, 1968.

Johannes vom Kreuz. *Sämtliche Werke des heiligen Johannes vom Kreuz*. Neue deutsche Ausgabe in fünf Bänden von P. Aloysius ab Immaculata Conceptione und P. Ambrosius a Sancta Theresia, unbeschuhte Karmeliten. München: Kösel Verlag, 1957.

————. *Des heiligen Johannes vom Kreuz Dunkle Nacht: nach den neuesten kritischen Ausgaben aus dem Spanischen übersetzt.* Vol.2. Translated by Aloysius Alkofer and P. Ambrosius a. S. Theresia. München: Kösel Verlag, 1979.

Johnson, Julian. *Der Pfad der Meister.* Aus dem Englischen übersetzt von Radha Soami Satsang Beas Deutschland e.V. New Delhi: Baba Barkha Nath Printers, 1999.

Rituale pro vestitione et professione monialium ordinis sancti Benedicti. (Ritus der Jungfrauenweihe). Paris: Desclee & Socii, 1927.

Langton, Stephen. *Pfingstsequenz.* Zitiert in Missale Romanum (Schott-Messbuch). Freiburg Basel Wien: Herder Verlag, 1961.

Mechthild von Magdeburg. *Das fließende Licht der Gottheit.* Eingeführt von Margot Schmidt. Einsiedeln Köln: Benziger Verlag, 1956.

Merton, Thomas. *Berg der sieben Stufen.* Übersetzt von Hans Grossrieder. Einsiedeln Zürich Köln: Benziger Verlag, 1950.

————. Zitat *Christ in der Gegenwart,* June, 1983.

Monchanin, Jules and Henri Le Saux (Abhishiktananda). *Eremites du Saccidananda.* Paris: Casterman, 1957.

Monchanin, Jules and Henri Le Saux (Abhishiktananda). *Eremiten von Saccidananda.* Übersetzt von M. Mayr und M. Vereno. Salzburg: Otto Müller Verlag, 1962.

Nikolaus von der Flue [Niklaus von Flüe]. In *Bruder Klaus.* von Werner T. Huber. Zürich und Düsseldorf: Benziger Verlag, 1996.

Nikolaus von Kues [Cusanus]. *De docta ignorantia (Die belehrte Unwissenheit).* Bd.1. Hamburg: Meiner Verlag, 2002.

Otto, Rudolf. *West-östliche Mystik: Vergleich und Unterscheidung zur Wesensdeutung.* 3. Auflage. München: Verlag C.H. Beck, 1971.

Pascal, Blaise. *Vermächtnis eines großen Herzens: Die kleineren Schriften.* Übertragen und herausgegeben von Wolfgang Rüttmann. Wiesbaden: Dieterich's Verlagsbuchhandlung, 1947.

Philokalie. *Kleine Philokalie, Betrachtungen der Mönchsväter über das Herzensgebet.* Gesammelt und übersetzt von Matthias Dietz. Düsseldorf: Patmos Verlag, 2006.

Plattner, Felix. *Indien.* Ostfildern: Mathias Grünewald-Verlag, 1963.

Rahner, Karl. *Schriften zur Theologie.* Bd. 7. *Zur Theologie des geistlichen Lebens.* Zürich/Einsiedeln/Köln: Benziger Verlag, 1971.

Scheeben, Matthias Joseph. *Die Mysterien des Christentums.* Mainz: Matthias-Grünewald-Verlag, 1931.

Schneider, Reinhold. *Die Sonette von Leben und Zeit, dem Glauben und der Geschichte.* Köln & Olten: Verlag Jakob Hegner, 1954.

Schott-Messbuch (Missale Romanum). Freiburg/Basel/Wien: Herder Verlag, 1961.

Spink, Kathryn. *Mutter Teresa: Ein Leben für die Barmherzigkeit.* Übersetzt von Michael Larrass. Bergisch Gladbach: Gustav Lübbe Verlag, 1997.

Stebler, Vincentius. *Der benediktinische Weg zur Beschauung.* Olten: Verlag Walter, 1947.

Teresa von Avila (Theresia von Jesus). *Sämtliche Schriften der hl. Theresia von Avila.* 6 Bände. Übersetzt und bearbeitet von P. Aloisius Alkofer Ord. Carm. Disc. 6. Auflage. München/Kempten: Kösel Verlag, 1963.

———. *Obras Completas de Santa Teresa de Jesus.* 9th ed. Madrid: Biblioteca de Autores Cristianos, 2003.

Theresia von Lisieux (Die heilige Theresia vom Kinde Jesu). *Geschichte einer Seele von ihr selbst geschrieben.* Kirnach-Villingen, Baden: Verlag der Schulbrüder, 1925

Thomas von Aquin. *Summe der Theologie.* Herausgegeben von Joseph Bernhart. Leipzig/Stuttgart: Kröner Verlag, 1985.

Tilmann, Klemens. *Die Führung zur Meditation: Ein Werkbuch.* Bd. 1. Zürich/Köln: Benziger Verlag, 1974.

————. *Leben aus der Tiefe: Kleine Anleitung zur inneren Versenkung und christlichen Meditation.* Einsiedeln: Benziger Verlag, 1975.

Underhill, Evelyn. *Mystik.* Herausgegeben und übersetzt von Ernst Reinhardt. München: N.p.,1928.

Weihnachts-Singbuch. Berlin/Freiburg I.Br.: Christophorus-Verlag Herder KG, 1942.

Wolke des Nichtwissens, Die. Das Buch von der mystischen Kontemplation, genannt die Wolke des Nichtwissens, worin die Seele sich mit Gott vereint. Übertragen und eingeleitet von Wolfgang Riehle. 6. Auflage. Einsiedeln: Johannes Verlag, 1999.

Yoga Sutra. *Yoga Sutra, Sanskrit/deutsch, der Yoga-Leitfaden des Patanjali.* Übersetzt aus dem Sanskrit, Einleitung und Anmerkungen von Helmuth Maldoner. Hamburg: Papyrus Extra GmbH, 1987.

BOOKS BY SSRC

BOOKS ON MYSTICISM
A Treasury of Mystic Terms,
Part I: The Principles of Mysticism (6 volumes) – John Davidson

PERSONAL EXPERIENCE
A Soul's Safari – Netta Pfefier
Adventure of Faith – Shraddha Liertz

VEGETARIAN COOKBOOKS
Baking Without Eggs
Creative Vegetarian Cooking
The Greenway to Healthy Living
Meals with Vegetables

ORIGINS OF CHRISTIANITY – John Davidson
The Divine Romance
The Gospel of Jesus
The Odes of Solomon
The Prodigal Soul
The Song of Songs

BOOKS BY RSSB

SOAMI JI MAHARAJ
Sar Bachan Prose (The Yoga of the Sound Current)
Sar Bachan Poetry (Selections)

BABA JAIMAL SINGH
Spiritual Letters

MAHARAJ SAWAN SINGH
The Dawn of Light
Discourses on Sant Mat
My Submission
Philosophy of the Masters, in 5 volumes
Spiritual Gems
Tales of the Mystic East

MAHARAJ JAGAT SINGH
Discourses on Sant Mat, Volume II
The Science of the Soul

MAHARAJ CHARAN SINGH
Die to Live
Divine Light
Light on Saint John
Light on Saint Matthew
Light on Sant Mat
The Master Answers
The Path
Quest for Light
Spiritual Discourses, in 2 volumes
Spiritual Heritage
Thus Saith the Master